after effects
in PRODUCTION

A companion for Creating Motion Graphics

Trish & Chris Meyer

CMP **Books**

DEDICATED

To the memory of **Kevin McGrath** (1921–2001)
You loved to learn new things, and we loved you for it. Braithimid uainn thú. – Trish

CMP Books
1601 West 23rd Street, Suite 200
Lawrence, Kansas 66046
USA
www.cmpbooks.com

CMP Media LLC
Publishers of DV magazine

Distributed in the U.S. and Canada by:
Publishers Group West
1700 Fourth Street
Berkeley, California 94710
www.pgw.com

ISBN 1-57820-077-6

02 03 04 05 06   05 04 03 02

Table of Contents

PART 1 // TUTORIALS

This extensive but easy-to-follow tutorial builds a high-energy opening title combining Illustrator files and movies, and uses Sequence Layers, time remapping, transfer modes, and the Radio Waves effect. **(4.1/5.0)**

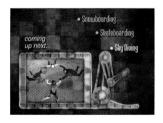

How to employ the new 5.0 feature Parenting to animate a multisegment robot arm. Includes importing Premiere projects as compositions, the new Slip Edit tool, and motion blur. **(5.0)**

A trio of text tricks: using Vector Paint to reveal characters of a word, keyframing a slam-down animation, and elementary 3D. **(5.0PB)**

An exercise in employing the Motion Tracker to attach sensor icons to live footage. Includes working with D1 footage, 3:2 pulldown, and 16–235 luminance ranges. **(4.1PB/5.0PB)**

PART 2 // CASE STUDIES

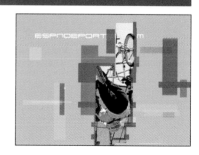

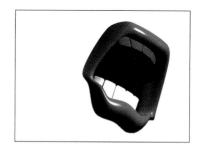

Artists and Their Tools

In our first book – *Creating Motion Graphics with After Effects* – we focused on the details of how to master this incredible program. We tried to do this against a backdrop of how you would employ its features artistically on real jobs.

Response to *Creating Motion Graphics* has been overwhelming. Thank you to everyone who bought it, and to the many who have written us personally or who publicly recommended it to others. This response has encouraged us to write the book you are now holding: *After Effects in Production.*

This book is our chance to explore the many ways After Effects can be employed in real-world productions. It contains a dozen in-depth tutorials that demonstrate a number of techniques you can apply to your own work. Several of these tutorials also provide gentle introductions to significant new features and effects that were added to After Effects version 5.0, including 3D Space, Cameras, Lights, Parenting, Expressions, SWF Export, and Vector Paint.

When we create a tutorial, it is always a challenge to balance clarity and conciseness against our desire to share all of the little tweaks and layers of detail that are necessary on real jobs. As a result, several of the tutorials include bonus sections that walk through such enhancements, or present a more complex project that builds on the concepts taught.

We're also proud to include six case studies of broadcast spots created by leading studios such as ATTIK, Belief, Curious Pictures, The Diecks Group, and Fido, as well as our own studio, CyberMotion. These case studies demonstrate different ways that After Effects has been used to combine film and video, 3D models, and elements as organic as water and wooden puppets, to realize a client's goal. The intention behind these studies is to inspire: As wonderful as it is, After Effects is merely a tool that helps you channel your own creativity into reality. We hope this book helps you realize that potential.

Trish and Chris Meyer

CyberMotion

October 2001

How to Use This Book

This book was designed for people who already have some experience using Adobe After Effects. Its goal is to help you build on that experience by sharing a number of tricks and techniques in an artistic context.

That said, we've endeavored to make the instructions for each tutorial easy to follow, without assuming too much. The first tutorial in particular – *Atomic Café* – is a good starting point for beginners. You can then fill in the information behind a feature by referring to the manual, online Help, or our first book *Creating Motion Graphics with After Effects*.

Each tutorial follows its own path. Some feature step-by-step instructions for how to build a project from scratch; others begin with several elements already in place, then show you how to put them to work. Some provide exercises on general concepts, then walk you through a more complex project that uses those same concepts; a couple encourage you to build on our base and customize the project on your own. There are a handful of two-part tutorials, which either are continued on a PDF file on the CD, or which form the base for the next tutorial in the book. There are even occasions when we purposely lead you down the most common blind alleys, just to make sure you know how to find your way back out.

The case studies should be of value to any motion graphics artist or producer, even if you don't use After Effects for your own work.

The Ground Rules

Before you start each tutorial, we recommend you copy its folder from the CD to your hard drive. This will speed up file access and allow you to save your own intermediate versions of the project as you work – something we suggest you do often. The QuickTime movies of the finished pieces will also play back more smoothly.

If files become "unlinked" for some reason, they will appear in *italics* in the Project window. Simply double-click the first missing item: This will bring up a standard file navigation dialog where you can locate that item. Select it and click OK. Provided the folder relationship between the project and its sources has not changed, After Effects will now search all folders for the other missing items and link them in as well.

You should read the Overview box on the first page of each tutorial: It will alert you to any free third-party effects you need to have installed before you open After Effects, and to the project files you should load. If you open a project and After Effects warns you that some effects have been removed, you either forgot to install one of these plug-ins, or the project requires a Production Bundle effect while you're running the Standard version.

Each tutorial is broken down into a number of Parts, which cover certain features or building blocks in the final project. Inside these Parts are numbered Steps. Our definition of what fits into a Step is pretty loose; in general, you will find that Steps in a tutorial start out short and easy and become more involved as you proceed.

There is no set amount of time that it should take to finish a tutorial – some are very long and involved and might take several hours and more than one session; others are relatively quick and breezy (well, one is anyway…).

Therefore, each tutorial project typically contains a folder of prebuilt compositions that represent where your progress should be at the end of Parts or after significant Steps. Feel free to use these to compare against your own work to make sure you understood a section. If you want to pick up a tutorial from the middle, you can also use one of these prebuilt comps as your starting place.

What's in a Name?

There are so many different elements in an After Effects project, we've tried to establish a set of typographic conventions that we hope will make it easier to understand what we are talking about and when:

• **Words in bold** refer to the specific names of folders, files, or layers you are using, or an effect that you should apply.

• **[Words in bold and in brackets]** are the names of compositions, as opposed to layers in a composition.

• "**Words in bold and in quotes**" are text you should enter – such as the name for a new composition or solid.

• **Words in bold and in this alternate font** are pieces of code used in Expressions.

• Most figures start with a number that tells you which Step they are referring to. Keep a lookout for the After Effects selection arrow shown in these figures: It often points to the values or switches being discussed.

• When there is a chain of folders or effects you have to navigate through, we separate links in the chain with a > symbol: For example: **Project>Sources>Proxies**.

• We use keyboard shortcuts extensively throughout this book. The Macintosh shortcut is presented first (followed by the Windows keystrokes in parenthesis). "Context click" means to hold down the Control key while clicking on the Macintosh, and to right-mouse click on Windows.

Iconography

The content inside each chapter is usually presented in a linear fashion. However, you will find numerous asides throughout. In addition to sidebars, which focus on specific ideas or techniques, you will also see:

 Tips: Useful tricks and shortcuts, or info on optional third-party effects we recommend.

 Factoids: Tweaky bits of specific information that might help demystify some subjects (or at least provide interesting party gossip among your tweaky friends).

 Gotchas: Important rocks you might trip over, such as special cases in which a feature might not work.

 Connects: If you want more background information on a subject or section of the program used in the tutorial, these refer you back to chapters in *Creating Motion Graphics* where you can read more.

 Production Bundle: After Effects comes in two versions: Standard and Production Bundle. Whenever a chapter or section of a tutorial *requires* the Production Bundle, you will see this icon. In some cases, we provide workarounds or otherwise suggest you could perhaps skip this section. If you have the Standard version, read on a little bit before giving up.

Installation

Most of the free After Effects plug-ins on this CD – including all of the Macintosh versions – don't require an installer: Just drag them into the After Effects Plug-ins folder. If the Windows version ends in .aex, you can drag it directly (although if an effect fails to serialize you may need to unlock it on your disk). If it ends in .zip, it needs to be uncompressed first; if it ends in .exe, then it is an installer that you need to run. A summary of the free plug-ins with a guide to their installation is included in the Free Plug-ins folder as a PDF.

System Requirements

We assume you already have a copy of After Effects 4.1 or later installed – if not, a try-out copy of the version 5.0 Standard program is included on this book's CD. Our requirements are not that much different from what Adobe recommends for After Effects.

If you already have a full version of After Effects, then you have already installed QuickTime, which is required to run the program. If you are using the try-out version and don't already have QuickTime installed, download it from Apple's Web site (www.apple.com/quicktime/).

The rule of thumb with After Effects is that the more layers and compositions you are using, and the bigger those layers and comps are, the more RAM you need allocated to the program. Also, the amount of RAM you have allocated has a direct relationship to how long of a segment of time you can RAM Preview in a composition.

We strongly recommend that you allocate more RAM to After Effects than the default amount. Most of these tutorials were created with 150 to 250 Megs reserved for After Effects alone. Consider 128 Meg a safe minimum; try to assign 256 Meg for projects with full video size frames, such as *Auto Tracker*, *The Planets*, and *Cosmopolis*. We personally allocate 300 to 400 Meg for video production work; more for film and high definition.

After Effects takes up a lot of screen real estate. Most of these tutorials should work okay at a screen resolution of 832×624 pixels, although you will be happier if you can work at 1024×768 pixels. If you are using version 5.0, we suggest you check out the Window>Workspace function, where you can save a specific arrangement of your windows – this will allow you to quickly reconform how we have saved each project to the way you personally prefer to arrange your screen.

We assume you are using an extended keyboard, as many great time-saving shortcuts take advantage of the function keys and numeric keypad. The Macintosh operating system may try to steal the use of some of the function keys away from you; the fix we use is to remove the **Keyboard** extension from **System Folder>Extensions** and restart the computer. If you don't have an extended keyboard, buy one – it will be one of the best time-for-money purchases you will make.

As for the speed of the computer, faster is always better – it results in less time wasted waiting to see the results of your work. Most of the projects have been built at smaller frame sizes to reduce the rendering time needed. If they are still too slow, consider using a lower Resolution – such as Half – which will greatly reduce your rendering time while still letting you see what's going on. We also have heard some reports of Windows computers bogging down when thousands of keyframes are displayed, as is the case in sections of the *Just an Expression* tutorial. If you have this problem, either zoom into the timeline (resulting in fewer keyframes being seen), or quickly inspect then twirl up the layers with the offending keyframes.

Many of the additional files on this book's CD are in PDF format and require Adobe Acrobat Reader. If you don't already have a copy of Acrobat Reader, an installer is included on your After Effects CD, as well as on the CD for *Creating Motion Graphics*; you can also download the latest version for a variety of platforms from Adobe's website (http://www.adobe.com/products/acrobat/readstep2.html)

If you do not already have a copy of After Effects 5.0 or later, we have included a try-out version of the Standard version on the CD, courtesy of Adobe. Copy the folder with the version for your operating system to your hard drive, decompress the archive, and then run the installer. More recent versions may be downloaded as they become available from Adobe's Web site (www.adobe.com/products/aftereffects/demodnld.html).

Version Compatibility

Whereas several of the tutorials demonstrate features introduced in After Effects 5.0, others feature concepts that can also be employed in 4.1.

We have made an effort to make each tutorial compatible with as many different versions of After Effects as possible – for example, half of the tutorials and all of the case studies may be used in version 4.1. The version compatibility of each tutorial is indicated in several ways:

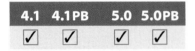

- The first page of each tutorial has a series of compatibility checkboxes: **4.1**, **4.1PB**, **5.0**, and **5.0PB** (the PB designation means Production Bundle). A check mark means this version is suitable for undertaking this tutorial. A blank box means this version is not compatible. Some tutorials recommend the Production Bundle, but in those cases we note which steps are optional.

- The tutorials are also color-coded based on which version is recommended: Red means 4.1 or 5.0 Standard version, Blue means 4.1 or 5.0 Production Bundle, Green means 5.0 Standard version, and **Purple** means 5.0 Production Bundle.

Keep Up to Date

www.cybmotion.com/training

The above Web page includes information on our books, video, and training classes. The books page includes an errata page for our first book, *Creating Motion Graphics with After Effects*. We will also add an "errata" page for *After Effects in Production* to address any errors discovered after the book has been printed.

We love to hear from our readers as to what they enjoyed – and didn't enjoy. Please email your feedback to: books@cybmotion.com. Please note that we cannot answer technical questions unrelated to the content of the books.

- All of the case studies are color-coded Turquoise and were saved using the 4.1 Standard version. If you are opening them in version 5.0, After Effects will convert these projects for you. The one exception is a bonus project in Fido's case study, which requires the version 5.0 Production Bundle.

- The tutorial project files include designations such as _4 or _5 indicating which version they should be opened in; the Production Bundle version adds a **PB** to the end of the filename.

Many of the tutorials can be performed in a lower version of the program if you are willing to skip certain sections, or if you have a required effect that used to be available from a third party. These details are noted in the Overview box for each tutorial.

If you are using version 4.1, make sure you set File>Preferences>Time>Display Style>Timecode Base to 30 frames per second (fps), Non-Drop Frame as your starting point. Unless otherwise noted, all of the tutorials are built at the NTSC standard rate of 29.97 fps, and assume Non-Drop Frame numbering. (These preferences are saved with the project file as of version 5.0.)

Since we have tried to focus on artistic concepts as much as version-specific tricks, we hope this book earns a place on your bookshelf for years to come. You should be able to open all of these projects in future versions of After Effects; just click OK when it tells you it is converting the project from an earlier version.

The Point

We imagine you've heard the saying that if you give a person a fish, you've fed a person for a day, but if you teach a person how to fish, you've fed them for the rest of their lives. As a result, you will find this book short on tables of numbers to enter, and long on explanations of *why* you might enter a certain range of numbers. Without this background information, we fear tutorials turn into magic incantations: You may know how to repeat them to reproduce a specific effect, but are left not knowing how to apply them to your own projects. We want you to come away from *After Effects in Production* with a better understanding of how to efficiently realize the original ideas in your head.

CD ROADMAP

The enclosed CD contains all of the tutorials and case studies discussed in the book, plus a number of other useful resources. Here's what is in each folder:

1_Tutorials

The project and source files for each of the 12 tutorials, along with a movie of the final animation. Many tutorials include bonus projects and supplemental PDF files, which are also contained in these folders.

2_Case Studies

The project and source files for each of the six case studies, including QuickTime movies of the spots being discussed; you can play these or step through them frame by frame.

Also from CMP

A free chapter from a new title in the DV Expert series from CMP Books, the same folks who publish our books.

Credits and Info

Information about the guest artists, stock footage houses, and audio sample sources you will see and hear throughout this book. Also contains the End User License Agreements that you agree to when you're using the media and software provided on the CD – a must-read.

Goodies

Contains a pair of articles on timing video to audio, which is relevant to several of the tutorials; a series of Illustrator film and video templates, which will come in handy when you're designing your own titles; a PDF called *Hidden Gems*, which is packed with After Effects tips and shortcuts; and a wonderful HTML document by JJ Gifford which provides lots of information on the Expressions language.

Free Plug-ins

Boris Effects, Media 100, Pinnacle Systems, The Foundry, and Trapcode have generously provided a series of free plug-ins which are used throughout this book:

- **Boris AE Mosaic** and **Tint-Tritone:** You may recognize these mainstays from the *Creating Motion Graphics* CD. The latter in particular is one of our favorite tools for colorizing footage.

- **Media 100 FE Sphere:** In the *Postcards* tutorial, we will show how to use expressions to make the sphere it creates track a 3D camera.

- **Pinnacle Systems Knoll Light Factory LE:** This useful lens flare and "scratch" effect is featured in several tutorials.

- **The Foundry T_LensBlur:** A blur that more naturally mimics the "blooming" effect of an out-of-focus camera. You'll use this on everything…

- **Trapcode Swedish Plug-ins:** Created especially for this book, these proxy effects provide controls that make it easier to manage expressions.

You'll also find information on other effect packages mentioned in these pages, as well as Toolfarm's cross-referenced Buyer's Guide of After Effects plug-ins.

_ After Effects Try-out

Contains a try-out version of After Effects 5.0 for Macintosh or Windows. If you don't already have After Effects, decompress these archives and run the installer so you can load the projects!

CD Technical Support

If your CD becomes damaged or won't load for any reason, please email CMP Books at books@cmp.com to arrange for a replacement.

Atomic Café

Creating energy through the use of Time Remapping, Transfer Modes, stock footage, and a pair of plug-ins.

In this tutorial, you will create a fun video intro that draws on retro themes from the '50s and '60s such as atomic power and psychedelic light shows. Underlying this goal are several important tricks: using the Sequence Layers keyframe assistant to auto-edit a large number of sources at once; Time Remapping to create a dramatic speedup; and layering stock footage of various graphics with your own elements which were created with plug-in effects, using Transfer Modes and Opacity.

If you're the type who likes to peek ahead before you get started, go ahead and explore the various compositions in the project's folder **_Atomic Cafe** * **prebuilt** to get an idea of where you will be going.

OVERVIEW

Main Concepts:

These are the features and concepts we will be focusing on in this project:

- Importing Photoshop and Illustrator files as Comp
- Sequence Layers keyframe assistant
- Time Remapping a comp
- Blending with Transfer Modes
- Nesting a composition
- Precomposing
- Animating Scale and Opacity
- The Wiggler *(optional)*
- Motion Blur
- Using "pyro" special effects movies
- Knoll Light Factory LE effect*
- Radio Waves effect *(optional)*

Requirements:

After Effects 4.1 or later standard version; Production Bundle is optional (it's only necessary for the step using the Production Bundle's keyframe assistant The Wiggler). Version 5.0 needed for the Radio Waves effect, but this is also optional.

Third party effects: Knoll Light Factory LE effect (included on this book's CD).

Getting Started:

* Be sure to install the Knoll Light Factory LE effect from Pinnacle Systems (www.pinnaclesys.com) included on the accompanying CD in the **Free Plug-ins** folder.

Inside the **Tutorials** master folder on the accompanying CD, locate and copy the folder **01_Atomic Cafe** to your hard drive.

In the folder **Final Movie**, double-click on and play **AtomicCafe.mov** in QuickTime Player. Inside the **Project** folder you'll find the finished After Effects project file.

Depending on the version of After Effects you are using (4.1 versus 5.0 or later), open the project **AtomicCafe_4.aep** or **AtomicCafe_5.aep**. This is your starting point; we suggest you save under a new name after each major section.

This folder contains copies of the compositions you will be building, saved after significant step numbers or at the end of whole parts. These should make it easier for you to make sure you're still on the right track. As this is a long tutorial, these prebuilt comps will also make it easier for you to jump into the middle of this tutorial later: Just find a prebuilt comp close to the step number where you want to jump in, duplicate it, rename it as if it was your own, and continue with the next step.

When you're finished exploring, close all the Comp and Timeline windows (Window>Close All) before you dive in below. As noted in the Getting Started box, this tutorial can be done in After Effects 4.1 or later; we'll alert you when the directions may diverge depending on the software you have. There are also some optional steps exploring The Wiggler keyframe assistant and the Radio Waves effect.

A frame from the final Atomic Café animation. The background uses movies from Artbeats/Soap Film CD and Bestshot/Retrocities CD, while the Radio Waves effect adds more radiating circles.

The Tasks

This is what you will be doing in the various parts of this tutorial. Since this is a fairly long tutorial, feel free to take breaks between parts:

PART 1: Import a layered Photoshop file of atomic icons and spread them across time using the keyframe assistant Sequence Layers.

PART 2: Import the soundtrack, alter the playback speed of the atomic icons using Time Remapping and have them scale over time, altering their speed by manipulating keyframe velocity curves.

PART 3: Mix stock movies using transfer modes to create an interesting background, and precompose them.

PART 4: Import the layered Illustrator file containing the title, and animate it using Scale, Opacity, and Motion Blur. An optional section uses The Wiggler from the Production Bundle to add further bounce to one of the words, or you can wiggle values using an expression in 5.0.

PART 5: Create additional lighting effects using stock footage and Pinnacle's Knoll Light Factory LE effect.

PART 6: An optional section using the Radio Waves effect (from the 5.0 Production Bundle) to further enhance the background.

Sources Diversion

In version 5.0 or later, newly imported sources are automatically directed to whatever folder is currently selected in the Project window, or the folder where a selected source resides. After Effects can help you stay organized: Select the **My_Sources** folder in the Project window before you import a new source – that way you'll always know where it went!

Part 1: Getting Some Assistance

One of the central elements of this animation will be a series of stylized atomic symbols that accelerate as they play back. Oh, and the client wants short crossfades to occur between each symbol; no simple sequence or hard cuts. Your first thought might be "Well, *this* is going to be a lot of keyframes…" and you'd be right. However, After Effects features a Keyframe Assistant called Sequence Layers that will create those keyframes for you automatically.

Sequence Layers has a couple of advantages over just bringing in a series of images as a sequence. First, you can have the images crossfade, or even leave gaps between them, rather than just switch at a speed determined by the sequence's frame rate. Second, it works with moving footage as well as still images (you can't import a set of movies as a sequence, but you can use Sequence Layers to create a video montage).

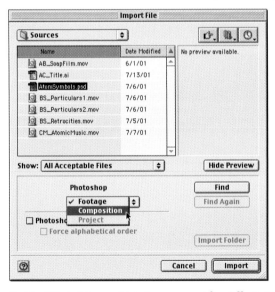

1 After Effects 5.0 consolidated several Import options – including Photoshop as Comp – into one dialog. Make sure you select the correct option from the Import As popup at the bottom of this dialog.

Sequencing Layers

STEP 1: We've created a layered Photoshop file for you, with one symbol per layer. You need to get these layers into After Effects, separated into individual footage items. The directions to do this vary slightly between After Effects 4.1 and 5.0:

After Effects 5.0 or later:
• Select the folder **My_Sources** in the Project window, select File>Import>File, and locate the file **AtomSymbols.psd** from the **01_Atomic Cafe> Project>Sources** folder. Choose Composition from the Import As popup at the bottom of the import dialog. Click Import (Open). After Effects will create a folder and a composition – both named **AtomSymbols.psd** – for you. Drag the comp [**AtomSymbols.psd**] into the **My_Comps** folder.

After Effects 4.1:
• Select File>Import>Photoshop as Comp and locate the file **AtomSymbols.psd** from the **01_Atomic Cafe>Project>Sources** folder. Click Open. After Effects will create a folder and composition – both named **AtomSymbols.psd** – for you. Drag the folder into the **My_Sources** folder in the Project window, and the comp into **My_Comps**. As you import sources and create comps later in the tutorial, stay organized by dragging them into their folders.

STEP 2: Double-click the composition [**AtomSymbols.psd**] to open it. There are a total of thirty layers in this comp, none of which you can see right now – because they are black, on a black composition background. Change the color of the comp's background to white (Composition>Background Color).

STEP 3: You should now see a huge blob! Remember that the 30 layers are on top of each other, because each starts at the beginning of the comp – but they will play one after the other in a moment…

Double-click individual layers to view them in the Layer window, or in After Effects 5, turn on their Solo switch in the Timeline. Option+click on Mac (Alt+click on Windows) the Solo switch to turn off any other Solo switches. Close the Layer window or toggle off all Solo switches when you're done.

When you import a layered Photoshop file as a composition, each layer is automatically trimmed to the exact size of the image portion of the *layer*. In comparison, when you import an Illustrator layered file as a comp, each layer is the same size as the *composition*. This auto-sizing of Photoshop layers is not a problem for this tutorial, but it may be a problem if you were to apply an effect that didn't properly draw outside the layer boundary. If effects are being clipped by the edge of the layer, you can Layer>Pre-compose using the Leave All Attributes option, then increase the size of the layer's new precomp in its Composition Settings. The effect will now be applied to the precomp layer, and it will be fooled into thinking the layer is larger than it was in the original composition.

3 At first, the comp looks like a blob (above), because you're seeing all the symbols at once. Open a few individually (below). These symbols were created by the Atomica illustration font from P22 (www.p22.com).

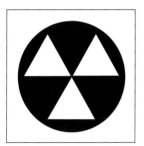

STEP 4: The duration of your comp will depend on the settings you last used to make a new comp. To adjust these settings, select Composition> Composition Settings or use the shortcut Command+K (Control+K). Rename the comp "**My_Atoms_precomp**", set the Frame Rate to 29.97 frames per second (fps) and change the Duration to 40:00. (The width and height of 300×300 and the pixel aspect ratio are set automatically by the size of the Photoshop file, and are fine as is.) Click OK.

• The timecode base we prefer for NTSC production – namely 30 fps, Non-Drop Frame – has been saved with the After Effects 5.0 version of this project (via File>Project Settings). If you are using version 4.1, check that time is being counted the same way in the File>Preferences>Time dialog (set the Timebase Base popup to 30 fps, and NTSC to Non-Drop Frame). Click OK to close dialog.

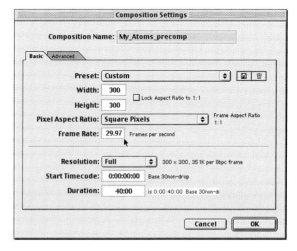

4 Edit the Composition Settings to give this comp a new name, a duration of 40:00, and a frame rate of 29.97 fps.

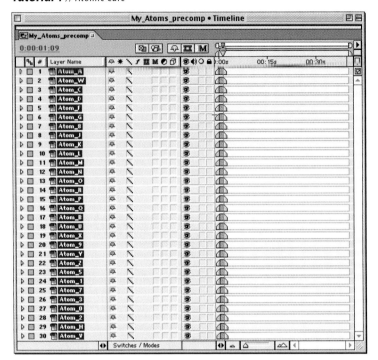

• If the original comp was shorter than 40:00 in duration, the timeline will be zoomed in, showing a smaller segment of time. If that's the case, zoom out in the timeline by hitting – (the minus key on the normal keyboard, not the numeric keypad) as many times as necessary until you're viewing the entire forty seconds.

You can view layer names as Source Name or Layer Name by clicking on the panel at the top of the layer name column. Layers originating in Photoshop and Illustrator are shorter and easier to read if they are viewed as Layer Name. (However, some of our figures appear viewed as Source to reflect its origins.)

5 To trim all of the layers at once, select them all, move the time marker to 01:09, and use the shortcut Option+] on Mac (Alt+] on Windows) to trim their out points to the current time.

STEP 5: The plan is to trim each layer to 1:10 in duration, then stagger them in the timeline so they fade up and down over ten frames. Go to time 01:09, Select All using the shortcut Command+A (Control+A), and press Option+] (Alt+]) to trim all selected layer out points to 1:09.

If we wanted a duration of 01:10, why did we trim the Out Points to be at 01:09? Because all the layers currently start at 00:00, which counts as one frame of their duration. After trimming the layers at 01:09, they will play until just before 01:10, for a total duration of 01:10.

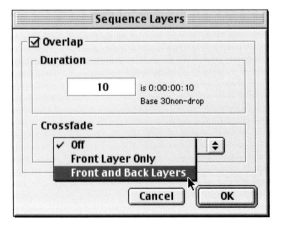

STEP 6: With all the layers still selected, context+click (Control+click on Mac, right-mouse click on Windows) on any layer in the Timeline window and select Keyframe Assistant>Sequence Layers from the context-sensitive menu.

6 Set the Sequence Layers options to be Overlap, duration 10 frames, Crossfade Front and Back.

• The Sequence Layers dialog defaults to having the Overlap option unchecked, which means that the layers will sequence end to end. Since the client has asked you to soften the transitions between symbols by crossfading between each layer, turn on Overlap, and set the Duration to 00:10 (ten frames).

• Our Atom symbols are Photoshop layers that all have alpha channels, so it's important that one image fades out as the next fades in. To achieve this, set the Crossfade popup to Front and Back Layers. Click OK.

The layers should now rearrange themselves along the timeline from 00:00 to about 30:00, with a little overlap. If they don't, use Undo and apply Sequence layers again, double-checking your settings as you go.

If the layers we were sequencing were simple full-frame images or movies, you would use the Crossfade>Front Layer Only option in the Sequence Layers dialog. This is recommended for images that are full frame, as it avoids having two semi-transparent layers in the middle of the crossfade. Depending on how they were stacked (top to bottom, or bottom to top), the frontmost layer would either fade out (Opacity keyframes 100–0%) to reveal the layer below, or fade in (Opacity keyframes 0–100%) to hide the layer below.

STEP 7: With the layers still selected, twirl down their Opacity property by hitting T. Notice that each layer fades in and out, with the exception of the first layer (which only fades out) and the last layer (which only fades in). Press T again to twirl up Opacity, and Deselect All (shortcut: F2).

STEP 8: Move to time 30:00 and make a note of the last image in the sequence, layer **Atom_V**. You want this layer to hold at the end of the sequence. Extend the out point of this layer to the last frame of the comp by dragging the end of the layer to the right.

STEP 9: Making sure the time marker is at 30:00, hit N to end the work area at 30:00, and RAM Preview (0 on the keypad). When the preview plays back, you'll see each image for approximately one second. Note that this timing is fairly arbitrary: We chose 1:10 duration with a ten-frame overlap so that we could RAM Preview each image for a second, which is enough time to see who's who and whether the sequence is nicely balanced for variety and size (you could rearrange or resize individual layers if not). We also liked the balance of ten frames of fade up, twenty frames for the image fully on, and ten frames to fade down.

Save your project now – and often! If you got lost along the way, check out our prebuilt comp, [**Atoms_after Step 09**]; *you'll find it in the* **Atomic Cafe * prebuilt>_compare comps_after Step ##** *folder.*

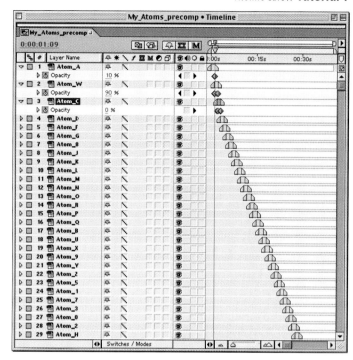

6 *complete:* After you've executed Sequence Layers, each trimmed layer will be offset in time with a ten-frame overlap. The Opacity keyframes show each layer fades during these overlaps.

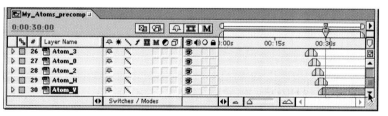

8 Extend the Out Point for the last layer – **Atom_V** – to the end of the comp. (Note that any frames that extend past the end of the timeline are trimmed off, so you don't have to carefully drag to the last frame.)

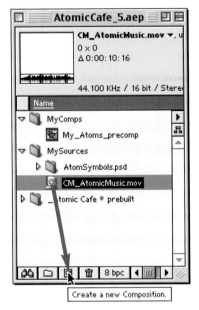

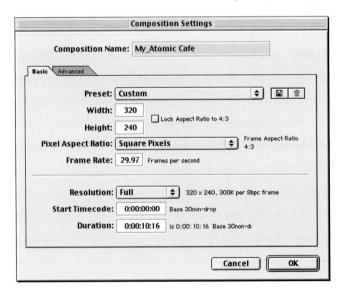

11 To automatically create a new comp the same duration as a footage file, drag the file to the Create a New Composition icon at the bottom of the Project window (where the cursor is pointing).

12 Give this new comp an appropriate name, and set its size to 320×240.

Part 2: Remapping Atoms

The design calls for the images to play back slowly, then get faster and faster until they culminate in a big bang as the title explodes onto the scene six seconds in. No, really...

To accomplish this, you're going to use the Time Remapping feature, timing the speedup to the soundtrack we've also provided. The atoms will also scale up over time to emphasize the gathering-energy feel. First, you need to create a new composition to hold this action, and to become familiar with the music.

Starting the Assembly Comp

STEP 10: Import the file **CM_AtomicMusic.mov** in this tutorial's **Project>Sources** folder. Make sure it ends up in the project's **My_Sources** folder. Note its duration in the Project window: 10:16.

STEP 11: You want to create a composition that is the same length as this soundtrack – this is where you will be building the main parts of this tutorial. You could remember the duration, Command+N (Control+N) to create a new comp, and type it in, but we're going to use a handy shortcut instead.

Select **CM_AtomicMusic.mov** and drag it down to the Create a New Composition icon at the bottom of the Project window. This will automatically create a new comp with the duration of the footage file you dragged to it, and open its associated windows.

STEP 12: Open the Composition Settings (under the Composition menu), and rename this comp "**My_Atomic Cafe**". Set the Width to 320 and Height to 240. Verify that the Pixel Aspect Ratio is Square and the Frame Rate 29.97. Click OK.

In the Project window, drag this new comp to the **My_Comps** folder. (Yes, we're sticklers for organization.)

STEP 13: RAM Preview the comp to hear the music, or press . (period on the keypad) to preview the audio from the current time. You can also twirl down the soundtrack's audio waveform (shortcut: select the layer and type LL – two Ls in quick succession), to get visual reinforcement for where the loud sections and other beats land in time.

If the audio cuts out before the end, set the duration of Audio Preview to around 12:00 in Edit>Preferences>Previews in After Effects 5.0, or File>Preferences>General in version 4.1.

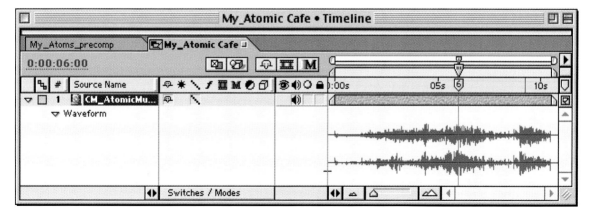

The music has seven measures overall, with a major downbeat hitting at 06:00 at the start of the fifth measure. Move to this time, and type Shift+6 (on the keyboard, not the keypad) to create a comp marker at this frame. Now whenever you need to return to 06:00, just hit 6 on the keyboard. Go ahead and twirl up the waveform display – it takes up a lot of room, and needs time to redraw.

13 After adding the audio track, a comp marker is created at 06:00 to make it easier to locate back to this major beat in the music.

The position of the music layer in the layer stack in the Timeline window is irrelevant, since it does not appear in the Comp window. However, we usually position the music layer at the top of the layer stack so that when the waveform is twirled down, chances are good you won't also need to scroll the Timeline window to see it.

Speeding Up Atoms

Truth be told, we didn't fancy trying to work out some tricky timing of how the Atoms sequence would speed up over time – for instance, Image #1 gets twenty frames, Image #2 gets nineteen frames, and so on hoping that somehow it will magically all add up to Image #30 hitting exactly at 06:00 – and then calculating faster transitions as the images speed up… You get the idea of what a headache that would have been. Instead, now that you've sequenced the images to play back one every second, we'll use Time Remapping to create the speedup trick.

Time Remapping is an underused feature that allows you to keyframe time – a pretty strange concept at first. The advantage of Time Remapping over a layer's normal Time Stretch parameter is that you can change the time-stretch percentage of a layer over time – even make a layer pause by adding Hold keyframes. Another advantage is that After Effects calculates the results of Time Remapping before looking at the other animation keyframes, so you don't have to worry about your keyframes moving about just because you changed the speed. It's the perfect tool for the accelerating playback trick we want here.

Music Credits

The music for this tutorial was arranged by co-author Chris Meyer, using copyright-cleared samples from Keith LeBlanc's *Drum & Bass Carnage*, Zero-G's *Malice in Wonderland* (both available from Sounds Online: www.soundsonline.com) and Spectrasonics' *Distorted Reality 2* (available from Ilio Entertainment: www.ilio.com). Its tempo is 160 beats per minute, which works out to 1.5 seconds per measure. You'll notice a lot of the keyframes you create in this tutorial will be set to multiples of this duration.

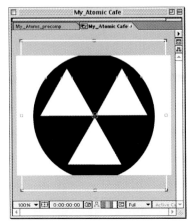

14 Nest [**My_Atoms_precomp**] into [**My_Atomic Cafe**]. Now you can treat the sequence of atomic symbols as just one piece of media (above and right).

Scrubbing the Timeline

After Effects is capable of rendering on the fly as you move the time marker. In After Effects 4.1, hold down the Option (Alt) key while dragging the time marker. In After Effects 5.0, realtime previews happen automatically, though you can revert to 4.1 behavior by selecting Use Wireframe Interactions while Option Key is "Up" in Edit>Preferences>Previews.

STEP 14: With the [**My_Atomic Cafe**] comp forward and the time marker at 00:00, select the [**My_Atoms_precomp**] comp from the Project window and nest it into [**My_Atomic Cafe**] by dragging it to either the Comp or Timeline window (in After Effects 5.0, make sure you drag it to the left side of the Timeline window; If you release the mouse somewhere in the timeline, it will start at that time).

You can also use the keyboard shortcut Command+/ (Control+/) to add it without dragging. Another way to nest is to drag the precomp icon to the [**My_Atomic Cafe**] comp icon directly in the Project window.

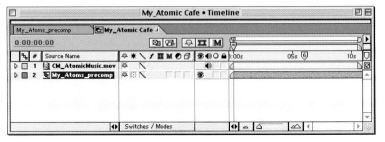

The [**My_Atoms_precomp**] now appears as a single layer in [**My_Atomic Cafe**], and can be manipulated as a group. However, any individual atom symbol can still be edited back in the precomp, and any changes made will ripple up through the second comp. This is the beauty of nesting: Think of it as a way to "group" multiple layers together so they can be effected or transformed easily.

STEP 15: Select the **My_Atom_precomp** layer and apply Layer> Enable Time Remapping. Type RR (two Rs in quick succession) to twirl down just the Time Remapping property. You'll notice one Time Remap keyframe is assigned automatically to the first frame of the layer (time 00:00), and the keyframe navigator indicates a second keyframe that you can't see. That's because it was assigned to the last frame of the layer (time 40:00). We'll deal with it later.

Twirl down the Time Remap velocity graph and note that the speed is running at 100%, which is realtime (one second in the precomp is one second in this comp).

15 Enable Time Remapping, type RR to reveal this property in the Timeline window, and twirl it down to further reveal its velocity graph.

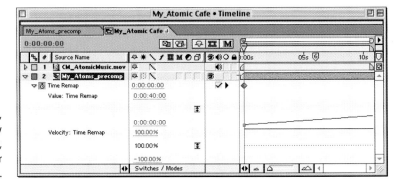

STEP 16: Hit 6 on the keyboard (not the numeric keypad) to jump to comp marker 6 at 06:00. Click on the Time Remap property value in the Timeline window and change its value from 06:00 to 30:00. This tells the layer to play back thirty seconds of the precomp by the time it reaches 06:00 in this comp's timeline. The result is the equivalent of time-stretching the layer about 500% (thirty seconds now plays over six); because the keyframes are currently Linear, the speed change is consistent.

16 Locate the time marker to 06:00, click on the Time Remap property (where the scrub cursor is pointing), and enter 30:00. Notice that the velocity curve now has a steeper slope, and that the numbers along the left indicate the layer is playing back at 500% of normal speed.

STEP 17: Remember back in Step 8 when you extended the last atom layer to play back from 30:00 through the end of [**My_Atoms_precomp**]? The result of this, plus the time remap you performed above, means that as of 06:00 in [**My_Atomic Cafe**], that last atom image will hold until the end of the comp – even though the time remap keyframes are interpolating between a value of 30:00 at time 06:00 (the new second keyframe) and a value of 40:00 at time 40:00 (that last, hidden keyframe). Even though the image is by all intents and purposes a "freeze frame" from time 06:00 to the end of the comp, it's still taking rendering time to calculate. This is because the precomp needs to be sampled at each frame to see what's going on.

To change this to a more efficient freeze frame, locate to the last Time Remap keyframe at 40:00 by clicking on the right arrow in the keyframe navigator, then delete the keyframe by unchecking the keyframe checkbox. Notice that the speed after 06:00 now reads 0% per second, indicating a true freeze frame. Go ahead and return to time 00:00 (hit the Home key).

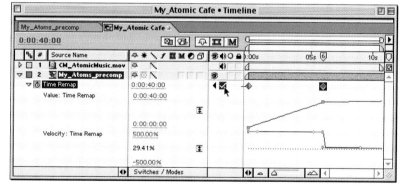

17 Use the navigation arrow to move the current time-marker to the last keyframe at 40:00 (which is otherwise past the end of the comp), and uncheck it to remove it. When you check and uncheck the keyframe box, you're affecting the keyframe at the current time (40:00); the second keyframe selected at 06:00 is not affected by this action.

Since no other keyframe follows the one at 06:00, the source image at 06:00 will be cached in RAM, and the precomp will be ignored from that point on. As a general tip, enabling Time Remapping for a precomp and then freezing on the last moving frame is a great way to optimize rendering when the precomp has lots of layers, but has otherwise stopped moving early on in the timeline. A example of this would be a precomp with a multi-layered title that animates on with many slow-to-render effects before resolving to a final resting place – but the effects are still being "polled." Time Remap can freeze this last frame for a faster render.

Even Easier!

If you're easing the first or last keyframe of an animation, you don't need to be particular about applying Easy Ease Out and Easy Ease In – just hit F9 for Easy Ease (this will ease both in to and out of the keyframe).

STEP 18: Set the work area from 00:00 to 07:00 and RAM preview. All 30 atom images will now play back faster over six seconds – albeit at a consistent pace. It's now time to match the action of the images to the music, which builds in intensity until the downbeat at 06:00.

If you've had trouble following the use of Time Remapping, compare your result with the prebuilt comp, [**AtomicCafe_after Step 18**]. *You can rename and continue with our comp, if you wish.*

Tweaking Speed

STEP 19: To add a speedup, the general idea is to ease out of the first keyframe, and speed up into the second keyframe. The first part is easy: Select the first Time Remap keyframe and apply the Keyframe Assistant>Easy Ease Out to it. In 5.0, it's under the Animation> Keyframe Assistant menu (in 4.1, it's under Layer>Keyframe Assistant).

STEP 20: Move to time 05:00, and read the Velocity percentage value at this point in the animation – it should read somewhere between 600% and 700% (it's a little faster than the original 500%, because you slowed down the beginning – and that delay has to be made up later).

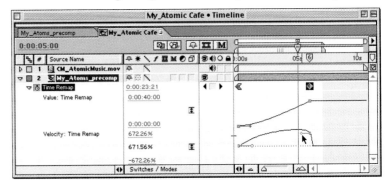

20 You need to reshape the velocity curve from having a slowdown right before the second keyframe to constantly increasing in speed. The cursor points to the velocity handle you need to grab and move up.

You will also notice a hump in the velocity curve, indicating that it speeds up but then slows down again slightly before reaching the second keyframe.

    Drag the velocity handle for the second keyframe upward until the speed reads around 900% at time 05:00 (see figure on the next page). It's okay if you drag beyond the area (or "cell") where the velocity curve is visible; it will redraw correctly when you let go of the mouse. While you're doing so, be careful not to drag the influence handle too far to the left or right, or you will unduly increase or decrease the amount of influence this new keyframe value has. Keeping the handle end right around the 05:00 mark works well. The result will speed up the play-back of the atoms as it interpolates into the second keyframe. RAM preview and see how you like it.

Velocity Dip

When you're editing the velocity or value graph, holding down the Shift key restrains the velocity curve from dipping below the center line to a negative value. In the case of Time Remapping, that means time would run backward…

> You might think you could apply Easy Ease In to the second keyframe, but that would be the opposite of what you need. Instead of slowing down to zero speed, you want it to speed up.

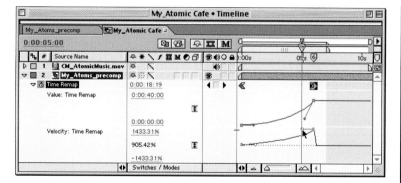

20 *complete:* Drag the handle for the second keyframe upwards until it reaches a velocity of 900% at time 05:00. It's okay to drag above the "cell" area – after you've released the mouse, the velocity curve will rescale itself to fit into the display area again.

STEP 21: When you preview the result of your velocity edit, if you were to find fault, it would be that the start of the animation is now too slow. Scrub the first two seconds of the timeline, and notice that the second atom image (at 1:10 in the precomp) doesn't appear until about 1:14 – which means that the beginning is playing slower than realtime. Let's speed up the takeoff by modifying the ease out values precisely, rather than just dragging the handles.

All the Easy Ease keyframe assistant does is plug in a default velocity and influence for a keyframe – otherwise, there's nothing special about it. You have free rein to go in and edit what it did. Option+double-click (Alt+double-click) the first Time Remapping keyframe at 00:00. The Keyframe Velocity dialog will open, showing the values that the Easy Ease assistant produced:

● Outgoing Velocity: 0 seconds per second

● Influence 33.33%.

21 The Keyframe Velocity dialog lets you precisely edit the speed of parameter change at a keyframe, and how much influence that speed has before and after the keyframe. You can access this dialog by Option+double-clicking (Alt+double-clicking) a keyframe, or from the Animation menu in version 5.0 (or the Layer menu in After Effects 4.1).

Under the Influence

The amount of influence assigned to a keyframe decides how strongly it affects the velocity curve coming into or going out of that keyframe. A linear keyframe has zero influence, meaning only the keyframe value matters; the incoming and outgoing velocity values for the keyframe are meaningless. You could think of the length of the influence handles as deciding when the speed change begins to take place.

You can roughly tell the amount of influence a keyframe has by the length of the influence handles in the velocity graph. Influence of 100% means the keyframe affects the rate of parameter change all the way to halfway between the current keyframe and the one before or after (depending on whether you are editing incoming or outgoing velocity, respectively). Seeing how far the keyframe handles reach to this halfway point, tells you how much influence it has. Easy Ease keyframes change the velocity to 0 and apply a 33.33% influence, meaning the parameter eases into and out of stopping at its keyframed value.

In Step 20, there are six seconds between keyframes. A three-second-long influence handle would be 100% influence. In this case, you want about a 33% influence (the classic "easy ease" value), so you would try to keep the influence handle roughly one second long (one-third of three seconds). That's why we instructed you to keep it around the 05:00 mark – one second before the keyframe you were editing.

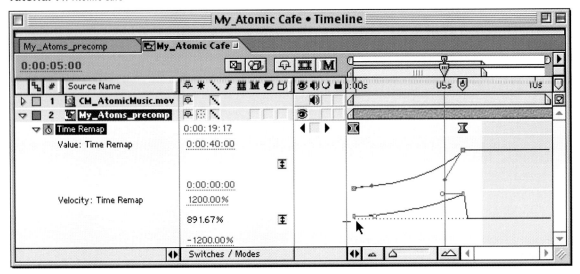

21 *complete:* The final velocity curve. The cursor is pointing to the fact that the velocity is now above the centerline, which means it is always faster than zero speed.

The Keyframe Velocity dialog is context sensitive, which means the configuration of the Velocity parameter display depends on the type of keyframe selected. The Continuous checkbox indicates whether or not the incoming velocity matches the outgoing velocity. In this case, the Incoming values are irrelevant, since this is the first keyframe.

Change the Outgoing Velocity value from 0 to 1 second per second, and click OK. The result will be that the layer will start playing back in realtime (one second per second), and get only faster from that point on. Look closely at the velocity graph: It should be raised a little off the centerline now, indicating that the speed is faster than before.

RAM Preview again and Save your project. If you need to, compare your result with prebuilt comp [**AtomicCafe_after Step 21**].

Scaling Back Your Expectations

The way we perceive the scaling of an object differs from its keyframe velocity. If an object scales up at a linear rate of speed, this scaling will appear to slow down as it reaches its final, larger size. This makes sense when you think it through: A 10% difference in Scale means a lot if you're increasing from 0% to 10%, but it means much less if you're increasing from 90% to 100%.

The Production Bundle contains a Keyframe Assistant called Exponential Scale which performs this correction for you. Although it is mathematically the most precise approach, it has the downside of creating a keyframe on every frame in the timeline, making further adjustments to Scale difficult. We try to use Exponential Scale only when the animation is locked down, and only when a simple velocity curve just doesn't work out.

Scaling Atoms

You now have the speed portion of the animation down. Next is reinforcing the impression of gathering energy by scaling the atom sequence up in size.

STEP 22: You want the atom sequence to scale up as it plays back, continuing to scale a little past 06:00. By going a little past the downbeat at 06:00, the atoms will continue scaling as the main title builds on, adding more interest. This also gives you a bit of "handle" to fade the atoms out. (On a real job, you might think of little touches like that later. But we thought we'd save you some work now.)

• Make sure the **My_Atoms_precomp** layer is still selected. At time 00:00, press S to twirl down Scale, and turn on the keyframe stopwatch for Scale. Enter a value around 15% so the first symbol is small but still readable.

• Move to 06:10 and scale up to around 75%, which will confine the last atom image to roughly the Title Safe area (use the ' apostrophe key to toggle these guides on and off).

> It's never a bad idea to create elements at a larger size than you'll end up using later (within reason, of course; we consider about twice as big as you think you'll need it to be the edge of reason). Having some headroom to scale from 75% to 100% offers you more options when you're animating – especially when you're using pixel-based sources such as those from Photoshop, where scaling above 100% will soften and degrade the image.

• To make the scaling speed up over time to match the sequence speed, select the first Scale keyframe and apply Keyframe Assistant> Easy Ease Out. If you like, you can also tweak the velocity of the second keyframe to emphasize this acceleration, just as you did for the second Time Remap keyframe earlier. We personally twirled down the velocity graph and dragged the second keyframe's handle up until its speed was about 22% per second.

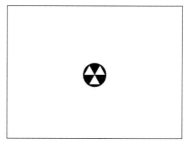

23 The atom sequence scales from 15% (above) to 75% (below) over time, to add further excitement.

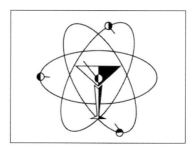

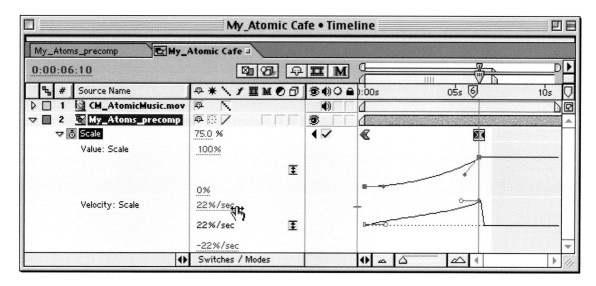

Step 23: Toggle the layer to Best Quality (shortcut: Command+U on the Mac, Control+U on Windows). This will antialias the layer smoothly as it scales. RAM Preview if you like. When you're done, twirl up the Scale property to clean up the Timeline, and return to time 00:00.

You know the routine: If you want to compare your version with ours, or pick up this tutorial in the middle, check out [**AtomicCafe_after Step 23**]. *And don't forget to Save your project…*

23 *complete:* The first Scale keyframe eases out, and the handles are adjusted to accelerate into the second keyframe. The layer is set to Best Quality so that it antialiases nicely.

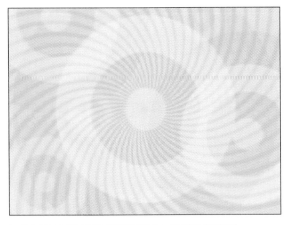

24 Two movies you will be using to create your background. The first is a movie of graphical circles from the Bestshot/Retrocities CD (top), which is looped two times in the Interpret Footage dialog (above). The second movie from the Artbeats/Soap Film CD is then added to the comp (below).

Part 3: Get Back!

In this section, you will build the background for the overall piece. While you're at it, you'll have a little fun combining different layers with transfer modes to create a melded '60s flashback look. You'll start out building this background in the same comp as you've been speeding up the atoms, then move it to its own comp later.

STEP 24: Select the **My_Sources** folder and import **BS_Retrocities.mov** – it should be in the same folder as the soundtrack and atoms. (*4.1 users:* Move the movie to the **My_Sources** folder in the Project window.) While it's selected in the Project window, observe that it's only 7:06 in duration – too short for your 10:16 final comp. Fortunately, it was created as a seamless loop, so you can repeat it as often as necessary. With it selected, open the Interpret Footage dialog (File>Interpret Footage>Main) and set its Looping parameter to Loop 2 Times. Click OK, and note that its new duration is 14:12.

STEP 25: Add **BS_Retrocities.mov** to [**My_Atomic Cafe**], starting at time 00:00, and drag it to the bottom of the stack in the Timeline window. Scrub the timeline, and notice there is no jump at 07:06 as the movie loops back to the first frame.

STEP 26: Import **AB_SoapFilm.mov**, which has a longer duration of 16:01. Add this movie to your comp, also at time 00:00, and place it just above the **BS_Retrocities.mov** layer. Scrub the timeline to see the multicolored liquid flow (see the sidebar *Soap Film* to learn how this was made). We'll use this second movie to add some texture and color to the underlying yellow movie.

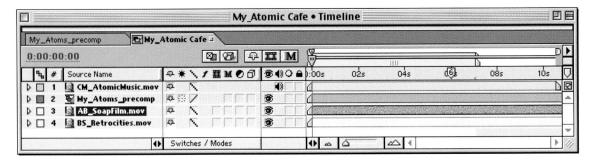

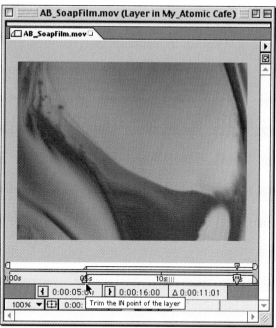

STEP 27: Double-click the AB_SoapFilm.mov to open it in its own Layer window, and scrub along the timeline to check out the entire movie (16:01 duration). The movie is longer than the comp's duration of 10:16, and the second half of the movie is more turbulent than the beginning. Since we like the more turbulent look, trim the layer so the 10:16 portion you need comes from the later portion:

• In the Layer window, drag the layer's in point to around 05:00 until the duration reads about 11 seconds. You can also trim the in point by moving the time marker to 05:00 and clicking the In switch (which looks like an open squiggly bracket). By trimming the clip in the Layer window, the layer's in point in the timeline (00:00) is maintained. Close the Layer window when you're done trimming.

27 The **AB_Soap Film.mov** layer starts off with larger shapes (above left), and progresses over 16 seconds to more interesting shapes near the end of the movie (above right). To include more of the more turbulent flow, you can trim out the first five seconds. In the Layer window, drag the in point (where the cursor is pointing) to around 5:00, leaving a duration of just over the 10:16 you'll need.

Soap Film

The Soap Film collection from Artbeats (produced and directed by Ted Kinsman of Kinsman's Physics Productions) contains an explanation of the physics behind soap film images. In short:

"The brilliant displays of color are created by the wave nature of light as revealed in a thin sheet of soap. This same effect is often seen in a wet parking lot where a few drops of oil spilled on the pavement and a rainbow is seen in the water. The clips show optical interference of light waves as they reflect from a very thin moving sheet of soap. The colors are linked to varying thicknesses in the sheet of soap. As rocks in a stream create eddies in the water, obstructions placed in the flowing sheet of soap are transformed into infinitely complex changes in color and pattern."

And you thought it was just another pretty background…

Blending Layers

Combining multiple layers
with Transfer Modes works best
if the sources are not super busy.
If one layer is dominating the
balance of the mix, don't be
afraid to reduce its opacity or
desaturate its color.

Step 28: We often combine multiple layers of imagery using Transfer Modes to create a new image. Your goal here is to end up with a bright, colorful background that shows the twirling lines in the **BS_Retrocities** movie, but also blends in some of the flowing nature and the bright color of the AB_SoapFilm movie. You don't want to make it so busy that the atoms sequence in front is overshadowed; you also need to keep it light and bright so that the black atoms continue to stand out well against this background. Here's how we achieved a blend that we liked (by all means experiment a bit to arrive at a mix that suits your own tastes):

• If the Modes panel is not already visible in the Timeline window, expose it by pressing F4. Set the mode for the **AB_SoapFilm.mov** layer to Overlay. This is going in the right direction, but now the soap layer is not showing up as well as we'd like…

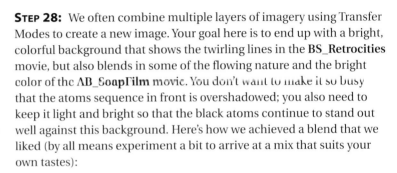

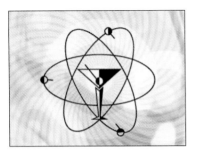

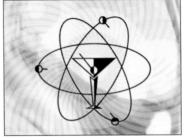

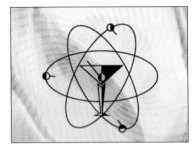

28 To create different looks, try using different combinations of transfer modes. The first image (left) shows one copy of **AB_SoapFilm** in Overlay mode on top of the **BS_Retrocities** layer; the second (center) shows a second copy of **AB_SoapFilm** in Overlay mode with 50% opacity; the third (right) shows a third copy of **AB_SoapFilm** on top in Color mode. The Timeline window (below) illustrates this layer stack.

• Duplicate the **AB_SoapFilm.mov**. This duplicate retains the same mode, so it is also set to Overlay. The blend is getting more intense… perhaps too intense. Press T to reveal the Opacity of the duplicate, and blend it down to about 50% Opacity. You now have a nice blend of texture between the flowing liquid and the swirling lines.

• To add more color, select the duplicated **AB_SoapFilm.mov** layer, and duplicate it again. This time, set its transfer mode to Color. This maintains the luminance values of the layers below, but mixes in the Hue and Saturation of this third soap-film layer. Scrub the Opacity value and set to taste (we used 50% again).

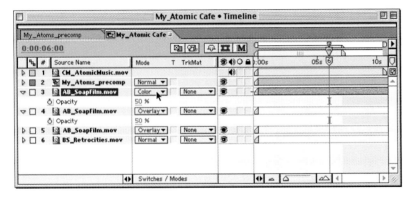

Note that when you duplicate a layer, the copy always goes above the source. Go ahead and play around with changing the order of these three copies of the soap film movie – note that when the Overlay layers are on top, the result is more intense colors. We personally left the Color version on top, going for a more pastel look.

Save your project. Compare your version with our [**AtomicCafe_after Step 28**]. *As this section was more "to taste," don't be too concerned if yours looks different. But if you want to make sure your results match the illustrations from here on, duplicate ours, rename it* [**My_Atomic Cafe_28**], *and continue.*

Precomposing the Background

Once you've finalized your mix of the background layers, it's time to give them their own composition. This will tidy up the timeline by consolidating (or "grouping") the four layers down to one, and make it easy to turn the background on and off as a group.

STEP 29: Select the four background layers – they should be the four bottom layers in the Timeline window – and Layer>Pre-compose them, or use the shortcut: Command+Shift+C (Control+Shift+C). Be sure to give the precomp a useful name, such as "**My_Background_precomp**," and click OK.

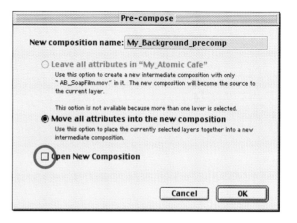

> The Pre-compose dialog usually offers more than one option of which details to send back to the precomp along with the layer. Because you've selected multiple layers, the only option available is to precompose using the Move All Attributes option. This creates a precomp based on the size and duration of the current comp, and moves all the attributes (for example, the trim points, transfer modes, and Opacity values) back to the precomp.

The four background movie layers will now appear as one layer: a nested comp called **My_Background_precomp**. You can bring this precomp forward for editing at any time by Option+double-clicking (Alt+double-clicking) the nested comp layer. You can also open it by double-clicking it from the Project window, just like any other comp.

RAM Preview or scrub through the comp, and then Save your project. You've now completed Part 3 of this tutorial. Compare your version with our [**AtomicCafe_after Step 29**]. *To pick up this tutorial at Part 4, rename this comp to* [**My_Atomic Cafe_29**] *and continue from here.*

29 To reduce clutter in your comp, select the four layers that make up the background and Layer>Pre-compose them (above). The result is one layer in [**My_Atomic Cafe**] (below). In After Effects 5, you can check the Open New Composition box (circled in red) if you want the precomp to appear as a tab item at the top of the Comp and Timeline windows after it is created.

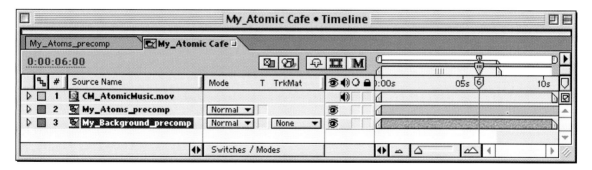

Part 4: Atomic Café Title

The stage is now set for you to add the main title. As we've been alluding, the intention is for it to make an impact around 06:00 in the timeline to match the explosion and change in the music.

There are three sections to this animation: bringing on the word "Atomic," bringing on the word "Café" and making it animate, and fading out the atom symbols that got us to this point.

STEP 30: Import the layered Illustrator file **AC_Title.ai**. Since you want to access its individual layers, you'll need to import it as a composition, as you did with the layered Photoshop file back in Step 1. As before, the instructions vary slightly depending on what version of After Effects you're using:

After Effects 5.0 or later:

• Select the folder **My_Sources** in the Project window, select File> Import>File, and locate the file **AC_Title.ai** from the **Project>Sources** folder. Be sure to choose Composition from the Import As popup at the bottom of the import dialog. Click Import (Open).

• After Effects will create a folder and a composition, both named **AC_Title.ai**. Drag the comp [**AC_Title.ai**] into the **My_Comps** folder.

Background Quickie

To quickly change the comp's background color to something other than black, open its dialog, select the eyedropper, click on the gray area of the dialog, then click OK.

30 The title was created in Illustrator. Atomic uses the font Axiom from T.26 (www.t26.com); Café was created with the font Telegram Plain from Fontek (www.fontek.com).

After Effects 4.1:

• Select File>Import>Illustrator as Comp and locate the file **AC_Title.ai** from the **Project>Sources** folder. Click Open.

• After Effects will create a folder and composition, both named **AC_Title.ai**. Drag the folder into the **My_Sources** folder in the Project window, and the comp into **My_Comps**.

STEP 31: Open the [**AC_Title.ai**] comp, and change the background color (Composition>Background color) to something other than black so you can see the text clearly.

• This comp contains two layers of interest: **Atomic** and **Cafe**. Turn on Best Quality for both layers. You can ignore or delete the **Guides** layer.

• Deselect all layers (shortcut: F2) to ensure that no properties are selected, then select both the **Atomic** and **Cafe** layers, and Copy.

STEP 32: Bring the [**My_Atomic Cafe**] comp forward, and at time 00:00, Paste the layers. Turn off the Video switch (the eyeball) for **Cafe**; you'll be animating the **Atomic** title first.

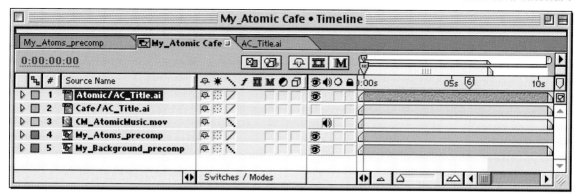

Animating the Atomic Title

STEP 33: First, you're going to animate the Scale of the **Atomic** layer to make it spring on the scene. It will have a primary action, where it first appears, and a secondary action, where it drifts a bit to keep the viewer's attention.

- Move to time 05:25, select the **Atomic** layer, and press [(left bracket) to move the layer's In Point to the current time. Check to make sure the layer extends to the end of the comp – if not, drag the Out Point to the end.

- With the **Atomic** layer still selected, press S for Scale, turn on the animation stopwatch for this property, and set its value to 15%.

- Press 6 to move to the comp marker at 06:00 – where the downbeat of the music hits – and scale the layer up to 70%. This zooms the type quickly toward the viewer in five frames.

- Move to time 07:00 and hit Shift+7 (on the keyboard, not the keypad) to set comp marker #7 at this time. This will make it easy to return later to this point.

- Set the Scale value to 100%. The title will continue to "drift" for another second, adding interest while the viewer digests the meaning of the word.

32 Import the Illustrator artwork as a comp, copy the two layers **Atomic** and **Cafe**, and paste them into **[My_Atomic Cafe]**. Turn off the **Cafe** layer's Video switch for now; you'll be animating **Atomic** first.

33 The Atomic title (shown solo) scales quickly from 15% (left) to 70% (center), then drifts slowly to 100% scale (right).

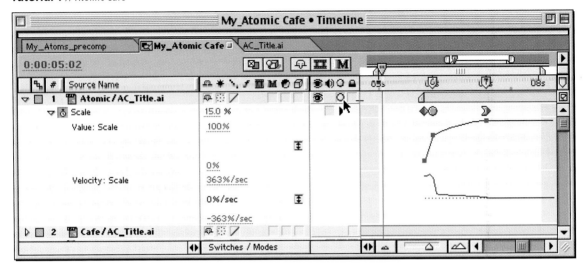

33 *complete:* The interpolation for **Atomic**'s scale-up has been edited to smoothly go through the second keyframe, and ease into the third. The cursor is pointing at the Solo switch – new in After Effects 5.0 – which makes it easy to temporarily view the animation of select layers.

Diamonds Aren't Forever

To return a temporal keyframe back to Linear after applying Easy Ease or otherwise changing it, Command+click (Control+click) on the keyframe until it reverts back to the familiar diamond icon.

• Set the work area to extend from about 05:00 to 08:00 (either drag the work area handles, or locate to these two points in time, hit B to set the beginning of the work area, then N to set the end). RAM Preview this section. In After Effects 5.0 or later, you can set the Solo switch for the **Atomic** layer to remove the distractions of the other elements. You should notice that by using the Linear interpolation method, there will be a hitch in the speed as it reaches each keyframe.

• To refine the Scale keyframe interpolation, select the third keyframe (the one at 07:00) and apply Easy Ease In. This will create a gradual slowdown as the title interpolates from 70% to 100%. RAM Preview and note the result.

There's still a slight hitch to the animation around the second keyframe. A good keyframe interpolation type to use in cases like this is Auto Bezier, which smoothes the transition through a keyframe by averaging the parameter velocity at this point, and giving this average speed a 16.7% influence.

• Command+click (Control+click) on the second keyframe in the Timeline to change its interpolation type from Linear (the diamond icon) to Auto Bezier (circle icon). RAM Preview again, and see if you like the smoother result. Twirl down the Velocity graph to see how the Value graph is now rounded. (You can Undo back a few steps to compare what the graph looked like with the previous Linear keyframes; just be sure to Redo back again or repeat the Easy Ease and Auto Bezier actions.) Twirl up the Velocity and Value graphs when you're done.

> Depending on the placement of the Anchor Point for a layer, scaling can cause a layer to appear to drift in position as it scales away from the center point defined by the anchor. In this case, we already centered the word Atomic in the Illustrator file, using our center guides for placement, so its anchor would end up centered in the word in After Effects. However, you can change the position of a layer's Anchor Point in After Effects if necessary.

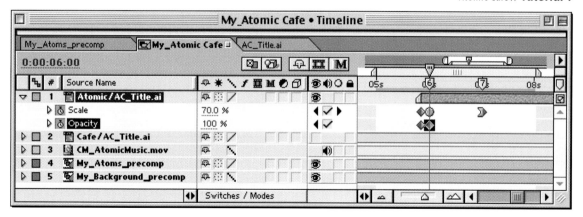

STEP 34: There is a slight visual "pop" when the word Atomic comes on, because it is starting at a Scale larger than 0%. This can be smoothed over with some quick Opacity keyframing:

• Make sure the **Atomic** layer is still selected, and press I to move back to the layer's in point at 05:25.

• Press Shift+T to twirl down Opacity while keeping the Scale property open as well. Turn on the animation stopwatch for Opacity, and set its initial value to 0%.

• Press 6 to move to 06:00, and set the Opacity back to 100%. Editing its value will automatically create the second keyframe.

• If you're using After Effects 5.0 or later, turn off the layer's Solo switch so you can see all the other layers again.

Atoms Be Gone

STEP 35: As the Atomic title is zooming up, you want the atoms behind it to quickly fade down. Simple enough; just add some more Opacity keyframes.

• Select the **Atoms_precomp** layer. If the layer's keyframes are not already visible, hit U to show animated properties.

• Move to time 05:25, press Shift+T to also view Opacity, and turn on its animation stopwatch to create a keyframe at 100%.

• Note the position of the Scale keyframe at 06:10. Click on the keyframe navigator right arrow for the Scale property to jump to 06:10, and scrub the Opacity value down to 0% (see also figure on next page).

When you're synchronizing keyframes, use the keyframe navigator arrows to jump to certain keyframes – that way you can be sure that new keyframes created for another property synchronize exactly with the existing keyframe(s). It also avoids errors where extra keyframes are created one frame to the left or right of a keyframe you were trying to edit...

34 To smooth over the visual pop when Atomic comes on, quickly fade up its opacity. However, having both the atomic symbols and the word Atomic on at the same time is visually messy; you'll straighten that out in the next step.

Scrubbing Values

5.0 makes it easy to scrub values interactively, but you can still do this in 4.1. Press Option (Alt) and click on the name of the property in the Timeline window. In most cases, a slider will pop up that allows for interactive editing. It's particularly useful for Opacity.

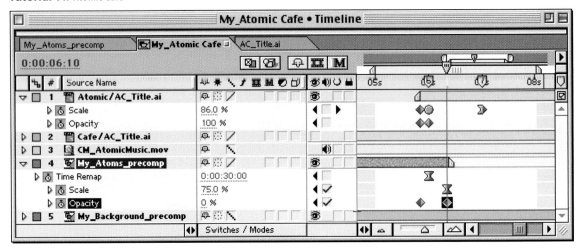

36 The **My_Atoms_precomp** layer fades down to 0% as the title builds on, and is trimmed out at 06:10.

STEP 36: Even though the layer is at 0% Opacity and therefore is taking no rendering time, it's still a good idea to trim layers that have faded down – this will help you know who is playing at what point in time just by glancing at the Timeline window.

With **My_Atoms_precomp** still selected and with the time marker at 06:10, press Option+] (Alt+]) to trim out the end of this layer.

Save the project and twirl up the **My_Atoms_precomp** *layer. Compare your version with our* [**AtomicCafe_after Step 36**]. *Remember you can select a layer and press U to view its keyframed properties.*

Animating the Café Title

The word Café will get a different treatment. It will scale and fade up after the word Atomic, stretching from the center of the frame rather than its own center. If you have the Production Bundle, you'll also take advantage of the keyframe assistant The Wiggler to make it continue to bounce around to attract attention, and to follow the talking, bouncy nature of the music after the big hit at 06:00. The last step in this part of the tutorial will then be adding a drop shadow to both words in the title.

More on Music

There is an article in the **Goodies** folder on the CD-ROM that came with this book – *Timing Video to Audio* – which goes into greater detail about matching animation moves to music.

To reduce the amount of clutter in the Timeline window, you can twirl up the animating properties for the other layers. Or, if you have a large computer monitor, go ahead and keep them exposed, and drag the Timeline window larger so you can see the timing interplay between layers.

STEP 37: Select the **Cafe** layer and turn its Video switch back on. Press 7 (on the keyboard) to jump to comp marker #7 at 07:00, and press [to move this layer's in point to the current time. Check to make sure that the layer extends to the end of the comp – if not, drag the out point to the end.

STEP 38: With the **Cafe** layer selected, notice in the Comp window that its Anchor Point – the circle with an X through it – defaults to the center of the layer (which also happens to coincide with the center of the **Atomic** layer). If you have trouble seeing this, double-click on the layer to open it in its own Layer window, and make sure Anchor Point Path is enabled in this window's wing menu. This means that any scale or rotation applied will originate from this point.

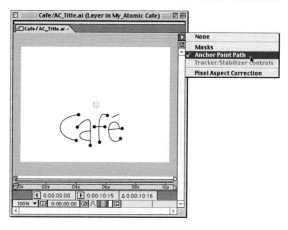

• With the **Cafe** layer still selected, press S to twirl down Scale, turn on its animation stopwatch, and reduce the Scale value down to 0%.

• Move to 07:15, and set the Scale to 90%.

38 Any scale or rotation a layer undergoes is centered around its Anchor Point – the icon of a circle with an X inside. It is often easiest to view it in the Layer window. (If you animate the Anchor Point, its motion path is editable only in the Layer window.)

STEP 39: With **Cafe** selected, press Shift+T to also twirl down its Opacity property in the Timeline window. You're about to add a fade-up that syncs with the Scale keyframes – but let's do it in reverse, to reduce the amount of parameter entry you have to do:

• Still at time 07:15, turn on the animation stopwatch for Opacity. This will set a keyframe value of 100%, its final value.

• Hit I to return to the in point of the layer at 07:00, and change the Opacity to 0%.

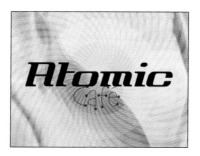

• RAM preview a work area around these two keyframes. The Café title will stretch out from the center of the comp.

• Save your project!

39 The Café title animates on after the word Atomic. Since its Anchor Point is set to the middle of the overall frame instead of the word Café, it seems to stretch out from the center of the comp.

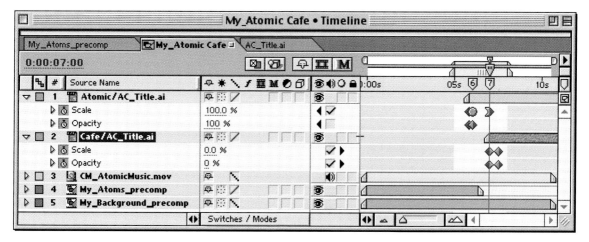

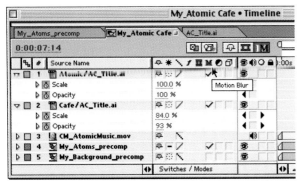

40 To enable Motion Blur calculations for a layer, set its M switch in the Timeline window (top). To preview the results in the Comp window, enable the larger M switch along the top of the Timeline window. The result will be a zoom blur on the titles as they scale up (above).

Motion Blur

When objects move quickly in the digital world, they can seem to strobe as they jump from one position to another, frame to frame. In the film world, the same objects appear more as streaks, because the shutter of the camera is open and still exposing film while they move. This latter look is considered more natural.

STEP 40: After Effects can simulate the open shutter streaking effect through its Motion Blur feature. When an object is animated by After Effects, it can calculate a streak along the vector the object is traveling at each frame. Let's employ this feature to improve the look of the title animation.

• Turn on the M (Motion Blur) switch in the Timeline window for both the **Atomic** and **Cafe** layers. This enables motion blur to be calculated for these layers during final rendering. If you can't find these switches, chances are your Timeline window is still displaying Modes instead of Switches (you called up the Modes panel back in Step 28); use F4 to flip this panel back to Switches.

• To see this blur in the Comp window, turn on the Enable Motion Blur switch (the large M button along the top of the timeline), and either RAM Preview or set the time marker to a point where the title layers are animating (such as 07:15 for the **Cafe** layer).

• You can optionally turn on the motion blur switch for the **Atoms_precomp** layer that's scaling up. Understand that the blur effect will be less on this layer since it is scaling at a much slower rate, and the motion blur effect adds considerably to your rendering time – it's a tradeoff you'll have to make a decision about.

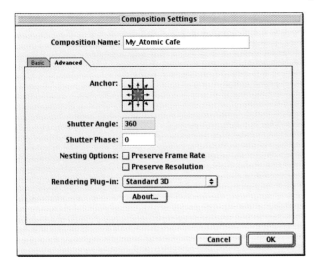

• Change the Motion Blur amount to 360° for longer streaks and more impact. In After Effects 5.0 and later, you can set this per composition by setting the shutter angle in Composition> Composition Settings dialog, under the Advanced tab. (In After Effects 4.1 and earlier, this is set in File>Preferences>General for all comps.) The Motion Blur angle can also be overridden in the Render Settings dialog in the Time Sampling section.

40 *complete:* After Effects 5.0 allows you to set different Motion Blur Shutter Angle values per composition. This parameter is hiding under the Advanced tab in the Composition Settings window.

Wiggle Expression

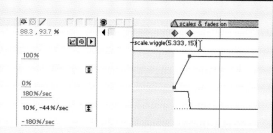

If you don't have the Production Bundle, but you do have After Effects 5.0 or later, there is a very simple expression that creates a result similar to The Wiggler in Step 41 below:

- Select the **Cafe.ai** layer and hit S to reveal its Scale keyframes.

- Option+click (Alt+click) on the animation stopwatch for Scale – this enables expressions, and enters the word "scale" in the expression field to the right.

- Place the cursor after the word scale, and type

.wiggle(5.333,15)

and hit Enter (not Return).

- Set the work area the same length as **Cafe.ai**, and RAM Preview.

Where did those numbers come from? The first is how many wiggles per second. As noted earlier, our music takes 1.5 seconds per measure. To make Café dance eight times per measure, you need to wiggle 8 ÷ 1.5 = 5.333 times per second.

The second value is how many units to wiggle by. Since our starting Scale is 90%, a value of 15 means the layer's Scale will bounce around between 75% and 105%.

(Note: Expressions are covered in detail in Tutorial 11, *Just an Expression*.)

The Wiggler *(Production Bundle)*

This next part is optional, as it requires that you have the Production Bundle version of After Effects. You'll be using a keyframe assistant in it called The Wiggler.

Cute name, but what does it do? The Wiggler takes previously existing property values and offsets them randomly. You can decide how often it does this (e.g. every five frames), and what is the maximum amount the parameter will be offset (e.g. ±10 pixels). It works between the keyframes you select. As a result, you need to select at least two keyframes for a property – even if there is no change in value between those keyframes – to use The Wiggler.

In this tutorial, you're going to use The Wiggler to randomize the Scale of the Café title. This will make it dance around during the last few seconds of this clip.

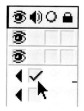

Forced Motion Blur

After Effects can add motion blur only to objects it animates – not to footage of moving objects. To add blur to footage, use a third-party plug-in like ReelSmart Motion Blur from RE:Vision Effects (www.revisionfx.com).

Step 41: Select the **Cafe** layer and hit End to go to the last frame of the comp (10:15). Press N to set the work area to end here as well. You can trim the start of the work area to 07:00 if you like, as you'll be focusing solely on the Café animation for now. Its Scale property should be visible (if not, hit S to twirl it down).

- Check the keyframe box for the Scale property to add another Scale keyframe at this time (10:15). It should have the same value as the previous keyframe: 90%.

Click the keyframe box for the Scale property to create a new keyframe at the current time (10:15).

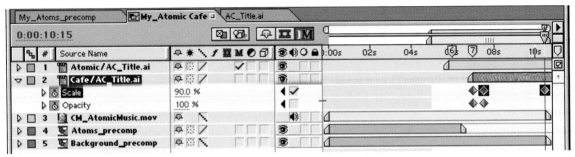

41 Set a third keyframe for Scale at 10:15 and select the last two keyframes before you apply The Wiggler.

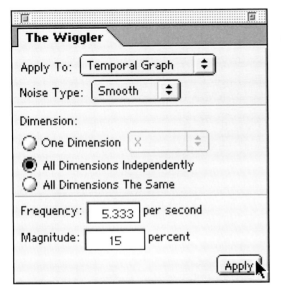

41 *continued:* The parameters for The Wiggler. These settings mean a new keyframe will be created 5.333 times a second, randomizing the X and Y scale independently by up to ±15%.

41 *continued:* The Wiggler creates new keyframes between the ones you selected (below). Note the Scale parameter (where the cursor is pointing): the X and Y dimensions were randomized separately. Zoom into the timeline to get a better view of the individual keyframes.

• This new keyframe will automatically be selected when you created it. Shift+click on the second keyframe back at 07:15 so that both the second and third Scale keyframes are highlighted. *Remember that you can use The Wiggler only when two or more keyframes are selected.*

• Select Window>The Wiggler to open its floating palette. Some of the default settings – namely, to Apply to>Temporal Graph, with Noise Type>Smooth, and All Dimensions Independently – are fine. The All Dimensions Independently setting is of particular interest: This means the X and Y scale randomizations will be independent of each other, which should result in some fun stretch and squash movements.

• To make the title dance in time to the music, you need to pick a Frequency that matches the tempo of the soundtrack. As noted earlier, our music takes 1.5 seconds per measure. To make Café dance eight times per measure, you need a Frequency parameter of 8 ÷ 1.5 = 5.333 wiggles per second. Go ahead and enter this value for Frequency.

• In the Magnitude field, enter 15%. This will keep the new scale keyframes created by The Wiggler confined to a range of ±15% from the current value (90%), or in a range from 75% to 105%. (Yes, any value over 100% will soften the type, but sometimes you have to live dangerously…and in reality, this is the outer limit; most keyframes will be well inside the maximum values of 75% to 105%.)

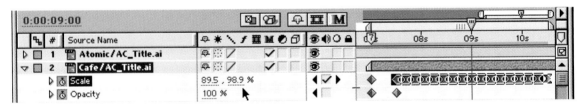

• Click Apply. Keyframes will be added along the timeline at a spacing decided by the Frequency parameter, with values randomly determined by the Magnitude parameter. Immediately RAM Preview. (It's best not to click around the timeline, as you'll fill up the Undo buffer making it harder to undo the Wiggler if you don't like it.)

• Remember that the Wiggler values are truly random! If you don't like the result – too subtle or too boingy – Undo until the extra keyframes disappear but the two Scale keyframes are still selected, then hit the Wiggler's Apply button again. You don't need to adjust any other Wiggler parameters. Feel free to RAM Preview, Undo, and Apply again until you arrive at a bounce pattern you find pleasing. Don't be surprised if it takes a few tries. If you find the RAM Previews are taking too long, turn off the Enable Motion Blur switch for this comp (the big M switch along the top of the Timeline window) – this will speed things up considerably. Remember to keep the individual layer M switches on, so Motion Blur will still be calculated during your final render.

• Close The Wiggler palette when you're done, and twirl up the layer properties for the **Atomic** and **Cafe** layers.

Compare your version with our [**AtomicCafe_after Step 41**]. *If you don't have the Production Bundle, you can use this comp – which already has Wiggler-generated keyframes – for the remaining steps.*

Drop Shadows

STEP 42: For the last step in this part, lift the title a bit off the background using shadows. Add Effect>Perspective>**Drop Shadow** to both the **Atomic** and **Cafe** title layers, and set the shadow parameters to taste.

A subtle alternate to a drop shadow is a dark diffuse glow. Use the Drop Shadow effect, but change the shadow's Opacity value to 100%, distance to 0.0, and softness to taste (around 20 to 30 should work).

We saved an Effect Favorite with these settings. Select one of the title layers, invoke Effect>Apply Favorite, navigate to the **01_Atomic Cafe>_Favorites** folder, and select **DropShadow_diffuse.ffx**. A drop shadow with our settings will be applied to the selected layer.

41 *complete:* The Production Bundle's The Wiggler creates a fun stretch/squash animation.

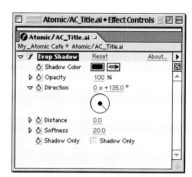

42 Apply a dark diffuse glow with the Drop Shadow effect to finish off the title layers at the end of Part 4.

End of Part 4! RAM Preview, Save your project, and close the Effect Controls window. Compare your comp with our [**AtomicCafe_after Step 42**] *if you got lost.*

Part 5: Sparks and Flares

The basic animation is now finished. For the remaining steps, you'll be spicing up this spot. First, to further emphasize the "energized" feeling of the piece, you'll be adding various lighting effects such as sparks and lens flares. Two different approaches will be employed: using stock footage elements, and applying plug-in effects. (That plug-in effect will be Knoll Light Factory LE which we suggested you install back in the Overview box at the beginning of this tutorial. If you haven't installed it yet, save, quit, install, restart After Effects, and reload your project.)

Particle Movies

STEP 43: First, let's light the fuse that will lead up to the big hit at 06:00:

• Import **BS_Particulars2.mov** from the **Project>Sources** folder.

• Add it to [**My_Atomic Cafe**] and set it to start at 01:15 (remember that you can also move to 01:15 and hit [to move its in point to this time). Position it directly above **Atoms_precomp** in the layer stack.

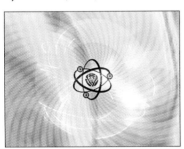

43 The **BS_Particulars2.mov** file (courtesy of Bestshots/Particulars 2 CD) is a set of particles swirling in a figure-eight pattern (above). When applied in Add mode, the black background drops out, and the particles illuminate the layers behind (below).

> A new feature in After Effects 5.0 is the ability to drag a footage item to a specific time and layer stack position in the Timeline window. To do this, drag the movie to the right side of the Timeline window, watching for the black insertion bar within the layer stack for positioning. The current time (top left of window) will display the layer's in point.

• Scrub the timeline and you'll see particles swirling around in a figure-eight pattern. The problem is that it obscures all that's behind it. You need to drop out its black background, and keep just the particles.

• Make sure the Modes panel is exposed in the Timeline window (shortcut: F4 to toggle between Switches and Modes), and select the Add transfer mode for the **BS_Particulars2.mov** layer.

> The Add mode reveals the layers behind, adding to them the color values of the selected layer. Since the color value of black is zero, it adds nothing to the layers behind, revealing them untouched. The bright particles will greatly brighten the background where they're swirling. If you find this effect too bright, use Screen mode – it's a tamer version of Add.

• These particles are supposed to fade away when the title comes on. Press 6 to move to time 06:00. With the **BS_Particulars2.mov** layer selected, press T to reveal its Opacity, and click on its corresponding animation stopwatch to turn on keyframing. This will create a first keyframe with a value of 100%.

• With the particles still selected, press the letter O to jump to this layer's out point, and change its Opacity to 0% to fade the movie out.

• With the **BS_Particulars2.mov** selected, press Command+Option+B (Control+Alt+B) to set the work area to the duration of the layer. RAM

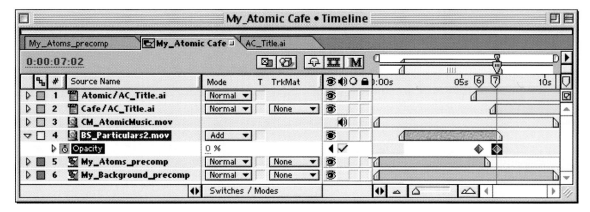

Preview and observe the result. If you feel the particles linger a little too long after the word Atomic comes up, you can move the second opacity keyframe earlier in time, or try applying Easy Ease In to it to taper the fade. When you're done, twirl up the layer (or press T again).

Notice how the particles appear to wrap themselves serendipitously around the atoms. This is emphasized because the particles are composited on top of the atom symbols as well as the background. To compare, drag the **BS_Particulars2.mov** layer below **Atoms_precomp** in the layer stack and you'll see that the interaction between the two is reduced. Undo to move the particles back above the atoms layer again.

Step 44: As if that wasn't enough pizzazz, we have a second particles movie for you to apply. It will be treated much like the particles in the step above, but will add spice to the Atomic Cafe title section.

• Import **BS_Particulars1.mov**, and add it to [**My_Atomic Cafe**].

• Press 6 to move to 06:00 and hit [to start **BS_Particulars1.mov** at this time.

• Position this new movie above the **Atomic** and **Cafe** title layers (the top of the layer stack).

• Set its Transfer Mode to Add.

• With the movie still selected, press Command+Option+B (Control+Alt+B) to set the work area to the duration of the movie, and RAM preview. The particles build from the center out, creating a horizontal energy whorl.

  Notice that this movie has a built-in "fade up" as the particles gain momentum, and a natural "fade down" as the particles dissipate, so there is no need to add Opacity keyframes.

Save! We took some shortcuts in the explanations of the steps, as we figured you already knew the basic dance by now. If we assumed too much, compare your version with our [**AtomicCafe_after Step 44**].

43 *continued:* The particles layer starts at 01:15, the beginning of one of the measures of the soundtrack, and fades out after the bang at 06:00 when the title starts to build.

Work Area Snap To

Use Command+Option+B (Control+Alt+B) to set the work area to the duration of the selected layer(s).

44 A second particle movie (from the Bestshots/Particulars 1 CD) adds an energy whorl around the word Atomic.

45 Create a new blank layer –
a Solid – that's black, and the
same size as the composition.

Light Manufacturing

To further emphasize the big musical hit at 06:00, you're going to create
a flare effect to temporarily blind the viewer as the word Atomic comes
up. Well, maybe not *blind*, but at least make a statement…

Like many of the other elements so far, this one will start just before
the downbeat, ramp up quickly for impact, then fade down to make
room for other elements. In this case, you'll be animating some of the
Knoll Light Factory LE parameters to create this effect, instead of the
Scale and Opacity you have been using so far.

If you want, go ahead and close the other comp windows aside from
[**My_Atomic Cafe**] – you're done with them, and it will reduce screen
clutter as you focus on these last few effects.

STEP 45: Locate to time 05:25 in your comp, just before that downbeat. Create a new Solid by either using the shortcut Command+Y
(Control+Y) or the menu item Layer>New>Solid (in After Effects 4.1,
it's Layer>New Solid – no intermediate menu). Give the solid a good
name such as "**My Flare**," click on the Make Comp Size button, and
select black as its color. Click OK.

STEP 46: With the new layer selected, choose the plug-in Effect>
Knoll Light Factory>**Light Factory LE** (provided free with this book
courtesy of Pinnacle Systems). A nice bright spark, with a series of
lens reflections, will slash across your black solid. Go ahead and try
out the different Flare Types available in the Effect Controls window;
we're going to stick with the Warm Sun Flare default.

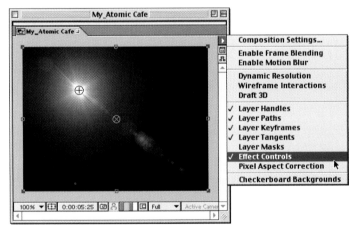

46 The default Light Factory LE
lens flare. Make sure you can see the
Effect Control for its Light Source
Location in the Comp window; you'll
be dragging this to the center of the
comp to create a pure spark effect.

• *Make sure the effect is selected in
the Effect Controls window.* This will
cause its control point for the Light
Source Location to appear in the
Comp window: It will be a circle with
a + symbol in the middle, right where
the sparks originate. if you can't see it,
make sure the option Effect Controls
is selected in the Comp window's wing
menu. Draw an imaginary line from
this Light Source Location through the
center of the layer; notice how the lens
reflections are drawn along this
imaginary line.

• In this case, you don't want all those reflections; you just want the
spark. The way to make the reflections go away is to align the Light
Source Location with the centerpoint of the layer. Drag it in the Comp
window until they align, or type in the value X160, Y120 for the Light
Source Location in the Effect Controls window.

• Scrub the Angle parameter in the Effect Controls window. Notice how it makes the rays in the spark rotate and create new patterns. You'll be using this to create additional excitement in your flare. Set it back to 0.0 when you're done.

• You want the spark to start from nothing, so scrub its Brightness parameter down to zero.

STEP 47: Time to animate your flare:

• Still at time 05:25, turn on the keyframe animation stopwatches for the Brightness, Scale, and Angle parameters; you will be animating all of these. In After Effects 5.0 and later, you can set these stopwatches directly in the Effect Controls window. (In After Effects 4.1, Option-click (Alt-click) on each of these three parameters to turn on their stopwatches.) After you've set this trio of stopwatches, press U to reveal these keyframes in the Timeline window.

• Press 6 to locate to comp marker 6 at 06:00 in the timeline.

• Increase the Brightness parameter to somewhere over 100. You want the flare to illuminate most of the frame, with just a bit of dark in the corners. We chose a value of 140.

• Increase the effect's Scale parameter. This increases the size of the center of the flare, increases the overall illumination, and makes the individual rays more pronounced. We settled on a value of 2.00.

After this initial blow-out, you want the flare to reduce in size over the next couple of musical beats, as the word Atomic comes up underneath. (You can't see the word Atomic right now – it's obscured by the black solid you created for the flare. We'll deal with that shortly.) We mentioned earlier that one measure of the music was 1.5 seconds, which is about 45 frames; let's fade out the flare over half a measure.

• Go to time 06:23. Reduce the Scale parameter back down to 1.00, and the Brightness back down to 0.0. Trim the out point of this layer by making sure it is still selected and pressing Option+] (Alt+]). Then press Command+Option+B (Control+Alt+B) to set the work area to equal the length of this layer, and RAM preview it.

Pretty cool! But the rays aren't doing anything other than growing and contracting.

• With **My_Flare** still selected, press the letter O to locate to its out point, and increase the Angle parameter to give the rays a bit of movement. A little goes a long way; we chose to animate from 0° to 45° – but you can use more if you like. RAM Preview and adjust to taste.

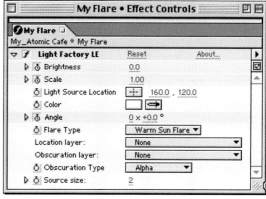

46 *complete:* After you've set the Light Source Location to equal the center of the layer (X160, Y120), reduce the Brightness to zero. In Step 47, enable keyframing for the Brightness, Scale, and Angle parameters at 05:25.

47 At maximum brightness, the flare should just fill the frame, with some dark falloff visible in the corners.

Flares Galore

If you like this free Light Factory LE effect, you should check out the full Knoll Light Factory package from Pinnacle Systems (www.pinnaclesys.com). A demo version is included in the Free Plug-ins folder on your CD. Yes, it was created by the same John Knoll who has supervised special effects for numerous blockbuster films.

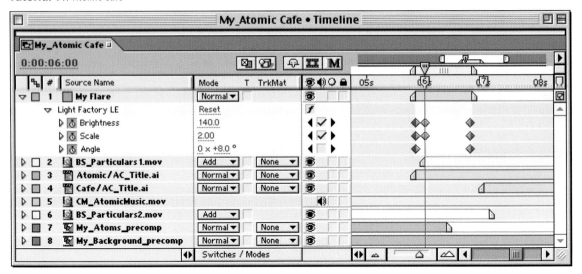

47 *complete:* The parameters of Light Factory LE have now been animated to make the flare grow and contract in time with the pivotal hit in the music. Pick a transfer mode that works for you in Step 48.

STEP 48: Now finish the effect off by using Transfer Modes to blend your flare over the logo and background.

• Press 6 to locate to the point of maximum brightness. Make sure the Switches/Modes panel in the Timeline window is set to Modes (press F4 if it isn't). There are a few Transfer Modes which are ideally suited to blending in layers on black backgrounds: Add, Screen, and Color Dodge. (Lighten, Difference, and Exclusion also work with black backgrounds, but they give pretty weird results.) Screen is the most

48 Different Transfer Modes create different blending effects. Here are Add (left), Screen (center), and Color Dodge (right).

middle-of-the road, and it creates an easier-to-watch effect. Add mode is the one that will temporarily blind your viewer. Color Dodge is psychedelic. Go ahead and experiment with all three, RAM Previewing as you go, and choose the one you like the best. We personally took the safest route and chose Screen: It did the best job of preserving our original colors, while still adding a lot of light to the scene.

Save, twirl up all layers, and Preview. Compare your version against [**AtomicCafe_after Step 48**]. *If you had trouble creating the flare animation, you can cheat: At Step 46, select your new solid, choose Effect>Apply Favorite, and use our preset* **Favorites>LightFactory.ffx.** *This includes the keyframes in Step 47; just add the Mode in Step 48.*

Part 6: Radio Waves *(optional)*

You could end this tutorial at this point, and be very happy with the result. Make sure you either RAM Preview or render the whole thing, so you can see all the parts strung together. However, if you want to push on and add one more layer of interest to the piece, we've got one more effect to add: Radio Waves.

Radio Waves generates geometric patterns that can animate. The most common use for it is to create a series of concentric circles that expand from a central point, yielding the common graphical representation of radio waves emanating from an antenna. That's what we'll use it for here – but as you learn the basics, keep in mind it's a very flexible plug-in that can be used to create a wide variety of shapes.

This Part calls for either After Effects 5.0 or later, or the Atomic Power Evolution plug-in set and After Effects 4.1. The instructions below will be for version 5.0, noting the differences for 4.1 where we can.

STEP 49: Just like Light Factory LE in Steps 45 through 48, the Radio Waves effect will be applied to a solid layer, and tweaked to taste. The idea is to complement the circles that appear throughout the background thanks to the **BS_Retrocities.mov** layer you added back in Steps 24 and 25.

• Hit 6 to move to time 06:00. Create a new Solid just as you did back in Step 45 (same size as the comp, black in color), and name it "**RadioWaves_solid**."

• Drag this new Solid down the layer stack in the Timeline window so that it sits directly above the **Background_precomp** layer.

• Apply Effect>Render>**Radio Waves**. (In After Effects 4.1 with the Atomic Power Evolution plug-ins, it would be Effect>Evolution>**Radio Wave**.) Rather than compositing on top of the black solid as Light Factory LE did, Radio Waves defaults to creating its own alpha channel, so you see only the effect, and not the black solid it's applied to. The waves draw on over time, so they are not yet visible at 06:00.

• Solo the **RadioWaves_solid** layer so that previews are fast, and you can see more clearly what you are doing. (In After Effects 4.1, you might want to turn off the other layers.) At this point, all you should see is the comp's white background. Set the work area from 06:00 to the end of the comp, and RAM Preview. The default settings produce a thin, fast-moving blue wave pattern. You'll need to change some settings to create thick, slow-moving, light-colored waves.

STEP 50: You'll start by tweaking the frequency and speed of the waves. In the Effect Controls window, twirl down the Wave Motion section of the effect (called just Wave in the Evolution version). The Frequency parameter sets how often a new wave is "born," while the

49 The idea is to use the Radio Waves effect to create additional animating circles, which will serve to reinforce the circles that appear in the background you built earlier.

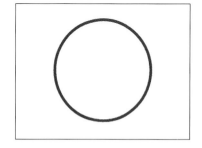

49 *complete:* Apply Radio Waves to the new solid layer and Solo the layer. When you first apply Radio Waves, the default settings create a thin blue wave, which you can see if you advance a few frames or RAM Preview.

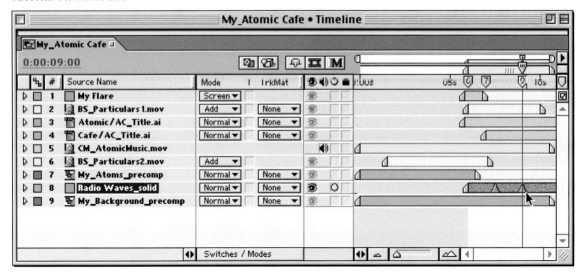

50 The **Radio Waves_solid** layer sits above the background layer and is set to Solo. To help time out where you want new waves to appear, set layer markers at 07:15 and 09:00. Also place comp marker 9 at 09:00 by pressing Shift+F9.

Expansion value sets how fast it moves. Remember that the speed dictates how long each wave will be onscreen before it moves outside the edges of the comp. This in turn defines how long of a "life" each wave appears to have (though we'll change the Lifespan to match the apparent life span of the wave in a moment).

• Since a measure of music is 1.5 seconds or 45 frames long, it would work well to create a new wave every measure. And because a downbeat falls at the start of the layer at 06:00, you will want a second wave to start at 07:15, and a third one to start at 09:00. Move to time 07:15, and with **Radio Waves_solid** still selected, hit the asterisk key on the extended key-pad to add a layer marker. Do the same at time 09:00; also press Shift+9 (on the keyboard) to set a comp marker at 09:00.

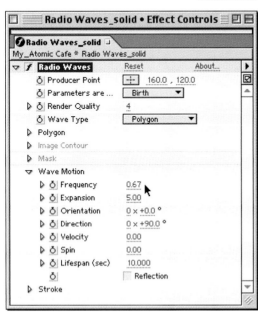

50 *complete:* To generate a new wave every 1.5 seconds, set the Wave Motion>Frequency parameter to 0.67.

• Scrub the timeline, starting at 06:00, and you'll notice that the third wave starts at around 08:00 instead of 09:00. By 09:00 it's quite evolved. This confirms that the waves are being produced too often, as we suspected.

• Hit 9 to jump to 09:00, and change the Frequency value from 1.0 to 0.90 – notice how the third wave moves back toward the center. Try 0.80, and then 0.70. A value of 0.67 should place the beginning of the third wave at exactly 09:00. RAM preview, and see how the waves are now timed to start on beats of the music.

Why a value of 0.67? If you want one wave to start every 1.5 seconds, that means the frequency at which the waves should be generated is 1 wave ÷ 1.5 seconds = 0.67 waves per second.

STEP 51: The speed at which the waves travel from the center is controlled by the Expansion value, which defaults to 5. This pacing is so fast that the first wave is completely off screen before the second one even starts. To create more overlap, slow down the wave Expansion value to 2. When scrubbing values in 5.0, press Command (Control) to scrub in fine increments. RAM Preview again to confirm that this new Expansion rate works better, and that altering it did not affect the Frequency (how often they trigger) – the waves still sync to the music.

STEP 52: Scrub the timeline and you'll notice that the first wave, which started at 06:00, exits the comp at around 09:10. This tells you that each wave has an "onscreen time" of about 03:10. You might consider this to be the lifespan of the layer, but the actual default for the Lifespan parameter – how long the Radio Waves plug-in considers a wave to be around, whether you can see it or not – is 10 seconds. Change Wave Motion>Lifespan to 3.5 seconds so it more closely matches the timing of your waves. This will make the effect more intuitive to deal with when you're setting values that defer to Lifespan. For instance, the Fade-in and -out parameters, as well as the Start and End Width values, take their cues from Lifespan – they don't look at your animation, decide what point the wave moves outside the comp area, then consider that to be the "end" or "out" point!

STEP 53: The waves will now appear faded, due to the default settings in the Stroke section. Twirl down Stroke in the Effect Controls window, and change the Fade-out Time from 5 seconds to 1 second. This will make the wave fade out between 2.5 and 3.5 seconds in its lifespan, or just when it reaches the edges of the comp. Since the wave is outside the comp when it's 03:10 old, it will never fade completely to 0% even as it moves outside the frame.

The Fade-in Time fades up the wave as it starts to move out from the center – it can remain at 0 (no fade in) for this project since the title and particles will obscure the center of the Radio Waves layer.

53 To reduce the amount of fading you saw in the previous figure, reduce the Stroke>Fade-out Time (where the cursor is pointing) to 1.000 seconds.

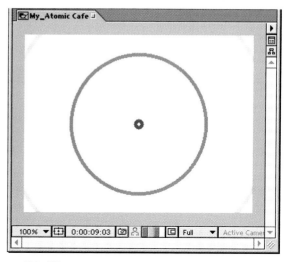

51–52 The Expansion rate has been slowed down so more waves appear onscreen at the same time, and the Lifespan parameter has been reduced to roughly the length of time one wave is visible – note how it fades out as it gets close to the edge.

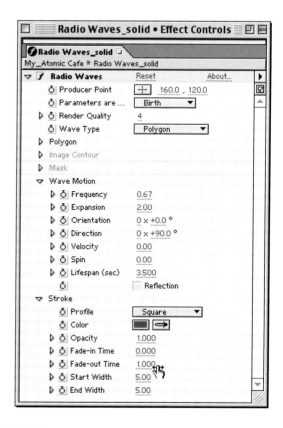

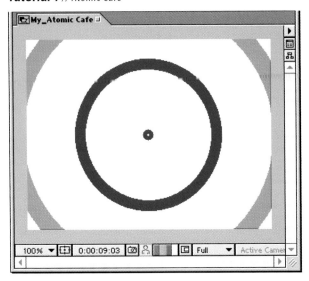

54 By setting a larger End Width than Start Width, the waves grow in thickness as they expand.

STEP 54: There are also settings for the Start Width and End Width. These defer to the duration of the Lifespan, with the Start Width interpolating to the End Width over the course of 3.5 seconds. Leave the Start Width at 5, but change the End Width to 25, or to taste. RAM Preview again, and tweak the fades and width settings until you're happy with the general look. As you can see, it's important to set the Lifespan value first, as it has an impact on other parameters.

STEP 55: All that's left is to set the color and Transfer Mode:

• Set **Radio Waves_solid** to Best Quality to smoothly antialias the waves, and turn off its Solo switch in the Timeline window to view the waves in context with the other layers. (If using After Effects 4.1, turn back on any layers you turned off in Step 49.)

• Under the Stroke section, change the effect's Color to a soft yellow that you think will blend well with the background.

• Experiment with the Transfer Mode for this layer. We used Soft Light, as it blended the yellow waves in a way that they rendered subtly in the background.

• If the waves are still too prominent, set the Opacity of the Radio Waves layer to taste. Somewhere around 75% will help them sit more into the background. You can either use the regular Opacity, or set Radio Waves' own Stroke>Opacity parameter to 0.75, if you prefer.

55 A soft yellow color (below left) blends well with the background. To blend it in even more, choose a transfer mode such as Soft Light, and reduce the opacity a touch (below right).

• And now, the moment of truth: Do a RAM Preview with all layers on from 06:00 to the end, and see if the Radio Waves perform their function (adding interest without overwhelming anyone else).

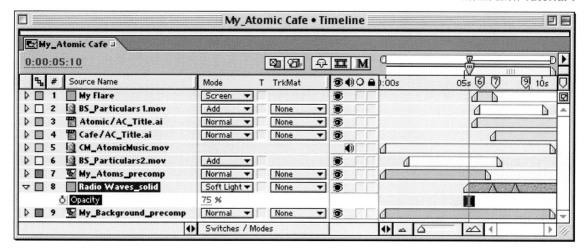

STEP 56: There's just one problem with our well-planned wave element: the timing. Although each new wave starts on a downbeat, you don't *see* each wave until it's about twenty frames old because the waves are partially hidden behind the title.

Yes, what you did above is technically correct, but now it's time to cheat to make it visually correct as well. To make the waves hit the beats of music as far as our final composite is concerned, you'll need to slide the layer back in time by about twenty frames:

- Hit 9 to move to time 09:00, where the third wave starts to trigger. Slowly drag the layer bar for **Radio Waves_solid** to the left (earlier in time) until you see the wave appear over the top of the Atomic title. Watch the Info palette as you drag (if it's not visible, open it by pressing Command+3 on Mac, Control+3 on Windows); the in point for the layer should end up around 05:10 (twenty frames earlier).

- RAM Preview again, and adjust the in point to taste.

When you're timing to music, don't be afraid to slip and slide elements so they work better visually, even if they don't precisely hit the beats of music. Sometimes there's a cue in the instrumentation or vocal track, or an accent drum beat, that is more fun to hit. Just listen, look, and tweak.

Save your project and RAM Preview the entire comp one last time. If you got lost, compare your settings with those saved in the prebuilt comp, [**Atomic Cafe_final**]. *The Radio Waves settings are also saved as an Effect Favorite in the* **Atomic Cafe>_Favorites** *folder (the "_4" version is for 4.1 owners who own the Atomic Power Evolution effects).*

Feel free to render your movie to disk (Composition>Make Movie); name your movie, select the Render Settings>Best Settings template, and set the Output Module appropriately for your hardware.

56 Project complete: The final Timeline window. The Radio Waves solid is moved earlier to start at 05:10.

Connect

For more information on topics covered in this tutorial, check out the following chapters in *Creating Motion Graphics*:

Importing Photoshop files as Comp: *Working with Photoshop*

The Sequence Layers keyframe assistant: *Trimming the Fat*

Nesting a comp: *Nesting Compositions*

Time Remapping: *Time Remapping*

Keyframe velocity manipulation: *A Matter of Time and Space*

Layer modes: *Transfer Modes*

Precomposing layers: *Precomposing*

Importing Illustrator files as Comp: *Working with Illustrator*

Animating Scale and Opacity: *A Trio of Transformations*

The Wiggler: *Our Trusty Assistants*

Motion Blur switch: *Motion Blur*

Lens flare on black solids: *That Ol' Black Solid*

RoboTV

Employing Parenting to animate a multi-segment robot arm, and adding a Premiere-edited video montage to the inset screen.

One of the most significant features added to After Effects in version 5.0 is Parenting, which lets you attach one object to another and animate both while they remain linked. This feature is particularly useful for character-style animation, as it makes anthropomorphic chains of objects much easier to manage.

In this tutorial you will employ Parenting to control a robot arm to use as a pointing device in a bumper for a hypothetical sports program. You will link the different segments of the arm and animate it to point at different places in the frame. We'll lead you through the first set of keyframes; you can animate the rest on your own if you like.

OVERVIEW

Main Concepts:

These are the features and concepts we will be focusing on in this project:

- Importing Photoshop as Comp
- Anchor Point and Rotation
- Parenting
- Importing Premiere as Comp
- Relinking missing footage
- Trim Comp to Work Area
- Slip Editing, Overlay Edit
- Vignetting the background
- Mask Feather and Mask Expansion
- Importing Illustrator as Comp
- Motion Blur and Shutter Angle
- Typing on with Path Text
- Boris Mosaic effect* *(optional)*
- Fractal Noise effect (PB) *(optional)*
- Boris Tint-Tritone effect* *(optional)*

Requirements:

After Effects 5.0 or later standard version.

Third party effects: Boris Mosaic, Boris Tint-Tritone (included free on this book's CD in the **Free Plug-ins** folder).

A bonus tutorial on the CD requires the effect Fractal Noise, which is available in the version 5 Production Bundle.

Getting Started:

** If you don't already own the third-party effect set Boris AE (www.borisfx.com), be sure to install the Boris Tint-Tritone and Mosaic effects included on the accompanying CD in the **Free Plug-ins** folder.*

Inside the **Tutorials** master folder on the accompanying CD, locate and copy the folder **02_RoboTV** to your hard drive.

In the folder **Final Movie** which is inside this main folder, open **RoboTV.mov** in the QuickTime Player and preview it.

Inside the **Project** folder you'll find the finished After Effects 5 project file **RoboTV_5.aep**. Open this project file: This is your starting point; we suggest you save under a new name after each major section.

You will also learn different approaches to editing a sequence of shots to use in After Effects, including importing Adobe Premiere projects and using some of the new video editing tools introduced in After Effects 5.0. Of course, we'll be throwing in a few design tips along the way, including a guided tour of the finishing touches we applied. An optional bonus tutorial on this book's CD demonstrates using the Fractal Noise effect to create abstract backgrounds.

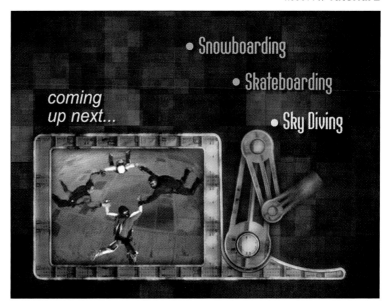

A frame from the final *RoboTV* animation. Footage from the Artbeats volume Skydiving.

The Tasks

This is what you will be doing in the various parts of this tutorial. Since this is a fairly lengthy tutorial, feel free to take breaks between major sections:

PART 1: Import the layered Photoshop file containing the robot arm, set anchor points for correct rotation, and build the parent/child hierarchy.

PART 2: Import the soundtrack, import a Premiere project with an already-edited video sequence, make further changes to this sequence, nest this video edit comp into your main comp, and position it inside the robot's frame.

PART 3: Composite the background plate out of a combination of three layers to create various lighting tricks.

PART 4: Add the text and slide it to match the video edits, animate the robot arm using different interpolation types, and render the final.

PART 5: Take a guided tour of additional touches we added to the finished project, including color correction, adding shadows, tweaking the timing, animating Path Text to type on an additional subtitle, and using Boris Mosaic to transition into the first piece of video.

CD BONUS TUTORIAL: A bonus step-by-step tutorial showing how we created the fractal noise elements used in Part 3 with the Fractal Noise plug-in included in the After Effects 5 Production Bundle.

Part 1: Building the Robot

Your first task will be building the robot arm, including creating a parent/ child chain for it. By now you should have the project **RoboTV_5.aep** open. In its Project window you will find folders named **My_Comps** and **My_Sources** to keep your own work organized. There is also a folder called **_RoboTV * prebuilt** which contains this project paused at various steps so you can compare your own work. Feel free to explore some of the comps in it ahead of time if you like, but make sure you close all windows except for the Project window before starting in below.

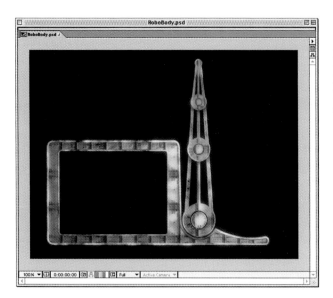

1 Import the layered Photoshop file **RoboBody.psd** as a composition. This comp will contain four pieces: the frame and three arm segments. If you want to check what each layer looks like, use the Solo switch in the Timeline window (where the cursor is pointing below).

Importing the RoboBody

STEP 1: Select the **My_Sources** folder in the Project window, then select the menu command File>Import>File by hitting Command+I on Mac (or Control+I on Windows). Locate the **02_RoboTV>Project>Sources** folder on your drive, and select **RoboBody.psd**: a layered Photoshop file. At the bottom of the Import dialog, be sure to set the Import As popup to Composition; it defaults to Footage, which is not what you want in this case. Click Import (Open), and both a folder and composition with the same name as this file will be added to the **My_Sources** folder in the Project window. (If instead you got a dialog asking you to choose a layer, you missed the Import As Composition popup; cancel and try again.)

• The folder called **RoboBody.psd** contains the individual pieces of the robot arm. Drag the comp to the **My_Comps** folder, and double-click it to open it. This comp includes four layers: the **Frame**; and **Big**, **Medium**, and **Small Arms**. All layers will be aligned with each other, just as they were in Photoshop. If you want, solo the individual layers to get a feel for which piece is which. You can Option+click on Mac (Alt+click on Windows) on a Solo switch to turn off other Solo switches.

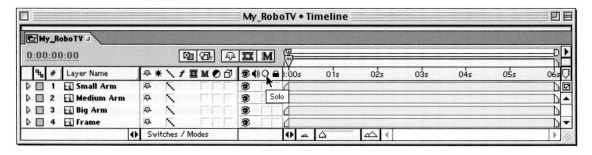

STEP 2: Press Command+K (Control+K) to open the Composition>Composition Settings dialog, and set the following:

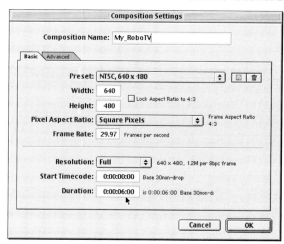

- Change the name of the comp to "**My_RoboTV.**"

- The width and height (640×480) and pixel aspect ratio (square) is dictated by the size of the original Photoshop file, and should not be changed.

- The frame rate should read 29.97 frames per second (fps) – the NTSC video rate.

- Set the Duration to 06:00 seconds. This is the length of the animation you'll be creating. (Photoshop and Illustrator files imported as compositions use the duration of the last comp you created or edited.)

- Make sure the Composition is in Full Resolution, and click OK.

  The Resolution can be set to Full in the Composition Settings, or changed at any time by selecting View>Resolution>Full or using the shortcut Command+J (Control+J).

STEP 3: If your composition was originally shorter than 06:00 in duration, you will need to zoom out the timeline and trim all layers to last the full six seconds.

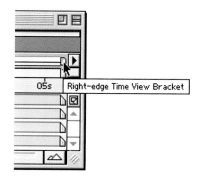

- Zoom out the timeline by pressing – (minus key on the keyboard), dragging the right edge Time View Bracket (the topmost brackets above the timeline's ruler area in the Timeline window), or using the zoom controls below the timeline in the same window.

- Hit End to move to 05:29.

- Select All layers by using the shortcut Command+A (Control+A).

- Hit] (the right square bracket key) to trim the Out Point of all layers.

- Press Home to return to 00:00.

3 Make sure you can see all six seconds of your timeline. One way to set this view is to drag the Time View Brackets in the Timeline window (where the cursor is pointing).

Setting the Anchor Points

In After Effects, all the rotations and scalings a layer undergoes is centered around its Anchor Point. In order for the robot animation to work correctly, each arm must be set to rotate around a sensible point, such as where it would join to the previous robot piece, before you begin setting up the parenting hierarchy.

When you're setting the anchors in the next step, make sure you're viewing all the pixels available. Set the comp's Resolution to Full and its Magnification to 100% – there are popups along the bottom of the Comp window where you can set these. If you're short on monitor space, resize the window to focus in on each arm as needed but still view at 100%.

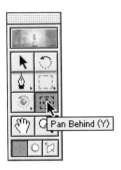

4 Solo the **Big Arm** layer, select the Pan Behind tool (above), and use it to move its anchor to the middle of its lower joint (below).

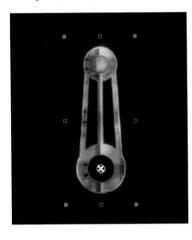

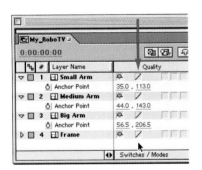

7 Drag your cursor down the row of Quality switches to turn on Best Quality for all layers.

When a layer is selected, its Anchor Point can be seen in the Composition window as a circle with an X in the center. This is what you will be moving:

STEP 4: To see each arm's joints more clearly, we recommend you solo each layer as you work on each arm. This temporarily turns off all other layers.

• Select the **Big Arm** layer, and solo it.

• Select the Pan Behind tool (also known to some as the Anchor Point tool) from the Tool palette; the shortcut is Y. If the Tool palette is not visible, type Command+1 (Control+1) to reveal it.

• In the Comp window, drag this layer's anchor to the center of the *lower* joint – the one you would expect it to pivot around. Zoom in to 200% or more if you need to see the area more clearly.

Any rotation will now occur around this area. If you want to verify this, select the Rotate tool (shortcut: W) and spin the layer around in the Comp window. When you're done, Undo until the arm is back in its original position, and reselect the Pan Behind tool.

STEP 5: Select the **Medium Arm** layer and Option+click (Alt+click) on the Solo button to solo this arm only. Repeat Step 4, moving this layer's anchor point to its lower joint.

STEP 6: Select the **Small Arm** layer and Option+click (Alt+click) on the Solo button to solo this arm only. Repeat Step 4 again, moving its anchor point to its lower joint.

The Anchor Point should now be set for all three arms. To turn on all layers again, turn off the Solo switch for the **Small Arm**. *Don't turn on all the Solo switches to see all layers again* – if you do, any new sources you add to the comp will not be visible!

Revert to the Selection tool (shortcut: V) when you're done.

You do *not* want to have the Pan Behind tool selected except when it's needed. It may look like a friendly "mover" tool, but you can create a big mess by trying to move layers with it! This is even worse if the layers have masks applied, as its true purpose will reveal itself: panning an image behind a mask shape, and changing the Position value automatically...

STEP 7: Turn on Best Quality for all layers by dragging down the row of Quality switches in the Timeline window, or select them all and press Command+U (Control+U). If zoomed in, return to 100%.

Save your project. We've prebuilt a version with the anchor points already set up and named it [**RoboTV_after Step 07**]; *you can find it in the* **RoboTV * prebuilt comps>_compare comps_after Step ##** *folder. If you're not sure whether you've set your anchor points correctly, compare your Anchor Point and Position values with our version.*

The Parenting Chain

Parenting is the ability to link one object to another. Once this bond has been established between parent and child, the two are grouped together as one complex object – if you move, scale, or rotate the parent, the child is affected in the same way. A child can still have its own animation; if the parent happens to be animating as well, the child just follows it around while it also does its own thing.

In several ways, Parenting is similar to nesting compositions. Before After Effects 5, the best way to group objects was to place them in their own composition, then nest this entire comp into a master comp. This works great if you want to move several layers as one group, but it becomes a pain if you need to build a chain where one object is grouped (linked) to another, which is then linked to another – such as your robot arm here.

There are two different ways to establish Parenting links between layers: a popup menu, and a pick whip tool. We'll try out both.

Parent Panel Position

You can drag the Parent panel to a new position in the timeline by dragging its column header left or right. We like to position it close to the layer names, as it makes using the pick whip more convenient.

STEP 8: Spend a moment thinking through what relationship between the robot pieces would make sense: For example, what should be attached to the **Big Arm** piece? Should **Big Arm** be attached to anyone else?

• Make sure the Parent panel is visible in the Timeline window. Shift+F4 is the easiest way to toggle it on and off; you can also select it from the wing menu of the Timeline window under Panels>Parent.

• In the Parent panel for the **Big Arm** layer, there is a popup menu that initially says None. Click on it, and you will see the names of all the other layers in the current comp. Select the **Frame** layer as the Parent. This way, you can later reposition or scale just the frame, and all of the attached arms will follow along.

• Time to try out the other tool. In the Parent panel for the **Medium Arm** layer, note the spiral icon to the left of the popup menu: This is the *pick whip* tool. Click on it, and drag the cursor to the name of the layer you want to be the parent – in this case, the **Big Arm** layer.

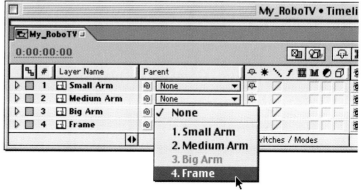

8 To assign a parent for a layer, you can use either the popup menu under the Parent panel (above), or the pick whip tool to click and drag to the parent of your choice (below).

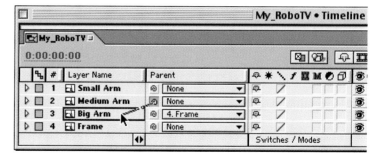

• The last step is hooking up the **Small Arm** layer to the **Medium Arm** layer. Go ahead and use the tool of your choice – menu or pick whip.

You can re-assign a layer's parent at any time, or reset it to None by using the popup menu or Command+clicking (Control+clicking) on its pick whip icon. A parent can have multiple children, but each child can have no more than one parent.

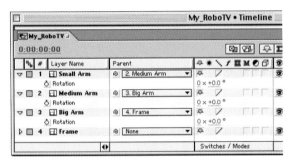

STEP 9: The point of setting up the Parenting chain is so that you can later rotate the position of any one of the robot arms, and know the others will follow along naturally without you having to animate their position as well. You will build an animation based on this in Part 4; for now, let's test this theory and make sure your chain works:

• Select all three arms, and hit R to twirl down just their Rotation property in the Timeline window. Deselect the layers by hitting F2.

• Scrub (click and drag) the rotation value for the **Big Arm** layer, and watch the other two arms follow in the Comp window.

• Scrub the rotation value for the **Medium Arm**, and watch the **Small Arm** also react.

• Since the **Small Arm** is the end of the chain, rotation affects only this one layer.

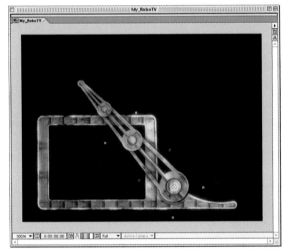

• If an arm seems "out of round" when you rotate it – the hole for its pivot wanders off from the pivot point underneath – you might want to readjust your anchor point for that layer. Return its rotation to zero, select the Pan Behind tool again, nudge the anchor, and scrub that layer's rotation again.

9 After you've correctly built the Parenting chain (top), the other two arms will automatically follow when you rotate the **Big Arm** layer (above).

• If the layers appear jagged, check that Best Quality is on for all layers so that they will look nicely antialiased when they're rotated.

• Return all Rotation values to zero when you're through experimenting, and twirl them up in the Timeline window. Later on you'll animate the rotation values so that the arms will reach different words in a title, appearing to trigger different video events. But next, you're going to import the video layers that will fill that hole in the RoboTV frame, and build the background.

Save your project. If you are completely lost, open our prebuilt comp [RoboTV_after Step 09] *from the* **RoboTV * prebuilt comps> _compare comps_after Step ##** *folder and compare your results. Feel free to drag this comp to the* **My_Comps** *folder, rename it "My_RoboTV_09", and use it to continue with the tutorial.*

The Making of RoboBody

The video frame and robot arm were much easier to build than it might seem at first glance. The original shapes were drawn in Adobe Illustrator, then swept to create an inset look using the Zaxwerks EPS Invigorator plug-in (www.zaxwerks.com) for the 3D program Electric Image (www.electricimage.com). The surface detail was not modeled; it's just a combination of a texture map from the Plaid Companion library by Dedicated Digital plus fractal-based procedural shaders. Shades of gray were used while in the 3D program, to maintain flexibility for tinting later on.

The main texture for the frame and arm pieces came from the Plaid Companion library by Dedicated Digital.

The camera was positioned far away, with a high amount of zoom. This reduced perspective-based distortions. Each piece was then soloed and rendered one at a time. These pieces were imported into After Effects and tinted individually using the third-party effect Boris Tint-Tritone (free on the CD that came with the book, in the Free Plug-ins folder). The Production Bundle's Stylize>Glow was added for warmth, and a diffuse Perspective>Drop Shadow effect was added to give the perception of depth.

This shadow was centered on each object so they could be rotated freely without the shadow's direction appearing to change.

The file was exported from After Effects as a Photoshop layered file (type: PSD). The advantage to passing it through the Photoshop PSD file format is that each layer was automatically trimmed by the Photoshop process to just the size of its visible area after the effects were applied. This saves on rendering time, as each layer does not have wasted space. We then opened the file in Photoshop and masked out some of the glow that bled into the center of each arm's pivot, to better reveal the joint of the arm piece underneath.

Part 2: The Video Montage

After Effects has traditionally been weak at editing video. It used to be a common practice to pre-edit video segments in another system, render that project, and use the result as a single clip inside After Effects.

This situation has improved considerably in recent versions of After Effects. For starters, you can import an entire Adobe Premiere project and have it converted into an After Effects composition. Specific transitions don't come across, but it works fine for cuts-style editing. After Effects 5.0 has also added several very useful video editing tools. We'll explore both of these approaches in this part. But first, let's load in the groove…

Adding Music

Step 10: Select the **My_Sources** folder in the Project window, and press Command+I (Control+I) to File>Import the music track **CM_RoboMusic.mov** from the **02_RoboTV>Project>Sources** folder that came with this tutorial. Double-click it in the Project window to open the QuickTime player for it, and audition it. Close the player,

Playing With Others

Third parties have made it possible to load in edit lists other than Premiere as After Effects compositions. Media 100 (www.media100.com) has its own plug-in to load its projects. For Avid users, Automatic Duck (www.automaticduck.com) has created a plug-in to load Avid-compatible OMF files into After Effects.

Music Credits

The music for this tutorial was arranged by Chris Meyer. Rather than the harsh guitar rock or skittering "drums & bass" dance music commonly used for extreme sports shows, we opted for something more surreal that played up the robotic angle. This soundtrack employs copyright-cleared samples from Spectrasonics' *Distorted Reality 2* (the main groove) and *Bass Legends* (the half-speed Marcus Miller bassline) plus Zero-G's *Malice in Wonderland* (the ascending hi-hat-ish riff), servo sounds from The Producers' *Science Fiction 1*, and a startup whine courtesy of sound designer Alan Howarth.

11 When you import the Premiere 6 project as a composition, two items will be added to the Project window – a folder of sources and a composition. The source footage will be missing (indicated by the color bars and italics), and will need to be relinked.

then drag it from the Project window into the [**My_RoboTV**] comp so that it starts at 00:00. Where it lands in the layer stack is unimportant; we tend to place sound files at the top of the stack to make it easier to view their waveform (shortcut: LL in quick succession) when we want.

Importing Premiere Project

For the sake of this tutorial, let's say a coworker has already used Adobe Premiere 6.0 to edit together the video montage to be used for this spot. She's saved her Premiere project, and given you all the clips she used. Your first task will be importing these into After Effects as a composition:

STEP 11: Select the **My_Sources** folder in the Project and Command+I (Control+I) to open the Import dialog, then locate the **Montage.ppj** file inside the **Project>Sources> Montage** folder. Notice that the file type indicates that this is an Adobe Premiere Project and that the Import As popup says Premiere Composition. Click Import (Open), and two items will be added to the Project window:

- You should have a *folder* called **Montage.ppj**. Twirl down this folder and you'll see a subfolder called **Bin 1**, which is the bin from the Premiere project. If you twirl this folder open, chances are you will note that the icons for all the footage items are color bars, and their names are in italics – this means the links between the footage and project have been lost. To fix this, double-click on each one of these footage items, and locate the corresponding file in the same **Montage** folder where you found this project.

> Unlike Photoshop and Illustrator files imported as Compositions, Premiere projects include "links" to the footage sources, instead of the actual sources. These links include the name of the original drive and folders they were placed in when the Premiere project was saved. If you rename folders or sources, or drag them to a disk with a different name than they were created on, you will need to relink these sources. With most relinked sources, After Effects will scan the entire folder and automatically relink to any other missing footage it finds. (Sadly, this is not the case with Premiere projects.)

- You should also have a *composition* called **Montage.ppj**, the same name as the original Premiere project. Drag this comp to the **My_Comps** folder in the Project window, hit Return, and rename it "**My_Montage_precomp**." Hit Return again to accept the new name.

- Double-click [**My_Montage_precomp**] to open the comp, which includes four video layers your coworker already captured, trimmed, and edited. Note the additional layer called **Timeline Markers**; it

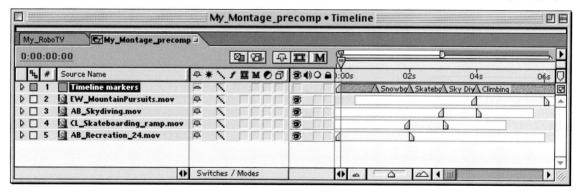

contains layer markers that have the same name as the Timeline Markers in the original Premiere project – a nice touch (documenting your projects is particularly helpful if you're sharing them with others).

RAM Preview to see the action. The montage consists of:

• Two seconds of snowboarding (**AB_Recreation_24.mov** – we added the suffix to indicate it was shot on 24 fps film)

• One second of skateboarding on a bowl-style ramp (**CL_Skateboarding_ramp.mov**)

• One second of sky diving (**AB_Sky Diving.mov**)

• Two seconds of rock climbing (**EW_MountainPursuits.mov**)

11 *continued:* The new composition includes the four source movies, and an additional layer which contains the Timeline Markers that were created in Premiere. The timeline has been zoomed in by pressing + (from the keyboard, not the keypad). We'll remove the extra space at the end of the timeline in the next step.

STEP 12: The Premiere project imported with extra space in the timeline, clocking in with a duration of 13:00 instead of the required six seconds. To reduce potential confusion later, trim off the unwanted extra time in [**My_Montage_precomp**]:

• Go to time 05:29 and hit N to end the work area.

• Select the menu command Composition>Trim Comp to Work Area. Or, context+click on the center of the work area bar and select Trim Comp to Work Area. (Hands up if you never noticed *that* one before…)

Footage for this tutorial was generously provided by (left to right): Artbeats (Recreation & Leisure CD and Sky Diving CD), EyeWire (Mountain Pursuits CD, shot by Philip and Karen Smith), and Glen Darcy of Creative License (the skateboarding footage).

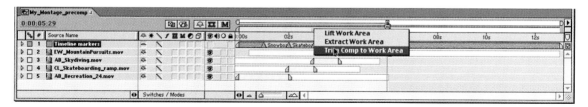

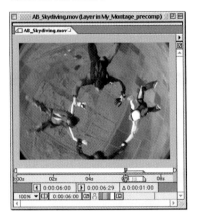

13 The Layer window indicates that the movie has been trimmed to a one-second section from 06:00 to 06:29.

13 *complete:* Placing the cursor beyond the currently used portions of a clip activates the Slip Edit tool (below), which allows you to slide the section of the clip you want to use while occupying the same slot in the overall timeline. The new in point will be the frame where the skydiver in red just starts to lift his hand (above).

Slip and Slide

Several features added in After Effects 5.0 have made it much easier to change your edit decisions after you've already imported your cuts. The first of these we'll explore is the Slip Edit tool.

STEP 13: The full version of **AB_Sky Diving.mov** is over eight seconds long, but your animation allows for only one second to be used – from 03:00 to 03:29 in the timeline. Of course, you want to use the best one second of action.

Double-click the **AB_Sky Diving.mov** layer to open the movie in the Layer window, hit Home to return to 00:00, and hit the spacebar to play the entire clip. Notice the one-second section that's currently being used (from 06:00 to 06:29) as defined by the Layer window's in and out points. Also notice that shortly after this "select," the diver on the left side raises his hand and waves at the camera. Your coworker thought this was a bit corny, but wouldn't you know – this was your client's favorite bit of the entire shot. You've been asked to change the edit to get it back in.

In previous versions of After Effects, you would have had to edit the In and Out Points either in the Layer window or the Timeline window, then spend a few more clicks resetting the in and out points in the timeline. But technology marches on…

- Close the Layer window, and move to time 03:00 in [**My_Montage_precomp**] where the movie of the skydivers (**AB_Sky Diving.mov**) starts.

- Place the cursor just to the left of the layer's in point, and note that the normal cursor changes to a double-arrowed icon.

- Drag the empty layer bar area to the left. This "slides" the movie along the layer bar, while maintaining the clip's relative position in the timeline. Move it left until you reach the frame where the diver's hand just starts to break away from the group.

- Scrub the timeline from 03:00 to 03:29 and check that you selected the full hand wave action in the space of one second.

You can also slide the layer while the time marker is parked at any point in the clip; just remember to drag the layer from the "empty bar"

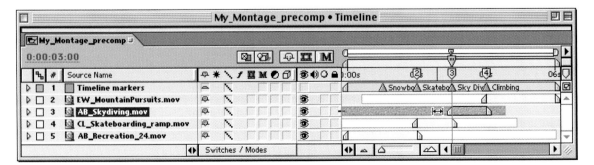

Slippery Keyframes

If the layer already has keyframes applied to it, you can choose whether or not keyframes move as well when you slide the video with the Slip Edit tool:

• If you don't want keyframes to move when you slip a layer, make sure they're deselected (shortcut: select the layer, then type Shift+F2). The keyframes will then remain attached to the same point in the overall timeline, rather than the source footage. For example, two Opacity keyframes at the head of a clip for a fade-in will remain locked to the layer's in point, regardless of what time in the clip that in point is.

• If you want keyframes to also slide along the time-line, select those keyframes first, then slip the layer.

• Only selected keyframes will slide, so you could slide some keyframes and not others. For example, if you had rotoscoped a figure by setting mask shape keyframes, these keyframes need to travel with the frames they are masking. On the other hand, you might have a fade or a special effect that's synchronized to the beginning or end of a clip or another layer in the timeline, in which case you'll want these keyframes to remain locked to the same point in time.

Before you slip a layer, we recommend you twirl down all keyframes by using the shortcut U and decide which, if any, keyframes need to be selected so they remain attached to the source frames.

• Beware of hidden selections: If you've just edited a keyframe and twirled up the layer, that keyframe will still be selected, even though you can't see it! If you then slip the layer, that hidden, selected keyframe will slide too – potentially causing much confusion later… So be sure to deselect keyframes (Shift+F2) when in doubt.

section – you won't be able to slide it if there is no handle left to the clip. More tips on using the Slip Edit tool can be found in the sidebar *Slippery Keyframes*.

Overlay Edit

RAM Preview the entire six seconds of the [**My_Montage_precomp**]. It often helps to listen to the soundtrack while you're editing video, so go ahead and add the **CM_RoboMusic.mov** layer from the **My_Sources** folder to this comp as well, again making sure it starts at 00:00. (We'll remind you to turn it off when you nest this precomp in the main comp later, so the music won't be doubled up.)

The clients are happy with the skydiving edit now, and in particular they love the way the snowboarder takes off as the music starts up. However, they note that while they can focus on the individual athletes in most of the shots, the current skateboarding shot has a lot of dis-tracting people in the background. They say "Do something to fix it," and cheerily wave their hands as they leave.

You go knock on the door of the coworker who made the original edit, and ask if she has any solo skateboarding shots. She's busy editing another piece, but gives you a file for a street-style skateboarder she thinks will work. It's up to you to edit it in.

STEP 14: Select the **My_Sources** folder and Command+I (Control+I) to import a file. Locate and import the **CL_Skateboarding_street.mov** inside the **Project>Sources>Montage** folder.

Sliding Up Close

If you've zoomed way into the timeline to where an empty portion of the layer bar is not visible – but you still need to Slip a layer – press Y to select the Pan Behind tool. The cursor will change to the Slip tool when it's placed over the layer bar in the Timeline window.

From the Project window, Option+double-click (Alt+double-click) to open this movie in the special After Effects Footage window. New in After Effects 5's Footage window are trimming tools and the Ripple Insert Edit and Overlay Edit buttons.

If you simply double click the movie, it opens in a QuickTime Player window, with no timecode or in and out points. Another bonus to the After Effects Footage window is that it also premultiplies any alpha channel so that edges in an RGB+Alpha movie look correct.

STEP 15: Play the movie. Note that the most exciting part seems to happen around the middle of the clip's duration. Pick your favorite one second of action, and trim the movie to those frames by setting the In and Out Points. We picked the section from 1:15 to 2:14, but you can choose a different section if you like.

You can trim footage by dragging the triangles at the left and right of the main timeline (the top timeline is just for zooming in time, which is handy for a very long clip). You can also trim by moving the time marker to a frame, and clicking the In or Out buttons (these are the { and } squiggly brackets). The Duration readout will update to reflect your changes.

16 Trim the new clip in its Footage window to use a second of material out of the middle. Click on the Overlay Edit button (where the cursor is pointing in the lower right) to add the trimmed clip to your comp. Skateboarding footage courtesy of Creative License.

STEP 16: This is a great time to take advantage of the new Overlay Edit feature to add the trimmed clip directly into the video montage:

• Bring [**My_Montage_precomp**] forward, and move the time marker to 02:00 where the new skateboarding movie will begin.

• Turn off the Video switch for the old **CL_Skateboarding_ramp.mov** layer.

• Bring the Footage window for **CL_Skateboarding_street.mov** forward.

At the bottom of the Footage window it should say "Edit Target: My_Montage_precomp" which means that if you use the Overlay Edit button, the trimmed clip will be added to this – the most forward – comp. If a different comp is showing up as the Edit Target comp, verify that [**My_Montage_precomp**] is indeed the forward composition, and select the Footage window again.

• Click on the Overlay Edit button in the bottom right-hand corner of the Footage window. The one-second portion you trimmed this clip to will be added to the top of [**My_Montage_precomp**], starting at 02:00.

There's nothing special about this clip after you've added it; the result is not unlike adding the original clip to the comp, then trimming it down to one second afterward. Overlay Edit is just another tool that can occasionally save a few clicks. The Overlay Edit tool can also be handy for pretrimming a folder of clips while you're just checking them out, without having to add them to a comp first.

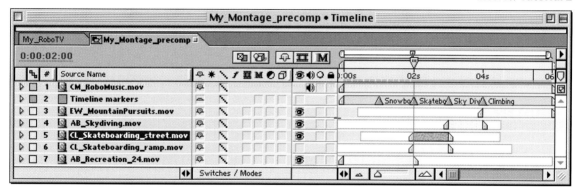

Overlay Edit also makes it easy to add the same trimmed clip to multiple comps: If you reopen the Footage window, the trimmed area will still be active but it is not "live" – changing the trim points will not update the footage already in use in a comp. This means you could retrim the layer and Overlay Edit a different section to the same – or even a different – comp. If you add the clip to a comp normally (by dragging it from the Project window rather than by using Overlay Edit), the trim information from the Footage window will be ignored.

16 *complete:* The final timeline for the video montage. Note that we've turned off the layer Video switch for the old skateboarding clip so it won't accidentally render, but have kept it around just in case we need it again.

• Drag the new clip down the layer stack so that it sits in place of the old one and Save your project. Go ahead and leave the previous skateboarding clip in the composition (just in case the clients change their mind) – since it's turned off, it won't take up additional rendering time. RAM Preview, and see if you're happy with the new montage. If you'd like to tweak the new clip's in and out points some more, practice using the Slip tool you learned back in Step 13.

Ripple Insert Edit

In addition to the new Overlay button covered in Step 16, After Effects 5 features another tool for adding pretrimmed source footage to a comp: **Ripple Insert Edit** is similar to Overlay Edit, except that when you add footage to a composition, all the other layers move down the timeline to accommodate the new footage.

To access this feature, hold down the Option (Alt) key and double-click a source from the Project window to open it in After Effects' Footage window. If necessary, trim the in and out points in the Footage window to remove unwanted frames.

In the Composition, move the time marker to where you'd like the new footage to be inserted. Back in the Footage window, click the Ripple Insert Edit button (the one immediately to the right of the Duration value). The trimmed movie will be inserted

in the timeline at the current time, and all other layers will move down the timeline. If the time marker is placed in the middle of a layer, that layer will be split and the new footage inserted in the middle. Lock any layers if you don't want them to be affected (moved or split).

Nesting the Video Montage

The video editing is done; the next step is nesting this video montage into your main composition. To remember where the video cuts were, we'll add comp markers along the timeline; these will convert to layer markers when you nest it into [**My_RoboTV**].

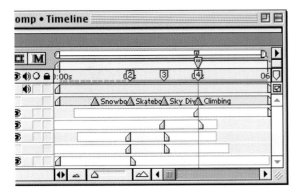

STEP 17: While you're still in [**My_Montage_ precomp**], locate to the following times and set corresponding comp markers:

- At 02:00, press Shift+2 to create comp marker #2
- At 03:00, press Shift+3 to create comp marker #3
- At 04:00, press Shift+4 to create comp marker #4

Once set, press just the number 2, 3, or 4 to jump to these markers. You can also hold down the Shift key while dragging the time marker along the timeline to "snap" to markers and In/Out Points as it gets near them. Use these features to locate easily to specific frames.

17 Set comp markers at the various video edits, to make it easier to remember their locations when you nest this comp into your main composition.

STEP 18: Bring the [**My_RoboTV**] comp forward. If its time marker isn't already at 00:00, hit Home to locate there. You'll nest the edited video sequence and place it into the TV frame.

Select [**My_Montage_precomp**] from the Project window and drag it to the bottom of the layer stack in the [**My_RoboTV**] Timeline window. This will nest [**My_Montage_precomp**] into [**My_RoboTV**], starting at 00:00, and sorted behind the robot body layers.

As of After Effects 5.0, you can drag a layer to the timeline and place it anywhere in the layer stack – in previous versions, new layers were always added on top. If you drag and drop to the left side of the Timeline window (in the Source/Layer name column), the in point for this new layer will start at the current position of the time marker, same as before. If you drag the new layer to somewhere in the timeline area, the point at which you release the mouse determines the in point for this layer as well as its order in the layer stack. This feature can be annoying until you get the hang of it, then you'll integrate it as another click-saver. Dragging new footage to the Comp window will always start it at the current time and add it to the top of the layer stack, as will the Command+/ (Control+/) shortcut.

18 Nest the video montage into the [**My_RoboTV**] comp, starting at 00:00, placed at the bottom of the layer stack. Note that the comp markers you created in Step 17 appear as layer markers here. Remember to turn off the Audio switch for this layer (where the cursor is pointing).

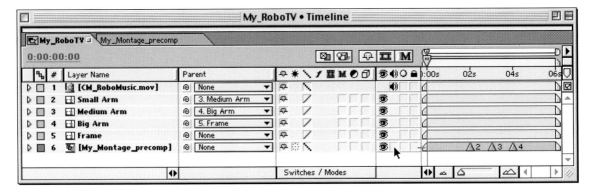

[**My_Montage_precomp**] will now appear as one layer, so you can manipulate the entire montage as one group. Notice how the comp markers in the precomp appear as layer markers when they're nested. These markers are not linked back to the original comp in any way, though – changing a comp marker in the precomp will not update the layer markers here.

Don't forget to turn off the Audio switch for the nested layer! You don't want to double up the music track or you will introduce distortion.

STEP 19: You'll need to position and scale the [**My_Montage_ precomp**] layer so that it fits nicely behind the TV screen.

• In the Comp window, drag the montage layer so it's centered behind the screen. It's just a bit too large at its default size; you will have to scale this montage layer down so that you see the maximum image area inside the screen.

19 The video montage defaults to being too large and out of position (above); center it behind the opening in the robot frame, and scale it down so it just fills the hole (below).

• Verify that the **My_Montage_precomp** layer is the one selected. Drag one of its corner handles in the Comp window to scale the layer, then add the Shift key to maintain its aspect ratio. If you have the Info floating window open, it will update as you drag to display the current Scale value; about 83% should work nicely.

> There are some handy shortcuts for scaling layers in small increments. You can increase the Scale amount in 1% increments by holding down the Option key (Alt in Windows) and using the + or – keys on the numeric keypad. Add the Shift key for 10% increments. If you don't use the Option (Alt) key, you'll rotate the layer instead of scaling it.

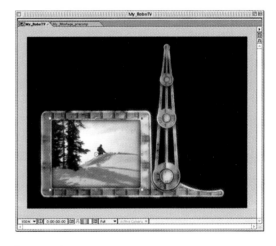

• Set the [**My_Montage_precomp**] layer's Parent popup to Frame, so it becomes part of the RoboBody group.

• Save the project. As a final reminder that **Frame** is the main parent of all the visible layers in this comp, try moving or scaling the **Frame** layer and notice how the entire RoboTV – frame, three arms, and the inset movie – are treated as a group. Be sure to Undo any changes.

Synching Comps

Turn on "Synchronize time of all related items" in General Preferences to synchronize the time marker in nested comps.

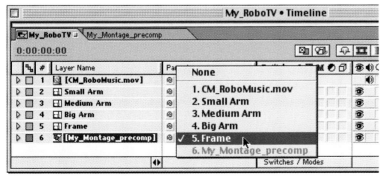

19 *complete:* Make the video montage layer a child of the **Frame** layer.

Part 3: Background Noise

The background consists of two movies, both previously created with the Fractal Noise effect (included in the After Effects 5.0 Production Bundle only; it originally appeared in the now-discontinued Cult Effects 1.5 set). One instance of the effect created a blocky pattern, while a second layer rendered a soft blurry pattern that will serve as a subtle lighting effect. These effects have been prerendered as movies because (a) you may not have the Production Bundle, and (b) using live effects for the background slows down the previews.

This tutorial's folder on the CD contains a copy of the project that was used to create these layers, along with a PDF bonus tutorial on how they were created. In the meantime, take advantage of the pre-rendered movies:

Go Home!

To force layers to start at 00:00 in After Effects 5.0, select them and hit Option+Home.

20 Add **FractalNoise_blocky.mov** behind all of the other layers in **[My_RoboTV]**.

21 The **FractalNoise_soft.mov** will provide a lighting effect for the blocky pattern background.

STEP 20: Select the **My_Sources** folder and Command+I (Control+I) to import a file, locate to the **Project>Sources** folder for this tutorial, and import the movie **FractalNoise_blocky.mov**.

• Open it from the Footage window and scrub through it to become familiar with it. It consists of an abstract, randomized series of blocks that seem to zoom slowly toward you. Close the Footage window when you're done.

• Add the movie to your [My_RoboTV] comp and drag it to the bottom of the layer stack, starting at 00:00.

STEP 21: Select the **My_Sources** comp again and this time import the movie FractalNoise_soft.mov.

• If you like, open it from the Footage window and scrub through it to become familiar with it. This movie contains a hazy, cloudy pattern that you will use to add a lighting effect to the blocky background above. Close the Footage window when you're done.

• Add this movie as well to your [**My_RoboTV**] comp, also at time 00:00, and drag it down the layer stack so that it sits above the FractalNoise_blocky.mov layer.

STEP 22: All that's left for your lighting trick to work is to change the transfer mode for the **FractalNoise_soft.mov** layer to Overlay. Toggle the Switches/Modes panel to Modes (shortcut: F4) and change its mode from the default Normal to Overlay.

To get a feel for what effect this is having, turn the Video switch for **FractalNoise_soft.mov** on and off, and observe the changes in the Comp window. Leave it switched on when you're done, and Save the project.

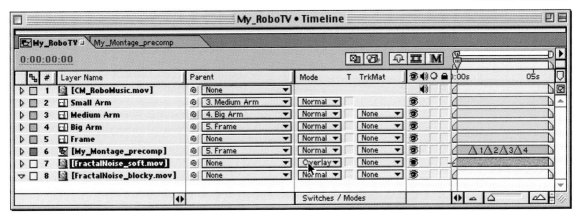

Overlay is a useful mode for boosting the contrast and apparent saturation of a composite. If the source layer has 50% gray, these areas will have no effect on the layers underneath. Where the source layer is brighter, it will brighten the underlying layers akin to Screen mode; where the source is darker, it will darken the underlying layers akin to Multiply mode. It works great with grayscale sources; interesting hue shifts occur if the source has color in it as well.

Expanding Masks

Step 23: To finish off our background, add a "vignette" effect by using a black solid with a soft-edged mask to darken the corners:

• With the time marker still located at 00:00, press Command+Y (Control+Y) to create a new Solid layer. Name it "**Vignette solid**," click the Make Comp Size button, make sure the color is black, and click OK.

• Drag the black solid down the layer stack so that it sits above the two Fractal Noise movies you imported earlier.

• Pop open the wing menu in the upper right corner of the Comp window and verify that Layer Masks is checked on. If not, enable it now – it needs to be on for the next trick to work…

• Press Q once to select the Mask tool in the Tools palette; if the Rectangle Mask is active, press Q again to toggle to the Oval Mask tool. (You can also click and hold on the Rectangle Mask until the Oval Mask tool pops out.) With your new solid layer still selected, double-click the Oval Mask tool to add a new full-frame oval mask to this layer. (If Layer Masks was not enabled, the mask tools would have been grayed out.)

22 The **FractalNoise_soft.mov** sits above the **FractalNoise_blocky.mov** in the Timeline window (top) and is set to Overlay mode. Result shown above.

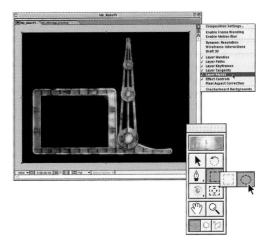

23 Make sure that Layer Masks is toggled on in the Comp window's wing menu, and select the Oval Mask tool from the Tools window.

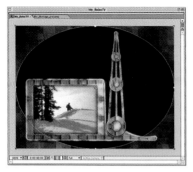

23 *continued:* A vignette effect which darkens the corners of the frame is built by applying an oval mask to a black solid (top), inverting the mask, feathering it, and using Mask Expansion to push it out to the corners (above).

• Type MM (two Ms in quick succession) to twirl down the Mask options in the Timeline window; you should see the Mask Shape, Mask Feather, Mask Opacity, and Mask Expansion properties.

• Check the Inverted switch so that the black solid is opaque outside the mask, and transparent inside the mask.

• Scrub the Feather tool, setting the value to a nice soft value of 100. Notice how the feathered edge affects the inside and outside of the mask.

We'd like to reveal more of the corners. One approach would be an even larger feather amount, but that may eat away too much from the inside of the mask. Time to use another new feature introduced in version 5.0: Mask Expansion.

• Scrub the Mask Expansion value. Notice how the feathered edge moves in relation to the mask outline in the Comp window. Set the Expansion value to around +50 or to taste to move the feathered edge outside the mask edge.

• From the Comp window's wing menu, toggle Layer Masks off so you can see the edge of the mask without the yellow border.

• Turn on Best Quality to antialias the mask more smoothly. Tweak your Feather and Expansion values if you like.

And that's it for the background – you can now turn your attention back to the robot arm and the text items it will be pointing to. Go ahead and twirl up any property that may be open in the Timeline window to reduce distractions.

That completes Part 3 so Save your project. You can compare your work against our prebuilt comp [**RoboTV_after Step 23**]. *If you want to pick up this tutorial at this point and focus on animating the robot arm, rename our comp to "My_RoboTV_23" and continue.*

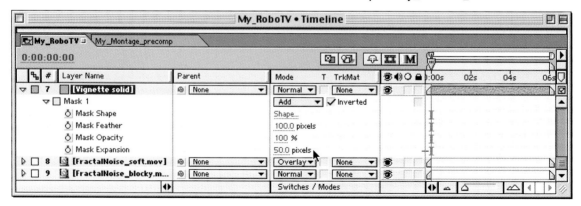

23 *complete:* Your mask should end up with roughly these settings. The cursor points to the new Mask Expansion parameter.

Part 4: Rotation Motivation

Remember way back in Part 1, when you set up the Parenting chain for the robot arm? Time to put that groundwork to use in animating the arm. But first, you have to give it some targets to hit in your animation moves.

As we mentioned earlier, the idea behind this spot is a bumper that will lead into the next section of a sports program. There are four sports highlighted in the next section; the title of each will come on as the arm swings to it to illustrate it.

Adding the Titles

STEP 24: Select the **My_Sources** folder in the Project window and hit Command+I (Control+I) to bring up the Import dialog. Select the layered Illustrator file **SportsTitle.ai** from this project's **Sources** folder. At the bottom of the Import dialog, be sure to select Import As: Composition. Click Import (Open), and two new items will be added to the Project window:

• A *folder* called **SportsTitle.ai**, which stores the individual source layers.

• A *composition* also called **SportsTitle.ai**. Double-click it to open it. The comp includes four title layers: **Snowboarding**, **Skateboarding**, **Sky Diving**, and **Climbing**. All layers are filled with white, and were aligned along an arc in Illustrator.

24 The Project window after importing **SportsTitle.ai** as a comp.

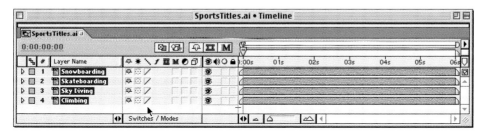

25 The names of the four featured sports have already been typeset in an arc in Illustrator. The font is Conques Demi from T.26 (www.t26.com).

STEP 25: In the comp [**SportsTitle.ai**], select the **guides only** layer and Delete it (hit the Delete key). The guides are only visible when inside Illustrator, where they indicate the position of Title Safe areas.

• Select the four title layers by using Command+A (Control+A), and turn on Best Quality by pressing Command+U (Control+U).

• With all layers still selected, Copy them.

STEP 26: Bring your [**My_RoboTV**] comp forward, and Paste.

• All layers will paste to the top of the layer stack starting at 00:00, so drag them down the stack until they sit above the **Vignette solid** and the fractal background layers.

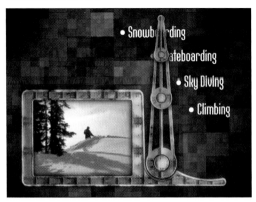

26 Paste the titles into **[My_RoboTV]** and drag them down the layer stack to be just in front of the background layers.

• If your [**SportsTitle.ai**] composition had been shorter than 06:00 duration, the pasted layers will appear trimmed shorter than needed in this comp. If that's the case, extend all layers to the full six seconds: with them still selected, go to the end of [**My_RoboTV**], and hit Option+] (Alt+]).

Timeline Markers

The idea is that each title pops on as its respective movie plays. Fortunately, back in Step 17 you placed comp markers at these edit points, which rippled through as layer markers when you nested [**My_Montage_precomp**] into your main composition. Problem is, just numbers came across – you have to remember which number corresponds to which sport. However, there was a layer back in that precomp that contained additional notes carried over from the original Premiere project…

STEP 27: In [**My_RoboTV**], Option+double-click (Alt+double-click) the layer [**My_Montage_precomp**] to open its original composition.

• Select the **Timeline Markers** layer – which identifies which movie starts when – and Copy.

• Bring your [**My_RoboTV**] comp forward, and Paste.

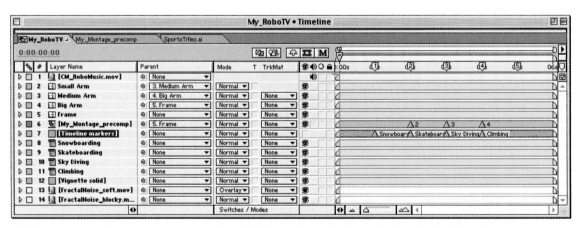

27 Copy the layer with the Premiere notations from **[My_Montage_precomp]** into **[My_RoboTV]**, and add comp markers at every second through 05:00 to speed up navigation to the video edit points.

• Drag this layer down the layer stack so it sits below the [**My_Montage_precomp**] layer, above the four title layers. You'll now have the benefit of the notated markers in the main comp, indicating at what point each title should start.

• Just as you did back in Step 17 for the [**My_Montage_precomp**] comp, feel free to add comp markers 1 through 5 at 01:00, 02:00, 03:00, 04:00 and 05:00. You'll then be able to return to these marked frames by simply typing their respective numbers. Hit Home to return the time marker to 00:00 when you're done.

Twisting Your Arms

You may want to take a moment here and play the final **RoboTV.mov** again (you can even import it into the project, so that you can play it from inside After Effects). If you get stuck wondering how the arms could possibly rotate so they align with each sport's bullet point, you can always refer to our finished movie. However, there is no right or wrong way to animate the arms – provided they hit their marks, and seem to be having fun!

If you're not there already, you'll probably want to set the Comp window to display in Full Resolution and 100% Magnification for the following arms rotation steps, so you can see the titles clearly. Feel free to turn off the Video switch for the background layers to speed up previews; we also toggled the Switches/Modes panel back to Switches by pressing F4.

STEP 28: With the time marker at 00:00, select the **Small Arm**, **Medium Arm**, and **Big Arm** layers and hit R to twirl down Rotation.

• Turn on Rotation animation stopwatches for all three. You can drag the cursor across all three stopwatches in the Timeline window in one movement, or use the Set Rotation Keyframe shortcut Option+R (Alt+R). This will create the first keyframe for each arm at time 00:00.

• Press F2 to deselect the arms to avoid accidentally editing all three arms at once.

Now here's where the fun starts: You need to change the rotation values for all three arms to create a starting position which has them "tucked in" along the right side of the TV screen.

There are a couple of ways to edit the Rotation values. We personally prefer scrubbing these values in the Timeline window; hold down Command (Control) to scrub Rotation in finer increments. Or, you can use the Rotation tool (W is the shortcut for the Wotation tool) to rotate the arms by dragging them in the Comp window.

We'll give you some clues to get started, then you can complete the animation using your own ideas on what would be fun moves. For example, the arms at 00:00 would tuck in alongside the screen with these settings:

• **Big Arm** rotated –10°

• **Medium Arm** rotated –170° and

• **Small Arm** rotated +160°

Of course, you can always enter in these exact values for the Rotation property for each layer – but where's the fun in that.

Switcheroo!

To switch the Switches and Modes panel back and forth, press F4.

Finer Increments

If you're scrubbing the Rotation values to animate the arms, remember that holding the Command (Control) key when you're scrubbing will cause it to rotate in finer increments.

28 The initial, folded-up starting point for the arms at 00:00; the background layers have been turned off to speed up RAM Previews.

STEP 29: Once you're happy with your first set of keyframes, move to time 01:00 by typing 1 to locate its corresponding comp marker. Change the rotation keyframes for all three arms so that the tip of the small arm hits the bullet at the beginning of the **Snowboarding** title. We suggest you animate the big arm a little clockwise, but make big

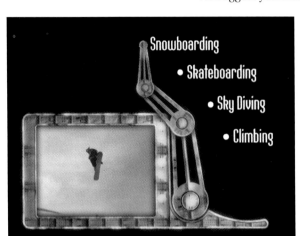

dramatic moves for the medium and small arms so that they swing out to the right and up (if they swing left as they ascend they will obscure the TV screen). Getting it right will take some tweaking; feel free to nudge the title into position if you can't get the arm to reach the bullet point exactly – just be careful not to disrupt the arrangements between words to the point where it starts to look sloppy.

Our example reaches the bullet with the following settings:

- **Big Arm** rotated $-6°$
- **Medium Arm** rotated $-1 \times -41°$ and
- **Small Arm** rotated $1 \times +45°$

29 The arms are rotated to hit the first sport's bullet point at 01:00, creating the second set of keyframes.

STEP 30: Once you're happy with the placement of the arms at 01:00, hit N to End the Work Area at 01:00 and do a RAM Preview (shortcut: hit 0 on the keypad) to see how the animation looks.

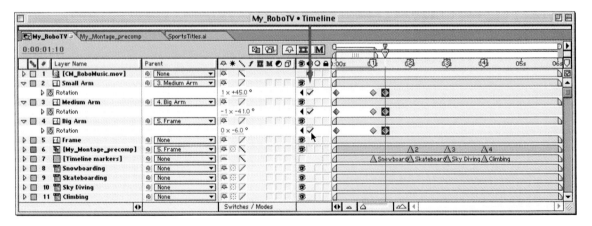

30 After animating the first move, go to time 01:10 and check another set of keyframes to hold the arms in place for ten frames. You can drag across all three keyframe checkboxes in one mouse movement.

- If you're happy with the movie, press Shift+Page Down to advance ten frames to time 01:10. Add Rotation keyframes to all three arm pieces by checking their keyframe boxes. This should ensure that they have the exact same values as the keyframes at 01:00. This will make the arms "freeze" for ten frames between 01:00 and 01:10.

In Step 33, we'll convert the keyframe at 01:00 to a real "Hold" keyframe, which will ensure that the Rotation value holds steady until the next keyframe is encountered.

STEP 31: As your aerobics instructor would say (if you ever got to the gym), "this is the pattern": The arms reach up to the title at the top of the second, freeze for ten frames, then move to the next title for twenty frames. So have fun completing the animation as follows, doing a RAM Preview after each title as it is reached:

• At 02:00, animate the arms to reach the **Skateboarding** title. Give the movement some personality – for example, feel free to rotate the **Small Arm** around a full turn. Once you're happy with the placement, hit N to reset the End of the work area, and RAM Preview. (Use this technique to RAM Preview each section as you go – making changes to a section in the middle is difficult once you've completed the progression of keyframes.) If you like the way the arms swing around, Shift+Page Down to advance ten frames.

• At 02:10, check the Rotation keyframe checkboxes to duplicate the values and introduce a freeze between 02:00 and 02:10.

• Move to 03:00, and rotate the arms to reach the **Sky Diving** title. RAM Preview this section and tweak if necessary. Then Shift+Page Down to advance ten frames.

• At 03:10, check the Rotation keyframe checkboxes to duplicate the values.

• Move to time 04:00, and make the arms reach the **Climbing** title.

• At 04:10, check the Rotation keyframe checkboxes to duplicate the values.

• At 05:00, animate the arms back into a tucked-in position, similar to the beginning.

• RAM preview the entire animation when you're done, and switch back to the Selection tool (V) if the Rotation tool is currently active.

*Save! If you're having trouble creating an animation you like, feel free to pick up our prebuilt comp [**RoboTV_after** Step 31] and call it your own…we won't tell. Just be sure you know how we arrived at this point.*

Easy Does It

STEP 32: All the rotation moves so far use Linear keyframes – the default interpolation type when you create temporal keyframes. Although we have a "robotic" design, we don't necessarily want the robotic motion that results from linear interpolation. A quick way to add some elegance (and to make this animation a little more realistic, as a "real" robot arm wouldn't be able to start and stop instantaneously) is to add some ease in and outs to the rotation keyframes.

• Make sure the Rotation properties are still exposed for all of the arm pieces in the Timeline window.

Bullet Hole

When you're animating the arms to hit the bullets, if you temporarily reduce the Opacity of the **Small Arm** layer, you'll be able to see the bullet point underneath. Return Opacity back to 100% when you're done.

At 02:00, the arms reach Skateboarding.

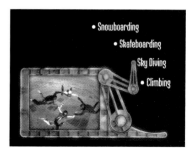

At 03:00, the arms move to SkyDiving.

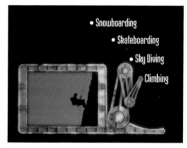

At 04:00, the arms tuck into Climbing.

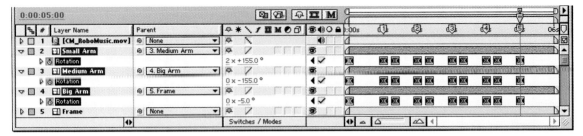

32 After all the Rotations keyframes have been selected, press F9 to apply Easy Ease to them.

• Click on the word "Rotation" for the **Small Arm** layer. This will select all the Rotation keyframes for this layer. Now Shift+click on the word Rotation for both the **Medium Arm** and **Big Arm** layers, so that all Rotation keyframes are selected.

• Press F9 to apply Easy Ease to all selected keyframes, or apply it from the menu using Animation>Keyframe Assistant>Easy Ease.

• Deselect All (shortcut: F2).

Parent Power

To toggle the Parent panel on and off, press Shift+F4.

Looking Square

STEP 33: Since the Rotation keyframes at 01:00, 02:00, 03:00, and 04:00 for all three layers are freezing for ten frames, it would be helpful if they looked like Hold keyframes in the timeline (Hold keyframes have square icons, or if converted from Linear will have a square shape on the outgoing side). Although it's not necessary for this particular animation, this is an example of "defensive" animation in which you're reducing the chance of accidentally screwing something up later.

> Hold style keyframes say "do not vary the value of this parameter until the next keyframe." Even if two successive keyframes have the same value, it's still possible for drift to occur between them through mistakes with their velocity curves. It's also a problem with Position keyframes, where errant handles in the motion path can introduce wobbly animation.

33 Select the Rotation keyframes at comp markers 1, 2, 3, and 4 by holding down the Shift key and dragging a marquee around them (shown in progress).

• Drag a marquee around the three keyframes at 01:00.

• Hold down the Shift key and drag a marquee around the keyframes at 02:00, 03:00, and 04:00 to select them as well.

• Once these keyframes are selected, Command+Option+click (Control+Alt+click) on any one of the selected keyframes to toggle

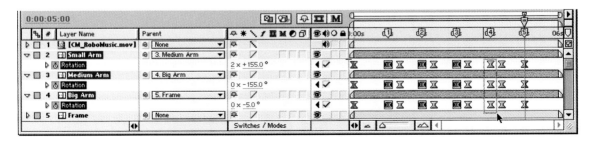

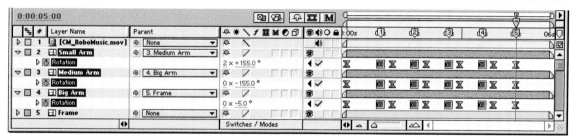

them all to Hold keyframes (or use Animation>Toggle Hold Keyframes menu command). Deselect the keyframes again by pressing F2.

- Rotation is now complete, so twirl up all layers and Save your project.

STEP 34: Since the idea is that the arm reaches up and "turns on" each title, you will need to next move the In Point for each title to its "cue in" time. One approach to this is using the In Panel in the Timeline window.

- Context+click on the column headers in the Timeline window and select Panels>In, or select Panels>In from the Timeline window's wing menu. If you're running short of screen space, close the Parent panel (Context+click on Parent heading and select Hide This from the popup, or press Shift+F4).

It helps to drag the In panel close to the layer names so you don't inadvertently change the value for the wrong layer. Currently, all layers have an in point of 00:00:00:00 (or at least, they should!).

- For the **Snowboarding** title layer, click on the value for in point. The Layer In Time dialog will open; type "100" (you don't need to type the colon as in 1:00), and click OK. The in point value will be converted to the 00:00:01:00 display style.

- Using the same technique, set the **Skateboarding** title to start at 02:00.

- Set the **Sky Diving** title to start at 03:00.

- Set the **Climbing** title to start at 04:00.

- Save your project, and RAM Preview again to see the titles "pop on".

33 *complete:* The selected Rotation keyframes converted to Hold keyframes.

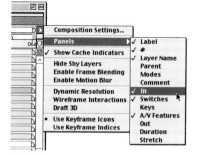

34 You can customize the Timeline window by opening just the In Time panel, giving you another tool to set the In Point of layers.

34 *complete:* Set the In times for the titles to equal when the robot arm hits their marks.

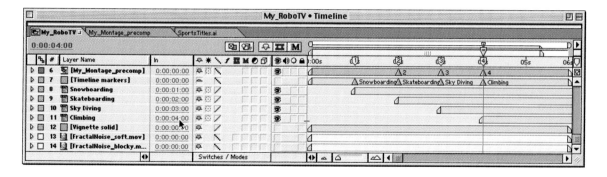

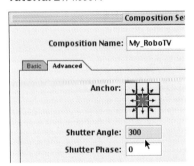

Motion Blur

STEP 35: Turn on Motion Blur (the "M" switch) for all three arm layers, then click on the master Enable Motion Blur switch along the top of the Timeline window so you can see this blur in the Comp window before you render. RAM Preview a couple of seconds to see how the arms look with motion blur applied.

You can set the amount of Motion Blur in the Composition Settings>Advanced section under Shutter Angle. We set our comp to a relatively high Shutter Angle of 300°.

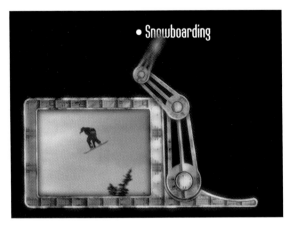

Since the Small Arm is moving more than the other arms, you should see the Small Arm blur more. Also, the pixels at the tip will usually be blurrier than the area near the joint, since these pixels are moving faster.

Notice how the motion blur fades away right before 01:00 as the arm eases into a stop when it reaches the **Snowboarding** title. The blur amount is based on the speed of each pixel, so the motion blur fades away as the layer slows down.

Motion Blur adds a considerable render hit, so turn off the Enable Motion Blur switch if you need faster previews. If you decide to render your final version of this tutorial, in the Render Settings dialog the Motion Blur popup should be set to

35 By enabling Motion Blur for the robot arm pieces, After Effects will automatically calculate more blur when the pixels in each piece move faster.

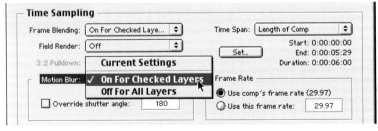

"On for Checked Layers" to ensure that layers with their M switch checked will render with motion blur in the final render. The Render Settings also includes an Override Shutter Angle field, where you can force the comp (and any nested comp layers) to render using a common shutter angle amount.

Shutter Angle

In 5.0, the Motion Blur Shutter Angle can be set as high as 720°, compared with the 360° limit of earlier versions. If you were field rendering the final output, remember that the intensity of the motion blur would appear cut in half; use larger values as needed.

STEP 36: Turn on any background layers you might have turned off to speed up your previews. You're done with all of the hard work for this tutorial. Save the project and RAM Preview your final animation.

In the next Part, we're just going to step through some additional enhancements we decided to make to the final animation. Feel free to try out your own variations to customize the result to your own tastes.

If you want to check the results of these final edits, compare your version with our [RoboTV_after Step 36].

RoboRender

STEP 37: Hit Command+M (Control+M) if you want to render your comp as a movie. (If not, skip ahead.)

• In the Render Settings dialog, make sure you choose Best Quality, Full Resolution, and set Field Rendering to Off (unless you have a video card capable of playing back 640×480 interlaced movies). Set the Motion Blur popup to On for Checked Layers.

• In the Output Module Settings dialog, set Channels to RGB, Depth to Millions of Colors, and Color to Premultiplied (Matted). The Format is up to you, given your hardware; for playback from hard disk, we personally like QuickTime Movie and the Photo-JPEG codec, with the Quality set between 60 and 99 depending on visual quality and disk space requirements (lower numbers equals lower quality and space). Don't forget to enable Audio Output.

If you suspect you'll have trouble playing back 640×480 29.97 fps movies from your hard drive, reduce the final render to a more manageable size, such as 320×240 pixels: In the Output Module, check the Stretch option, and set the Stretch To dimensions to 320×240. This will give you higher quality output than if you had rendered at Half Resolution.

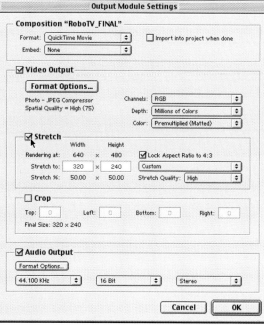

37 If you suspect a full-frame render will not play back smoothly, the highest quality way to create a smaller frame is to use the Stretch option in the Output Module. (But never stretch vertically if you field rendered in Render Settings.)

Part 5: Guided Tour to the Finish

That just about completes the RoboTV animation. There are a few finishing touches we added which we encourage you to explore. Select Window>Close All to reduce window clutter.

Play the **RoboTV.mov** again from the **Final Movie** folder for this tutorial and note the "coming up next" title that types on, and the white-to-yellow color changes in the titles to the right. To study these and other additions, in the **_RoboTV * prebuilt>Final Comps** folder in the Project window, open [**RoboTV_FINAL**], and note the following:

• Select the **Snowboarding** title layer, and hit U to twirl down animated properties if they're not already visible. We felt that the arms "sliding" into position with their ease-in animation called for a softer entry of the titles. So instead of popping on each title, we added a five-frame fade-up that began two frames before the original pop on time. For example: The **Snowboarding** title originally popped on at 01:00, but it now fades up from 00:28 to 01:03. All four titles were treated the same way. RAM Preview a section and see if you like the softer fade ups better. (Often the music will dictate whether layers should pop on or fade up, so try to listen closely for any such musical cues.)

The titles are set to fade up over five frames, and as each new title fades up, the previous title changes from white to yellow thanks to an animated Fill effect.

To start the spot, "coming up next…" types on while the first video is revealed through Effect>Boris AE>Boris Mosaic.

Natural Typing

Add Visible Character keyframes with velocity curves to a Path Text "typing on" trick to introduce natural pauses and subtle speed-ups and slow-downs.

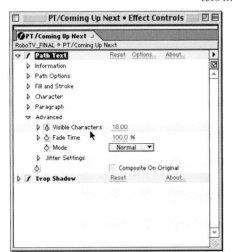

By animating the Visible Characters parameter in Path Text from 0 to 18, the "coming up next…" text appears to type on over time. Fade Time at 100% means that each character fades up instead of popping on.

• With the **Snowboarding** title still selected, hit F3 to open the Effect Controls window. We added Effect>Render>Fill to each title layer, and animated the Color from white to yellow over ten frames. Since the yellow has less contrast than white against the predominately blue background, this moves the emphasis to each new white title as it fades up. Select the **Skateboarding** title and hit T to reveal its Opacity keyframes. The timing is such that as each new title fades up to 100%, the previous title turns yellow. So in the case of the **Snowboarding** title, it fades from white at 01:23 to yellow at 02:03, while the second title – **Skateboarding** – fades up from 01:28 to 02:03.

• A small dark drop shadow (Effect>Perspective>Drop Shadow) was added to all titles to give them a little more lift from the background.

• On the left side of the frame just above the video inset, the words "coming up next" were typed on over twenty-five frames using Path Text (Effect>Text>Path Text). Select the layer, **PT/Coming Up Next**, and hit F3 to open the Effect Controls window. The effect was applied to a black solid, and Path Options>Shape Type was set to Line. The Fill Color is a very pale pink so it won't have quite the high contrast of the white titles.

• The "typing on" effect is created by animating the Visible Characters parameter in Path Text's Advanced section. There are eighteen characters in "coming up next…" (you need to count the Return and the three dots as characters); at time 00:00 the Visible Characters is set to 0 (no characters visible), and at 00:25 it is set to a value of 18. As the keyframes interpolate over time, the title types on. To make the typing fade on instead of each letter popping on, the Fade Time was set to 100%. Change it back to 0% and see the difference. The speed of the typing is set by the spacing between the two keyframes: move them apart to slow down the typing, or move them closer together to speed it up.

• From 00:00 to 01:00, the first video in the montage is already showing a snowboarder taking flight, but the **Snowboarding** title has yet to be revealed. To make the first video more "mysterious" for the first second of the animation, we added the Boris Mosaic effect to the **Montage_precomp_FINAL** layer. Select this layer and hit F3 to see its parameters. By animating the Pixelate X value from 50 at time 00:00 to 0 at 01:00, the mosaic fades out over time. There's no need to also animate the Pixelate Y value because the Lock Pixelation checkbox is on (this locks the Y value to whatever X is set to).

• We also added some more saturation to the snowboarding movie and tweaked the hue and saturation of the rock climbing movie to better match the blue-purple background. If you want to see before and after comparisons, Option+double-click (Alt+double-click) our [**Montage_precomp_FINAL**] nested layer to open our treated precomp. Drag its tab completely out of the Comp window to open a second Comp window where you can see both this comp and our final [**RoboTV_FINAL**] comp side by side. Resize and rearrange the windows as needed.

In the [**Montage_precomp_FINAL**] comp, move to time 01:00 and turn on and off the Effects switch (the "f" switch) for the **AB_Recreation_24.mov** layer – this will toggle the Hue/Saturation effect for the snowboarder. Compare the effect of adding more saturation against the background layers in the final composite. Press F3 to see the effect settings used and edit to taste.

Also in the [**Montage_precomp_FINAL**] comp, move to 05:00 and turn on and off the Effects switch for the **EW_MountainPursuits.mov** layer – this will toggle the Hue/Saturation effect for the climber movie. Compare the original turquoise blue sky against the blue-purple sky, which we feel better matches the blue in the fractal noise background. Press F3 to see the effect controls and edit to taste.

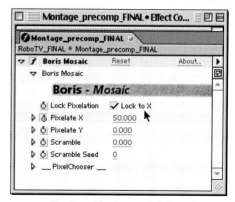

The first video is revealed through Effect>Boris AE>Boris Mosaic; the Pixelate X parameter is animated from 50 to 0; the Pixelate Y parameter follows as it is locked to X.

Going Farther & Bonus Tutorial

You can continue to tweak our final version, if you like. For example, to emphasize each new title appearing, experiment with animating a glow (perhaps using Effect>Tinderbox-Blurs>T_LensBlur, which comes free on this book's CD) to each title as the arm turns it on, or add a small light "sting" using Effect>Knoll Light Factory> Light Factory LE (which also comes free on the CD).

We've also included a bonus step-by-step tutorial called **Fractal NoiseBG_5PB.aep** with an accompanying PDF file, which are in the **02_RoboTV>_FractalNoise_Bonus Tutorial** folder. This shows how we created the backgrounds used in this project with the Fractal Noise plug-in included in the After Effects 5 Production Bundle. It also includes additional tips for creating animated seamless loops with the Fractal Noise effect.

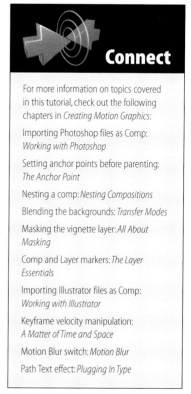

Connect

For more information on topics covered in this tutorial, check out the following chapters in *Creating Motion Graphics*:

Importing Photoshop files as Comp: *Working with Photoshop*

Setting anchor points before parenting: *The Anchor Point*

Nesting a comp: *Nesting Compositions*

Blending the backgrounds: *Transfer Modes*

Masking the vignette layer: *All About Masking*

Comp and Layer markers: *The Layer Essentials*

Importing Illustrator files as Comp: *Working with Illustrator*

Keyframe velocity manipulation: *A Matter of Time and Space*

Motion Blur switch: *Motion Blur*

Path Text effect: *Plugging In Type*

Some of the footage was further color corrected to better match the overall spot. For example, the snowboarder had some saturation added (left = before, right = after).

Hot but Cool

A trio of text animation tricks, starring Vector Paint.

This breezy tutorial shares three ideas for animating the words in the title Hot but Cool: jerkily slamming the word "Hot" into place, rotating "but" into position in 3D, and using the Production Bundle's Vector Paint effect to reveal "Cool" one character at a time. Vector Paint is nearly a mini-program unto itself, and will be our primary focus.

We will provide you with a starter composition that already has the Illustrator artwork for the title and a partially marked-up soundtrack in place. Step-by-step instructions will be provided for each text trick, with latitude for you to customize the animations to taste. We'll wrap up with a quick guided tour of touches we added to the final project, including layering together a pair of background movies and treating the entire composition with an interesting blur effect.

OVERVIEW

Main Concepts:

These are the features and concepts we will be focusing on in this project:

- Spotting music
- Vector Paint effect *(PB)*
- Anchor Points
- "Slam down" text animation
- Continuous rasterization
- Hold keyframes
- Masking in the Comp window
- 3D rotation
- Adjustment layers
- Transfer modes
- Tinderbox T_LensBlur effect*

Requirements:

After Effects 5.0 Production Bundle (required for Vector Paint effect); all other aspects of the tutorial could be completed with the 5.0 Standard version.

Getting Started:

** Be sure to install the Lens Blur effect from The Foundry (www.thefoundry.co.uk), included on the accompanying CD in the **Free Plug-ins** folder.*

Inside the **Tutorials** master folder on the accompanying CD, locate and copy the folder **03_HotCool** to your hard drive.

In the folder **Final Movie** inside this main folder, double-click and play **HotCool.mov**.

Inside the **Project** folder you'll find the finished After Effects project file **HotCool_5PB.aep**. Open the project file – this is your starting point. We suggest you save under a new name after each major section.

(Note: If you don't have the Production Bundle, the Vector Paint effect will simply be removed from the project; you can still use this project to complete the other tasks.)

The Tasks

This is what you will be doing in the various parts of this tutorial:

PART 1: Learn how to use Vector Paint to reveal an underlying title, including important tips on mastering its custom interface.

PART 2: Animate one word to slam into place using hold keyframes, then rotate another using simple 3D.

PART 3: Take a guided tour of our enhanced version of the title, where we add background movies as well as adjustment layers with Tinderbox's T_LensBlur effect to create a "blooming" effect that ties the elements together.

A different text trick is used to introduce each word of the *Hot but Cool* title. The background consists of movies from the Bestshot CDs ShapeFlow and Upbeat; the halos around the shapes are created with the Tinderbox T_LensBlur effect.

Part 1: Cool Painting

PB Since the Vector Paint effect is the centerpiece of this tutorial, we'll dive into it now. We've set up a few things already in a starter composition; you'll need to do a little more prep work before you get paint on your mouse:

STEP 1: Find the composition [**HotCool * starter**] in the Project window's **My_Comps** folder, and open it. It consists of four layers: Three words created in Illustrator and imported as a composition, and the soundtrack, which was added to this comp. We've already set Composition>Background Color to a sky blue similar to our eventual background layers so we can see the black characters clearly.

STEP 2: A recurring aspect of this tutorial will be timing your animations to music. Open the dialog for Edit>Preferences>Previews, and enter "**900**" to set the Audio Duration to 09:00. This will allow you to preview the entire 08:16 length of the comp, plus give you a half-second pause before it starts over again. Click OK to save this new value.

1 The starter comp already has the text imported; the comp's background color is a sky blue to make the black characters more visible.

2 Set the Audio Preview Duration to 09:00 by entering "900" – no colons are needed.

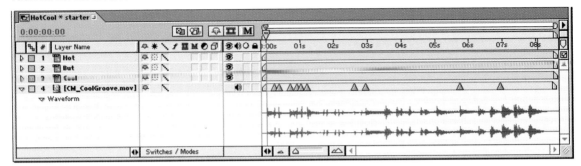

3 Some of the major beats in the music are marked with layer markers. To add more markers, select layer 4 and press * (the asterisk key on the keypad) to add a marker at the current time.

More on Music

To learn more about reading audio waveforms and spotting music, check out the article *Timing Video to Audio* in the **Goodies** folder on this book's CD.

4 Set the text layers to Best Quality, turn off **Hot** and **But**, and slide **Cool** to start at 02:28 – in time with the third section of the music.

STEP 3: The audio waveform for layer 4 – **CM_CoolGroove.mov** – should already be visible. If not, select this layer and type LL (two Ls in rapid succession) to reveal it.

Press Home to reset the time marker to 00:00, and press the decimal point on the extended keypad to preview the audio (hit any key to stop playback). The soundtrack has three main sections: a pair of drum rolls at the start, a drum "pickup" with a sax playing on top, then the main groove when the upright bass and drums play together.

Listen carefully as the time marker scrolls through the waveform in the Timeline so you can start to draw a correspondence between the beats and their spikes in the waveform. We've already created layer markers for some of the more important beats; feel free to create more.

Audio waveforms are slow to redraw in After Effects. After you have a handle on which layer markers correspond to which parts of the music, you can twirl the waveform up to save redraw time. Press LL again whenever you need to see the waveform again. We're going to leave the waveform open for some of the illustrations in this tutorial.

STEP 4: Illustrator artwork looks pretty crunchy in Draft Quality. Set all three type layers to Best Quality by dragging down their Quality switches in the Timeline window. Then turn the Video switch off for the **Hot** and **But** layers – we'll work on the **Cool** layer first.

• Type Command+G on the Mac (Control+G on Windows) to open the Go To Time dialog, enter 228, and hit Return to jump to 02:28. This corresponds to the marker we set for the beginning of the third section of the music – feel free to preview the audio from this point forward.

• Select the **Cool** layer, and press [(left square bracket) to start **Cool** at that time.

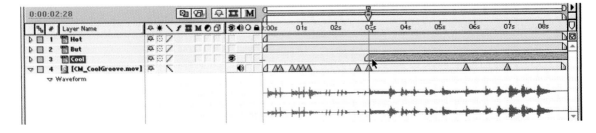

Painting to Reveal

Although the name of the plug-in is Vector Paint, often you will never see the paint strokes themselves. In this tutorial, you will be using it to paint a matte that will reveal the characters of your title underneath.

Vector Paint has modes that decide whether it uses the speed with which you draw your strokes, and the pauses between them. You can alter these speeds later. There are also different playback modes, in which you can choose if all strokes start drawing at once, or if individual strokes are tied to specific points in time. What's disconcerting about Vector Paint is that you don't see keyframes in your timeline that correspond to your strokes – so you have to do a bit of planning to use it in a predictable fashion.

For this project, you will be using a mode in which your strokes are played back with the general timing you drew them with, with no pause inbetween. Since you can change the playback speed later, your main focus will be drawing the strokes accurately and at an even pace.

STEP 5: With the **Cool** layer still selected, apply Effect>Paint>**Vector Paint**. Its Effect Controls window will open, and a special interface will appear along the left edge of the Comp window. This interface will be active only when you have the Vector Paint effect selected in the Timeline or Effect Controls window.

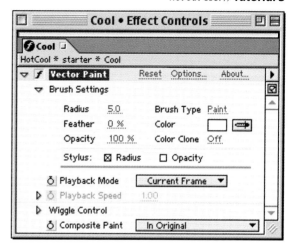

5 Apply the Vector Paint effect to the **Cool** layer (above). When this effect is selected, a special set of controls appears along the left side of the Project window (below).

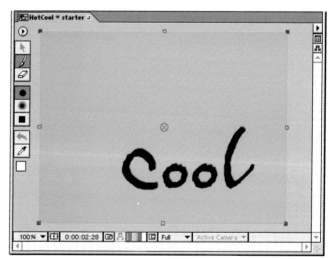

Music Credits

The soundtrack for this project was arranged by Chris Meyer of CyberMotion, using a trio of copyright-clean sampling CDs. The upright bass is played by John Pattitucci, and is from the Spectrasonics *Bass Legends* CD (distributed in the United States by Ilio Entertainment – www.ilio.com). The drums were played by Keith LeBlanc on his *Kickin' Lunatic Beats* CD (distributed by AMG – www.amguk.co.uk), and were edited to fit. The sax riff was transplanted from Zero-G's *Pure Trip Hop* (www.zero-g.co.uk).

Tablet Paint

Vector Paint supports graphics tablets – such as those from Wacom – which can be easier to use for drawing than a mouse. Tablet stylus pressure may also be assigned to vary the brush size or opacity.

6 Draw some test strokes with different radius settings, to make sure the brush will cover the characters cleanly.

7 Use either the Vector Paint wing menu or context-click in the comp window, and select Shift-Paint Records>Continuously.

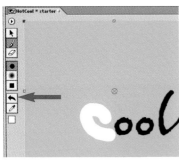

8 While you're holding the Shift key down, paint over the four characters using evenly paced strokes. When you're done, release the Shift key, and the Comp window will change to displaying your first stroke. If you need to start over, click the Undo button (where the arrow is pointing) to wipe out your strokes.

STEP 6: To test the size of paint brush you will need, dab the paint along one of the letters; the default radius of 5 pixels will be too thin. Change it to 14 or so, and try again. Although you can change the width of the strokes after they're drawn (an advantage that painting with vectors, instead of pixels, gives you), having a big enough brush radius to start with will require less work in the long run.

When you're satisfied with your brush size, delete your test strokes. Make sure the Comp window is forward and the Vector Paint interface is visible, press Command+A (Control+A) to Select All strokes (look closely in the middle of the strokes – you should see tiny dots, indicating they are selected), and hit Delete.

STEP 7: The last thing to do before you start is set the paint recording mode. This option can be accessed from the wing menu at the top of Vector Paint's Comp window controls (on the Mac, you can also Control+click in the Comp window while Vector Paint is active; on Windows, try right clicking on the Comp window's pasteboard area).

Open the Vector Paint menu and select Shift-Paint Records>Continuously. This means that if you hold down the Shift key as you paint, Vector Paint records each stroke in realtime, *and* removes the pauses between strokes. (Another available option – Shift-Paint Records> In Realtime – will faithfully record all those pauses.)

STEP 8: Vector Paint defaults to treating every stroke as a separate event. To treat a number of strokes as one long event, you need to hold down the Shift key while you're painting. That way, you can release the mouse (or lift your graphics tablet stylus) and move over to the next character without creating independent strokes that would all start at the same time.

With the time marker at the start of the **Cool** layer, hold the Shift key down and paint each stroke at a relaxed pace – don't worry about the pauses inbetween as they will be ignored. Make sure each character is covered completely. *And don't let up the Shift key until you're through painting over all the letters!*

If you make a mistake and want to start over, release the Shift key and click the Undo tool – the backward arrow in the Vector Paint tools – or type Command+Z (Control+Z); the strokes will be deleted. Press Shift again and start painting. Don't be afraid to do this as many times as necessary until you feel comfortable with your strokes.

When you're happy with your painting, release the mouse or stylus and the Shift key. If the Info window is open, it will note that you've drawn four strokes – one for each character. Whenever you release the Shift key, the Comp window displays your first stroke only on the first frame. (In the Effect Controls window, change the Playback Mode to All Strokes if you want to see all four strokes during the entire layer.)

STEP 9: Time to see how your strokes play back!

• Type B to start the work area at this point. In the Effect Controls window, change the Playback Mode popup to Animate Strokes – your strokes will disappear from the Comp window. Either hit the spacebar to play the comp, hit 0 on the keypad to RAM Preview, or scrub the Timeline to get a quicker preview of how long the strokes are taking to draw on.

Your strokes will probably draw on *very* slowly, perhaps finishing only halfway by the comp's end. No sweat: The Playback Speed slider sets the global drawing speed. Increase it to 2 or 3 and try again.

There is a shortcut to determining the correct speed: Say you want the strokes to finish by the beat of the music we marked at 05:22. Place the time marker there, and scrub the Playback Speed value until the painting just finishes covering the L in **Cool**. You can hold the Command (Control) key while you're scrubbing to get finer increments.

STEP 10: Hit I to jump back to the **Cool** layer's in point. Change the Composite Paint popup to As Matte, which makes the strokes affect only the alpha channel of **Cool**. RAM Preview, and the logo will be revealed over time as the paint strokes animate.

Another aspect of speed is when the stroke starts: Even with the Shift-Paint Records option set to Continuous, you might see a delay of a few frames before each stroke. Step through the start of the animation until you see the first bit of the C appear, and hit the keypad's asterisk key to place a layer marker at this point. Then slide the layer back until the marker lines up with the time at which you want playback to start – 02:28, in this case. Don't forget to return to the time you want the painting to finish by, and adjust the Playback Speed so that it still finishes at the same frame.

(If you make a mess, bring the Comp window forward, select all of your strokes, delete them as you did in Step 6, and start over with Step 8.)

If you're not sure you got the result you should, open our prebuilt comp [HotCool_after Step 10] *and compare your results. You can find it in the Project window's* **_HotCool * prebuilt>_compare comps_after Step ##** *folder. Save your project before continuing.*

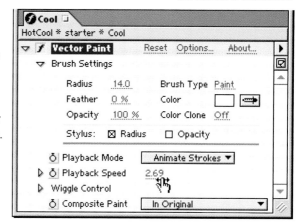

9 Set the Playback Mode to Animate Strokes (above), place the time marker where you want the painting to end, and scrub the Playback Speed until the last character is just covered by your strokes (below).

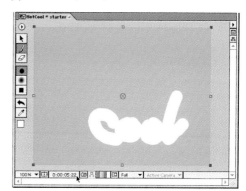

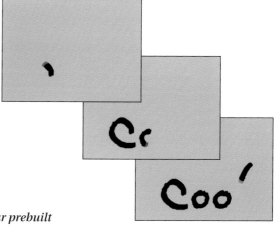

10 Change the Composite Paint popup to As Matte, and your strokes will reveal the underlying characters over time.

Playback Speed and Retimer

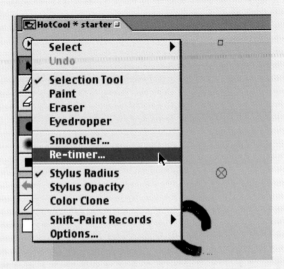

The online Help file contains extensive documentation on Vector Paint. It's quite a deep plug-in with lots of useful options; it just has a different way of thinking than you may be used to.

For example, Vector Paint contains two speed controls: Playback Speed, which controls the overall pace of your painting (including strokes and pauses), and Retimer, which allows you to alter the speed of individual strokes without altering the overall pace or the timing of the other strokes. Retimer is cumbersome to use, and most important of all, *you can't Undo it*. So *save your project* before trying out these steps, so you can Revert later on!

● RAM Preview, memorizing the pacing of when the letter C finishes and the first O starts.

● Go to the time when the stroke revealing the letter C is nearly finished. Make sure the Vector Paint effect is still selected, and click on its selection tool (the arrow) in the Comp window.

● Click where you believe the path for your C should be. This can be tricky; keep trying until you see a faint dotted line appear for your stroke.

Selecting stroke paths is tricky, and may take more than one try. When you have successfully selected a path, a faint dotted line will appear.

● Context-click on the Comp window or use Vector Paint's wing menu, and select Retimer. A dialog box will open; here you can enter a time stretch percentage for this stroke. Enter 50 and click OK. You will get a warning dialog that you can't undo your action; click OK again.

● RAM Preview. Note that the C reveals in half the time as before, but the timing for the other strokes – *including when they start* – does not change. Retimer

After you have selected the stroke you want to retime, select Retimer from Vector Paint's contextual menu.

edits the speed that you drew the selected stroke at, without affecting the Playback Speed.

● Repeat, but this time enter 300%. This will result in a longer time than your original speed (Retimer speed changes accumulate: 50% x 300% = 150% duration). RAM Preview, and note that the C's reveal now continues past when the first O begins. Again, Retimer affects only the selected stroke, regardless of what the other strokes are doing.

● Experiment with different Retimer and Playback Speed settings so you can see how they interact.

● File>Revert to return to your last saved project.

A last note about Playback Speed: It alters the timing of all of your strokes and pauses, regardless of where along the timeline you drew them. For example, in the prebuilt comp **[HotCool_after Step10_alt]** we drew the strokes individually (without the Shift key held down), relocating the time marker each time we drew a new stroke to time each character more tightly with the music. However, changing the Playback Speed moves when the later strokes start to play back. In this case, we used Retimer on each individual stroke to get them to end when we wanted, without affecting their start times in the timeline.

Part 2: Two Words

The animations for the first two words are much less complicated; they also have a degree of artistic latitude in how you animate them. For the word "Hot," we'll employ the popular "slamming down" technique you see in many high-energy animations. For the word "but," we'll use a simple 3D rotation and opacity fade, demonstrating that you don't need cameras and lights to do "basic 3D" in version 5.

Hot Slam

STEP 11: Turn off the Video switch (the eyeball) for the **Cool** layer, then turn **Hot**'s eyeball on.

We've decided to bring this word on in time with the second drum-roll at the start of the soundtrack. Return to 02:28 and press N to end the work area. Then move to 00:21 where we have the hits in this roll marked in the audio layer, and press B to begin the work area here. Press + (on the normal keyboard, not the keypad) to zoom in until the four layer markers around this time are easy to distinguish. Select **Hot** and press [to start it at the current frame, 00:21.

Favorite Strokes

To save a set of strokes and their timing for future reference, select Vector Paint and use Effect>Save Favorite to store them.

11 Set the **Hot** layer to start with the second drum roll at 00:21, and zoom in to the timeline area so you can see the individual beats.

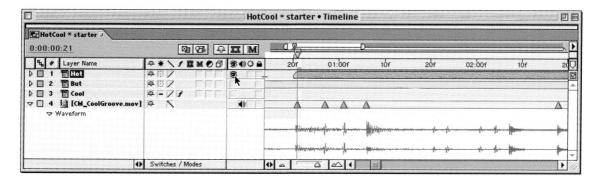

STEP 12: Each word started as individual layers in the same Illustrator file. Illustrator defaults to all layers being the same size as the overall document, with their anchor points in the center of that document. Since you'll be animating Scale, it's best if the anchor point is centered in the O of Hot.

• With the **Hot** layer selected, press Y to select the Pan Behind (also known as the Anchor Point) tool. Then drag the anchor point icon in the Comp window to the center of the O. Press V to return to the Selection tool.

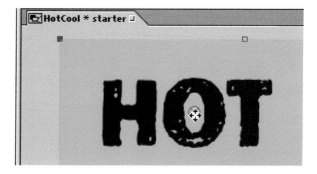

12 Press Y to select the Pan Behind tool, and move **Hot**'s anchor point into the center of its O.

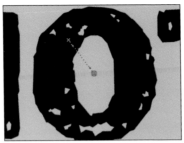

STEP 13: Move the time marker to 01:06 – the beat where **Hot** should land. Type P followed by Shift+S to reveal **Hot**'s Position and Scale properties, and turn on their animation stopwatches. This will create the keyframes for the landing position. Now have fun creating the "slam" keyframes:

13 Scale **Hot** to 400% and center it in the frame (above left). Turn on the Continuous Rasterization switch (below) for a sharp image (above right).

#	Layer Name	🔲 ✳ ↘ ƒ ▦ M
1	🔲 **Hot**	🔲 ✳ ∕
▷ ⓣ Position	200.5 , 149.0
▷ ⓣ Scale	400.0 %

• Press I to locate to the layer's in point at 00:21.

• Scale up **Hot** to around 400%, and reposition it until it the O is centered in the comp – that should be an attention-grabber…

• Scaling **Hot** larger than 100% makes it look pixelated. Since it is an Illustrator file, turn on its Continuous Rasterization button so it renders cleanly.

• Create alternate poses using Scale and Position to match the other drum beats. At a minimum, create keyframes for the major beats at

13 *complete:* Create additional Scale and Position keyframes for the other beats. Have fun bouncing the size smaller then larger again.

00:27 and 01:01; we also created keyframes at 00:24, 00:29, and 01:03. As a general rule, the scale values should decrease from 400% to 100% – but they don't have to do so in an orderly fashion. Have fun decreasing the size, then abruptly scale one keyframe larger again.

STEP 14: RAM Preview about a second or so of this animation. **Hot** slides quickly between your poses – but you wanted slams…

Select all of your Scale and Position keyframes, except for the last ones at 01:06. Then select Animation>Toggle Hold Keyframe. This will make the animation hold each pose until the next keyframe, resulting in a jerky slam movement. RAM Preview and note the difference!

14 Select all the keyframes except the last set, and use Animation> Toggle Hold Keyframe to create abrupt animation moves.

If you want to compare your slam keyframes with ours, inspect the prebuilt comp **[HotCool_after Step 14]**. *And remember to save!*

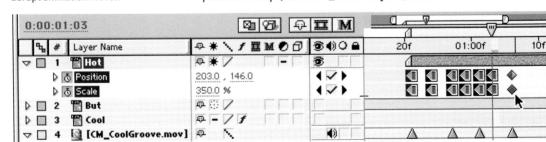

Simple 3D Rotation

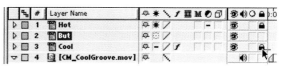

STEP 15: Twirl up the keyframes for **Hot**, and turn on the eyeball for the layers **But** and **Cool**. Since all three layers are the same size as the comp, it's hard to select **But** in the Comp window as it's underneath the **Hot** layer. To solve this, toggle on the Lock switch for **Hot** and **Cool**.

15 Turn on the Video switches for all three title layers. Lock the **Hot** and **Cool** layers to make **But** easier to select in the Comp window.

Then move the time marker to about where the saxophone comes in – we used 01:12. Select the **But** layer, and press [to slide its in point.

STEP 16: As we noted in Step 12, Illustrator layers default to having their anchor point (the circle with the X) in the middle of the overall file – not each specific layer.

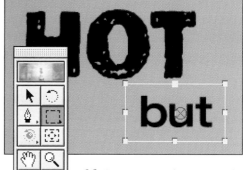

- Press Y to select the Pan Behind tool, click on the anchor point in the Comp window, and drag **But**'s anchor point to the center of the "u".

- To neaten things up, let's mask **But** down to just the part of the frame we're using. Make sure Layer Masks are enabled in the Comp window's wing menu (top right corner of window), select the Rectangular Mask tool, and draw a loose rectangular mask around the word "but" directly in the Comp window (new in 5.0).

16 Center **But**'s anchor point, and with the rectangular mask selected, drag a rough mask around **But** directly in the Comp window.

- Press V to return to the Selection tool, and turn the Comp window display of Layer Masks option off. (Note that when masks are applied, the Continuous Rasterization switch is not available.)

STEP 17: For this final animation, you want to rotate this word around its Y axis. This used to require an effect like Perspective>Basic 3D, but as of version 5.0 you can manipulate any layer directly in 3D space:

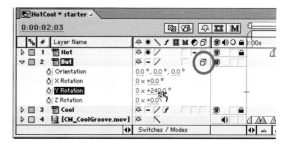

- Turn on the 3D Layer switch for **But** in the Timeline window. You don't need to create a camera or a light; After Effects provides default comp cameras and lights that work fine in simple cases like these.

17 Turn on the 3D switch (circled in red above), and scrub the Y Rotation value (above). Watch the **But** layer spin around in the Comp window (below).

- With **But** still selected, hit R to reveal its Orientation and Rotation properties. We'll get into the difference between them later in this book in the *Postcards in Space* tutorial; for now, focus on the Y Rotation value, which is in Revolutions and Degrees. Scrub the degrees while you're watching the Comp window to get a feel for what it does.

- With the time marker still at 01:12, reset Y Rotation to 0° and enable its animation stopwatch. You want to make one full revolution during the sax riff, so move to somewhere around 02:21 and set a second keyframe with a value of 1 Revolution (or 360°). With this keyframe selected, press the shortcut F9 – Easy Ease – to smooth out the end of this move. RAM Preview, and tweak this keyframe's timing to taste.

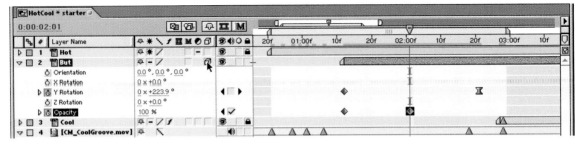

17 *complete:* The **But** layer was set to be 3D (where the cursor is pointing), with its Y Rotation animated. A simple fade-up was also added.

Finer Scrub

Hold the Command (Control) key while you're scrubbing to get finer adjustments.

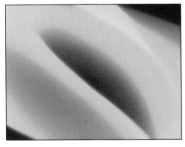

The background is based on **BS_Upbeat.mov** (top), with **BS_ShapeFlow.mov** (above) applied on top in Multiply mode to add shadow effects.

- **But** pops on a bit abruptly. Fix this by keyframing a simple Opacity animation from 0 to 100% over this layer's first 20 or so frames.

- Press – (minus key on the keyboard) to zoom out the Timeline to the full length again. Double-click on the ribbed area of the work area bar to set the work area to equal the length of your comp, and RAM Preview all three of your text animations.

That wraps up the steps in this tutorial. If you want to compare your animation with ours, check the prebuilt comp [**HotCool after Step 17**].

Part 3: All That Jazz

Now that you have animated the words in the title, feel free to finish the project off as you like – perhaps tint the words, add a background, and otherwise treat the final frame. We've included our own version for you to pick apart: In the Project window, look inside the **_HotCool ∗ prebuilt>Final Comps** folder and open [**HotCool_FINAL**]. Starting at the bottom, here are some highlights:

- The background consists of two movies. **BS_Upbeat.mov** (layer 8) is the base; **BS_ShapeFlow.mov** (layer 7) has been layered on top of it at 50% Opacity in Multiply mode to add shadow effects.

- The three words (layers 3 through 5) use Effect>Render>Fill to give them color, and Perspective>Drop Shadow to lift them off the background. The **Hot** and **Cool** layers have their positions animated to slowly drift across the frame after they come on.

There are two special points about these effects worth noting. The first is that **Hot** (layer 3) was set earlier to continuously rasterize, so it could be scaled up cleanly. Since effects cannot be applied to layers set to continuously rasterize, we needed to precompose this layer (select layer and Layer>Pre-compose) using the "Move All Attributes" option. We could then apply effects to the precomposed layer.

Second is that even though **But** (layer 4) has its 3D Layer switch enabled, we applied a 2D drop shadow to it rather than using a 3D light to cast the shadow. In version 5.0, this is the only way to have a 3D layer cast a shadow on the 2D background layers. We've also enabled Motion Blur (the M switch) for this layer.

• To lift the final look beyond simple line art, we applied a pair of adjustment layers using Tinderbox's T_LensBlur. This effect gives a "blooming" appearance, compared with the normal fuzziness of other blurs. We then used different transfer modes and tweaked their opacities so that these bloomed versions would interact with – rather than simply replace – the untreated frame underneath.

Experiment with turning layers 1 and 2 on and off to get an idea for what they are contributing to the overall look. Pay particular attention to the lines in the **BS_Upbeat.mov** layer, and the way the colors bleed between the title and background. Also try out different transfer modes: We used Color Burn and Hard Light, both of which make the frame darker; try some brightening modes such as Add or Screen.

Play with the Opacity properties of these layers to see how they were blended – higher values tended to make the overall frame darker than we wanted. Select these layers and press F3 to open their Effect Controls windows, and experiment with T_LensBlur's Radius and Bloom values to get different looks. In general, applying adjustment layers with effects on top of the final frame is a great technique for blending disparate elements, and pushing your design in a direction you might not have otherwise envisioned.

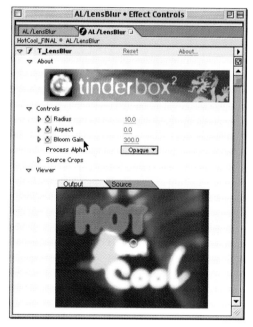

Tinderbox's T_LensBlur effect is great for creating a "blooming" appearance. The result is then transfer moded on top of the original.

The final animation (top left) was blended further by stacking two adjustment layers with T_LensBlur applied: one in Color Burn mode (above), and another in Hard Light mode (left).

Connect

For more information on topics covered in this tutorial, check out the following chapters in *Creating Motion Graphics*:

Spotting Audio: *Audio Basics and Effects*

Anchor Points: *The Anchor Point*

Continuous Rasterization: *Working with Illustrator*

Hold keyframes: *A Matter of Time and Space*

Fill and Drop Shadow effects: *Standard Effects Round-Up*

Transfer modes: *Transfer Modes*

Adjustment layers: *Adjustment Layers*

AutoTracker

Using Motion Tracking to composite graphical overlays onto live footage with 3:2 pulldown applied.

This tutorial is derived from a larger project CyberMotion executed for Perception Communications and American Isuzu Motors Inc. for Isuzu's new Axiom crossover vehicle. To illustrate the numerous sensors monitored by Isuzu's Torque on Demand system in the Axiom, we created a fanciful animation in which a number of sensor icons follow points on moving footage of the Axiom, adding numeric readouts down the side to indicate the information being conveyed.

To link these icons to the footage, we used the Motion Tracking feature of the After Effects Production Bundle. In this tutorial, we will walk you through tracking specific points on the footage and attaching the icons to them. You will also be encouraged to see how many other points you can track to create a full set of twelve. After the hard work is done, we will then walk you through the additional enhancements we made to the final frame.

OVERVIEW

Main Concepts:

These are the features and concepts we will be focusing on in this project:

- Removing 3:2 pulldown
- Managing 16–235 luminance ranges
- Motion Tracking
- Nesting compositions
- Adjustment layers
- Adding pulldown during rendering
- The Wiggler *(optional)*
- Stroke, Mosaic, Transform, Numbers, Basic Text, and Posterize Time effects *(optional)*

Requirements:

After Effects 4.1 or later Production Bundle.

Getting Started:

Inside the **Tutorials** master folder on the accompanying CD, copy the folder **04_AutoTracker** to your hard drive. Inside this is a folder called **Final Movie** – open it, then open **AutoTracker.mov** in the QuickTime Player to preview it.

Inside the **Project** folder you'll find accompanying After Effects project files. Depending on the version of After Effects you are using – 4.1 versus 5.0 or later – open the project **AutoTracker_4PB.aep** or **AutoTracker_5PB.aep**. This is your starting point; we suggest you save under a new name after each major section.

Some details of using the Motion Tracker changed between After Effects 4.1 and 5.0. The illustrations and primary instructions in this tutorial will be based on version 5.0, but we will note the differences and give alternate instructions for 4.1 users as needed.

Another significant subject of this tutorial is handling video footage that originated on film and that uses a luminance range different from what is normally employed by After Effects. You will learn how to remove 3:2 pull-down from footage and to add it back in when you render, as well as how to manage these common luminance range issues.

The Tasks

This is what you will be doing in the various parts of this tutorial:

Part 1: Import the footage, remove 3:2 pulldown, create a new composition at the resulting

special frame rate, translate its luminance range, and add the soundtrack. These issues relate to all versions of After Effects.

Part 2: Motion track the footage by trying different techniques, including picking up failed tracks from the middle of a clip.

Part 3: Import and attach the sensor icons, scale and apply transfer modes to them to improve their appearance, and exploit nested comps to swap them out quickly.

Part 4: Retranslate the luminance range for video output, and automatically add 3:2 pulldown during the final render.

Part 5: Take a guided tour of additional touches we added to the finished project, including creating a series of randomized numbers using the Numbers effect, and treating select areas of the original video using the Mosaic effect applied to an Adjustment Layer, with the Transform effect thrown in to compensate for odd comp sizes and non-square pixels.

A final frame from this sequence, featuring a number of graphical tracking boxes and faked numeric readouts. Axiom footage courtesy of Perception Communications and American Isuzu Motors Inc.

Standard Version

If you don't have the Production Bundle, you can still benefit from this tutorial. Complete Part 1, skip over Part 2, and pick up again with Part 3 using our prebuilt comp, **[Tracker_after Step 22]** where the tracking data is already complete.

Part 1: Pull Me Down

Not all of the footage items you receive for jobs will be ready to use in a composition as-is. In this case, the main footage was originally shot on 24 frame per second (fps) film, which introduces some interesting frame rate and field interlacing issues. It was also captured on a Media 100 nonlinear editing system, which passes along to the user a luminance range based on digital video transfer protocols, in which the black and white points are not where you might expect.

Removing 3:2 Pulldown

STEP 1: Select the **My_Sources** folder in the Project window, then select the menu command File>Import by pressing Command+I on Mac (Control+I on Windows). Locate the **04_AutoTracker>Project> Sources** folder on your drive, select **PC_Axiom.mov**, and click on Import (Open). If you are using After Effects 4.1, drag this source into the **My_Sources** folder to make them easier to find (continue to do this with other sources you import later on in this tutorial).

At the top of the Project window, the movie will report that it has a frame rate of 29.97 fps. After Effects 5.0 will also detect a tag in the file that says it has separated fields, lower field first. (If you are using version 4.1, select File>Interpret Footage>Main, and set the Separate Fields option to Lower Field First.) However, this is only part of the story…

1 After you import **PC_Axiom.mov**, the Project window will note it has a frame rate of 29.97 fps, Lower Field First.

STEP 2: Double-click the movie to open it in a QuickTime player window. Single-step through it using the left and right arrow keys, and look for signs of video field interlacing: alternating horizontal lines in the image that seem to be offset from each other, like the teeth of a comb. This is easiest to spot in the ivy hanging over the wall to the left early in the shot, since it has good contrast, and is the object moving most quickly in the image.

These offsets appear because the alternating lines from each field of the image are from different points in time – namely, 1/59.94th of a second apart (half the duration of a single NTSC frame). As you continue to step through the clip, you will notice, however, that only some of the frames exhibit interlacing. Keep stepping, and note the pattern: three "whole" frames with no interlacing, followed by two "split" frames with interlacing. By contrast, normal interlaced video exhibits these lines and split appearance in every frame.

Close the QuickTime window, and Option+double-click (Alt+ double-click) the same item to open it in After Effects' own Footage window. This special window shows you the footage after After Effects has separated the frame into two distinct fields. Step through these individual fields using the Page Up and Page Down keys. You should now notice a different pattern, in which an

2 As you step through this movie in a QuickTime player, you will notice some of the frames appear "whole" (left), while others are "split" with field interlacing lines clearly visible (right).

3:2 Pulldown

What is the cause of the strange patterns of repeated images you observed in Step 2? You're seeing the result of a process known as 3:2 pulldown. This footage was originally shot on film, at 24 fps. To transfer this shot to NTSC video with its frame rate of 29.97 fps, the film is first slowed down from 24 fps to 23.976 fps (the same ratio as between 30 fps black-and-white video and 29.97 fps color). The original film frames are then spread across video fields using a method in which the first frame is copied across two video fields, then the next frame is copied across three video fields. This creates a pattern of whole and interlaced (split) frames that matches what you saw in the QuickTime Player, as well as the pattern of two repeated fields followed by three in After Effects' Footage window after the fields have been separated.

   In most cases, you can treat this video the same as any other clip. However, when you have to track the detail in every video field – such as rotoscoping, or matching the motion of another layer to an object in

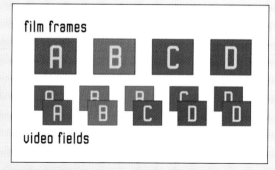

The 3:2 pulldown process spreads four film frames across ten video fields by repeating the film frames in a 2-3-2-3 pattern. When two different film frames end up in the same video frame, it is said to be "split" (S); when the same film frame is used for both fields of a video frame, it is "whole" (W). This illustration shows a WWSSW pattern.

this video – it is highly desirable to find a way to retrieve the original film frames: It's the difference between having to manage 24 frames or 60 fields of imagery for every second of the shot.

image is repeated for three steps, then the next image appears for two steps. (With normal video, you would observe a different image every field; if a progressive scan camera was used, you would observe a steady pattern of a different image every two fields.)

   You are witnessing the results of how most film is transferred to NTSC video, commonly known as 3:2 pulldown. This technique spreads every four film frames across ten video fields (for more details, see the sidebar *3:2 Pulldown*). Since the main point of this tutorial is to track the motion in this footage, it would require a lot less work to track only the unique source frames, and not the duplicated fields as well.

Step 3: Select **PC_Axiom.mov** in the Project window, and press Command+F (Control+F) to open its Interpret Footage options.

   We often refer to this dialog as "the money box" because making sure its options are set correctly can save you lots of time and/or money. For example, removing pulldown will reduce the number of frames you have to work on. And you can avoid correcting mistakes later in the process because the field separation, frame rate, or alpha channel interpretation were set incorrectly.

   The third panel in this dialog is named Field and Pulldown. At this point, the Separate Fields option should be set to Lower Field First (the most common setting for NTSC D1 or DV footage), and the

VideoSyncrasies

Interlacing, 3:2 pulldown, alpha channels, field rendering, non-square pixels, and other technical video issues are discussed and demonstrated in our tape, *VideoSyncrasies* from Desktop Images (www.desktopimages.com).

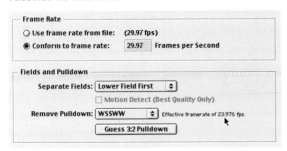

3 If a footage item has 3:2 pulldown, you can either manually remove it by carefully observing the footage and choosing an appropriate whole/split phase setting, or have After Effects guess for you. The cursor is pointing to an important message: that this footage now has effectively the same frame rate as the original film.

Remove Pulldown option defaults to Off. There are five possible whole/split patterns this footage could have. You could try each one by hand, or you can let After Effects try first:

Click on the Guess 3:2 Pulldown button. After a brief pause, the Remove Pulldown setting should change automatically to WSSWW, which After Effects thinks is the pulldown pattern or "phase" this footage was created with. Also notice that a line of text has appeared next to this setting, noting that the footage now has an effective frame rate of 23.976 fps after pulldown has been removed – this is the rate the film was running at when it was transferred to video. Click on OK.

Go back to the After Effects Footage window for this item, or re-open it if you already closed it. Now as you step through the source, you should see a new frame of movement for every step you make. Close the Footage window when you're done. (The QuickTime Player window will not show any change, since it presents the footage to you before it has been processed by the Interpret Footage settings.)

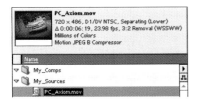

3 *complete:* After you've removed the pulldown, the pulldown phase and new effective frame rate will be noted in the Project window.

Occasionally, After Effects is unable to guess the correct phase – such as when the footage is fading up from black, or has little to no initial motion. You can either hand-count the phase and enter it yourself, or keep trying the different options until you no longer see split frames in the Footage window. If you can't find an option that works, there is always the chance that the phase was disrupted at some previous point in the chain, including placing an edit during the clip, or because the footage was time-stretched.

If you look at the top of the Project window again, you will note that the information for this clip has been amended to include the 3:2 pull-down phase, and you'll see the new effective frame rate (rounded to 23.98 fps for display purposes only).

Building the Main Composition

Removing 3:2 pulldown has reconstructed the original, whole film frames. The next steps include creating a composition that takes this special frame rate into account, adjusting for differences in luminance space that some video systems impose on their footage, and adding the soundtrack.

4 Drag the source footage to the New Composition icon at the bottom of the project window to have its size, length, and frame rate automatically copied into the comp's settings.

STEP 4: You need to create a composition with the same settings – size, duration, and frame rate – as this clip. You could copy down this information from the Project window, create a new comp from the Composition menu, and transcribe these parameters across, or you can let After Effects do the work for you.

• Drag the footage item **PC_Axiom.mov** to the New Composition icon at the bottom of the Project window, and release the mouse. A new comp with these settings will be created automatically for you.

• Drag this comp to your **My_Comps** folder in the Project window.

• With this new comp selected, press Command+K (Control+K) to open its Composition Settings dialog. Verify that the frame rate is 23.976 fps and change its name to "**My_Tracker**". The process of removing pulldown has left some less-than-ideal frames at the end; go ahead and alter the duration to 06:17 to trim these off. Click on OK.

STEP 5: This footage was originally captured on a Media 100 system, which passes its internal 16–235 luminance range directly to other programs. It is much easier to work with clips like these in After Effects if you first convert them to a 0–255 luminance range; that way, you don't have to watch out for accidentally creating colors that are too dark or bright for legal video on output.

• In the composition [**My_Tracker**] select the layer **PC_Axiom.mov**, and apply Effect>Adjust>**Levels**. This will automatically open an Effect Controls window for Levels. Note that the Histogram in this window shows very little visual information at the left and right extremes, giving a further clue that a reduced luminance range is in use.

• Type Shift+F5 to take a snapshot of the Comp window in its current state (in version 4.1, this shortcut requires Option (Alt), not Shift). You can also click on the camera icon at the bottom of the Comp window to take a snapshot.

• Set the Input Black parameter to 16, and the Input White parameter to 235. This will stretch the luminance for this clip back out to full range.

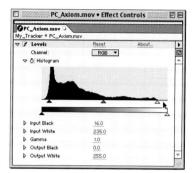

5 The Histogram in the Levels effect can give a clue as to the luminance range of a captured clip. Here, the cursor points to the gap in the white areas, indicating "true white" is probably at 235, not 255 (on a 0–255 scale).

Time Display

You can set the Timecode Base in Preferences>Time to 24 fps if you prefer the time readout to more closely match your frames. We left it at 30 Non-Drop Frame for this tutorial.

A Matter of Black and White

Have you ever received footage that looks more washed out than you would expect? Most digital video systems work with an internal luminance system where, in a range of 0–255, a value of 16 represents true black and 235 represents true white. This allows them to capture hot spots that were accidentally too bright (over 100 IRE), and to output so-called superblack video which is occasionally used to create mattes.

Some systems, such as the Avid and Digital Voodoo, automatically translate these internal values to the 0=black/255=white ranges most image software –

including Adobe After Effects – expects. However, some systems – such as the Media 100, older DDRs, and some DV codecs – pass along these unscaled internal values directly to other software.

This makes it your responsibility to manually translate to and from these alternate systems, stretching 16–235 out to 0–255 before you use a clip, and squeezing it back down to 16–235 again when you render.

Details on this are in *TechTip 04* on the *Creating Motion Graphics* CD; in this tutorial, you will be working through an example of this procedure.

5 *complete:* The original 16–235 luminance range movie displayed in a 0–255 colorspace looks washed out (left). After applying Levels and extending its luminance range, the contrast increases (right).

• Press F5 to compare this treated footage with the snapshot you took of the untreated version (or click the "man" icon at the bottom of the Comp window). The treated version should have a nicer contrast to it; you might even notice now that the paint is a subtle shade of gold or beige rather than silver.

• Close the Effect Controls window.

STEP 6: Select the **My_Sources** folder in the Project window, and type Command+I (Control+I) to open the Import dialog. Locate the file **CM_Tracker_music.mov** in the same **Sources** folder where you found the Axiom clip, and click Import (Open). Then drag this file to the [**My_Tracker**] Timeline, making sure it starts at time 00:00.

RAM Preview [**My_Tracker**] by pressing 0 on the numeric keypad to get a feel for the overall shot.

Music Credits

Chris Meyer of CyberMotion arranged the soundtrack for this tutorial. It includes rhythm loops from the Spectrasonics sampling CD *Metamorphosis* (distributed by Ilio Entertainment – www.ilio.com), plus an additional snare roll from *Chemical Beats* by Zero-G (www.zero-g.co.uk). The guitar chord was played by Peter Maunu for the Spectrasonics CD *Bizarre Guitar*, and was chosen to match the camera move that slides from a frontal to a partial profile view. The garbled communication voices are from the Sound Ideas *6000 Series* sound effects library (www.sound-ideas.com), and are intended to reinforce the data communication theme.

If you don't have enough RAM or a fast enough computer to preview the entire full-frame shot, reduce the Resolution to Half by pressing Command+Shift+J (Control+Shift+J), and reduce the Magnification to 50% by pressing Command (Control) plus the – symbol along the top of the keyboard. However, in doing so you may notice a quirk in After Effects (at least through version 5.0) in which fields reappear in footage with 3:2 pulldown applied when they're viewed at Half Resolution. Ignore it. When you're done, return to Full Resolution and 100% Magnification; you will need it for the next part of this tutorial.

To ensure your basic comp is built correctly, compare [**My_Tracker**] *with our version* [**Tracker_after Step 06**] *in the Project's* **_AutoTracker * prebuilt>Prebuilt Comps** *folder. If you like, duplicate our comp and rename it "My_Tracker_06" to use for the rest of this tutorial. And don't forget to save your project!*

Part 2: Getting On Track

 The portion of the video script that this shot was supposed to illustrate says: "While driving, the system monitors twelve different inputs, including engine RPM, the brakes, and throttle position. Changes in speed, throttle position, or braking alert the system to possible handling or traction challenges." This was the only guide we had for where to place the sensors.

In this part of the tutorial, we'll walk you through the process of tracking two of these points. The footage was not shot with special markers for us to track; we just chose what we thought would be the best piece of footage from a selects reel – so part of your challenge will be trying to find naturally occurring points in the image to track.

Forward Track

The first motion track we'll do will be fairly simple. We're looking for a section of the car that will be visible for the entire duration of the video, and which doesn't change shape too much during this time. The best shapes to track are ones with high contrast and distinct edges or boundaries. The middle of a line is bad, because it's hard to tell where you are along the line. However, where two lines cross is good, because the X formed at the cross is easy to identify and follow. Dots and the ends of lines are also good, unambiguous shapes to track. For this first track, we'll choose one of the crosses formed by the shape of the car's grill.

STEP 7: At this point, we haven't decided what the final tracker shape will be. However, the Motion Tracker will want to know what layer should be assigned to follow the point you're about to identify. Therefore, create a small Solid to use as a placeholder (once you've completed the tracking steps, you'll replace the solid with a sensor icon):

- Set the time marker back to 00:00.

- Type Command+Y (Control+Y) to create a new solid.

- Enter a name that makes sense, such as "**track 1**", set a small size such as 20×20 pixels, and pick a color that will be easy to see against the car – such as hot pink.

- Set both the movie and solid layers to Best Quality. The shortcut for this is to select both layers and type Command+U (Control+U). Then Deselect All (shortcut: F2).

> Best Quality renders the solid to subpixel positions and antialiases it. You will be tracking with subpixel accuracy; you might as well see this reflected in the Comp window during RAM Previews. More than once, we have thought we had a very jittery motion track, only to realize we forgot to set the tracking layer to Best Quality.

An Image Problem

The higher the image quality of the footage you are tracking, the better your results. In this tutorial, the footage has already been through a composite video dub, and compressed heavily to fit on this book's CD – not ideal conditions.

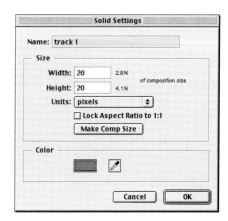

7 Create a simple solid to use as a stand-in for your tracking object.

8 As of version 5.0, the Motion Tracker/Stabilizer can be accessed from the Layer window's wing menu.

STEP 8: With your comp at Full Resolution, select the **PC_Axiom.mov** layer. In After Effects 5.0, select Motion Tracker/Stabilizer from the Animation menu; in version 4.1, it is under Layer>Keyframe Assistant. Also new to version 5.0 is that you can double-click on the item to open it in its Layer window, then bring up the Motion Tracker/Stabilizer from its wing menu. The additional functions for the Tracker/Stabilizer will now always appear when you open the Layer window, until you choose another option.

You will be presented with a window that shows your footage above, has a timeline in the middle, and contains a series of buttons and numbers below. If you look again at the image above, you will also notice a pair of boxes: This is the Tracker Region, which you will use to identify the feature in your footage you wish to track.

Set the Track and Stabilize Type popup to Track; make sure you check the Position option, but not Rotation. You will see a small + symbol appear in the middle of the Tracker Region. (In version 4.1, this window should default to Track Position, which is correct.)

8 *complete:* When you enable the Motion Tracker/Stabilizer, you will see a large window that contains your footage and a Tracker Region box, and additional parameters below. The arrow is pointing to the Track and Stabilize Type popup; set this popup to Track.

STEP 9: The frustration some experience with After Effects' Motion Tracker is often the result of using the default options. Click on the Options button, and choose the following settings:

• Make sure the Apply Motion To Layer popup near the top is set to **track 1**, or whatever you named the dummy solid you created in Step 7.

• The Time Options should be set to 23.976 fps, the effective frame rate of your footage after you removed its pulldown. This also eliminated its fields, so leave Track Fields unchecked. Also leave Tracks In Reverse unchecked; you'll try that out later.

• Under Track Options, change the Use option from RGB to Luminance. Most good track points have a strong contrast between light and dark; this is particularly true of the grill of this car, where the bumper is light silver and inside the grill is black: not much difference in color or saturation, but a big difference in luminance.

• The Track Adaptiveness parameter essentially asks: "How much is the tracking point going to change over the course of this shot?" Since the camera angle and zoom do change a little during **PC_Axiom.mov**,

No Tracker?

If the Track option is grayed out in the Type popup, you need to have a second video layer in your comp. In the Options dialog, if you can't select a layer to attach, it's because the Type is set to Stabilize.

we found a Track Adaptiveness value of 40% to be a good choice for tracking the grill.

• The higher the Subpixel Matching parameter, the more resolution used to determine the tracked position – and the longer the track will take. We personally don't like to use under 1/16 of a pixel. If you have a slow computer, choose 1/8; if you have a fast one and a bit of patience, try 1/32 or 1/64.

• Ignore the Process Before Match and Extrapolate Motion parameters; they are for shots that are far more problematic than what you're dealing with here.

• Click OK.

STEP 10: Make sure the time marker is set to 00:00. Drag inside the smaller square of the Tracking Region box (but not on the crosshair), and position the small crosshair in its center to the point where the thin central vertical grill piece just meets the middle horizontal bar of the grill/bumper combination. (If you don't see a small crosshair, make sure that the Track and Stabilize Type is set to Track, or that in After Effect 4.1 you chose Track, not Stabilize.)

The smaller box is known as the Feature Region: It encloses the pattern of pixels After Effects tries to match from frame to frame as it tracks. The smaller this region is, the fewer pixels After Effects has to match, so drag its corners to make it as small as you can, while still seeing a clear, high-contrast shape inside of it.

The larger box is the Search Region: It encloses all the pixels After Effects will search from frame to frame to find the pattern enclosed by the Feature Region. The trick here is to make this box as small as possible, while not making it so small that the point you're tracking does move outside of it between any two frames. The more drastic the motion in the original footage, the larger this box needs to be. Since we remember the car moved down and to the left of the frame during the shot, resize this box to contain a little extra room on this side.

STEP 11: Moment of truth: Click on the Analyze button (called Track in version 4.1), and watch how the Tracking Region boxes move from frame to frame. If you're both lucky and good, they should constantly recenter on that point in the grill you identified until it reaches the end of the clip. But if you see a sudden jump, something went wrong (as it often does in the real world); press any key to stop the track.

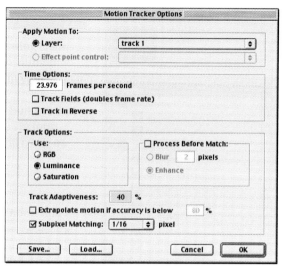

9 The default Motion Tracker Options are often unsatisfactory. Alter them as described; the Track Adaptiveness parameter (highlighted) often causes problems if it's overlooked.

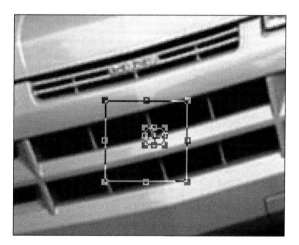

10 Reposition and resize the Tracking Region boxes to contain a good point to track, and allow enough room to follow its movements from frame to frame. If you have trouble seeing the regions you are setting, use Command (Control) plus the + and – keys along the top of the keyboard to zoom in or out.

11 We defined too large of a Search Region; as a result, After Effects jumped from the correct spot (left) to a similar-looking but incorrect spot below it (right).

In our first attempt, these boxes suddenly jumped to the lower portion of the grill around 01:20 in the timeline. If you did not resize the Search Region, the boxes will jump almost immediately. We made our Search Region too big, and After Effects accidentally thought another point was a better match.

You could go back to Step 10 and start over, defining a better Search Region. Or, you can save the work you've already put in, and redefine the track mid-stream to pick up from the last good point:

STEP 12: If your Search Region was close to the right size, there's a chance you don't have to do anything: Just back up the time marker to the last good tracked frame, and click on Analyze again. The tracker will adapt to this new "model" frame as it tracks subsequent frames.

But you may not be that lucky, so back up to this last good frame (around 01:20 in our case; your specific frame will depend on the size

of your Search Region box), then carefully resize the Search Region smaller so it no longer encompasses another similar section of the grill either to the left, right or below. Make sure you don't move the crosshairs in the middle of the Tracking Region, or you will confuse the resulting position data. Also, be aware that if you resize the Search region then move to another time, the boxes revert to their old size – so move the time marker first, then resize the box. (In version 4.1, you need to trim the layer's in point to match where you wish to restart the track – click on the { button just underneath the timeline to reset it. The boxes can only be moved at the in point.)

12 Reduce the size of the Search Region to miss the similar-looking section of the grill below (where the cursor is pointing).

When you've resized the box, click on Analyze again. You should make it to the end of the clip fine this time. If not, just repeat this step: Back up to an earlier good-looking track, adjust the Search or Feature region, and continue from there. If it seems hopeless, go back to Step 10…

Step 13: After the track is finished, you will notice a black line running underneath the timeline – this indicates what portions of the clip have been tracked. As you drag the time marker along this line, the box below will show some of the parameters for the Tracking Region, including a percentage for how accurate the tracking point was matched for each frame. In general, if this number drops under 70%, you might not have a very good track, and you probably want to do that region over again.

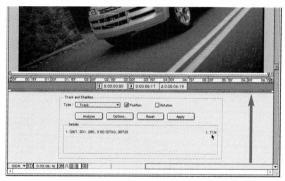

13 After the track is done, a black line should extend under the timeline, indicating which frames have been tracked. The cursor is pointing to a readout that shows how accurately the match was accomplished for each frame.

You may be tempted to click on the Apply button at this point. But before you do, click on Options instead. Inside this dialog, click on Save. This will create a file that contains all of your tracking data, including your options and all of the points tracked – which can prove to be invaluable if you want to go back later to try to improve a prior track. Once your data is saved, close the Options dialog, then click on Apply. Close the Motion Tracker window (in version 4.1, the Tracker window will close automatically).

Step 14: Select **track 1** (your dummy sensor icon), and hit U to twirl down its keyframes. You will see a Position keyframe for every frame of your video. RAM Preview the comp, and observe how the square stays positioned in the center of the grill.

> If you were trying to replace a portion of the car, such as a license plate or badge, you would need to be very critical of how precise the track is. For data readouts and other more fanciful graphics, you don't need to be as critical. This application is rather forgiving, so don't be upset if you have trouble creating rock-solid tracking data.

14 Tracking creates a Position keyframe for the dummy sensor icon on every frame of the original footage. If you select the layer, the resulting motion path is visible in the Comp window.

Save your project. If you are unsure of the results of your first track, compare your work with our prebuilt comp [**Tracker_after Step 14**].

Backtracking

Not all tracking points are polite enough to stay in the frame for the entire shot. We decided the centerpoints on the wheels would be good points to add sensor icons to, but they aren't visible during the first second of the shot. To work around this, you can try tracking them from the end of the shot backward, then decide how to gracefully cover up the beginning.

Step 15: Return the time marker to 00:00, and create another solid for a dummy sensor icon, with the same settings as in Step 7. Name it "**track 2**" and click on OK. Set it to Best Quality.

Apply!

Don't forget to click on the Apply button when the track is complete – don't just close the tracker window!

A Track of One

If you click the Analyze button, and After Effects stops after tracking only one frame, chances are the Track in Reverse switch inside Options is set to the opposite of what you need.

STEP 16: Select **PC_Axiom.mov** in the Timeline window and open the Tracker/Stabilizer window again. In After Effects 5.0 or later, just double-click it to open its Layer window; the Tracker/Stabilizer Controls option should still be enabled in its Wing menu, so this interface will automatically appear. In version 4.1, select Layer>Keyframe Assistant>Motion Tracker.

STEP 17: In version 5, set the Track and Stabilize Type to Track, click on the Reset button, then click on the Options button. (In version 4.1, select Track Position, and click on Options.) You can use essentially the same parameters as you did in Step 9, with a few important changes:

- Set Apply Motion To Layer to **track 2**.

- Under Time Options, select the Track In Reverse option.

- Under Track Options, continue to use Luminance, and the same Subpixel Matching value as you did before. Since the change in camera angle has a more drastic effect on the appearance of the wheel center than it did on the grill, try a higher Track Adaptiveness value, such as 75%.

- Click OK.

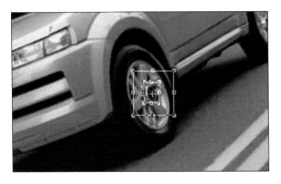

18 Set up the Tracking Region box to focus on the black insert in the front wheel, starting at time 06:16 in the shot.

STEP 18: Set the current time marker to 06:16. Click inside the Feature Region box (the inner one) but not on the Tracking Point crosshair, and drag it so the Tracking Point is centered on the black insert of the front wheel.

Resize the Feature Region box so it just encompasses that black insert, with about a pixel or two of silver as a border – this will create a nice, high-contrast spot to track. Resize the Search Region box, again remembering about how much the wheel moves from frame to frame. We chose an initial size about half the size of the tire, slightly biased to the right as this is the direction the wheel will slide off toward as we track backward through the shot.

19 The track started out well, but wandered down the wheel as the frames progressed. The Track Adaptiveness amount was probably too generous.

STEP 19: Click on Analyze (Track in version 4.1). Things start out okay, but the tracking region seems to slide down the wheel the farther we go into the track. Press any key to stop the track when you notice this happening.

This is different from the sudden jump we experienced when things went wrong with our first track. Drifting like this usually indicates the Track Adaptiveness parameter is probably inappropriate: By thinking too much of adapting to the track later in the shot, our large Track Adaptiveness percentage is allowing After Effects too much leeway when the track point isn't really changing that much.

Step 20: Return the time marker to 06:16, click on Options, and change Track Adaptiveness to a lower number, such as 25%. Click on Analyze again.

This time, the track should go much better. With the parameters and Tracking Region we chose, the track looked pretty accurate until about 01:21 (you will get different results depending on your Tracking Regions). We stopped the track when we noticed it had gone astray, and backed up until the last good-looking frame.

If you want, you can click on Analyze again at this point, as this will reset After Effects' memory of what it is looking for to match this frame. You can keep doing this, getting a few more good tracked frames at a time, until it is obvious there is nothing visible to track anymore.

In our case, we stared at the Tracking Region boxes and realized the change in camera angle had made the black centerpiece we were tracking appear larger and more elongated than it was when we started. We tugged on the corners of the Feature Region box to match this, making sure we didn't move the Track Point crosshair in the center, and continued from there. Try similar adjustments yourself. (In After Effects 4.1, you will need to click on the } button to reset the out point before you can edit the Tracking Region.)

20 If a track goes awry in the middle, back up to the last good frame, and adjust the Tracking Region – just be careful not to move the Track Point crosshairs. Here, we're reshaping the Feature Region to accommodate the black wheel insert's change in perspective.

The important concept to remember is that you don't have to get one, continuous, perfect track. Keep backing up and trying tweaks once the track goes astray. If you have something you think you might want to keep, go into the Options dialog and use the Save function to preserve it; then tweak away – you can always Reload your previous track if you like.

Step 21: After you have got the best track you can out of this point, click on Options and Save your track data. Back in the main Tracker interface, position your time marker on the last good frame of the track and remember the time (probably around 01:00). Click on Apply, and close the Tracker window.

Once you're back in the Timeline window, move the time marker to the last good frame you noted. With **track 2** selected, press Option+[(Alt+[) to trim this layer to begin at this last good frame. Later on, you can fade up this particular sensor icon from this time, which will also help cover any excessive jitter in the first few frames you kept.

Go ahead and RAM Preview your comp again and see if you're satisfied with this second track. If not, turn off this layer to keep it around as a backup, create a new solid, go back to Step 16, and try again. Motion Tracking involves a lot of trial and error work; don't be afraid to set a previous effort aside and try again.

21 Two tracks finished now. Select both solids to see their motion paths in the Composition window.

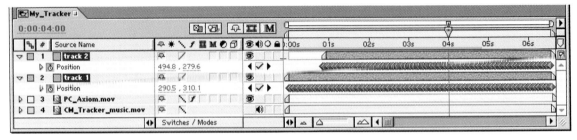

21 *complete:* Note how the second track is trimmed in the Timeline to begin later – the portion of the wheel we were tracking wasn't visible enough earlier.

This track probably jitters around more than your first one; the center of the wheel turns out not to be as good of a point to track as a crosshair in the grill. This amount of jitter would be unacceptable if you were trying to replace the wheel on the car, but will work fine for our purposes in this project. Part of motion tracking is knowing when to stop and move on...

STEP 22: Remember at the start of this Part, where the script said "the system monitors twelve different inputs"? You guessed it – you have ten more tracks to perform. Rather than lead you step by step through these remaining tracks, we're going to leave it up to you and your own creative devices to find ten more suitable points. Here are some tips:

22 Find 10 more features on the car to track.

• The sharp angles around the grill, bumper, and lights all present some excellent points to track.

• There are a couple of points along the side worth tracking, such as the back wheel, as well as the door lock or rearview mirror. As with the front wheel, you will probably need to track these in reverse, and trim them to start later in the comp.

• Running out of ideas? Start looking at points where the windshield meets the body pillars and hood.

• If you find a good track point where it otherwise would not make sense to place one of the sensor icons, you can place the Tracking Region around that good point, then move the Track Point crosshair to where you want the sensor to end up.

Oops – Wrong Layer

Don't forget to select the layer to be tracked, not the layer to be attached, before opening the Tracker dialog. Then open Options, and select the new layer to attach – otherwise it will default to the previous layer, overwriting your previous track.

• To keep better track of which solids are attached to which parts of the car, feel free to rename them: Select the solid, and press Command+Shift+Y (Control+Shift+Y) to re-open its settings dialog.

We encourage you to practice your tracking skills by completing all twelve tracks yourself. If you get too frustrated, look at our comp **[Tracker_after Step 22]** *for ideas on points to track. You can duplicate and rename it "MyTracker_22" if you wish to continue with our version rather than yours. For further comparison, we also saved some of our tracking data in a folder inside the tutorial's* **Sources** *folder; the "_4" or "_5" at the end indicates which version of After Effects it is for.*

Part 3: Iconography

In this part, you will replace the dummy solids you used for tracking with sensor icons. You will use a "defensive animation" technique that will make it easier for you swap out different icons later.

Standard Version

If you don't have the Production Bundle, continue with Part 3 using our prebuilt comp, **[Tracker_after Step 22]**. Duplicate it and rename it "**MyTracker_22**" and drag it to the **My_Comps** folder.

STEP 23: Select the **My_Comps** folder, and use Command+N (Control+N) to create a new composition. Set its size to 100×100 (make sure the Lock Aspect Ratio switch is off), square pixel aspect ratio, frame rate of 23.976, and a duration of 06:17 to match [**My_Tracker**]. Name it "**My_Sensor**" and click OK. Set its Composition>Background Color to black, to make the sensor easier to see.

STEP 24: Select the **My_Sources** folder, and use Command+I (Control+I) to open the Import Footage dialog. In the same **Project>Sources** folder where you found the video clip and the soundtrack, select **CM_sensor_crl.tif**. Depending on how you have your preferences set, you may get an Interpret Footage dialog asking you to choose an alpha channel type. If so, select Straight Alpha and click OK.

24 If you have the interpret alpha choice in Preferences> Import set to Ask User, when you import **CM_sensor_crl.tif** you will be asked to set the alpha type for this file. Choose Straight.

STEP 25: With [**My_Sensor**] open and the forward composition in your Comp and Timeline windows, select **CM_sensor_crl.tif** in the Project window and hit Command+/ (Control+/). This will automatically add the selected footage item to the forward comp. Select **CM_sensor_crl.tif** in [**My_Sensor**], and hit Command+U (Control+U) to set it to Best Quality.

26 Lock the original footage and soundtrack layers, to prevent accidentally swapping out or scaling them.

STEP 26: Bring [**My_Tracker**] forward. In the Timeline, turn on the Lock switch for the layers **PC_Axiom.mov** and **CM_Tracker_music.mov** so you don't accidentally swap them out or otherwise change them in the steps below.

Select your first dummy sensor – **track 1** – in the Timeline window. Then select [**My_Sensor**] in the Project window, and hit Command+Option+/ (Control+Alt+/) to replace the **track 1** layer with the [**My_Sensor**] comp. Your original solid will now be replaced with the real sensor icon.

Do this for each of your dummy solids. In After Effects 5.0 or later, you can take advantage of the ability to select all of these layers at once in the Timeline window, then just perform one swap to change all the selected layers at once.

26 *complete:* Swap [**My_Sensor**] in for all of the dummy solids you created during the tracking portion of this tutorial.

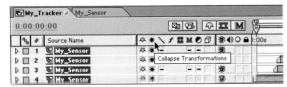

27 Set Collapse Transformations for all the **My_Sensor** layers in **[My_Tracker]**.

Circles and Eggs

The circular icons look elongated in the **[My_Tracker]** Comp window because they are being stretched to match the comp's D1 pixel aspect ratio. In version 5, select Pixel Aspect Correction from the Comp window's wing menu for a quick confidence check.

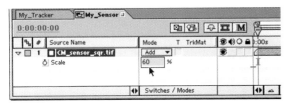

27 *complete:* The sensor icon has been scaled to 60% and set to Add mode in its precomp (above), which ripples through to all of the sensors in the **[My_Tracker]** comp (below).

STEP 27: These sensors are a big improvement over the pink squares, but they look a bit large, and could stand out more against the video. No problem:

• In [My Tracker], select all of the My_Sensor layers, and turn on their Collapse Transformations switch (the one that looks like a sun with rays). In 5.0 if you click on one switch, all switches will change (in 4.1 you need to Option (Alt) + click). This will allow changes in the [My_Sensor] precomp such as scalings and transfer modes to flow through to [My_Tracker] while maintaining maximum quality. Deselect the layers (shortcut: F2).

• Select the [My_Sensor] comp. If it occupies the same window as [My_Tracker], click on the [My_Sensor] tab in the Comp window, drag it outside its current window, and release the mouse – it will now have its own Comp window. Resize this new window and position it on your screen so you can see the Comp windows for [My_Sensor] and [My_Tracker] at the same time.

• In the [My_Sensor] comp, select **CM_sensor_crl.tif** and type S to reveal its Scale property. Experiment with different values. After you enter a new value, you will see all of the sensors in [My_Tracker] update to reflect the new size. We chose 60%.

• Still in [My_Sensor], press F4 to reveal the Modes panel in the Timeline window (or click on the Switches/Modes button at the bottom of the Switches panel). Change the mode for **CM_sensor_crl.tif** to Add mode.

Since you had turned on Collapse Transformations for this precomp's layer in [My_Tracker], all of the sensors in [My_Tracker] will redraw with this mode applied. This new mode will brighten up the appearance of the sensors and make them interact more with the video underneath, resulting in a more "phosphorescent" look.

STEP 28: RAM Preview [My_Tracker] to see how your new sensors look. If you had any tracks that did not extend to the beginning of the composition (as with our second track back in Step 21), you might be annoyed at the way these icons suddenly pop on. Smooth them out by adding some fade-ups:

• Select one of the sensor layers that starts later than 00:00.

• Press I to locate the time marker to its in point. Then move 10 or 15 frames past this point – in other words, a nice duration for a quick fade.

Planning for Change

When you have an element that is used multiple times and that may be changed later (either by you or the client), it is a good idea to put it into its own composition, and use this precomp in your final composition. Any changes made to the original element in its precomp will automatically ripple into any comp in which it is nested.

The sensor icon used in this tutorial is a good example. We created two different icons in After Effects, using a combination of solids, mask shapes, and Effect>Render>Stroke. However, you might want to create a different icon in a program such as Adobe Illustrator, use a "dingbat" type font in Effect>Text>Basic Text, or even create an animating icon. If so, place it in [**My_Sensor**], scale it to fit, and see how you like it in [**My_Tracker**]. In our sensor design, we purposely avoided anything that had too clear of a "crosshair" in the very center, as it might imply too specific of a region – as well as tip off the viewer that our tracks were not perfectly accurate.

If you are curious to see how we built our icons, check out the composition [**_sensor icon creation**] inside the Project window's **AutoTracker * prebuilt>Sources** folder. Even though we built them in After Effects, we prerendered them as stills to save rendering time later.

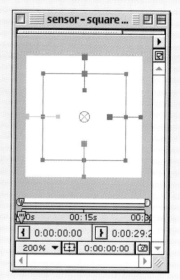

We built our sensors by drawing a series of mask shapes on a solid, then outlining them with Effect>Render>Stroke.

• Press T to reveal the Opacity property, and click on the stopwatch icon to set the first keyframe at 100%.

• Press I again to return to this layer's in point, and enter an Opacity value of 0%.

• Repeat this process for any other layers that start after 00:00, or Copy and Paste the Opacity keyframes to other layers, remembering to place the time marker at their in point before pasting.

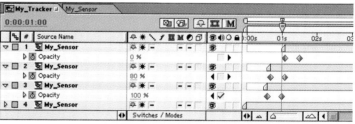

28 Add fade-ups to any layers where the tracks didn't extend back to 00:00.

• RAM Preview to see if you like this better. Twirl up the Opacity property to clean up your Timeline window again.

STEP 29: Everything is looking good…until you remember that the client told you the graphical theme in all the print materials is graph paper, and to use boxes whenever you can. Let's import a new square sensor icon and replace the circular icon layers. This is when you understand why you placed the sensor icon in a precomp:

• Bring the comp [**My_Sensor**] forward, and make sure the layer **CM_sensor_crl.tif** is selected.

29 By swapping one sensor image in **[My_Sensor]**, all twelve of the sensors update automatically in **[My_Tracker]**.

- Import the icon **CM_sensor_sqr.tif**. If you're asked, set its alpha channel type to Straight.

- With this item still selected in the Project window, type Command+Option+/ (Control+Alt+/) to swap it for the circular icon in **[My_Sensor]**. If you like, scale it down a little smaller to make it less imposing (we left it at 60%).

In this example, you could also have selected **CM_sensor_sqr.tif** in the Project window, and used File>Replace Footage>File to replace this source with the square sensor directly from disk. This would replace the icon throughout the project, even if it was used in multiple compositions. By comparison, importing a new source and using the Replace Layer shortcut lets you be more selective in replacing sources.

- If it's not already visible, bring the comp **[My_Tracker]** forward, and note that all of the sensors have been updated automatically.

Save your project. That finishes Part 3; the only task left is preparing for the final render. Compare your comp with [**Tracker_after Step 29**].

Part 4: Back to Video

The hard work is done. The final steps are getting back to where you started when you were handed this clip to enhance: Re-create the original luminance range, and impose 3:2 pulldown during render.

30–31 Add an Adjustment Layer to your comp, rename it "**luminance adjust**" and apply the Levels effect to it. (Creating a new Adjustment Layer really just creates a full-frame white solid with the half-moon switch turned on.)

STEP 30: In **[My_Tracker]**, return the Time Marker to 00:00. Add an Adjustment Layer to this comp (Layer>New>Adjustment Layer in version 5.0; Layer>New Adjustment Layer in version 4.1). Type Command+Shift+Y (Control+Shift+Y) and give it a name that makes sense such as "**luminance adjust**" and Click OK. If needed, press F4 to

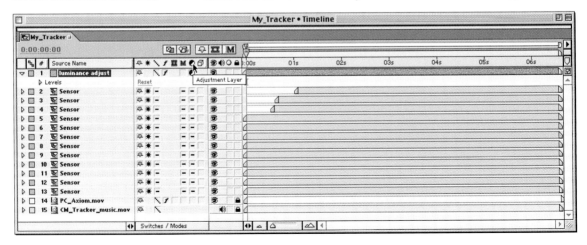

reveal the Switches panel in the Timeline window; notice that the half-moon Adjustment Layer switch is turned on.

STEP 31: With this adjustment layer still selected, add Effect>Adjust>**Levels**. In the Effect Controls window, set the Output Black to 16, and Output White to 235. This squeezes the luminance range back into what the Media 100 and some other systems expect. Your image will look a bit washed out in the Comp window, but will look normal on final output through your video system. Close the Effect Controls window.

STEP 32: Type Command+M (Control+M) to add [**My_Tracker**] to the Render Queue. Give it a name that makes sense, such as "**TrackerRender.mov**". In the Render Queue window, select Best Settings from the Render Settings templates popup, and click on the text "Best Settings" to open the dialog:

• Set the Field Render popup to Lower Field First, to match what most D1-size NTSC systems use.

• Set the popup for 3:2 Pulldown to any choice other than Off. The exact pulldown phase you choose is irrelevant for video work, and is only an issue if you are creating a video edit that needs to be conformed back to film later.

• The "Use this frame rate" section should now read "29.97". The line above will note that the comp is being sampled at 23.98 fps (really 23.976 rounded to two digits for display purposes). Click OK.

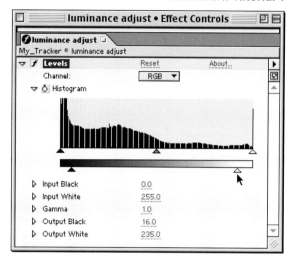

31 To reintroduce the luminance range the Media 100 expects, apply Levels, and set the Output Black and White parameters to 16 and 235 respectively.

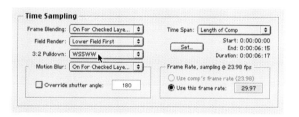

32 You can reintroduce pulldown at the render stage by selecting a field order and pulldown phase in the Render Settings, and setting the final frame rate back to 29.97.

• Choose an appropriate codec for your hardware in the Output Module, turn on the Audio switch, and proceed with the render.

The result of these settings is to instruct After Effects to render your comp at 23.976 fps. After it has rendered these frames, it will then spread them across video frames using the same two field/three field pattern discussed earlier when you removed pulldown from the original clip. After Effects then saves a 29.97 fps interlaced movie with this pattern. If you click on Render, you will observe this stuttering pattern in the timecode under the Current Render progress bar.

There are two advantages to working this way: The render goes much faster, because you are rendering only 24 frames rather than 60 fields per second; and any additional animation you have created – such as the tracking sensors – will be rendered at the same speed as the underlying footage, which will make the final motion appear more coherent.

D1 to DV

If you want to render to a DV NTSC codec, in the Output module set the Crop parameters to remove two lines from the top and four lines from the bottom. This will resize your rendered frame from 486 lines to 480, while maintaining the same field order.

Comp Background

When applying an adjustment layer with Levels to reintroduce the 16-235 luminance range, the Composition background color is not effected. Instead, use a background solid layer set to the color you want, and let the Levels effect perform the luminance adjustment.

Our final timeline, with all of our tricks revealed. Open the comp **[Tracker_Final]** to explore some of these tricks in more detail.

Part 5: The Scenic Tour

The work you performed in Parts 1 through 4 is enough to hand your client back the original clip with some tracker icons composited on top of the footage. However, we added some design touches to make the clip more than just a technical illustration.

In the Project window folder _Tracker * prebuilt>Final Comps, double-click on [**Tracker_Final**]. Here are some of the touches we added:

Pulsing to Music

We wanted to tie the graphics more closely to the music, which would add to the impact. We spotted some of the beats in the soundtrack **CM_Tracker_music.mov**, and noted the tempo averaged roughly 12.25 frames per beat (fpb) against a timebase of 30 frames per second. Since we could not track some of the sensor locations back to the start of the clip, we faded up a series of sensors – layers 7 through 10 – in time with the music. You know the saying: If life gives you lemons, make lemonade...

We then decided to make the sensors pulse in time with the music. We used the Keyframe Assistant The Wiggler to vary their Scale ±15%,

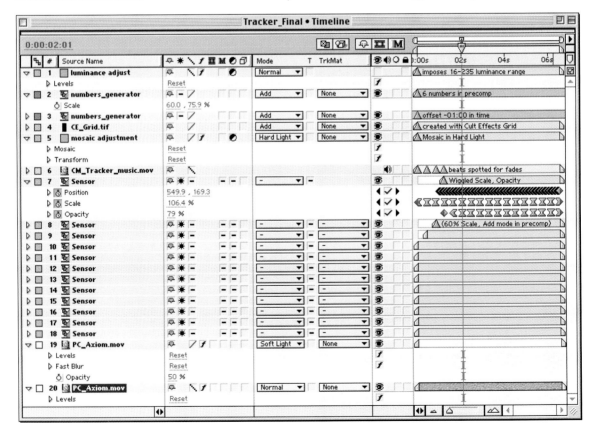

resulting in Scale values between 85% and 115%. It is normally a bad idea to scale past 100%, but since we collapsed transformations, the Scale value of 60% in the precomp gets factored in at the same time, resulting in a scale range of 51% to 69% (60 × 85 to 115%). Moreover, this scaling happens once, not twice, maintaining higher quality.

We also used The Wiggler to vary their Opacity ±50% from a starting point of 100%. Since a layer cannot become more opaque than 100%, this means each sensor was on full roughly half the time, occasionally dipping as low as 50% for the remainder. For the Frequency parameter, we used 30 fps ÷ 12.25 fpb ≈ 2.44 wiggles per second. Each sensor icon animating also helps reinforce the impression that each is measuring an ever changing value.

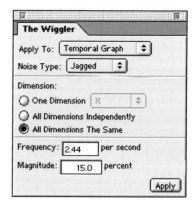

The Wiggler's settings to make the sensor icons randomly scale in time to the music. Note we checked the option All Dimensions The Same to preserve the aspect ratio of the sensors.

Grid Frame

To lend more structure to the frame, a graph paper-like grid element was added to the left side. This pattern was originally created using the now-discontinued Cycore Cult Effects plug-in CE Grid, using a spacing of 20 pixels. To keep the same "phosphorescent" look as the sensor icons, its Opacity was reduced to 75%, and the Add transfer mode was used.

We wanted to add more of a digital feel to this grid, so we added an adjustment layer that covered just the left portion of the frame, same as the grid layer. Effect>Stylize>Mosaic was employed to break the video into digitized boxes. The effect was made more subtle by using Hard Light transfer mode. Set mosaic adjustment's mode back to Normal to get a better idea of what the raw mosaic looks like.

Random Numbers

Next was creating a set of twelve randomized numbers and data read-outs to go with the twelve sensors. To save time, and to make it easier to adjust a group of numbers as a block, we set up a row of six of them in the precomp [**numbers_generator**].

Option+double-click (Alt+double-click) on one of these layers in [**Tracker_final**] to open this comp, and feel free to explore how we set it up. For the most part, we used variations on Effect>Text>Numbers, although we also used Text>Basic Text and hold keyframes to create a simple on/off sequence at the bottom. For the sake of this tutorial, we set the font to Courier Bold in hopes you would also have it installed on your system; feel free to try out other fonts if you don't – we used ITC's Conduit on the real job. Comp window guides were used to help align the different numbers.

Once we dragged this comp into our final, we realized the numbers were too big – to get twelve of them onscreen, they would extend outside the frame's safe areas. We scaled them vertically by about 75% so there would be one number for every 1.5 grid cells, and horizontally until we were happy with how they filled the available space. We used two copies of this precomp, and offset one in time so different numbers would appear for each copy of the precomp at the same point in the

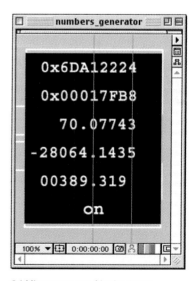

Grid lines were used in the Comp window to help us align the different types of numbers. The Proportional Spacing option was set in the Number effect to help hold their positions.

Aspect Adjustments

Getting the Mosaic effect and the grid to line up was trickier than you might think. We had to compensate for the composition's non-square pixel aspect ratio by hand.

The grid layer was created at a size of 140×486 pixels, with a grid spacing of 20×20 pixels. Once this source footage was brought into the D1 aspect ratio comp, After Effects automatically stretched it by 111.1% horizontally to compensate for the D1 pixel aspect ratio.

At first, we created a 140×486 pixel solid for the adjustment layer. However, this layer appeared skinnier in the comp than the grid layer. Since the grid had been automatically scaled 111.1% wide, it now covered approximately 155.5 pixels, not 140. Solids and adjustment layers do not receive the same automatic scale – the user has to do it by hand. So we increased the size of the adjustment layer to 155 pixels wide.

When you apply an effect to an adjustment layer, the effect thinks it's treating a layer the same size as the comp – not the layer it is applied to. When we applied Effect>Stylize>Mosaic, we set the number of Vertical Blocks to 720 pixels ÷ 20 pixels = 36. However, the resulting blocks were skinnier than the grid. Oops; we didn't take the aspect ratio into account again.

There are two ways to compensate for this. One would be to take the pixel aspect adjustment into account when we're deciding how many horizontal blocks we need: 720 x 0.9 (our pixel aspect ratio) ÷ 20 = 32.4 blocks. Unfortunately, Mosaic allows only whole numbers, and 32.4 is almost exactly between 32 and 33, meaning we would have a large round-off error no matter which one we chose.

Instead, we followed Mosaic with Effect>Distort> Transform (under the Perspective submenu in After Effect 4.1), and set the Scale Width to 111.1%. Changing the adjustment layer's own Scale value would not have the desired effect; it would only alter the region of the comp that is effected – not the effects themselves. To realign the Mosaic effect with the original footage, the Transform's Anchor Point and Position were both reset to X=0 so the stretch would start from the left edge of the frame.

The final bit of trickery involved the height. To calculate the Mosaic's Vertical Block size, we came up with 486 pixels ÷ 20 pixels = 24.3…but Mosaic takes only whole numbers, such as 24. We used this value instead, and scaled the **CE_Grid.tif** layer vertically by 486 ÷ 480 = 101.25% to cover this slight error. (We could also have scaled the Mosaic effect again with Transform, but enough is enough.) The vertical scale of the numbers precomps also needed to be tweaked by a similar amount.

Transform's Scale Width was set to 111.1% to perform the pixel aspect compensation for the adjustment layer. Its Anchor Point and Position were set to X=0 to align the results of this scaling to the left edge of the comp.

Our first shot at Mosaic resulted in blocks skinnier than our grid (left). We used the Transform effect to compensate for the comp's D1 pixel aspect ratio (right).

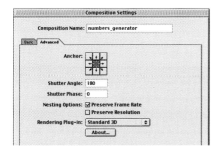

After Effects 5.0 added a new Comp Setting (above) that preserves the frame rate of the comp, even when it is nested in a comp with a different frame rate.

The final frame (right). We had to scale the numbers along the left skinnier than they are tall to get them inside the Action Safe area.

timeline. Again they were set to 90% Opacity with the Add transfer mode so that they would interact better with the image behind.

The Numbers effect defaults to updating every frame, which is often too fast. The old technique for slowing down Numbers was to precompose it, apply Effect>Time>Posterize Time to the precomp layer, then set the desired frame rate in the effect (this is what appears in our 4.1 project). As of After Effects 5.0, the Composition Settings dialog has gained an Advanced tab, where you can set a Nesting Option to Preserve Frame Rate. So we set our [**numbers_generator**] precomp to 12 fps in Composition Settings, and turned on Preserve Frame Rate. Now After Effects will obey this precomp's frame rate even when it's nested in another composition or rendered at a different frame rate.

Sex in Advertising

The last touch we added is our "instant sex" trick to make video look more like oversaturated, slightly overexposed film. To do this, we duplicated the footage layer **PC_Axiom.mov**, and set the copy on top to use Soft Light transfer mode to increase the apparent saturation. This copy was then blurred by roughly ten pixels to create the puffy, blown-out look, with its Opacity reduced until we achieved the desired effect.

End of the Track

We normally think of using After Effects' Motion Tracker for tasks in which part of the original scene has to be replaced. This usually requires a lot of preplanning, and the result can take many hours to get right. The shot provided here was not ideal for getting perfect tracks, but it was good enough to coordinate some fun graphical elements. With a few hours' work and a little imagination, we were able to deliver the client a scene with higher production value than the simple text overlays originally requested.

Connect

For more information on topics covered in this tutorial, check out the following chapters in *Creating Motion Graphics*:

Removing and rendering with 3:2 Pulldown: *3:2 Pulldown*

Managing 16–235 luminance range footage: *Luminance and IRE Issues* (TechTip)

Motion Tracking: *Motion Tracking*

Nesting a comp: *Nesting Compositions*

Collapse Transformation: *Collapsing Transformations*

Non-square pixels: *Working with D1/DV NTSC*

Blending images: *Transfer Modes*

Adjustment Layers: *Adjustment Layers*

The Wiggler: *Our Trusty Assistants*

Levels, Stroke, Mosaic, and Transform effects, plus "instant sex" trick: *Standard Effects Round-Up*

Numbers and Basic Text effects: *Plugging In Type*

Posterize Time: *Time Games*

3D Mechanic

Recombining the layers of a multipass 3D render in After Effects to create a more realistic composite.

The best 3D scenes are rarely finished "in camera" in a 3D application – they are massaged further in compositing programs such as After Effects. Performing this layering in After Effects is faster and more powerful than attempting it inside your 3D program.

You may already be familiar with the techniques of rendering separate diffuse, specular, and reflection passes to later mix inside After Effects, or adding some "grunge" to your surfaces to make them more realistic. In this tutorial, master 3D animator Alex Lindsay of dvGarage takes these concepts to the next level, focusing on details you might not

OVERVIEW

Main Concepts:

These are the features and concepts we will be focusing on in this project:

- Multipass rendering from a 3D program
- Combining the diffuse, specular, and reflective properties of a surface
- Alpha edge issues
- Transfer modes
- Track mattes
- Faking light wrap and edge feather
- Comp snapshots
- Adjustment layers
- Conforming frame rates
- Nesting comps
- Displacement Map effect (PB) (optional)
- Compound Blur effect (PB) (optional)
- FE Vector Blur (optional)

Requirements:

After Effects 4.1 or later standard version; Production Bundle recommended.

Third-party effects: FE Vector Blur (free on the *Creating Motion Graphics* CD in the **Free Plug-ins** folder) is an optional replacement for the Production Bundle.

Getting Started:

Inside the **Tutorials** master folder on the accompanying CD, locate and copy the folder **05_Mechanic** to your hard drive.

In the folder **Final Movie** inside this folder, double-click on and play **Mechanic.mov**.

Inside the **Project** folder you'll find the finished After Effects project file **Mechanic.aep**. Open the project file that is appropriate for your version of After Effects: 4.1 or 5, Standard (S) or Production Bundle (PB). This is your starting point; we suggest you save under a new name after each major section.

If you do not have the Production Bundle, but do have the book *Creating Motion Graphics*, install the free effect FE Vector Blur as a workaround for Step 26.

Credits:

The artwork for this project was created by Alex Lindsay of dvGarage (www.dvgarage.com).

have ever considered, but which contribute to making a photorealistic image. Not every 3D job you have will require this much planning and thought, but it's good to at least be aware that these issues exist.

The structure of this tutorial is a bit different from others in this book. Because the final image is essentially a still and involves a lot of layers, we've already imported all the layers for you, and arranged them in their respective compositions. You will perform the mixing of these layers, using a combination of track mattes, transfer modes, and simple effects such as blurs. A final version of this work is included in the project file for browsing or comparison when you're done.

A comparison between a simplistic 3D render (left) and one that uses a variety of techniques to create a more realistic scene in After Effects (right). Photograph and model courtesy of Alex Lindsay of dvGarage (www.dvgarage.com).

The Tasks

This is what you will be doing in the various parts of this tutorial:

PART 1: Build up the surface for the spaceship in its own composition, using track mattes, transfer modes, and blurring to combine separate diffuse, reflective, specular, grunge, and occlusion render passes.

PART 2: Finish two additional precomps that will serve as luminance mattes for faking edge feather and light wrap effects.

PART 3: Composite the spaceship over its background; create a more realistic shadow and the lighting effects mentioned above.

PART 4: *Optional for Production Bundle users:* Use a particle system render to create exhaust heat effects.

Attention To Detail!

Before you get started, play the two **AttentionToDetail** QuickTime movies in the **AttentionToDetail Movies** folder inside your After Effects project; these review important information on the subject of multipass rendering and layering. These movies are part of dvGarage's *Attention to Detail* series, and they provide an excellent overview of the techniques employed in this tutorial – especially from the 3D preparation and rendering side of the equation. Additional tutorials may be found on the Web site: www.dvgarage.com.

Part 1: Perfecting Imperfections

The general concept is that the ship was constructed with a metal that has a dull surface, and was then plated with chrome. However, time and use has worn some of the chrome plating away. Therefore, there are two different surface properties you will be balancing against each other:

Mech_diff_hard The diffuse (underlying) surface, lit by an overhead light to simulate the sun.

Mech_diff_dome The diffuse surface lit by a form of global illumination such as a dome light, simulating light from the sky.

Mech_grng_base The model with a "grunge" map placed in the luminance channel, representing the aging of the surface.

Mech_background The image you will composite the ship in front of; also used as a reflection map.

Mech_refl_blur The result of using a blurred version of the background as a reflection map, representing the diffuse surface's reflections.

Mech_refl_shrp A sharp version of the background reflected, representing the chrome surface's reflection of its surroundings.

Mech_occlusion A ray-traced occlusion map for the model. This will be discussed in more detail later.

Mech_spec_soft Softer, broader specular highlights for the underlying surface of the object.

Mech_spec_hard Harder, tighter specular highlights for the chromed surface of the object.

• The diffuse character of the underlying model. Light is scattered or absorbed by this surface.

• The harder specular character of the chrome surface. Light is reflected back to the eye by this surface.

You will be building up the ship from the underlying dull surface to the chrome plating, with reflections and specular highlights on top. As a result, we have rendered eight different passes of this ship (as shown on the opposite page).

Step 1: In the Project window, twirl open the **Sources** folder. Double-click the files to open them in their Footage windows, if you want to get a better idea of what they look like. You might notice that many are set to have their Alpha channel ignored (see figure), and have rough-looking edges as a result of rendering with a Straight alpha channel but viewing just the RGB channels. You will be transfer moding multiple copies of these files on top of each other, which can lead to artifacts in antialiased edges. Therefore, one copy with its alpha intact will be used as a stencil over the final stack to clean up the edges. You should still render these layers from your 3D program with a Straight alpha; otherwise, their edges will be premultiplied, and also will not add up correctly. (Straight alpha channels are also covered in *The Planets* tutorial.) When you're done, close any open files.

The Diffuse Surface

Step 2: In the Project window, double-click on the comp [**1_Ship Composite**]. It should have only the bottom layer (#14) turned on: **Mech_diff_hard.tif**. This represents the sun reflecting off the duller underlying metal surface of the ship.

Step 3: Turn on the eyeball (the Video switch) for layer 13, **Mech_diff_dome.tif**. This layer represents the broader illumination from the sky hitting the underlying metal surface.

Since this ship has seen some wear, this surface should not look clean. Above it in the layer stack is a copy of our grunge-mapped ship, **Mech_grng_base.tif**. Turn on its eyeball; this is where the aging is going to come from.

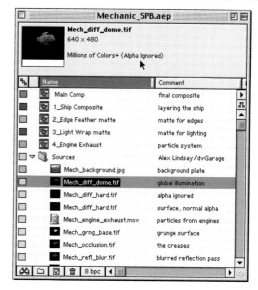

1 Many of the layers have had their alpha channels turned off. Their edges will be recut with a Stencil layer later, to make sure they are clean.

Navigation Aids

These are a few general concepts that will aid your navigation of this project:

• We've used the Labels feature in After Effects to color-code all the layers and comps to help you keep track of them.

• The layer property you'll be editing most often is Opacity. The shortcut to reveal it is to select the layer, and press T – we're going to assume you remember this rather than drive you crazy by repeating it throughout.

• You will be toggling the Video switch for many layers to make them visible. We tend to refer to this switch as the "eyeball" as that's what its icon looks like.

• Finally, many of the layers have both effects and transfer modes applied. For this reason, we took advantage of a feature introduced in After Effects 5 that allows you to have both the Switches and Modes panels open at the same time in the Timeline window. If you don't see both, context+click (Control+click on the Mac, right-click on Windows) on any other panel in the Timeline window and enable both Switches and Modes. If you are using version 4.1, use the shortcut key F4 to toggle back and forth between these two panels.

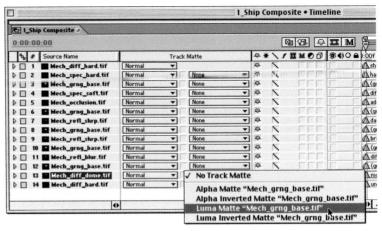

3 Use the grunge map of the ship as a luma matte for the dome light pass (right). This will reduce the sky's illumination where the ship has been beat up (above).

Grunge

The grunge map used in this tutorial – plus numerous others – is from dvGarage's Surface Toolkit CD-ROM. Grunge maps are essential tools for aging surfaces in 2D or 3D.

Make sure the Modes panel is visible, and set the track matte (TrkMat) popup for layer 13, **Mech_diff_dome.tif**, to Luma Matte; the Video switch for layer 12 (the matte) should turn off automatically. This will have the effect of reflecting the sky's illumination only where the ship has not been dinged and nicked. The underlying diffuse image is still visible; toggle layer 14 on and off if you want to check.

STEP 4: Turn on the Video switch for layer 11: **Mech_refl_blur.tif**. This blurred copy of the reflection map represents how the underlying surface is colored by the rest of its environment, not just the sun and sky.

This blurred reflection pass will also be matted by a copy of the grunge pass, already sitting above it in the layer stack. We want these colors to appear in the opposite places that the dome light illumination occurred. Therefore, set layer 11's track matte option to Luma Inverted Matte. Some of the pits created in Step 3 will now have reflected bits of color in them.

Reflections add illumination to a surface. To simulate this effect, set **Mech_refl_blur.tif**'s Mode to Screen. The result is too bright: You just want some subtle highlights at this point, since this is not the main chrome reflection. Reveal this layer's Opacity (select it and hit T), and reduce its value to somewhere around 32%.

4 Use the grunge pass as an inverted matte to reveal blurred reflections in some of the pits (above). Reflections add illumination to a surface, so use Screen mode, and reduce the layer's Opacity to blend it in subtly (right).

The Reflective Surface

STEP 5: Time to turn your attention to the chrome surface of the ship. Turn on layer 9: **Mech_refl_shrp.tif**. Reflections in a hard surface like chrome are much sharper than in a dull surface, so an unblurred map was used for this pass.

5 For the chrome, a sharp version of the reflection map is matted with the grunge layer (upper left), then set to Screen mode and reduced in opacity (upper right).

By now you should be seeing a pattern: A copy of **Mech_grng_base.tif** is sitting above **Mech_refl_shrp.tif** in the layer stack, just waiting to weather it. Set the track matte for layer 9 to Luma. This will add pits to the chrome.

As noted in Step 4, reflections add their coloration to a surface. Set layer 9 to Screen mode. Reveal its Opacity property, and turn it down to blend it in – somewhere around 63% is good.

STEP 6: A common trick to enhance the richness of 3D images is to duplicate them and apply an "intensifier" transfer mode such as Overlay, Hard Light, or Soft Light to the copy on top. This adds saturation and contrast, yielding a warmer version of an object or its environment than mathematically correct renders will.

Turn on layer 7, which is a copy of **Mech_refl_shrp.tif**. Since this copy should occupy only the same areas of the model as the underlying version, yet another copy of **Mech_grng_base.tif** is sitting above it. Set the track matte for layer 7 to Luma, and experiment with these different intensifier modes. Reveal this layer's Opacity, and reduce it to tone down the effect. We chose Hard Light mode, and an Opacity of 35%.

6 A copy of the mottled hard reflection pass is applied using an intensifier mode such as Hard Light. This helps warm up the image, adding saturation and contrast.

Occlusion

STEP 7: At this point, the ship still looks like a toy dipped in chrome that has been batted around a bit. Phong-rendered reflection maps are a great, quick-and-dirty way to reflect an environment onto a model without enduring the long render times that raytracing often incurs. However, they have a bad habit of appearing in the creases where the model should be dark. Therefore, we're going to use a bit of raytracing to give us a layer that indicates where those creases are, so we can make them dark like they should be.

Turn on layer 5: **Mech_occlusion.tif**. This special pass indicates whether a section of the ship is reflecting the environment or just another portion of itself, such as spaces in the creases.

7 An occlusion pass (upper left) can be thought of as revealing where an object shadows itself inside its various folds. Apply this using Multiply mode with Opacity to taste (above) to darken these folds (upper right).

Set **Mech_occlusion.tif**'s transfer mode to Multiply – this will darken the underlying image where the occlusion pass is dark. The result is a bit extreme; reveal this layer's Opacity, and dial back to taste. We chose 45%.

Specular Highlights

The final touches include adding specular highlights: "hotspots" where the light sources are reflected strongly back to the eye. As has been the case for the other surface properties of the ship, the underlying surface and the chrome surface will get different specular treatments.

STEP 8: Turn on layer 4: **Mech_spec_soft.tif**. This is a render pass of just the specular highlights, with a relatively wide, soft falloff. This corresponds to the highlights from the duller, underlying metal surface of the ship.

As is the case with most of our other surface properties, a copy of the grunge pass – **Mech_grng_base.tif** – has already been positioned above the soft specular layer, ready to be used as a track matte.

Since this softer specular pass is supposed to appear only where the chrome has been pitted or worn away, you will want to use the inverse of this pass. Set the track matte popup for **Mech_spec_soft.tif** to Luma Inverted.

Specular highlights further brighten the surface of an object, just as reflections do. Therefore, set the transfer mode for **Mech_spec_soft.tif** to Screen. You can leave its Opacity at 100%; its effect is already pretty subtle.

8 A relatively soft, broad specular highlight pass (upper left) is used for the underlying surface of the ship. The grunge pass is used as an inverted luma matte, so these highlights appear only where the chrome has been worn away (upper right).

STEP 9: The chrome surfaces of the ship get a harder, tighter specular highlight. Turn on layer 2, **Mech_spec_hard.tif**, and note how this differs in the intensity of the hotspot from **Mech_spec_soft.tif** (double-click layer 4 to view it in the Layer window, closing this window when you're done).

Set **Mech_spec_hard.tif**'s transfer mode to Screen, as you did above. We chose not to use the grunge pass to matte this layer, because this harder specular highlight is already pretty tight and does not spill over into some of the areas illuminated by the softer specular highlight in Step 8.

Highlights are often perceived as "blooming" – usually the result of film or video being overexposed by the bright hotspot of the specular highlight. Select **Mech_spec_hard.tif**, and apply Effect>Blur & Sharpen>**Gaussian Blur**. Experiment with small amounts of blur to soften the bright highlight. We settled on a value of 2.0; you can use a touch more if you want a softer look.

9 A tighter, hotter specular highlight pass (upper left) represents the light hitting the chrome surface. It is also applied in Screen mode, and blurred slightly (upper right) to give the impression of slightly over-exposed film or video.

STEP 10: You might have noticed that the edges of the ship look ragged or aliased. All of the render passes you have been layering together so far have had their alpha channels ignored, to avoid potential problems with transfer modes incorrectly adding multiple antialiased edges. Time to clean them up.

Double-click layer 1 – a copy of **Mech_diff_hard.tif** – to open it in its Layer window. Click on the Show only Alpha channel switch along the bottom of this window (it's the white tab). Note how the edges look clean; this is a copy of the diffuse pass with its alpha channel turned on and interpreted correctly.

Close this Layer window. Set layer 1's transfer mode popup to Stencil Alpha. This tells After Effects you wish to use this layer as a cookie cutter, and to trim the alpha channels of all the layers underneath with this layer's alpha. To have the stencil take effect, turn on this layer's eyeball, keeping an eye on what happens in the Comp window – the edges of the ship should clean up nicely.

10 The alpha channel of **Mech_diff_hard.tif** layer will be used as a Stencil Alpha to clean up the edges for the underlying layers in this comp.

*This completes the surface of the spaceship. Save your project under a new name before you continue. If you are concerned you missed a step, compare your composition with our prebuilt [**1_Ship Composite-FINAL**] in the Project window's* **3D Mechanic * prebuilt** *folder.*

10 *complete:* The rest of the layers in this comp have had their alpha channels ignored, displaying an aliased edge (left); using this top layer in Stencil Alpha mode cleans them up (right).

Part 2: Life on the Edge

Building the surface of the ship was over half the work you'll be doing in this tutorial. But before you move on to compositing the ship over its background, you need to prepare some precomps that will be used in this final composite.

Edge Feather Fake

An important technique for compositing an object over a new background is to feather the edges of the foreground object, causing that object to "melt" into the scene. This replicates the way light naturally bends around the edges of real objects. Effect>Blur & Sharpen> Channel Blur has an option to blur just the alpha, but it spreads the alpha to be larger than the layer was originally. You want the edge feather to just cut into the alpha – not enlarge it. Here's a workaround:

11 A copy of the ship render, with alpha channel intact, is filled with white. This is the start of creating a luma matte for the feathered edges.

STEP 11: In the Project window, open the comp [2_**Edge Feather matte**]. It contains two copies of the version of **Mech_diff_hard.tif** where we kept the alpha channel – same as you used in Step 10.

Select the second copy (layer 2), and apply Effect>Render>**Fill**. This replaces the normal color channels with the color of your choice, while keeping the layer's alpha channel. An Effect Controls window should have opened when you added this effect; change the Color parameter from its default red to pure white.

STEP 12: Turn on the Video switch for layer 1. It contains another copy of **Mech_diff_hard.tif** with its alpha channel intact. You will use this copy to cut a hole out of the underlying layer, resulting in just a feathered edge around the outline of the ship.

Make sure the Modes panel is open in the Timeline window. Set the transfer mode popup for layer 1 to Silhouette Alpha. This inverts the alpha channel for the top layer, making it transparent where the ship would be and opaque beyond it, and uses the result to cut out the alpha for the layer below. The only piece of the underlying ship layer you can see is a faint line where the antialiased alpha channels of the two layers combine (zoom in if you need to take a closer look).

12 To use the first copy of **Mech_diff_hard.tif** to punch a hole out of the second copy below, set the layer on top to Silhouette Alpha (above). The result is a thin white outline where their antialiased edges are trying to cancel each other out (left).

STEP 13: This thin white outline is the beginning of the feathered edge you will need later – but it needs to be wider. Select layer 1, and apply Effect>Blur & Sharpen>**Gaussian Blur**. (You can use Fast Blur if you are working on a slower machine; just make sure the layer is set to Best Quality so Fast Blur will render more cleanly.) In its Effect Controls window, increase the Blurriness parameter until you start to see a small, soft white rim in the Comp window, outlining where the ship should be. When you're scrubbing the value in version 5, press Command (Control) to scrub in fine increments. We used a value of 6.

> In version 5.0, when you're editing the Gaussian Blur effect, if you turn off Dynamic Resolution from the wing menu of the Timeline window you will see slower but full-resolution, real-time previews rather than faster low-resolution dynamic previews as you scrub the Blurriness slider. Turn Dynamic Resolution back on either from the same menu, or from File>Preferences>Previews.

Note how this rim has a hard edge around the outside, and feathers off only toward the inside. (If you see the opposite, you probably applied the blur to layer 2, not layer 1.) This result will be used later as a luminance matte to fake the feathered edge effect we're after.

STEP 14: In the Project window, double-click the [**3_Light Wrap matte**] comp to open it. The Comp window should look very similar to your result for [**2_Edge Feather matte**], with just a wider edge. The only difference is that the Gaussian Blur applied to the top layer has been set to a Blurriness of 10. (Since it is otherwise identical, we saw no point in making you go through the same steps again.)

In addition to feathering the edges of the ship, we want to give the impression that light being bounced from the ship's new surroundings is wrapping around or "contaminating" the surface of the ship. You will use this wider feathered edge as a track matte for this effect.

*Save your project. If you need to, compare your results for [**2_Edge Feather matte**] with its corresponding final version in the Project window's* **3D Mechanic * prebuilt** *folder.*

13 Blurring the top layer results in a feathered edge that is cropped by the alpha of the layer underneath. This will be used later as a luminance matte.

14 The comp [**3_Light Wrap matte**] is virtually identical to [**2_Edge Feather matte**], with just a wider blur to create a larger area to contaminate the edges of the ship with faux reflected light from its new background.

Composite Wizard

If you regularly need to composite 3D objects over new backgrounds, or work frequently with bluescreen or greenscreen images, check out the Composite Wizard effects set from Pinnacle Systems (www.pinnaclesys.com). It includes powerful plug-ins for edge blur, edge feather, and light wrap which are easier to use than the workarounds discussed here.

Part 3: Blending In

To blend the spaceship into its new environment, you will need one more special render pass in addition to the precomps you built in the previous two sections. We'll also cover some tricks using blurs and transfer modes to further erase the line between models and perceived reality.

Shadow

STEP 15: From the Project window, open the comp [**Main Comp**]. Although it contains nine layers, only one is turned on right now: the new background, which was also used for the ship's reflection map.

Double-click layer 7 – **Mech_shad_base.tif** – to open it in its Layer window. This is a special render pass that shows just where the shadow from the ship would fall on the imaginary ground in 3D. Close this Layer window after you've become familiar with the render.

STEP 16: You may be tempted to fill the shadow layer with the color black and use it as is. In reality, shadows are seldom simple pools of darkness – instead, they appear as shadings of the surface they fall on. To simulate this, we've placed **Mech_shad_base.tif** above a copy of the background layer so we can use the shadow pass as a track matte for a treated version of this background.

Turn on the Video switch for layer 8: a duplicate of **Mech_background.jpg**. To help keep all of our copies of the background image straight, click on the name for this layer to select it, hit Return, type in a more descriptive name such as **"BG for shadow"** and hit Return to accept it. Then set its track matte popup to Alpha Matte (Luma Matte would work as well, since our shadow pass was rendered as white against black). Nothing will appear in the Comp window yet, since at this point you just have an exact copy of the background.

With layer 8 selected, choose Effect>Adjust>**Levels**. This is what you will use to change the contrast of the shadow. In the Effect Controls window, drag the gray arrow under the center of the Histogram display

15 To create a more realistic shadow, render a special pass from your 3D program that shows just where the ship's shadow would fall.

16 Use the shadow pass as a track matte for a copy of the background.

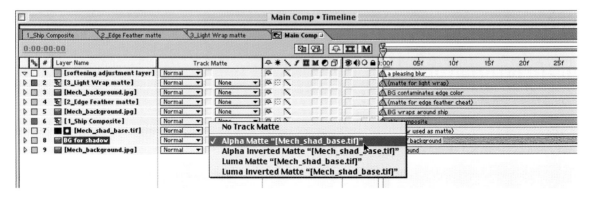

to the right to decrease the Gamma value. This will shift more of the image toward levels below 50% gray. Watch the Comp window; you will see the shadow appear.

This may be the only adjustment you need to make to create a realistic shadow. However, if there were any bright white areas inside the shadow's area, adjusting the Gamma may not make them dark enough. If this is the case, lower the Output White value to pull them down.

These are "to taste" parameters; when you're deciding how dark to make your shadow, take into account how strong the light sources would be. Because the scene is evenly lit by an overcast sky, we used a Gamma of 0.8 and Output White to 174 to create a relatively subtle shadow.

Edge Feather

STEP 17: Turn on the Video switch for layer 6, which is the precomp [**1_Ship Composite**] you built in Part 1. Since it uses the same image for its reflection map as is used for the background, it already matches fairly well. But look closely at its edges: They're a bit sharply defined, which is usually a giveaway that an object has been composited over a new background. In reality, the light being reflected by the background should wrap around and soften those edges. Click on the Take a Snapshot icon along the bottom of the Comp window or press Shift+F5 to store a reference copy of the current image.

In Part 2, you built a precomp – [**2_Edge Feather**] – to use as a matte to blend the background into the edges of the ship. Note that we've already nested this precomp as layer 4, and have positioned another copy of the background as layer 5 underneath it.

Select layer 5, hit Return to rename it, type in a more descriptive name such as "**BG for edge feather**" and hit Return to accept it. Turn on the Video switch for this layer, and set this layer's track matte popup to Luma Matte. You should notice a subtle lightening and feathering of the ship's edges, as a portion of the background is matted over them. To compare, press F5 or toggle the Show last Snapshot button along the bottom of the Comp window.

You can decide how strong this effect is by revealing the Opacity property for **BG for edge feather** and reducing it; try 50%. Press Shift+F6 to take a second snapshot of this intermediate result.

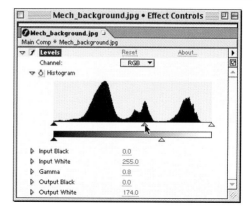

16 *complete:* The Levels effect (top) is used to darken a copy of the background copy to create a subtle shadow (above).

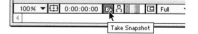

17 After turning on the ship, take a snapshot of the Comp window to compare the effect of adding an edge feather treatment.

17 *complete:* Before (below left) and after (below) adding the edge feather effect.

18 A matte with a broader feather is used for the light wrap effect. Transfer modes alter the color of the ship based on the background. But study the feet of the ship: We're seeing too literal a copy of the background cutting through them…

19 Blurring the light wrap effect gives a softer, more diffuse look (above). Your Timeline (below) should now have two sets of edge treatments active on top of the main ship.

Light Wrap

In addition to feathering the edge of the foreground object, another common compositing trick is to give the appearance that reflections from the background are wrapping around or "contaminating" the edge color of an object. This trick is especially useful if the background layer includes a light source that would be naturally illuminating the foreground object, but we can use it in this purely reflective example as well.

STEP 18: Check out layers 2 and 3 in the Timeline window: One is the precomp [3_Light Wrap matte] you inspected in the previous section, and the other is yet another copy of our background plate. Select the name of the latter (layer 3), hit Return, give it a more meaningful title such as "**BG for light wrap**" and hit Return again. Turn on its eyeball, and set its track matte popup to Luma Matte just as you did for the edge feather pair earlier.

The Comp window will show a fuzzier version of your edge feather application in the previous step. But rather than feather the edges, you want to change the color of them – so start experimenting with different transfer modes for **BG for light wrap**. If the background had a light source, you might use Add or Screen to further illuminate the ship. In this case, where you want color and contrast instead of light, try out Overlay, Soft Light, and Hard Light to see which coloration you prefer. Press F6 to call up the snapshot of the feather-only version from the last step to compare the effects.

Remember that you can always tweak the Opacity of this light wrap layer, or change the width of the wrap by changing the Blurriness parameter for the first layer back in [3_Light Wrap matte]. In the end, we chose Hard Light, with 100% Opacity. Press Shift+F7 to store a snapshot of this result.

STEP 19: This lighting effect is supposed to be suggestive, rather than a literal reflection of the background. Select **BG for light wrap** and apply Effect>Blur & Sharpen>**Gaussian Blur**. Increase its Blurriness to around 10 or until the effect softens; press F7 to compare your results with your previous preblur snapshot. A good area of the ship to focus on is along the top, where the left wall cuts behind the ship; the white parking stripes that cut through the feet of the ship are another area to watch.

Press Shift+F8 to store a copy of your final light wrap result. If you like, browse through your snapshots saved under F5, F6, F7, and F8 to review your progress at blending the ship into its new scene.

	#	Layer Name	Mode	T	TrkMat		
▽ ☐	1	☐ [softening adjustment layer]	Normal ▼				
▷ ☐	2	[3_Light Wrap matte]	Normal ▼		None ▼		
▽ ☐	3	BG for light wrap	Hard Light ▼		Luma ▼		*f*
		▷ Gaussian Blur				Reset	*f*
▷ ☐	4	[2_Edge Feather matte]	Normal ▼		None ▼		
▽ ☐	5	BG for edge feather	Normal ▼		Luma ▼		
		♢ Opacity				50 %	
▷ ☐	6	[1_Ship Composite]	Normal ▼		None ▼		
▷ ☐	7	☐ [Mech_shad_base.tif]	Normal ▼		None ▼		
▷ ☐	8	BG for shadow	Normal ▼		Alpha ▼		*f*
▷ ☐	9	[Mech_background.jpg]	Normal ▼		None ▼		

If in a hurry on a particular job, you can combine the edge feather and light wrap treatments in one pass. For example, turn off **BG for light wrap**, set **BG for edge feather** to Screen mode to provide the illumination, and reduce its Opacity to 30%. The result is not as nuanced, but still helps blend the spaceship into its background.

Through the Mist

There's one more trick we'll employ to finish off this composite. If reality is full of imperfections, our attempts to re-create it are even more imperfect. If you were to visit the set of a film production or television show, you might be surprised how rough many of the set pieces and props appear (including some of the human talent). Directors of photography use various tricks to slightly soften the image they shoot in an attempt to smooth over these imperfections. One technique is to apply a spray called ProMist to the camera lens. Here's a way to re-create the digital equivalent of this technique:

STEP 20: The topmost layer in [**Main Comp**] is a white solid with the same dimensions as the composition. You want to turn it into an Adjustment Layer. This means any effect applied to it will be applied to the composite of all the layers underneath.

To do this, in the Timeline click on the switch box under the "half moon" icon for this layer. Then enable the eyeball for this layer. You won't see any change yet, because you haven't applied any effects to it.

STEP 21: Select **softening adjustment layer**, and apply Effect>Blur>**Gaussian Blur**. If you have not applied any other effects since Step 19, you can also use the keyboard shortcut Command+Option+Shift+E (Control+Alt+Shift+E) to apply the last effect used. Increase the Blurriness parameter until you see the image go slightly soft; about 2 pixels should do the trick.

Then set the transfer mode for **softening adjustment layer** to Lighten. This means the blur will have an effect only where the blurred pixels are lighter than the pixel underneath, resulting in a slightly puffy look. The result is a subtle softening of the creases in the spaceship, lightening of the graffiti on the rear wall, and brighter white lines on the ground; press F8 to compare it with the snapshot you took at the end of Step 19.

Some compositors use more blur, or a brighter transfer mode such as Screen; however, you've done enough work with the edge feather and light wrap layers that you can get by with this light-handed treatment. If you find the result too soft or blurry, reveal the Opacity property for this layer, and scrub it until you have a look you like. We settled on an Opacity value of 40%.

Meet Doris

One nickname for this blur-it-when-you-shoot-it technique is Doris, supposedly named after techniques used to make a popular but aging actress appear perpetually young.

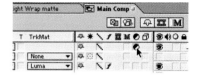

20 Enable the Adjustment Layer switch for the topmost layer.

21 An adjustment layer with a slight blur, applied with Lighten mode, performs the final blending for the scene.

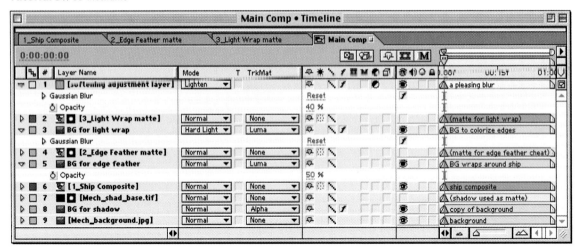

21 *complete:* The Main Comp's Timeline window after all our blending tricks have been applied.

Save your project. If you're using the Standard version of After Effects, this completes your work, so compare your result with the prebuilt comp [**Main Comp_FINAL**] *to see if you ended up with the same image. Close this comp and twirl up the* **3D Mechanic * prebuilt** *folder.*

Part 4: Exhausting Measures

Third-Party Heat

Several third-party plug-in vendors, such as Boris FX and Pinnacle Systems, supply alternate Displacement Map and Compound Blur effects. The Foundry offers a Heat Haze effect in their Tinderbox 1 set.

This final section is optional, and requires the After Effects Production Bundle for the two effects you will be applying: Displacement Map and Compound Blur. However, if you have the FE Vector Blur effect installed (part of Media 100's ICE'd Final Effects Complete; also free on the *Creating Motion Graphics* CD-ROM), you can create a similar look.

This trick covers using a separate particle system render pass to fake the heat wave distortion that would be caused by the engine exhaust from the ship.

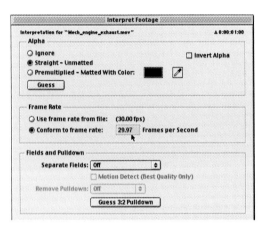

Exhaust Particles

STEP 22: In the Project window, open the **Sources** folder, select the footage item **Mech_engine_exhaust.mov**, and type Command+F (Control+F) to open its Interpret Footage dialog. This short movie was rendered out of the 3D program at 30 frames per second (fps). However, NTSC video rate is 29.97 fps – so its frame rate was set to conform to 29.97. Close this window when you're done, and twirl the **Sources** folder back closed.

22 Many 3D scenes are rendered at 30 fps, even though the proper frame rate for NTSC video is 29.97 fps. You can enforce the correct frame rate in the Interpret Footage dialog.

STEP 23: Still in the Project window, double-click on the comp [**4_Engine Exhaust**] to open it. Hit 0 on the numeric keypad to RAM Preview it.

This series of green and yellow dots was created with a very simple particle system in 3D. The model of the ship was used to create a hole in the alpha of the particles, leaving just dots. You will later use the green color to decide how much to displace the background image for the heat effect. It is important that this pass be rendered with an alpha channel, instead of over a black background; otherwise the Displacement Map effect will interpret the black background to mean it should displace pixels in a negative direction.

STEP 24: These dots are too well defined to create a hazy heat effect. Therefore, you will need to blur them. Compound effects, such as Displacement Map and Compound Blur, require that any treatments applied to a layer that will be used as a map must be done in a precomp – otherwise, these attributes will be ignored. That's why we've dedicated a composition to just apply effects to these particles.

In this comp, select **Mech_engine_exhaust.mov**, and apply Effect> Blur & Sharpen>**Gaussian Blur** (or Fast Blur, if you want to save render time – this is the least image-critical blur you've applied in this project, so you can cut some corners). Adjust the Blurriness parameter until the dots become fuzzy and blend together, but not so much that they fade away. A value around 5 works well.

STEP 25: You will be using this result as an image map layer for a pair of compound effects in the final composite. In the Project window, drag the icon for [**4_Engine Exhaust**] onto the icon for [**Main Comp**]. This will nest the exhaust comp into your primary comp. Open [**Main Comp**], turn off the eyeball for the new layer **4_Engine Exhaust**, and drag it to the bottom of the layer stack – we like to tuck our maps out of the way, to reduce the chances that we might turn them on by accident. If this layer does not already start at 00:00, drag it there; in version 5.0, you can select it and type Option+Home (Alt+Home).

Heat Wave

STEP 26: Select layer 9 – the original copy of **Mech_ background.jpg** that serves as the main backplate for the composite – and change its name to "**Background (with Displace)**." Then choose Effect>Distort>**Displacement Map**. (If you don't have the Production Bundle version of After Effects, but do have FE Vector Blur installed, jump to Step 26 Alt below.) In its Effect Controls window, set its Displacement Map Layer popup to layer 10, **4_Engine Exhaust**. You should now see some fairly obvious waves to the right of the ship's engines.

23 A simple particle system with green and yellow dots were rendered blasting from where the engines would be, with a hole cut in their alpha channel by the ship's body.

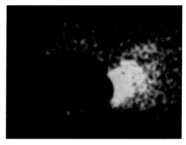

24 Blur the particle by about 5 pixels to create a blurred map to use in the final composition.

25 In the Project window, drag the icon for [**4_Engine Exhaust**] onto the icon for [**Main Comp**] to nest it.

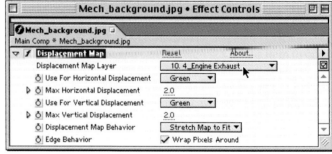

26 The engine particle system creates some nice, animating heat waves behind the ship (left) when it's first applied with the default values of 5.0 pixels. We reduced the displacement amount to a more subtle 2.0 pixels (right). Note the settings for the popups – especially Displacement Map Layer – if you are having trouble getting this to work.

Displacement Map includes a pair of popups that give you a choice of which properties of the Displacement Map Layer to use when you're deciding how much to displace an image. Since the engine particles were green, choose Green for both Horizontal Displacement and Vertical Displacement.

Then adjust the Max Horizontal Displacement and Max Vertical Displacement parameters until you have obvious, but believable, heat waves behind the ship. RAM Preview to check how they animate: They will be a lot more obvious when they're moving than when you're viewing them as a still frame. We settled on values of 2.0 for both Max Horizontal and Max Vertical Displacement.

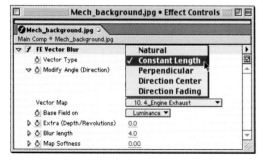

26 *Alt:* FE Vector Blur is also capable of creating heat wave distortion effects. The choice of Vector Type is important; the default setting blurs the entire image.

STEP 26 ALT: If you have FE Vector Blur installed, you can use it as an alternative to Displacement Map. Select layer 9, and apply Effect>ICE FE>**FE Vector Blur**. For its Vector Map popup, select **4_Engine Exhaust**.

Experiment with its Vector Type options. The first three – Natural, Constant Length, and Perpendicular – will introduce blur just where the engine particles are, and not the rest of the background image. Each gives a different look; we chose Constant Length. Then set its Blur length and Map Softness parameters to taste. We found that a Blur length of 4.0 and Map Softness of 0.0 worked well for us.

Alex Lindsay and dvGarage

Alex Lindsay has worked in computer graphics since the mid-1980s. He spent three years at LucasFilm subsidiaries JAK Films and Industrial Light and Magic working in roles from pre-visualization to creating shots for the movie *Star Wars: Episode 1*. His credits also include *Titan AE*, and the *ABC Hockey Night* opening title sequence.

Lindsay is one of the founders of dvGarage (www.dvgarage.com), a company dedicated to the development of the next generation of visual media artists. dvGarage products, such as its Surface Toolkit and 3D Toolkit, were used in the creation of this tutorial. Two examples of dvGarage's excellent online training are included in this project's folder on the CD.

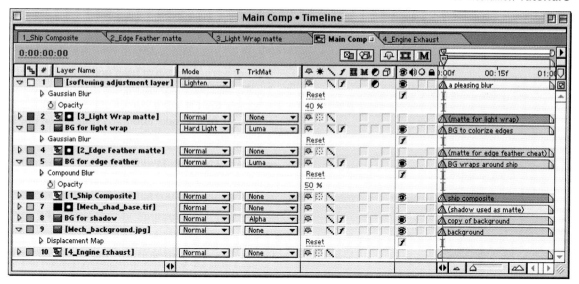

The Final Fake

This final trick is very subtle, but is another example of the kind of attention to detail (to borrow a dvGarage phrase) that will make a viewer's eye less likely to pause and note that "something's not quite right…"

The Displacement Map effect has been applied to the main background plate. However, this is not the only place where we see a portion of the background image – it was also feathered over the edges of the ship back in Step 17. To create the most accurate image, you should displace or blur this edge where the exhaust is just leaving the ship.

STEP 27: Select layer 5 – **BG for edge feather** – and apply Effect>Blur & Sharpen>**Compound Blur**. In its Effect Controls window, set the Blur Layer popup to use layer 10, **4_Engine Exhaust** precomp. The default Maximum Blur setting of 20 is a bit extreme; we chose a value of 4.

RAM Preview one more time and compare your result with [**Main Comp-FINAL**] *to verify you made the air move as you should.*

It's All in The Details

As Alex Lindsay of dvGarage notes, it is the subconcious detail that whispers to a viewer's brain whether or not it should believe what it is seeing on the screen. The overall goal is to create 3D composites and effects shots that are so convincing, that the brain can turn its attention back to the storyline and the message being conveyed.

It's true that you may have difficulty seeing the result of some of these tweaks at video resolution with this particular model, but it is good to get into the habit of thinking about such fine points. The day may come when you have to do a job like this at high-definition or at film resolution for a major motion picture…

27 The final Timeline window for [**Main Comp**]. Note the combination of track mattes, transfer modes, Opacity settings, and effects.

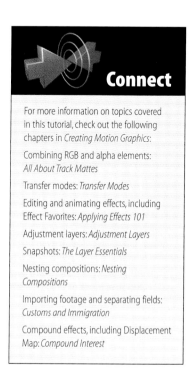

Connect

For more information on topics covered in this tutorial, check out the following chapters in *Creating Motion Graphics*:

Combining RGB and alpha elements: *All About Track Mattes*

Transfer modes: *Transfer Modes*

Editing and animating effects, including Effect Favorites: *Applying Effects 101*

Adjustment layers: *Adjustment Layers*

Snapshots: *The Layer Essentials*

Nesting compositions: *Nesting Compositions*

Importing footage and separating fields: *Customs and Immigration*

Compound effects, including Displacement Map: *Compound Interest*

Piccadilly Circus

Employing lights, shadows, and transfer modes to create a graphical look with 3D.

The client brief for the next two tutorials is to create graphics for a travel series that uses the London Underground (the subway, also known as the "tube") as a central theme. Each segment of the show focuses on the shops, sites, and tourist attractions around a particular tube stop, such as Piccadilly Circus.

There are two parts to the overall design, each of which will be covered in this and the following tutorial: The first is a centerpiece graphic that blurs the lines between flat, print-style art and dimensional 3D through lighting tricks; the second consists of additional graphical dressing based on sequences of words and moving elements. This tutorial is intended to be a gentle introduction to the concepts of using 3D space and lights, which are significant new features that were

OVERVIEW

Main Concepts:

These are the features and concepts we will be focusing on in this project:

- Creating and animating solids
- Importing Illustrator files as Comp
- Using Null Objects for Expressions and Parents
- Setting up a master color with Expressions
- Parenting
- Creating 3D layers
- 3D material options
- Light Options
- Animating a Light
- Saving a Comp as a Proxy

Requirements:

After Effects 5.0 or later standard version.

Getting Started:

Inside the **Tutorials** master folder on the accompanying CD, locate and copy the **06_PiccadillyCircus** folder to your hard drive.

In the folder **Final Movies** inside this main folder, double-click on and play the movies **PiccadillyCircus.mov** and **Underground.mov**. The first movie is what you will be creating in this tutorial; the second shows you how you will use it in the next tutorial.

Open the file **PiccadillyCircus_5.aep** inside the **Project** folder – this is your starting point; we suggest you save under a new name after each major section.

added in After Effects 5. Working in 3D doesn't mean you have to suddenly start flying around in space; you can use these features to subtly enhance what otherwise would be a flat, 2D design.

In this tutorial, you will create the comp [**Centerpiece**], which includes all the 3D elements such as the moving solids, the main title, plus the lighting tricks. In the next tutorial, you will add 2D layers such as the text animations along the top and the graphic element at the bottom.

While you could complete the entire tutorial in one comp, by splitting it in two you can pre-render the 3D comp and use it as a Comp Proxy, a very useful time-saving feature. This significantly speeds up creating the final comp.

Another reason we split this project across two tutorials is version compatibility. *Piccadilly Circus* requires After Effects 5 standard, while the next tutorial, *Underground Movement*, creates the final composite and can be completed using After Effects 4.1 or 5.0 standard versions.

A frame from the final Centerpiece animation. The movie you create in this tutorial will be used as a source in the next tutorial, *Underground Movement*.

The Tasks

This is what you will be doing in the various parts of this tutorial (since this tutorial is quite lengthly, feel free to take breaks between sections):

PART 1: Create and animate a set of solids to create the interweaving panels for the background, and assign them a master color through the use of a null object and expressions.

PART 2: Add a light to the scene, adjust shadow properties of the light and solids, add a background to catch the shadows, and adjust the Z depth of each object to increase the shadow interplay.

PART 3: Import the layered Illustrator file with the title elements, parent them to a null object, add expressions to them so that they follow the master color, and edit their Material Options to alter how they react to the light.

PART 4: Animate the title pieces.

PART 5: Animate the master color.

PART 6: Animate the light.

PART 7: Render, and create a composition proxy for the next tutorial, *Underground Movement*.

Sources Diversion

Newly imported sources in After Effects 5 are automatically directed to whatever folder is currently selected in the Project window, or the folder where a selected source resides. To stay organized, select the **My_Sources** folder in the Project window before you import a new source – that way you'll always know where it went!

Part 1: Building a Better Background

The main idea behind the centerpiece you will be creating in this tutorial is animating a series of overlapping, semi-transparent solids to create a shifting background for the main title. The trick here will be using 3D space, lighting, and shadows in slightly less than obvious ways to achieve a rich mix of what are otherwise simple elements. In the process, you will learn a fair amount about animating lights and setting the surface attributes for 3D layers in After Effects.

We've created **My_Comps** and **My_Sources** folders for you to put your own work into – they will help keep it separate from the prebuilt versions. When you select the appropriate folder before importing a file or creating a composition, After Effects will automatically add your new elements into that folder for you.

1 Start by building a new comp, 320×240, 3:01 long, at 29.97 fps.

Animating the First Solid

Step 1: In the Project window, select the **My_Comps** folder. Create a New Composition, 320×240 pixels in size, square pixels, a duration of 03:01, 29.97 frames per second (fps), and name it "**MyCenterpiece**". Notice that the comp will be created inside the **My_Comps** folder, which will help you stay organized.

Step 2: Change the Composition>Background Color to white. Your final animation will be over white; setting the background color to match will allow you to see your initial pieces in context, without having to build a background layer first.

Step 3: The animated stripes that go behind the title will be created using a total of six solids: three moving left to right, and three moving right to left. Each will be slightly different from the other in width and opacity.

Create the first solid by selecting Layer>New> Solid or use the shortcut: Command+Y on Mac (Control+Y on Windows). Make it 50 pixels wide by 300 pixels high, and name it "**Left to right/50**" (try to give everything a name that will make it easy to remember what it does).

You would normally set the color for a solid in this dialog; so for now, go ahead and select a nice blue, and click OK. In what should be a reflex action, press Command+U (Control+U) to set it to Best Quality.

3 Give solids a helpful name: The first solid will move left to right when animated, and is 50 pixels wide – hence the name **Left to right/50**.

You may have noted that we instructed you to make this solid taller than the composition. This is a bit of planning ahead: When you start to arrange objects in 3D space, quite often you will move some of them farther away from the virtual camera. This results in objects that previously filled the frame appearing smaller after the move. By starting out with solids taller than you may need, you reduce the chance they may be too small later.

STEP 4: Animate this solid from left to right by setting Position keyframes so that it moves from somewhere around the center of the comp at time 00:00 to the right side of the comp by 03:00. For beginners, here are the steps:

• To reveal Position in the Timeline window, select the layer and hit P; this reveals its animation stopwatch.

Go Home!

If you drag in a layer, or create a new solid, light, or null object, and it doesn't begin at 00:00 as you'd like, press Option+Home (Alt+Home) to move the selected layer(s) to start at the beginning of the comp.

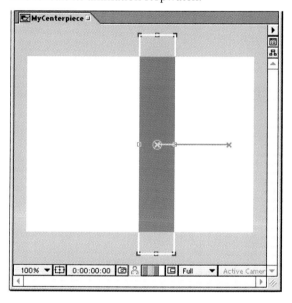 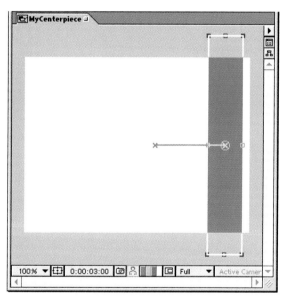

• Turn on the stopwatch for Position at time 00:00 to set the first keyframe, and make sure the solid is roughly in the center.

• Hit the End key to move to time 03:00, and drag the solid to the right side of the comp. Hold down Shift after you start dragging to move the solid in a straight line. Press Home to get back to time 00:00.

If you're curious, we personally chose the positions X184, Y120 at time 00:00 and X285, Y120 at time 03:00 – but the result is supposed to look somewhat random, so don't sweat the details quite yet.

If you'd like to check that you're on track so far, this first solid and its animation are saved in a prebuilt comp, **[Centerpiece_after Step 04]**, *which can be found inside the* **Piccadilly * prebuilt>_compare comps _after Step ##** *folder. And remember to save your project as you go…*

4 The first of six solids have been added and animated. The gray horizontal line in the Comp window shows the animation path. Hold down Shift after you start dragging to move the solid in a straight line, or scrub the Position X value in the Timeline.

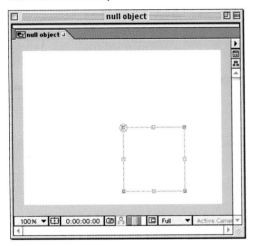

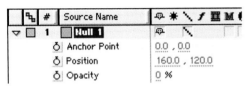

Null objects are 100×100 pixel solids set to 0% Opacity (so they don't actually render) with their Anchor Point defaulted to coordinates X0, Y0. Normally used in parenting chains, they also make great masters for expressions. Although a null doesn't render, it does have a width/height value, which affects how it appears in the Comp window. Open Layer> Solid Settings and you can set the size of the null's display box.

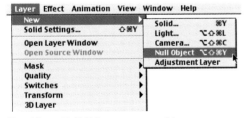

5 Adding a Null Object to a composition is no more difficult than adding a Solid or an Adjustment Layer.

A Null Swatch; A Master Color

There is an old saying: Measure twice, cut once. The same applies to building animations. Quite often it pays to sit back and think about what you are going to be doing, and if anything repetitive jumps out, to consider if there is a way to save some work before you actually do it.

In the case of this design, you will have six solids with the same color. Since clients are known to change their minds about details such as color, it would be nice if there was a way to change that color only once. Same goes if you decide to animate that color: Wouldn't it be great to animate only one set of color keyframes, instead of six?

A new feature, Expressions, was introduced in After Effects 5, and it's perfect for just these applications. In its simplest form, an expression is a way to have one parameter follow another. That way, you can change just one parameter, and have others slave along behind it.

Expressions can be applied to any parameter you can keyframe in the Timeline window. Note that the color of a solid is *not* a parameter that fits this description. However, there are several keyframeable effects that give you control over a layer's color. A good one for this job is the Fill effect.

Now that you know how you're going to make a solid's color your slave, the next question is, Who should be the master? You can designate one of the six solids to be the master and the rest slaves; we find it easier to keep track of an animation if the master is separate from one of the objects being animated. For this, we like to employ another feature introduced in After Effects 5: the Null Object.

A *null object* is essentially a small (100×100) solid that defaults to having an Opacity of 0%, so it does not render – even though you can still see its outline in the Comp window if its Video switch (the "eyeball") is turned on. Nulls are great tools for parenting chains, but they also make great masters for expressions.

Now that you've had a chance to think, instead of creating and animating five more solids first and figuring out how to coordinate their colors later, let's build a master color object and slave the color of our first solid to it. It will then be easy to duplicate this first solid, master color expression already in place, and save time creating the next five.

STEP 5: Select Layer>New>Null Object to create our master null. Make sure it starts at time 00:00 in your time-line. As a null does not render, it is not necessary to set it to Best Quality.

- While it's still selected, press Command+Shift+Y (Control+Shift+Y) and enter a new name, such as "**null/master color**".

- Since we don't need to see the null in the Comp window, go ahead and turn off its Video switch to hide its distracting outline.

STEP 6: Apply Effect>Render>**Fill** to your new **null/master color** layer. In the Effect Controls, click on the Color swatch and change its default red to a tasteful blue (on Mac, we used Hue 220, Saturation 70, Lightness 55, which should be RGB 60, 113, 221 on Windows).

This Color property will be the master color that the six solids will follow. Select **null/master color**, press E to reveal the effect in the Timeline window, then twirl down the effect to reveal the color swatch parameter in the Timeline – you will need to see it to assign an expression to it.

Expressing Color

STEP 7: Apply Effect>Render>**Fill** to the **Left to right/50** solid layer. Ignore its current red color; it will be overridden by the expression you are about to create. Press E for Effects and twirl down the Fill effect in the timeline.

*This is saved as prebuilt comp, [**Centerpiece_after Step 07**]. You can refer to it if you need to compare your progress so far.*

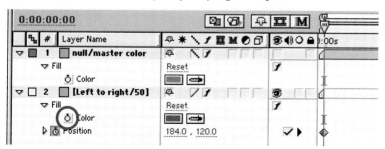

STEP 8: In the Timeline window, Option+click (Alt+click) on the *stopwatch* for the Color parameter in the Fill effect that was applied to the **Left to right/50** solid layer (see the stopwatch circled in the figure above). This adds a = symbol directly after the stopwatch and reveals the expression field. After Effects automatically fills the expression field with a default script, which we'll override by creating a new expression in our next step.

There are a number of ways to Add Expression to a property. You can also select the Color parameter in the timeline and choose Animation>Add Expression, or use the shortcut, Command+Option+= (Mac) or Control+Alt+= (Windows).

6 Apply the Fill effect to the **null/master color** layer, and change the Color from red to blue.

Sneaky Swatch

To reveal just the Color swatch in the Timeline, turn on its keyframing stopwatch in the Effect Controls window, press U to reveal keyframed properties in the Timeline, and turn keyframing back off by toggling the swatch's stopwatch again!

7–8 Both the master null and the first solid you created have the Fill effect applied. To Add an Expression to the solid Fill's Color property, Option+click (Alt+click) on the stopwatch for Color.

Express Yourself

Expressions are bits of software code, based on the JavaScript language, that create a value for whatever parameter you assign them to. These values are recalculated every keyframe, and are "live" – as you change another parameter the expression is looking at, the expression will automatically update the parameter it controls. If you aren't a programmer, don't worry: After Effects makes creating simple (but exceedingly useful) expressions very easy. If you *are* a programmer, you can really go to town!

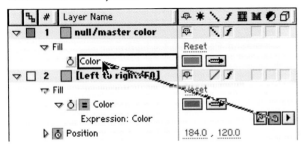

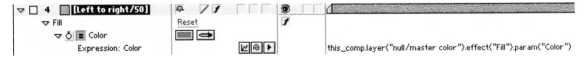

9 To create a simple expression, activate Expressions for the target parameter, and in the Timeline window drag its pick whip to the parameter that will be its master. After you release the mouse and press Enter, After Effects writes a corresponding Expression for you automatically.

EE for Expressions

To twirl down just Expressions, select layer(s) and type "EE" (two E's in quick succession). The über shortcut, U, will also twirl down Expressions since it's considered an animated track, but without the Expression text field displayed.

Swedish Swatch

On the enclosed CD we've included four dummy effects compliments of Trapcode (www.trapcode.com, makers of Shine). The "Swedish" set of plug-ins can be used as controllers for expressions. See the *Just an Expression* tutorial for more details.

STEP 9: Click on the Expression's pick whip (the center button that looks like a spiral symbol) and drag it to the word "Color" on the **null/master color** layer. This is a lot easier to do than to explain, so refer to the figure above. Release the mouse button, and press Enter (not Return) to activate the new expression.

After you press Enter, you will see that After Effects has written an expression for you. Without going into the depths of writing JavaScript, you can still read this expression and make sense of what is going on. One hint is to try reading it backward, using the periods as breaks in the phrasing. What the expression

> this_comp.layer("null/master color").effect("Fill").param("Color")

is really saying, is that the parameter Color, of the effect Fill, applied to the layer named **null/master color**, in this comp, now controls the Color parameter for the Fill effect on this layer.

To test that the expression is working, click on the Color swatch for the **null/master color** layer, and change the color to something quite different from blue. The color of the solid should also change, as its Fill Effect follows along. Be sure to Undo to return to that nice blue color…

If you got lost along the way, check out our prebuilt comp, [Centerpiece_after Step 09].

Three-up Solids

At this point you need to build up this centerpiece comp by duplicating the first animated solid layer and creating variations. Being that we're venturing into The Land of Repetitive Work here, if you're short on time you can be forgiven if you just read these steps, then use our prebuilt comp [Centerpiece_after Step 12] to continue with Part 2.

On the other hand, if you feel that Practice Is Good, then follow through with Steps 10 through 12 – though we'll leave some of the animation decisions up to you:

Step 10: Select the layer **Left to right/50** and duplicate it by selecting Edit>Duplicate. Press U to reveal the animated parameters for this duplicate. You'll notice that the expression was duplicated as well. Edit this copy as follows:

• Rename and resize the solid copy by selecting Layer> Solid Settings. We varied the width of each solid to be between 30 and 60 pixels wide. Rename the solid by changing the number at the end of its name to reflect the width you've chosen. For instance, if you change the width to 40 pixels, rename your duplicate solid "**Left to right/40**". Click OK.

• Edit the Position keyframes for the duplicate layer so that the solid starts somewhere left of center at 00:00, and ends up right of center at 03:00. Make sure the solids don't overlap at these keyframes; you're going for variety, and you want to cover a good deal of the comp with your solids rather than leave large white spaces.

• Repeat the Duplicating step again, set a different width and name for the third solid, and animate it so it starts on the far left at 00:00 and ends up left of center at 03:00.

• RAM Preview and check that the solids don't overlap and that all have slightly different speeds (otherwise they will look like a group of three solids moving in tandem).

Step 11: Set the Opacity property of each solid so they have a different value, somewhere between 25% and 60% (see figure below). This partial transparency will come in to play later as we overlap solids traveling in the other direction.

Save your project before moving onto the next step.

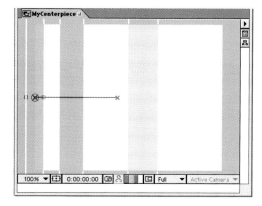

10–11 By duplicating the first solid, you can easily create two more; just edit their Position keyframes to vary their animation. Don't forget to also vary their widths and give each a different Opacity value. Here you see the third solid selected at time 00:00 (above) and at 03:00 (below).

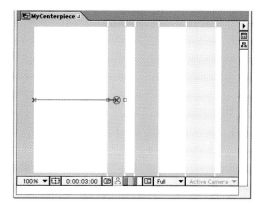

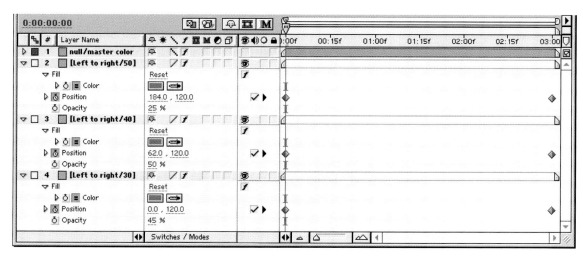

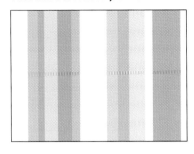

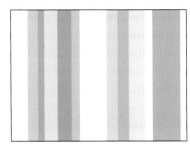

12 By now you should have six solids of varying widths and opacity, animating to cross over each other. To make the stripes appear a little darker when they overlap, change their transfer mode from Normal (top) to Multiply (above).

Six-up Solids

Step 12: You should now have three solids animating from left to right with different opacities. To create the next three, continue to duplicate one that's already built, but this time edit each so that:

• You have three solids that animate from *right to left*, spacing them apart in more or less a mirror image as you did the first three solids.

• Again, vary the width of the three new solids between 30 and 60 pixels wide, and rename the solids appropriately – i.e., "**Right to left/50**".

• Choose new Opacity values for each solid between 25% and 60%.

• Tweak all six solids so that you have a pleasing animated group, and RAM Preview to check that you end up with a group of solids with differing speeds, widths, and opacities.

• Simple opacity is often the least visually interesting way to blend together multiple objects. Get in the habit of trying out different transfer modes in search of more interesting looks. In this case, select all six solids and change the transfer mode for any one of them from Normal to Multiply; this will change all the modes at once. Multiply mode will make them appear even darker when they cross over each other.

You can change the transfer mode for a layer in a number of ways. The easiest is to select the Modes panel, then select a mode from the Modes popup. To open the Modes panel, click on the bottom of the Switches/Modes panel to toggle to Modes, or press F4 to toggle back and forth. To see the Switches and Modes panels side by side, context-click on any panel heading and select Modes from the Panels popup. Rearrange the panels by dragging the headers. Hide any Panel by selecting Hide This from the Panels popup when you context-click a panel heading.

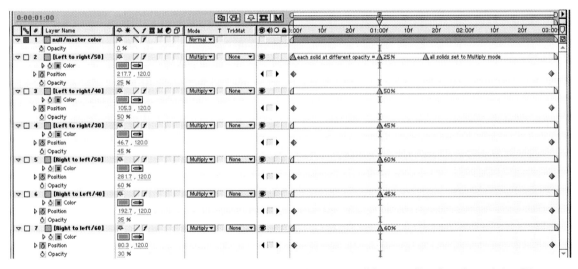

12 *complete:* Your Timeline window will now include seven layers: the master null for controlling the color, and six solids with animating Position, as well as Expressions applied to their Fill Color. Note that we've opened the Modes panel as well.

*Save your project and twirl up all layers in the Timeline window. If that all seemed a bit tedious, then you're probably glad we've prebuilt those last few steps for you! If you want to use our version, open the comp [**Centerpiece_after Step 12**] and rename it "MyCenterpiece12" in Composition>Composition Settings. In the Project window, drag this comp to the **My_Comps** folder and continue with Part 2.*

Part 2: Let There Be Light

After the previous step, you will have six solids animating: three from left to right, and three from right to left, all with different opacities and widths. They've all been set to Multiply mode, and the colors of all six solids are controlled by the **null/master color** layer. But let's be honest…it looks pretty flat, with not enough subtlety to really create interest. Let's liven things up by adding a light source so that shadows are falling all around.

Light Setup

STEP 13: In order for lights and shadows to work properly, you have to set up a number of items:

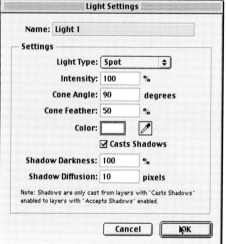

• Start by adding a Light. The procedure is simple: Click on the Layer menu or context-click in the Timeline window, and select New>Light. Use these Light settings (see figure): Spot, Intensity 100, Cone Angle 90, and Cone Feather 50. Make sure Casts Shadows is checked on and set the Shadow Darkness to 100% and Shadow Diffusion to 10. The Light Settings dialog also gives a tip at the bottom that's well worth noting as we'll see later: "Shadows are only cast from layers with 'Casts Shadows' enabled to layers with 'Accepts Shadows' enabled." Click OK, and make sure the layer has been set to start at time 00:00 – otherwise, the light will not switch on until it reaches the layer's starting point.

• Depending on whether you have added a light since you started up the program, and how you set an option, After Effects may warn you that some of your layers need to be in 3D for lights to have any effect. And it's right – so switch the six solids from being 2D layers

13 To add a light to a comp, select Layer>New>Light. Be sure you enable Casts Shadows, and heed the warning at the bottom of the dialog to set up the shadow options for your 3D layers. Once you've edited these settings, they'll be used the next time you make a new light.

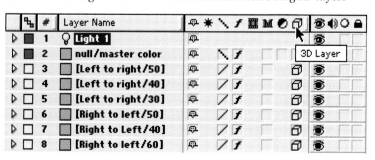

13 *continued:* To interact with cameras and lights, layers must be set to 3D mode – a simple switch in the Timeline window.

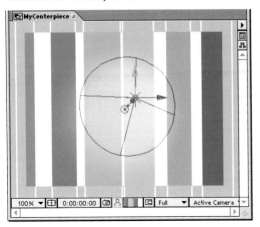

13 *complete:* The Material Options for a 3D layer decide how it interacts with Lights. Set Casts Shadows to On for all six solids in your project.

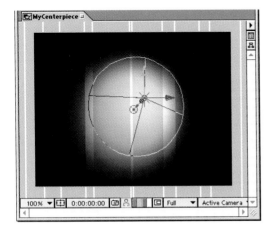

14 Once you've added a comp-sized white solid as a background layer and switched it to 3D mode, you can see the effect of the light on the entire comp.

13 *continued:* After you add a Light and switch the solids to 3D, you will notice their shading changes, as the cone of the spotlight falls off toward the edges of the comp.

(the default) to 3D layers. All this requires is toggling their 3D Layer switch to be On in the Timeline window. You can drag down a row of multiple switches to set them all in one swipe of the mouse.

Immediately, you will notice a difference in the way the layers are shaded in the Comp window. This is the result of how the light is interacting with them. But we still don't have our shadows…

• Select all six solids, and type "AA" (two As in quick succession) to twirl down their Material options. These options are available only for 3D layers. You'll notice that all the solids have Casts Shadows set to Off – this is the default. With all the solids still selected, click on any one of the words "Off" next to Casts Shadows, and all six layers will toggle to Casts Shadows = On. You can also use the shortcut for Toggle Casts Shadows: Option+Shift+C (Alt+Shift+C).

Hmm. Still not looking anything like our finished movie? That's because while the shadows are being cast, there's nothing to catch them. You're going to tackle this issue next, by placing another solid behind them in space. Twirl up all layers before moving on.

Cones and Feathers

If you look closely at the results so far, you might notice that the light has created some shading on the blue stripes, but not on the white background. Lights affect only 3D layers – not 2D layers or a comp's background color. To have the light affect the entire visible area of the comp, you'll need to create another solid to use as a backdrop. Once that's in place, it will be easier to adjust the light's characteristics to get the look you want.

STEP 14: Create another solid as you have above, but this time click on the Make Comp Size option, and change its Color to white. Name it "**white background**" and click OK. Drag this white solid to the bottom of the layers stack, set it to Best Quality, and turn on its 3D layer switch. Now you should notice the light's falloff shading the background as well. If nothing else, a spotlight is a nice way to add a vignette look to a comp.

If you are new to setting up lights and materials, compare your comp with [**Centerpiece_after Step 14**]. *As always, you can duplicate our comp and just continue from there.*

STEP 15: Nice effect, but the corners are probably quite dark if you used our initial settings. If you want the light to illuminate more of the comp, you can either change the light's position, or in the case of a spotlight, the size of its light cone and the way it falls off. Let's experiment with the latter approach:

• Select the light in the Timeline window and type AA (two As in quick succession) to reveal its Options.

• To see what Cone Feather does, scrub its value in the Timeline. Compare the result of values between 0% and 100%. Lights take a little while to render; be patient and pause on different settings to see their results. Leave this value set to 0% where the light edge is very hard for now – this will make it easier to see the results of Cone Angle adjustments.

• Scrub the Cone Angle value, and compare values from 0° (light contracts to nothing) to 150° (at which point the comp should be covered with light). Since your goal is to have the light cover the entire comp, with a nice falloff around the edges, set the Angle to somewhere around 135°, where the outer reaches of the cone just extend beyond the comp's edge.

• Now go back and tweak the Cone Feather to get a nice falloff that focuses attention back toward the center of the comp. We personally liked 65%.

Save your project before the next step.

15 *in progress:* The Cone Feather parameter adjusts how softly the light falls off from its outer reaches to its center. A Feather value of 0% (left) compared with 100% (right).

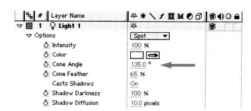

15 *complete:* By setting a slightly larger Cone Angle of 135°, (above) the center of the comp is lit more evenly (below). The Feather value is set to 65%. You can also enter these values directly in the Light Settings by double-clicking the light layer.

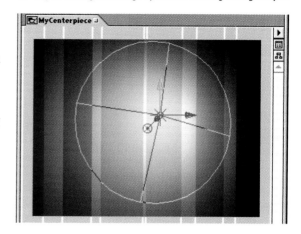

3D View Shortcuts

Press F10 to switch the Comp window to Top view, F11 for Custom View 1, and F12 for Active Camera. To choose your own views for these function keys, switch to a different view, and select View>Set 3D View Shortcut>Replace… For this tutorial, try changing the (F11) shortcut to the Right view, and use the function keys to quickly switch your view.

Shadow Depth and Darkness

Nice light falloff – but still no shadows. For shadows to be visible, you need to create some gaps in depth between the layers. These gaps from front to back create room for a shadow to be cast from one object onto another.

STEP 16: To get a true sense of depth, objects need to be different distances from the virtual camera. This means moving them to different positions along the Z axis, which defines closer/farther compared to X's left/right and Y's up/down.

By the way, where is this camera? When you create a comp, After Effects automatically creates a default camera. You can't see it in the Comp or Timeline windows, but it's there. In the event you're interested, it is based on a 35mm film camera with a 50mm lens and a field of view of 46.8°. It has automatically been positioned back in Z so that a layer the same size as the comp positioned at Z=0 perfectly fits what the camera sees; in the case of a 320×240 comp, this works out to a distance of Z value of –462.28 (the diagonal size of the comp × 1.1557). We hope you got all that, because there's a quiz later on…

So although you can create a camera with custom settings, since you're not going to be animating or otherwise editing the camera's settings for this tutorial, you might as well use the comp's default camera and keep things simple.

When you switched these layers from 2D to 3D mode, their Positions automatically added a Z parameter with a default value of zero. Negative values of Z will move the solids closer to you and the virtual camera; positive Z values move them farther away. A slight complication in this plan is that you already set up pairs of position animation keyframes for most of these solids, so you will need to edit the Z value for both keyframes to keep the solids at the same relative distance from the camera as they animate from side to side.

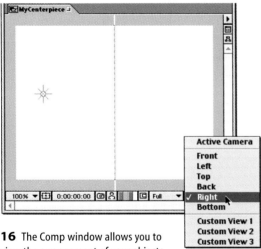

16 The Comp window allows you to view the arrangement of your objects several different ways. In the Right view, the solids default to the center, with the light and virtual camera off to the left.

The best way to approach creating these gaps is to change the Comp window's View popup from Active Camera to Right, via the popup at the bottom of the Comp window. Once you're in the Right view, you'll see the side view of the solids in the center of the Comp window, and the icon representing the light on the left side. In this view, positive Z values are toward the right; negative Z values (closer to the light and virtual camera) are to the left.

• Select all the animating solid layers, including the **white background** layer (but not the **null/master color** layer), and press P to view their Position values.

• Deselect all the layers (F2), and in the Timeline window click on the word Position for the first solid (which is probably **Left to right/50**) – this will select *both* of its Position keyframes.

• Press Home to return to 00:00 (if you're not already there), then *use the right arrow key* to nudge the layer's Position value in Z; as the value for Z increases, the layer moves right in the Right view, and thus farther away from the light. Double-check that both Position keyframes remain selected, indicating that both keyframes are being changed.

> When you're editing the value for Position, you can't simply scrub the value or change the value – this will change the value of Position only *at the current time*. If the time marker is parked on a keyframe, this will change just that keyframe, leaving the other keyframe unchanged (and deselected). If the time marker is between keyframes, you'll add a new keyframe at that point in time and deselect the existing keyframes. Using the arrow keys to nudge the layers in the Right or Left view is an easy way to move both keyframes in Z at the same time. Just be sure the time marker is parked on an existing keyframe, as nudging between keyframes will add a new keyframe.

Assume for now that later on your title layers will be placed somewhere around 0 on the Z axis. Therefore, you'll need some separation between the colored stripes and the background so they will cast shadows on each other. You'll also need a little separation between the title and these solid layers if the title is to cast shadows on them as well. So edit the Z values for the first solid to 20. Press End to move to 03:00, and double-check that the Z value for the second Position keyframe is also set to 20.

16 *continued:* 3D layers have an additional Z parameter for Position. Set the first solid to a Z position of 20. Make sure both Position keyframes get this Z value.

• Continue with the other five solids down the layer stack, setting their Z values to 55, 35, 80, 95, and 125 respectively. (These values aren't science – the idea is just to have some separation between layers. As long as the Z values range between 20 and 125, the tutorial will work as expected.) Before nudging, be sure to click on Position to select *both* keyframes for each layer and make sure that the time marker is parked at either 00:00 or 03:00.

16 *continued:* All of the solids have been arrayed varying distances from the light so that shadows will now be visible as they fall from the forward layers to the ones behind.

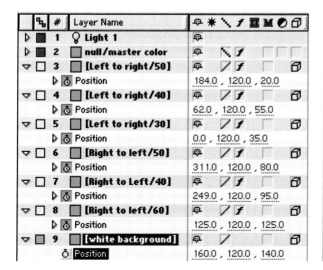

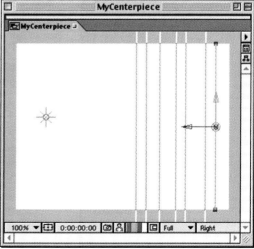

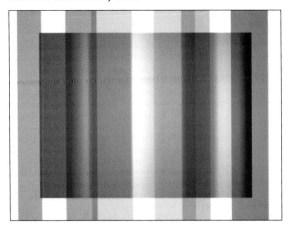

16 *complete:* Moving an object farther away from the camera makes it appear smaller. This is a problem in the case of your white background, which was supposed to fill the frame.

Nudging Nuances

Remember that nudging increments are based on screen pixels. Set the Comp window to 200% magnification to nudge in half pixels, or 50% to nudge two pixels at a time. Hold down Shift as you nudge with the arrow keys to move layers ten screen pixels at a time.

18 The background has been made larger, and the Shadow Darkness parameter backed off to a more subtle value of 25%.

• Set the white background solid to a Z distance around 140 so it is the farthest away from the light. This means it will catch the shadows for all of the animating solids in front of it.

Once the Z positions are set, press Home and End a couple of times and compare Position values – the Z values should be the same for the first and last keyframe for each solid. Only the X values, indicating left-to-right movement, should be changing, and the Y values should all remain at 120 (the center of the comp).

Select Active Camera again from the Comp window View popup; you'll notice that the shadows are finally starting to take shape. Move to different points in time to see how the solids and their shadows interact. There's just one small thing (isn't there always)…

Save your project. If you want to compare your progress, check out our prebuilt comp [**Centerpiece_after Step 16**].

STEP 17: Remember way back in Step 3, where we said it was a good idea to create 3D layers larger than you think you'll need them just in case you move them farther away from the camera? And remember we didn't do that in Step 14, when we created the background solid? That came back to bite us here. Now that you've moved the **white background** solid to 140 on the Z axis (away from you), the 320×240 solid is too small. (Look closely, and you'll notice one of the colored solids reaches just short of the top and bottom as well.) If you recall the final design we previewed at the start of this tutorial, this isn't so much of a problem vertically, since in the next tutorial you will mask it down to use just a center stripe for the final frame – but you still need the background solid to reach the left and right edges.

Select the **white background** layer, and open its Solid Settings using the keyboard shortcut Command+Shift+Y (Control+Shift+Y). When you eyeball the comp, you can guess that making this solid half again larger should more than do the trick; change its size to 480×360 pixels.

STEP 18: Shadows, by definition, create dark areas in the image. Twirl down the Light Options (or type AA) and scrub the value for Shadow Darkness. We think you'll agree that 100% darkness is a bit extreme; notice how lower values brighten up the image. Set it to about 25%. RAM Preview your comp, twirl up all layers, and Save your project.

Compare your comp with our prebuilt comp, [**Centerpiece_after Step 18**], *if your result doesn't seem to match the illustrations. Feel free to use this comp instead if you got lost along the way; just rename it "**MyCenterpiece18**" and drag it to the* **My_Comps** *folder.*

Part 3: Title Treatments

You've used a combination of lights, shadows, and transfer modes to create a nice animating background. Now it's time to put the main title on top, taking further advantage of some lighting tricks. If you've been opening the various prebuilt comparison comps as you go, it would be a good idea to clean up your screen at this point and close all of them except for your current [**MyCenterpiece**] comp.

Import and Center

STEP 19: The title for this episode of our travel series is "Piccadilly Circus." Select the **My_Sources** folder in the Project window and File>Import>File the Illustrator file **PC_Title.ai** residing inside the folder 06-PiccadillyCircus> Project>**Sources**. Be sure to set the Import As popup near the bottom of this dialog to Composition, and click Import.

When it's imported, you will have both a folder and a comp called **PC_Title.ai.** Double-click the comp to open it. The title consists of two layers of black type against a black background color (so they won't be visible), and a guide layer (which you can ignore). Select the two type layers in the Timeline – **Piccadilly** and **Circus** – and Copy them.

• Bring your [**MyCenterpiece**] comp forward, Paste, and the two title layers will be pasted on top. Notice that these layers are a different size than this comp, as they were created at a size of 400×130 pixels in Illustrator. This size difference also caused them to come in off-center.

• You'll want to center the type in your composition as a starting point for performing your animation. With both layers still selected, press P and twirl down Position. Click on one of the values and enter X160, Y120 (the center of a 320×240 comp).

To find the center of a non-standard-sized comp, you don't need a calculator. Context+click on the value for Position and select the Edit Value option to open the Position dialog. Set the Units popup to "% of composition," type 50 in the X-axis field and 50 in the Y-axis field. Click OK and the layers will appear exactly in the center of the comp.

To change multiple layers at once, click on the word Position in the Timeline window, then Shift+click to select all other Position properties – merely selecting multiple layers isn't enough. Even though all Position keyframes are now selected, only the values at the current time are changed when you context+click and select the Edit Values option.

For single layers, you can open the Position dialog by using the shortcut Command+Shift+P (Control+Shift+P).

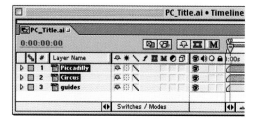

19 Open the 400×130 sized [**PC_Title.ai**] comp (above) and Copy the two titles layers. Bring the [**MyCenterpiece**] comp forward (below) and Paste . The titles paste in off-center because they retain their original Position values based on the 400×130 comp.

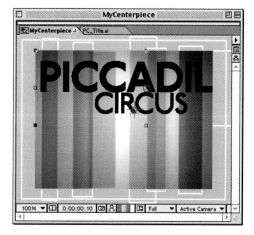

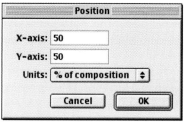

19 *continued:* To center the title, let After Effects do the math for you by using the "% of composition" option in the Position value dialog.

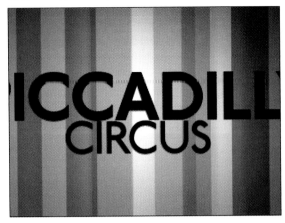

19 *complete:* The font used is Johnston's London Underground, from the foundry P22 (www.p22.com). It is based on Edward Johnston's original typeface design created for London Transport in 1916, which also became the model for the very popular sans-serif typeface Gill Sans.

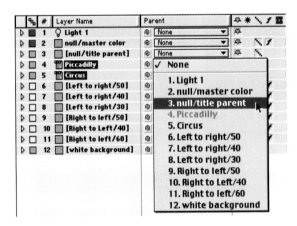

20 Assign a new parent for the Piccadilly and Circus type layers. This will make scaling and positioning them easier, without losing the ability to animate them independently.

• Drag the title layers down the layer stack so they are above the six solid layers and below the **null/master color** layer; this is mainly to help us keep organized.

• Turn on Best Quality so that the title layers are antialiased.

Control through Parenting and Expressions

Step 20: The title's too big for the frame; you're going to need to scale it down and tweak its position. You'll also be animating both words in the title separately from each other. A convenient yet flexible way to coordinate these actions is to group the two words together using a null object as a parent. Each word can then animate individually, while being scaled and positioned by its parent.

• As you did in Step 5, create a new Layer>New> Null Object. Rename it to "**null/title parent**" – Command+Shift+Y (Control+Shift+Y) will open Solid Settings. Turn off the Video switch for this null, to remove its distracting box from the Comp window.

• Again, to help keep things organized, drag this new null object down the layer stack so it sits above the two title layers.

• If the Parent column is not visible in the Timeline, use the shortcut Shift+F4 to reveal it, or context+ click on another panel and select Panels>Parent. Select both the **Piccadilly** and **Circus** layers, and set their parent to be **null/title parent**.

• Select the **null/title parent** layer. Press S to reveal its Scale property in the Timeline. Edit its Scale value to 90%, which will scale both title layers from their combined center.

If you feel your parenting skills are shaky, compare your work with [**Centerpiece_after Step 20**].

Step 21: The title is going to get the same color expression treatment you gave the background stripes in Steps 7 through 9:

• Apply Effect>Render>Fill effect to both title layers, leaving the settings at their defaults.

- Apply an expression to the Color parameter of these Fill effects so they also follow the Color swatch for the effect applied to the **null/master color** layer; refer back to Step 8 if you need a refresher.

- Select both title layers and change their transfer mode to Multiply (again, just as you did with the solids in Step 12). If you don't want to open the Modes panel, you can also select Multiply from Layer> Transfer Modes, or by context+clicking on the layer bar and selecting Multiply from the Transfer Modes in the popup menu.

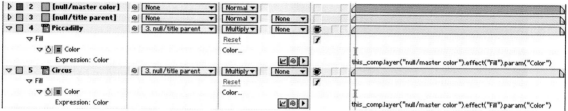

Reacting to Light

The title appears to be a different color blue from the solids because they are still 2D layers. By switching them to 3D layers, they will then interact with the comp's light, resulting in a more interesting look. But you can go even further than that, manipulating the shadows cast by the title and how the title reacts to the light hitting it.

STEP 22: Turn on the 3D Layer switch for both title layers. They will now react to the light. If you toggled the Switches/Modes panel to Modes to set their transfer mode above, you'll need to toggle back (shortcut: F4) to see the 3D Layer switch.

With both title layers selected, press Option+Shift+C (Alt+Shift+C) to change Casts Shadows to On. If you want to check that this worked, type AA to reveal the Material Options and the Casts Shadows setting.

21 Give the title the same treatment you gave the colored stripes: apply the Fill effect, use the pick whip to create expressions that slave the title's color off of the **null/master color** layer, and set them to use Multiply transfer mode so you get varying shades of blue as the title interacts with the background.

22 Toggling the 3D switch on for the title layers makes them interact with the light (left); change their Material Options to Casts Shadows (right).

Shadow Size

Whether the shadow is larger or smaller than the layers that cast it depends on how far away the light is from a layer compared with how far away the camera is. If the light is farther away than the camera, the shadows are smaller than the layer; if the light is closer, the shadows are larger.

STEP 23: The shadows for the title should now be visible. However, our starting point for the light set a Shadow Diffusion value of 10, which creates very soft shadows in this case. Here's how to adjust it:

• Select the **Light 1** layer, type AA to reveal its Options, and change its Shadow Diffusion parameter to 5. The shadows should now appear better defined.

The most visible portion of the shadow is being captured by the **white background** layer. Since the six blue stripes are transparent, the shadow is much less apparent on them. If you look closely, you can see broken-up echoes of the title's shadow on these stripes, which adds further visual interest – but the eye is definitely drawn to the main shadow on the background first.

To our eye, the shadow falling from the **Circus** layer is a bit large, to the point of distracting us from the first title layer **Piccadilly**. Closer spacings between layers results in shadows that are closer in size to the object casting them. To tighten the shadow just for the word Circus, you will need to move it closer to the background.

23 To make the shadows more defined, reduce their Shadow Diffusion setting (left). To make a shadow closer to the size of the layer casting it, move that layer closer to the layer catching it (right).

• Select the **Circus** layer and type P for Position. To achieve a better visual balance in the frame, select a Z value that places it somewhere between the **Piccadilly** layer and white background layers. We happened to choose a value of 30, but please experiment for yourself. Note that as you place it farther back, it will start to move behind some of the blue stripes. Due to a combination of their transparency and transfer mode settings, this is not as obvious as you might expect, but don't push your luck. When in doubt, check it at several different points in time as the stripes move about.

STEP 24: To finish up the look of the title, you can experiment a bit with the Material Options for each word (shortcut: AA). The Material Options affect the way a layer reacts to the light hitting it. By choosing different settings, you can get different looks out of layers that otherwise share the same light, without having to apply effects.

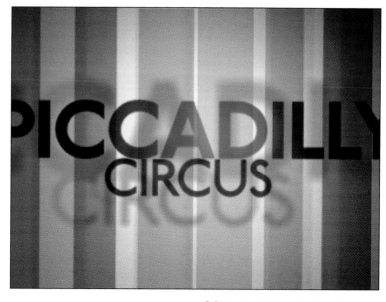

• The Diffuse and Specular settings determine how a light glares off a surface. To give the **Piccadilly** layer more punch, try higher values for either one of these parameters. In the end, we cranked Diffuse up to 100 and decreased Specular to 25, but feel free to set these to taste.

Note that higher Shininess values don't make an object shine more brightly; they tighten up the size of the glare.

• Rather than punch up the **Circus** layer as well, we want to make it recede more into the background. This can be done by reducing its Diffuse value, making it reflect less light back to the eye. We ended up with a value of 25 (see figure below of Timeline). Twirl up all layers and Save your project.

24 The Material Options for a layer define how it is illuminated by lights. By manipulating these, you can increase the glare on the word Piccadilly to make it punch forward more, and reduce the illumination on Circus to make it darker, without changing either layer's color.

We left some of those recent steps a little sketchy, since they repeated actions made earlier in this tutorial. If we lost you along the way, compare your result with our prebuilt comp [**Centerpiece_after Step 24**].

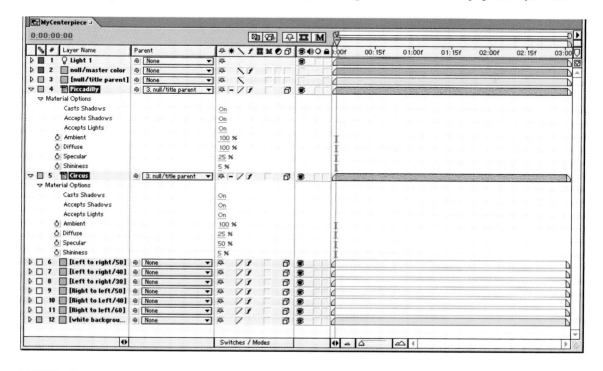

To make After Effects more responsive while working with 3D layers, you can turn on Draft 3D in the Timeline window (above). This will temporarily disable lights and shadows (below).

25 Piccadilly moves from right to left and is shown here at time 00:00 (below left) and 03:00 (below right). Title Safe guides (shortcut is ' – the apostrophe key) are turned on to help with placement.

Part 4: Animating the Title

Nice lighting – but the title just sits there. Now it's time for you to make it move. Working in 3D while lights and shadows are turned on is very slow, so turn on the Draft 3D switch for the next step to temporarily disable all lights and shadows. You temporarily won't have as rich a look, but scrubbing parameters and RAM Previewing your animation will be significantly faster in Draft 3D.

> Why not just turn off the Light's Video switch in order to work or preview faster? If you do, you will have to remember to turn it back on before you render. Draft 3D doesn't affect final rendering: Your lights and shadows will always render no matter how this switch is set, provided you render in Best Quality.

STEP 25: Select the **Piccadilly** layer and animate it from right to left:

• Return the time marker to 00:00 (shortcut: Home), select **Piccadilly**, and type P to reveal its Position property (if it's not already revealed). Remember to scrub just the X values; press Shift while scrubbing to move in larger increments or Command (Control) for finer increments.

• Move it along the X axis so the first character is well right of the left edge of the comp, and the last couple of characters are cut off by the right side of the comp. We liked somewhere around X = 60. Turn on the animation stopwatch to enable keyframing; this also sets the first keyframe to remember the current position.

• Press End to go to time 03:00 and move the **Piccadilly** layer left along the X axis until the last character nicely clears the right edge of the comp. We settled on an X value of –36; this meant the Position property in the Timeline window read –36,0,0.

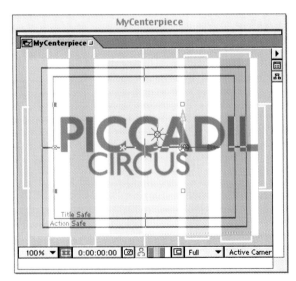

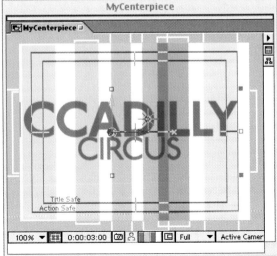

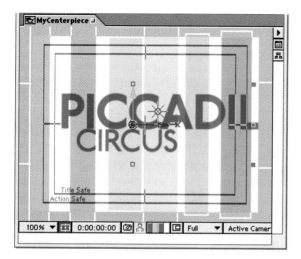
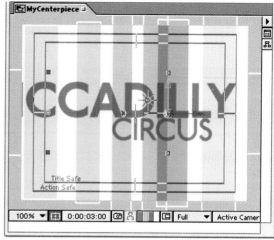

STEP 26: Now animate the **Circus** layer in the opposite direction:

• Reveal the Position property for **Circus**, and at time 00:00 move the layer left until its first character is just a bit to the right of the first character in the word Piccadilly. Its position should read something close to –20,0,30. Enable keyframing for the Position property.

• Move to time 03:00, and adjust the X value until the last character in Circus is just left of the last character in the word Piccadilly – somewhere around 55 should do. Don't just type in our values; use the scrubber in the Timeline window to get a feel for the faster screen update in Draft 3D mode.

RAM Preview and check the animation to see if you like the move. If you get lost, compare your version to our prebuilt comp [**Centerpiece_after Step 26**].

STEP 27: You'll eventually be taking just a center horizontal slice of this animation to use in the next tutorial. But after playing around with the positions of the words in the title, you can't be sure they're still centered vertically in the comp. Let's check that, and reposition it as necessary. Stay in Draft 3D mode during this step to speed things up:

• Look closely at the Comp window to see if the title seems vertically centered to you. For confirmation, either press the ' (apostrophe) key to turn on the Safe Areas overlay to get a center crosshair, or select View>Show Grid to overlay a virtual graph.

Since you've already set up animation keyframes for the words in the title, it would be a minor pain to

26 The Circus layer moves from left to right and is shown here at time 00:00 (top) and 03:00 (bottom).

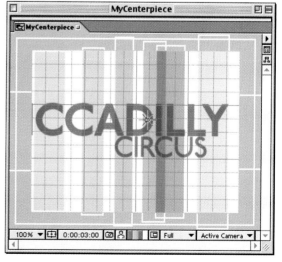

27 Turn on the safe area overlays or the grid (pictured here) to verify that the title isn't quite centered horizontally.

145

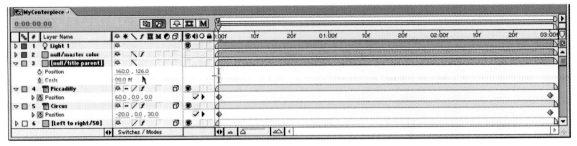

27 *complete:* By adjusting the Y Position value for the **null/title parent** layer, both title layers can be easily moved up and down in the comp – without affecting their individual left to right animations.

re-edit all of just them to recenter the title. So don't, and use the parent you set up earlier instead:

• Select the layer **null/title parent**, twirl down Position, and edit its Y Position value by scrubbing its value. Go for a better vertical position, remembering that the smaller layer **Circus** will take up less "weight" in the overall visual balance. By editing the parent layer in this way, you can move the entire title without messing up the keyframes already assigned to the children. Set the Y Position to about 126 (the Position of the null should now read X160,Y126).

> Note that the parent is a 2D layer, but the children are 3D layers. If you want to move the children as a group in Z, you would need to also turn on the 3D Layer switch for the parent null object. Since you are only moving layers in Y here, you can leave the parent in 2D.

The next steps involve tweaking the colors and animating the light, so turn off the Draft 3D switch so you can see the light's effect. Also turn off any guides or grids (View>Hide Grid) and Save your project.

Adjustment Layers vs. Expressions

You may be wondering why we didn't use an Adjustment Layer to set or animate the color of the layers below, rather than drag you down the path of using Expressions. Part of it is we wanted to give you some practice using Expressions. But there are a few advantages to the master color swatch concept described in this tutorial compared with Adjustment Layers, which may not be immediately obvious:

• The obvious one first: Adjustment Layers affect all layers below, which might

not be desirable if you want only certain layers to be effected. For instance, if you used an Adjustment Layer to change or animate the color of the bars, any background layers would change color as well.

• The master color swatch can be "expressed" to other layers in any comp, so you could control colors across multiple comps with just one swatch.

• A master color swatch that resides in, say, the Fill effect as in this tutorial, could be controlling a color swatch in any other effect,

such as the stroke color in the Stroke effect, or one of the replacement colors in a Tint effect.

• Adjustment layers are always 2D layers, and perform as "render breaks" in a 3D animation stack. This means that if you use an adjustment layer to apply an effect to the 3D layers below, these layers are rendered as a "group," and the result is a 2D composite. You cannot then have other 3D layers above the Adjustment Layer casting shadows or otherwise interacting with those layers below.

Part 5: Animating the Master Color

The advantage of setting up a master color as you did earlier is that it's easy to animate all the slaved layers at once. Let's take advantage of that:

STEP 28: Select the **null/master color** layer, and press F3 to open the Effect Controls window. With the time marker at 00:00, turn on the animation stopwatch for Color – this sets a keyframe for the original blue color at the start of the animation. Hit End to go to 03:00, and click on the color swatch to change the blue to a nice purple color.

> When you animate colors, After Effects interpolates between those colors by traveling in a straight line between them on the HLS color wheel. If you travel across the wheel in a way that brings you near the center (by using complementary colors), your intermediate colors will be grayish. A workaround is to add additional keyframes inbetween to guide it through more saturated colors.

Perform a RAM preview or test render. Note how all the colors change together, even though you had to set up only one pair of keyframes. Thus is the joy of using expressions to create master control layers! This will come in even handier if you have clients who are prone to change their minds about things like color. In our theoretical example of creating a series of graphics for a multipart travel show, you could also use this master to change colors for different segments.

Save your project and RAM Preview and check the animation to see if you like the move. If you got lost, compare your version with our prebuilt comp [**Centerpiece_after Step 28**].

STEP 28 OPTIONAL: Just because a master color is controlling your layers doesn't mean you can't introduce some variation in those slaves. For instance, you could add Effect>Adjust>**Hue/Saturation** effect to the **Circus** title layer and change the Hue to +25. Now when you change the master color, the **Circus** layer will follow as before, but always with a Hue offset by 25°. You can also write more complex expressions to do these offsets for you, but quite often it might be quicker and easier to just use a familiar effect.

28 By using expressions to create a master swatch, the color of eight layers can be animated together using two keyframes. Here you see the color at the beginning, middle, and end.

Color Theory

Color Theory from Toolfarm uses different formulas based on the traditional artists RYB color wheel so you can create color combinations easily . You can also import images with alpha channels (such as a logo) so you can see your color scheme in context.

You can then eyedropper the final color palette to CT Color Swatch (an effect consisting of just swatches), and use these as your master colors for Expressions. You can get more info on the accompanying CD in the **Free Plug-ins** folder or download a demo from www.toolfarm.com.

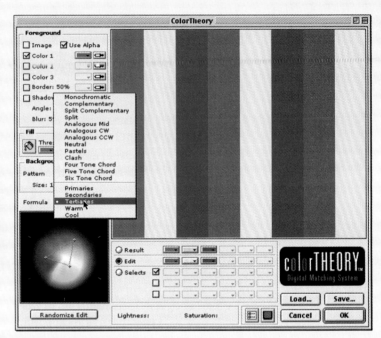

Part 6: Animating the Light

We've kept this tutorial fairly straightforward so far, with just a single light and the default camera. But you'll also notice a recurring theme of adding touches that create subtle visual interest. To further this aim we're going to animate the light, which will affect how shadows fall over time. This final effect is also much more "to taste" than some of the animation we led you through above, so we're going to discuss your options as much as tell you what to do.

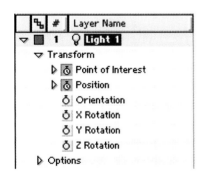

29 Lights have two steering wheels: the Position of the light in space, and the Point of Interest where the light is aimed. Turn on both stopwatches to animate the light for this tutorial.

Step 29: Be sure Draft 3D is off so you can see the effect of the light. At time 00:00, twirl down the **Light** layer in the Timeline window, then twirl down Transform. Turn on the stopwatch for *both* the Light's Point of Interest and Position properties.

> Unlike normal layers, lights and cameras have two "position" properties: one for where they are located in space, and a second Point of Interest for where they are aimed. It is true that you could achieve the same results with just one position property, then rotate the object to aim it where you want, but many find it easier to control cameras and lights with this two-position system. (Another technique is to attach a camera or light to a null object, then rotate the null – more on this in the *Postcards from Earth* tutorial).

Your goal is to set the first keyframe with the light highlighting the left side of the comp. You can do this by re-aiming its Point of Interest or its Position. Note that the relationship between the two decides

29, *at time 00:00:*
By animating the light, the areas that are lit and the resulting shadows will play across the title. Switch between Top View, Right View, and Active Camera to set up the light in 3D space. We start off pointing the light to the left side.

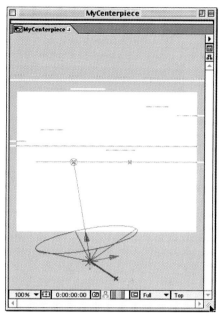

what direction the shadows will be cast. For example, if you moved the Point of Interest left and Position right, the shadows would be cast more to the left as the light raked across the title. If you were to move both the Point of Interest and Position of the light to the left, then the shadows directly under the light will be cast somewhat straight, while shadows farther away appear a bit more rakish.

If you're new to moving a light, check out the *Moving Lights 101* sidebar on the next page for some tips.

When you're happy with your look at the start of the comp (and verified that you remembered to enable keyframing), press End to move to 03:00, and move the Position and Point of Interest again so that the spotlight highlights the right side of the comp – in other words, so it scans across the word Piccadilly while it moves in the opposite direction.

The direction the light points as a result of the relationship between its Position and Point of Interest also affects whether the shadows are cast up or down the back wall you created with the layer **white background**. Moving the Position of the light closer to the title will also make the shadows grow in size, while moving it back will make them smaller. Feel free to experiment!

Save the project. To compare your results, open our prebuilt comp, [**Centerpiece**], *from the* **Piccadilly * prebuilt>Final Comp** *folder If you prefer our version, feel free to use it for rendering in the next step.*

29, *at time 03:00:*
The light has moved to point more to the right side of the comp, and also pulls farther away; this tightens the shadows closer to the title. Experiment until you find a move you like.

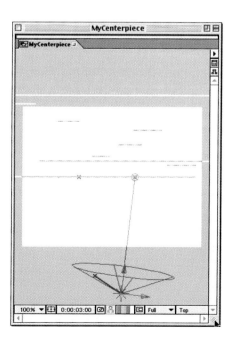

Moving Lights 101

There are a number of ways to move a light around in After Effects, which you should explore if you're new to using lights:

• Scrub the values in the timeline or enter values directly. Hold Shift down while scrubbing for larger increments; hold Command (Control) for finer increments.

• Drag the light directly in the Comp window while it's set to Active Camera view. If you avoid the three X/Y/Z axis arrows, you can move the light freely. If you drag one of the X, Y, or Z axis arrows (your mouse cursor will change to show you if you've

grabbed a particular axis), this will move both the light *and* the point of interest. However, you *can* move the light along a particular axis and *not* move the point of interest by holding down Command (Control) while you drag.

• If you make a mess, click Reset at the top of the Light's Transform section. This only resets the Transform values; it does not affect the light's options you've already set.

• Change the Comp window's view to Left or Top to get a better idea of how the light is pointing, and try moving the light or point of interest in those views. (Same rules apply regarding moving along the axes.) Return to Active Camera view to check your results.

Hold down Command (Control) as you move on one axis to move the Position without moving the Point of Interest.

The following tips for moving the light apply to moving any layer, but are particularly useful when you're moving layers in 3D when lights and shadows are slowing things down too much:

• Hold down Option (Alt) as you move the light to temporarily disable realtime updating in the Comp window.

• Turning on Wireframe Interactions (the switch directly to the left of the Draft 3D switch) will serve the same function as holding Option (Alt) by disabling realtime updating in the Comp window. When this switch is enabled, press Option (Alt) to regain realtime updating.

Part 7: Creating a Comp Proxy

This composition you've created will serve as a centerpiece inside a second composition for the finished design. You will build the rest of the project in the next tutorial. However, there's some final work you can do here that will make your life easier when you move on.

You may have noticed that your comp has been getting more sluggish as you add more layers, turn on shadows, and so on. This is because 3D in general and shadows in particular take longer to render than otherwise similar 2D compositions. You really don't want this render hit to be dragging you down as you try to work on other elements – especially since you've already finished this piece.

Therefore, it's a good idea to prerender this centerpiece comp so that the relatively slow 3D shadows don't try your patience later. In the next tutorial, rather than use your rendered movie directly, you will link in this movie as a Comp Proxy – that way, you can still go back and tweak this composition later if you feel the final design requires changes.

Proxies are footage items that act as stand-ins for other footage items or entire compositions. Most users employ them to temporarily link in draft or low-resolution versions of large footage items to speed up their work. However, they're a great tool when you are nesting a finished comp so that it becomes a source layer in another comp. You would render the first comp, link the render as a proxy for the comp, and now you don't have to wait for the first comp to render as you move around the second comp. Proxies are easy to turn off or remove, if you later decide to go back and edit the original first comp. Applying and working with comp proxies is covered in the next tutorial, *Underground Movement.*

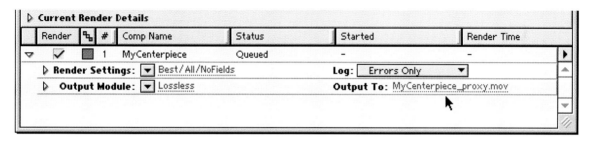

STEP 30: With your fully tweaked-out **MyCenterpiece** comp open, select Composition>Make Movie. Save the movie to this tutorial's folder on your hard drive, and name it "**MyCenterpiece_proxy.mov**".

• In the Render Queue, use the "Best" Render Settings template or similar (Best Quality, Full Resolution, No Fields).

• In the Output Module, use the Lossless template (you don't want to degrade the quality of a Comp Proxy movie by compressing it, since you will be using it in the final render).

• Save your project, and hit the Render button. Now go make a really nice cup of tea (you deserve it), as this comp will take a few minutes to render. If you like, play back your finished movie when the render is done so you can enjoy all the work you've put in throughout these pages.

To Be Continued...

Once you've given your brain and fingers a rest, move on to the next tutorial: *Underground Movement.* You'll finish off the title animation using tricks such as sequencing words created in Illustrator to create multiple layers of type, and turning a tileable graphic into a seamless "tickertape" that animates across the frame...

30 Render your final **Centerpiece** comp and you can use it as a Comp Proxy in the next tutorial, *Underground Movement.*

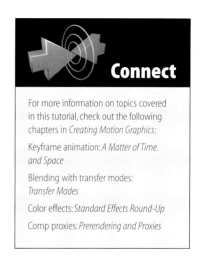

For more information on topics covered in this tutorial, check out the following chapters in *Creating Motion Graphics*:

Keyframe animation: *A Matter of Time and Space*

Blending with transfer modes: *Transfer Modes*

Color effects: *Standard Effects Round-Up*

Comp proxies: *Prerendering and Proxies*

Underground Movement

Using Comp Proxies to save time while maintaining flexibility.

Using precomps to hold complex portions of a final animation is a good way to manage your After Effects projects. However, those precomps might take a considerable amount of time to render every time you go to a new frame of your final composition. Some users will render these precomps and swap the resulting movies into their final comp. However, there's a smarter way to manage these intermediate renders: Comp Proxies.

Since the concept of comp proxies can be used in a wide variety of projects, we're going to take these pages to show how to apply and render with them. As a bonus, these steps are the starting point in finishing off the *Piccadilly Circus* animation you started in the previous tutorial.

OVERVIEW

Main Concepts:

These are the features and concepts we will be focusing on in this project:

- Using Comp Proxies
- Masking
- Importing Sequences
- Footage Frame Rates
- Looping in Time and Space
- Continuous Rasterization
- Timing to music
- Adjustment Layers
- The Offset effect

Requirements:

After Effects 4.1 or later standard version.

Getting Started:

Inside the **Tutorials** master folder on the accompanying CD, locate and copy the folder **07_Underground** to your hard drive.

In the folder **Final Movie** inside this folder, double-click on and play the movie **Underground.mov**. This is the final piece you will create in the PDF portion of this tutorial. Inside the **Project** folder you'll find the finished After Effects project file. Depending on the version of After Effects you are using (4.1 versus 5.0 or later), open the project **Underground_4.aep** or **Underground_5.aep** – this is your starting point; we suggest you save under a new name after each major section.

If you have After Effects 5.0 or later, we suggest you complete the *Piccadilly Circus* tutorial in the prior chapter first – it creates the centerpiece that appears in this project. You can start this tutorial with your finished project and composition from the prior tutorial, if you wish. But don't worry; we have also included instructions for jumping straight into this tutorial, and for those who are using After Effects 4.1.

The Tasks

This is what you will be doing in the various parts of this tutorial:

PART 1: Apply a comp proxy to save previewing time when a slow-to-render precomp is nested in a final comp. A sidebar includes tips for managing and rendering comp proxies.

The Set Proxy>File option is under the File menu.

PART 2: A quick overview of the final *Underground* project you can create by following the step-by-step bonus tutorial in the PDF file, **07B_Underground_Bonus.pdf**.

Part 1: Voting by Proxy

The title animation *Piccadilly Circus* was executed in 3D, using a light and shadows. These features slow down the responsiveness of the comp considerably. When you nest this 3D comp in a second comp to add the 2D elements, After Effects will have to render the 3D precomp every time you jump to a new frame of the final comp. To avoid this wait, you will attach an already rendered movie of the Piccadilly Circus title animation as a comp proxy. After Effects will then just grab frames from this finished movie as needed, which significantly speeds up the response in the second comp.

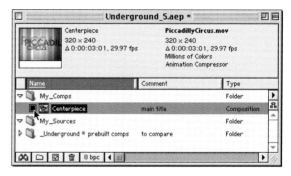

1 When a proxy has been assigned to a comp, specifications for both appear at the top of the Project window.

STEP 1: In the Project window, select and double-click the comp [**Centerpiece**]. Jump to different points in time; you will note it previews rather slowly. Bring the Project window back forward, and with [**Centerpiece**] still selected choose the menu item File>Set Proxy>File. When the Set Proxy File dialog appears, locate and select either the movie you rendered as the last step in the previous tutorial, or the file **PiccadillyCircus.mov** in the **07_Underground> Project>Proxies** folder. Click Import (Mac) or Open (Windows) to assign the proxy.

Once a comp proxy has been applied, you'll notice along the top of the Project window that the comp proxy movie's specifications appear to the right of the comp's own (you may need to open the window wider to see this). A square will also appear to the left of the comp's name. When this square is filled, the proxy is in use. Clicking on this box switches it to a blank box and turns off the proxy, but does not remove it.

1 *complete:* The Comp window looks the same with the proxy applied, but when you preview, the frames displayed are from the movie on disk. Be aware there is no indication in the Comp window that you are viewing a proxy, so if you edit any layers, the Comp window won't reflect those changes!

Comp Proxy Tips

Using comp proxies involves a certain amount of awareness. For instance, if you view a comp when a comp proxy is in use, the image you see in the Comp window is that of the prerendered movie – not the live composition. This is the whole point: Rather than render the layers that make up a comp, the proxy is used instead. Be warned, however – there is no indication in the Comp window (at least as of 5.0) that you are viewing a proxy rather than the real thing! If you later decide that a layer inside this comp needs editing, you could be making all sorts of blind changes – and wondering why on earth the Comp window doesn't reflect this… To avoid confusion, consider changing the name of a comp when it has a proxy assigned to it, or perhaps lock all of its layers – anything that reminds you that this comp is prerendered and is now displaying a proxy. Here are some additional tips on managing comp proxies:

• Render proxies using Best Quality, and save them in the best file format available, such as uncompressed. This will preserve maximum image quality, since you will potentially be re-compressing the proxy footage at the final render stage. If the comp you're rendering needs to have an alpha channel, be sure to render to a file format that supports alpha (such as QuickTime Animation, Millions of Colors+).

• Whether it's best to field render a proxy depends on your final output, and how the proxy is being used. If you are not field rendering the final movie, don't bother field rendering the proxy. If you *are* field rendering, and if the proxy will appear full-frame in the final image, then field render the proxy. When you assign an interlaced comp proxy, separate the fields of the proxy (via File>Interpret Footage>Proxy) just as you would treat any other interlaced movie source. If you're field rendering the final, but you won't be using the proxy full-frame, you will achieve the highest quality by rendering the proxy without fields, at twice the frame rate. This way, a full frame will be processed for each field of output.

• Another advantage proxies have over swapping in movies for precomp layers, is that when you archive your finished project, you can throw away these proxies: They tend to be large uncompressed movies, and you still have the underlying composition to edit or re-render if you ever need to open the project later. You can either remove the proxies from the After Effects project file before you archive, or after you re-open it and note they are missing. Either way, the project hierarchy remains intact.

• If you decide that a composition to which you have a proxy assigned needs additional changes, don't just turn off the proxy; if the prerendered comp proxy is no longer valid – *delete it*! Otherwise, you run the risk of using this now-outdated proxy when you perform your final render. To remove a proxy, select the comp in the Project window again, and use File>Set Proxy>None.

Rendering a Proxy

When it's time to render your final animation, pay attention to the Render Settings to ensure the **Centerpiece_proxy.mov** is used in place of the much slower **[Centerpiece]** composition. You need to set the Proxy Use popup to Use Comp Proxies Only. If the Proxy Use popup is set to Current Settings, this means proxies are used only if they are switched on in the Project window. That leaves your final render open to chance, as you might have accidentally switched it off. The Use Comp Proxies Only setting also ensures that any proxies assigned to footage items (which are usually low-resolution temporary files not intended for the final render) will be ignored – Current Settings doesn't assure you of that.

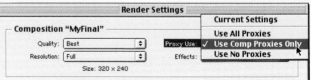

Set the Proxy Use popup in the Render Settings dialog to Use Comp Proxies, or Use All Proxies, to ensure the prerendered movie will be used in place of the precomp.

Part 2: Underground Overview

In this tutorial's **07_Underground** folder is a PDF file – **07B_Underground_Bonus.pdf** – that will lead you through using the Piccadilly Circus element as the centerpiece in a brief "chapter head" for a mythical travel show based around London's Underground. This bonus tutorial is relatively easy to execute, but includes several useful concepts such as Continuous Rasterization of Illustrator files and different tricks to loop elements. It's written for both 4.1 and 5.0 users. Highlights include:

• The Piccadilly Circus title will be masked down to occupy just the center of the final frame. If you have After Effects 5.0, this will provide a chance to use its new features which allows you to mask directly in the Composition window.

• We've created a sequence of Illustrator files that contains names of different "tube" stops along the Underground. This sequence will be layered on top of itself, using different sizes, opacities, and play-back rates. A couple of important tricks allow us to loop these copies for as long as we need them, and offset them so they appear to be different sequences.

• One of these text sequences will be scaled larger than 100%, and animate larger during the course of the composition (in time with the music). Scaling past 100% normally makes layers look blotchy, but since these files were created using vectors in Adobe Illustrator, you can use the Continuous Rasterization feature to keep them sharp. Since effects can't be applied directly to continuously rasterizing layers, you will then use an adjustment layer to further treat the large copy of this sequence.

• We've created an additional element based on the map symbols of the Underground, which tiles seamlessly in the horizontal dimension. You want this to scroll continuously along the bottom of the frame, like a ticker-tape. Rather than align and animate multiple copies of the layer, you will use the Offset effect, making the result easier to edit and control.

The end of this bonus tutorial goes on to suggest ways to further customize the final animation – so you can have some fun!

A frame from the final *Underground* animation. The "Piccadilly Circus" centerpiece was created in the prior tutorial using After Effects 5 lighting tricks. This tutorial teaches you how to manage this render as a Comp proxy.

The Illustrator sequence is used twice at different sizes and frame rates, with this larger version eventually becoming the background layer. Continuous Rasterization renders it cleanly even when scaled past 100%, and an adjustment layer is used to add a blur effect to the layer rather than precomposing it.

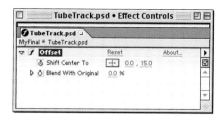

The unassuming Offset effect (above) makes it easy to animate a tileable layer, such as this tube track (below), as if it were a never-ending ribbon. Track created with the font Johnston Underground Extras from P22 (www.p22.com).

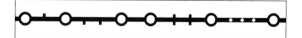

Postcards in Space

Using cameras and 3D space to create dimensional graphics.

This tutorial will serve as an introduction to using the new 3D space features introduced in After Effects 5.0, focusing on camera animation, as well as combining 2D and 3D layers.

It covers two separate projects: **Camera_5.aep**, where you will build a simple multilayer animation that will teach you the basics of manipulating layers and cameras in 3D (including nesting 3D pre-comps and collapsing their transformations), and a guided tour of the more complex **Postcards_5.aep**, which employs 3D space to build a

OVERVIEW

Main Concepts:

These are the features and concepts we will be focusing on in this project:

- 3D coordinates
- Alternate comp views
- Moving objects in 3D
- Layer rendering order
- Camera Angle of View and Zoom
- Continuous Rasterization
- Track Camera tools
- Moving and animating cameras
- Switching between multiple cameras
- Creating a viewer comp
- Orientation versus Rotation
- Layer intersections
- Precomposing
- Collapse Transformations
- Combining 2D and 3D layers
- Lights

Requirements:

After Effects 5.0 or later standard version.

Getting Started:

* Be sure to install the following plug-ins, included on the accompanying CD in the **Free Plug-ins** folder:

FE Sphere from Media 100 (www.media100.com)

Boris Tint-Tritone from Boris FX (www.borisfx.com)

Swedish plug-ins from Trapcode (www.trapcode.com)

Inside the **Tutorials** master folder on the accompanying CD, locate and copy the folder **08_Postcards** to your hard drive.

In the folder **Final Movie** inside this main folder, double-click and play both **Camera.mov** and **Postcards.mov**.

Inside the Project folder you'll find two After Effects project files: **Camera_5.aep** and **Postcards_5.aep**. Open the **Camera_5.aep** project file: This is your starting point; we suggest you save under a new name after each major section.

At the end of this tutorial, we'll direct you to a guided tour of the more complex **Postcards_5.aep** project.

more involved opening sequence for a fictional program. This second project includes additional tricks of interest, such as using expressions to integrate pseudo-3D effects into this new 3D space, and the intelligent use of nested compositions.

The next tutorial – *The Planets* – will extend these concepts by discussing the Auto-Orientation and Depth of Field options for the camera. Lights and shadows were covered in a previous tutorial, *Piccadilly Circus*. We will briefly cover lights in this tutorial as well.

The Tasks

This is what you will be doing in the various parts of this tutorial:

PART 1: Learn how to place layers in 3D space, including using different Comp views. We'll also cover render order concerns.

PART 2: Create a new camera and experiment with different presets, understand Angle of View and Zoom; learn tips on moving the camera and using the Track Camera tools to customize the Comp views.

PART 3: Add a background, employ different techniques to animate the camera, add a second camera, and switch between them.

PART 4: Understand the differences between Rotation and Orientation, including a side trip on the subject of layer intersections.

PART 5: Add more layers to your composition, precompose and collapse transformations for 3D layers, composite a 2D layer on top, and take a brief refresher course on adding a light.

PART 6: Read an overview of the more complex project **Postcards_5.aep**. A detailed walk-through of this project is included in a PDF file on the CD named **08B_Postcards_Bonus.pdf**.

In this tutorial, you will create a simple animation that involves a combination of 2D and 3D layers (left). We will then walk through a more complex project that uses the same principles (right).

The footage inside the "postcards" are from the Artbeats stock footage libraries Penguins, Under The Sea, Animal Safari, and Timelapse Landscapes 3; the texture map in the earth is from Digital Vision's Inner Gaze; the background in the complex project is a composite of movies from Artbeats' Digital Edge and from Digital Vision's Atmospherics.

Part 1: A Space Odyssey

1 Your initial image contains a pair of 2D layers: **Title.ai**, which was created in Adobe Illustrator using the font Childs Play Block from P22, and **Postcards_animals.tif**.

The plan for this and the next several sections is to use some of the elements from the *Postcards from Earth* project to create a simplified version of this opening title. Along the way, you will learn about 3D space and manipulating the camera. You do not have to exactly re-create the images shown here or the animation **Camera.mov**; feel free to experiment and pursue your own ideas of how you might use these tools.

In this first section, we will focus on placing layers in 3D, and becoming comfortable viewing and navigating around this space.

STEP 1: Make sure you have opened the project **Camera_5.aep**, not **Postcards_5.aep**. Then open the composition [**Camera*starter**]. It contains two layers – **Title.ai** and **Postcards_Animals.tif** – which are currently the type of 2D layers you are familiar with from previous versions of After Effects.

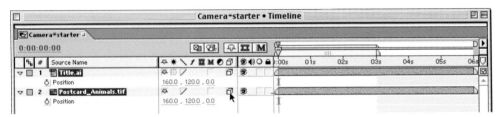

2 Layers default to 2D space, unless their 3D Layer switch (where the cursor is pointing) is enabled. Once set to 3D, their Position property gains a third value: Z Position.

STEP 2: Select both layers, and type P to reveal their Position properties in the Timeline window. Make sure the Switches panel is visible in the Timeline window; if not, hit F4 to reveal it.

Turn on the 3D Layer switch for both layers (its icon looks like a wireframe cube). In the Timeline window, you will notice that the Position properties have gained a third parameter: their Z Position. Where X is left and right, and Y is up and down, Z can be thought of as closer or farther away.

You should also notice that in the Comp window, 3D layers that are selected are drawn with three arrows extending from their Anchor Points. The colors of these arrows – red, green, and blue – correspond to which way their own X, Y, and Z axes are pointing. The blue Z arrow is hard to see right now, because it is pointed straight at you.

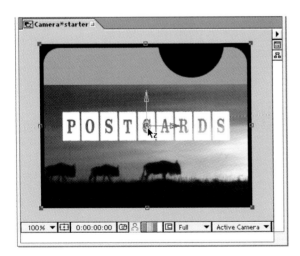

2 *complete:* When 3D layers are selected, they are drawn in the Comp window with a set of three axis arrows to tell you which way they are oriented. The blue arrow is hard to see in this view, because it is pointed straight at you along the Z axis.

You might also have noticed what *didn't* change: the position and size of the layers in the Comp window. Every composition has a default camera that ensures layers placed at Z = 0 that have not otherwise been rotated in 3D space (more on that later) appear the same way in 2D or 3D. In the next section, you will create a new camera, where you can change how it views these layers.

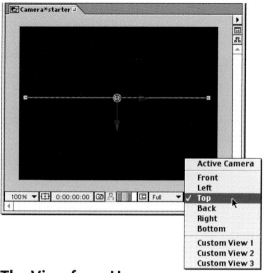

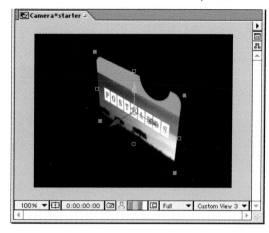

The View from Here

When you're working in a comp with 3D elements, the default view is the Active Camera, which is what will be rendered on final output. However, you will often want to look at your virtual set from different perspectives, such as from the side or from above.

STEP 3: Explore the different Comp window views either by using the menu item View>Switch 3D View, or the 3D View Popup along the bottom right of the Comp window. The first six views – Front, Left, Top, Back, Right, and Bottom – look at the scene from specific sides. For example, Top View is akin to floating above all of your layers. These six views, referred to as *orthographic* views, are also special in that they have no perspective distortion. They are useful for checking how your layers are truly arranged in 3D space, without having to take camera or perspective distortions into account.

The other three views – Custom View 1, 2, and 3 – give you different perspectives on the scene without having to create a camera and move it to that position. They include perspective distortion, which is more representative of how a camera will render on final output.

STEP 4: After Effects reserves the function keys F10, F11, and F12 to quickly jump between different views. You can decide what view each key jumps to: Set the view you want in the Comp window, then hold Shift while you press F10, F11, or F12 to assign that key.

For example, we like to use the Left view to see the Z Positions of layers: Positive Z values extend to the right; negative Z values to the left. Choose Left view from the popup at the bottom of the Comp window, and press Shift+F11. Verify that F10 is set to Top and F12 is set to the Active Camera; if they aren't, reassign them using the same procedure. Verify your key assignments by checking the View>Switch 3D View menu.

3 The 3D View Popup along the bottom of the Comp window allows you to see the layers from different angles, including Top view (left). Beneath the camera views are six *orthographic* views, with no perspective distortion – we use Top and Left a lot to help us see what is happening in Z space. The three Custom Views (right) allow you to examine a scene with perspective without having to move a camera there yourself.

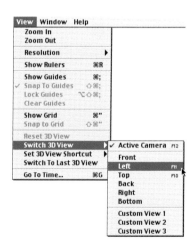

4 Set the current view to Left, and press Shift+F11 to assign this key to it. Verify your key assignments by looking under View>Switch 3D View.

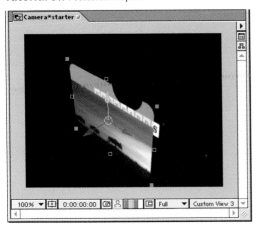

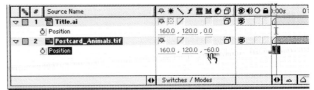

5 Scrub the Z Position value for **Postcard_Animals.tif** (above right) and notice how the layers separate in space (above).

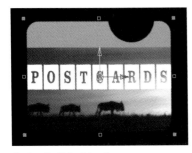

6 Set the Z Position for **Postcard_Animals.tif** to 100. Since it is farther away than before, it is drawn smaller in the Active Camera view.

Letter of the Law

Dragging an axis arrow automatically constrains movement to the letter of the axis that pops up next to the cursor – there is no need to hold down the Shift key while you're dragging.

STEP 5: Select Custom View 3 for the Comp window. In the Timeline window, scrub the Z Position for **Postcard_Animals.tif** while you're watching the Comp window. Notice how **Postcard_Animals.tif** separates from **Title.ai** in space.

If you set Z Position for **Postcard_Animals.tif** to a negative value, it will render in front of the **Title.ai** layer, even though it is below **Title.ai** in the Timeline window. Since their distance from the camera must be taken into account, 3D layers rewrite the old rules on which layers get rendered in front of other layers – see the sidebar *New World Order* for more details.

If layers do not move in the Comp window while you scrub their values in the Timeline window, check your Wireframe Interactions setting in the Preferences>Previews dialog (this option should be set to Up) or the Wireframe Interactions button along the top of the Timeline window (it should be off). Hold down Option on Mac (Alt on Windows) while scrubbing to temporarily get the opposite behavior of these settings.

STEP 6: Press F12 to return the Comp window to Active Camera view. Continue to experiment with scrubbing the Z Position for **Postcard_Animals.tif**. Notice that the higher the Z Position value, the farther away it appears, not unlike the effect of scaling a layer. This is part of normal 3D perspective. When you are done experimenting, set this layer's Z Position to 100; you will be using this arrangement later.

If you are still not clear on the implications of the orthographic views, change the view to Front. Notice that the layers look the same as they did before you changed the Position for **Postcard_Animal.tif**. This is because orthographic views such as Front, Left, and Top do not take distance perspective into account. Change back to Active Camera view when done.

STEP 7: Select the **Title.ai** layer and in the Comp window, click on the left or right side of the layer (away from the X, Y, and Z arrows), and drag it around in the Comp window while you're keeping an eye on its Position values in the Timeline window. Because you are looking straight on at the layer, moving it changes only the X and Y values, not the Z value. You can also press the Shift key after you start dragging to constrain movement to the X or Y axes. Also, if you move the cursor to either the red arrow (X axis) or green arrow (Y axis), you can drag the layer along a single axis. When you're done exploring, Undo until you return the layer's Position to 160, 120, 0, or enter these values directly.

New World Order

Before After Effects 5.0, it was easy to look at the Timeline window and know which layers would be rendered on top or in front of other layers: The layer at the bottom of this window renders first, and each layer farther up renders on top of the layers underneath. Stencils and Track Mattes cause minor but easily understood exceptions to these rules.

Although 2D layers still behave this way in version 5.0, 3D layers use different criteria: After Effects studies the 3D layers, calculates their relative distance from the active camera, and renders the layers that are farther away before the layers that are closer.

When you combine 2D and 3D layers in the same comp, the 2D layers break the 3D layers into groups that are rendered together. For example, say you had a composition with six 3D layers, and one 2D layer stacked in the middle of them in the Timeline window. All the 3D layers below the 2D layer would be calculated and rendered as a group. The 2D layer above them would then be rendered on top of this composite. Finally, the 3D layers above the 2D layer would be rendered as their own group, and composited on top of the layers underneath.

One important implication of these groups is when you have a light casting a shadow, and the 3D layers are also set to cast shadows: *shadows can fall only on other 3D layers in the same group.* (Shadows can never fall on 2D layers, and 2D layers don't cast shadows.) For purposes of rendering, Adjustment Layers are considered to be 2D layers; if they're placed between a number of 3D layers, they'll break those layers into groups above and below the adjustment layer.

So, even though the 3D rendering order is dependent on the distance of the layers to the cameras, you still need to be aware of the layer ordering in the Timeline when you're mixing 2D and 3D layers.

Move the cursor to the Anchor Point area of this layer until the cursor shows a Z beside it, and drag the mouse. Dragging up or to the right moves the layer closer (negative Z values); dragging it down or to the left moves it farther away (positive Z values) until it moves behind the **Postcard_Animals.tif** layer.

Although this works, it's quite difficult to control the movement along the Z axis in this view because it's straight on to the current view. If you want to move a layer on one axis, it's a good idea to pick the most appropriate view. For instance, press F10 or F11 to change the Comp's view to Top or Left views respectively. Now the blue Z axis is much easier to grab and move.

Return to Active Camera view (F12), and Undo until you return the layer to a Position of 160, 120, 0 – you will be relying on these values later.

Save your project. We have saved the composition at this point as [**Camera_after Step 07**]; *you will find it in the project folder* **Camera * prebuilt>_compare comps_after Step##**. *If you need to, you can compare your work with this one, or duplicate our comp and use it for the following sections.*

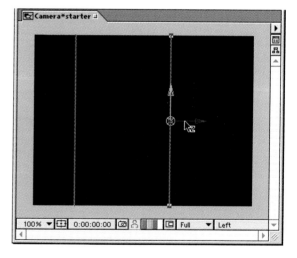

7 Although you can grab the Z axis arrow in a straight-on view (such as Active Camera view), it can be hard to see exactly what is going on. Get in the habit of switching views to see the axis you are interested in more clearly – such as the Left view to edit Z.

Part 2: Creating a New Camera

Now that you have some familiarity with objects in 3D space, in this section you will create a new camera and learn how to manipulate it around these objects. We will discuss some of the camera's settings, and several ways to manipulate it in the different Comp window views.

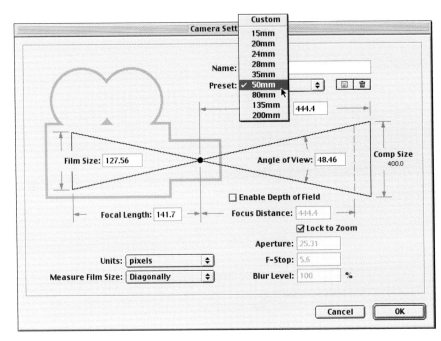

STEP 8: Make sure that the Comp window is in Active Camera view and that the time marker is at 00:00. Then create a new camera by selecting Layer>New>Camera.

This will open a large dialog box with a lot of parameters. If you are trying to match a scene in After Effects to one created in 3D or captured in real life, these parameters give you a lot of control. If you are a graphic artist who is just interested in cool imagery, they can be a bit daunting. If you fall into the latter category, you can ignore most of these parameters and just use different presets, or vary the Angle of View property to create different looks.

You are not committed to these settings; you can open this dialog again later, or access these parameters in the Timeline window. Pick the 50mm preset for now, and note the Zoom property directly below the preset popup: If the Units popup in the lower left of this dialog is set to Pixels, the Zoom value should equal 444.4. This property does not exist in a real camera, but it's handy inside the After Effects world – a layer this distance from the camera will appear to be the same size whether it is in 2D or 3D.

Click OK. With your new **Camera 1** layer selected, type P to reveal its Position property. Note that its Z Position equals –444.4: New cameras default to a Z Position equal to their initial Zoom setting (changing the zoom or selecting another preset later does not change the Z position to match).

The 50mm preset is very close to the comp's default camera. Save a snapshot of what this looks like by pressing Shift+F5 so you can easily compare what different camera presets look like.

8 Create a new camera, and select the 50mm preset.

8 *complete:* The 50mm preset has a look similar to the comp's default camera.

STEP 9: Everything else being equal – including the camera's position relative to the layers it is looking at – smaller lens presets equal a wider Angle of View. Wider Angles of View result in the layers appearing smaller in the frame, since the virtual lens would be taking in a wider overall image. A result of this is that the more layers are spaced apart, the greater the exaggeration in distance between the layers.

Double-click on **Camera 1** to re-open the Camera Settings dialog. Note the current Angle of View and Zoom settings, then pick the 28mm preset: The Angle of View will increase, and Zoom will decrease. Click OK. The two layers will appear much farther away. Press Shift+F6 to save a snapshot of this. Then note the Z Position parameter for **Camera 1**: It is still –444.4. Change it to –248.9, which corresponds to the Zoom parameter for the 28mm preset (and would have been the Z Position you would have gotten had you created a New Camera with the 28mm preset in the first place). Notice that the **Title.ai** layer – which is at Z = 0 in the comp – now appears about the same size as it did with the 50mm camera preset. You can press F5 to call up the 50mm snapshot to compare. However, the **Postcard_Animals.tif** layer appears farther away when you're using the 28mm preset: This is a result of the exaggerated perspective of using a smaller lens with a larger Angle of View.

STEP 10: Set **Camera 1**'s Z Position back to –444.4 so you have a common camera position to compare other lens presets with. Double-click **Camera 1** again, choose the 135mm preset, and click OK. This preset is more akin to a telephoto lens, resulting in the layers appearing much closer. Press F5 and F6 to compare it with the 50mm and 28mm presets, respectively.

STEP 11: The 135mm preset zooms so close to the layers that they are blown up past their original size, resulting in some fuzziness. However, **Title.ai** was created in Adobe Illustrator, and contains vector outlines instead of pixels. This means you can take advantage of the Continuous Rasterization feature to render it sharply at its new size. Click on the sunburst icon for **Title.ai** in the Timeline window, and notice how much sharper the title now appears.

9 The 28mm preset has a wider Angle of View, resulting in the layers appearing farther away if the camera is kept at the same position (above). When the camera is moved closer (below), you can see how perspective is exaggerated by the wider view angle.

10 – 11: If the camera is left at the same position, the 135mm lens preset works as a telephoto, magnifying the layers (far left). Unfortunately, this scales the images past their original size, resulting in a fuzzier image. Fortunately, **Title.ai** contains vector artwork; turn on its Continuous Rasterization button (above) and note how much sharper it appears (left).

11 *complete:* The 135mm preset with the Camera's Z Position set to –1200.

The 135mm preset has a much narrower Angle of View. To reinforce how this affects perspective, set the Z Position of **Camera 1** to –1200, which equals this preset's Zoom value. Notice the relative lack of perspective: The relative sizes of the two layers are almost the same as when they were both in 2D, even though **Postcard_Animals.tif** is placed farther back in Z. Set **Camera 1**'s Z Position back to –444.4 when you're done.

STEP 12: Open the Camera Settings one last time, choose the 35mm preset, and click OK. Be sure it's Z position is set to –444.4. This is the preset you will use for the remainder of this tutorial.

Save your project. If you suspect you may have crossed up your camera settings, compare your comp with [**Camera_after Step 12**].

Moving the Camera 101

Next you will be animating this camera around your layers, taking advantage of the resulting perspective to create more interest. If you already have experience moving the camera, you can skip ahead to Step 17. If you are not yet comfortable with the camera, here are a few techniques that are good to practice:

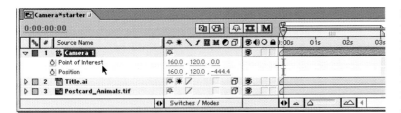

13 The shortcut key A reveals a camera's Point of Interest property – the point in space the camera is aimed at.

STEP 13: Select **Camera 1**. Its Position property should already be visible; press P if it isn't. Then press Shift+A: Instead of a normal layer's Anchor Point, this action reveals a second control point called the Point of Interest.

The Position of a camera can be thought of as where it is looking *from*, and the Point of Interest as where it's looking *to*. Some 3D programs, such as Electric Image, use this "two-point camera" approach. In many cases, this makes the camera easier to control, as you can explicitly set where it is looking – such as the center of a certain layer. You can also use a simple pick whip expression to tie the camera's Point of Interest to another layer's Position.

On the downside, this often means you have to keyframe both Position and Point of Interest when you animate the camera, which makes coordinating some moves more difficult. Later we'll discuss ways to turn off the Point of Interest if you find it is getting in your way.

P = Position only

When you're animating the camera, press P to twirl down Position and then Shift+A to twirl down the Point of Interest. Set the stopwatches for both properties, not just Position.

STEP 14: With **Camera 1** still selected, press F10 to switch to the Top view. Hit the comma key (,) to set the Magnification to 50%, and/or enlarge the window until you can see the camera in its entirety.

If the Info window is not open, press Command+2 on Mac (Control+2 on Windows) to open it – this will give you numeric feedback as you move the camera. Practice moving the camera using these different techniques:

• In the Timeline window, scrub the values for the camera's Position or Point of Interest.

• In the Comp window, grab and move the Point of Interest as you would a layer's anchor point.

• Still in the Comp window, you can drag the camera around freely provided you grab the camera icon where X, Y, or Z do *not* appear next to the cursor.

• Place the cursor near the camera's axis arrows until you see X, Y, or Z appear, then drag. *Both the camera and its Point of Interest will move together,* constrained to the axis indicated next to your cursor.

• To move the camera along a selected axis *without* moving the Point of Interest, place the cursor near the camera until you see either X, Y, or Z appear, then hold down the Command (Control) key as you drag.

Press F12 to toggle back to the Active Camera view to see the result of your new camera positions as you work, then F10 to go back to the Top view.

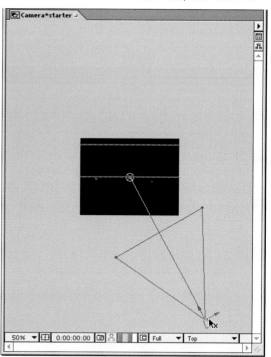

Track Camera Tools

The Comp window can be a bit cumbersome to handle in these alternate views: As you change its size or Magnification, it insists on recentering the rendered area inside the middle of the window. This rendered area provides only a limited preview of the frame in anything other than an actual Camera view, and there is a set of tools you can use to reposition your objects inside this area:

STEP 15: Change the Magnification back to 100%. Hitting the period key (.) is a shortcut to zoom up to the next level. Re-arrange your screen so you can still read Camera 1's Position property in the Timeline window while the Comp window is forward.

• Make sure the Tools window is visible; if not, press Command+1 (Control+1) to open it.

• Click and hold on the third tool down on the left. An additional window will pop open – these are the Track Camera tools. Select the rightmost one: Track Z Camera.

• As you move your cursor over the Comp window, it will change to an icon of this tool. Once it's over the Comp window, click and drag downward or to the left; the drawing of the camera and layers will get smaller. Drag until the camera and layers are about half the size they were when you started. If the camera is selected, you will see its wireframe outline; if it's deselected, you will see just a small box icon.

14 Alter the size and zoom level of the Comp window until you can see the camera and layers from the Top view, and practice moving the camera. The letters X, Y, or Z next to the cursor mean dragging is constrained to this one axis.

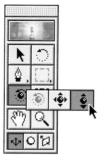

15 There are three Track Camera tools (from left to right): Orbit Camera, Track XY Camera, and Track Z Camera. Press C to select the Track Camera tool, and press C repeatedly to cycle through the three choices.

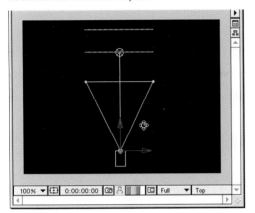

Keep an eye on the Timeline window while you're doing this; you will note that **Camera 1**'s Position property does not change. If you are not in a Camera view, the Track tools change only your view – not the positions of any object.

• Watch the Tool window, and press C twice. This will scroll through the track icons, landing on the Track XY Camera tool. Then drag upward in the Comp window until your objects are centered in this view.

Feel free to practice using these tools in the other orthographic and Custom views. You will quickly find that these are much better suited than Magnification for altering the view in the Comp window.

15 *complete:* The Track Camera tools allow you to zoom and reposition the objects in the orthographic or Custom views without changing the Position properties of any objects.

STEP 16: Press F12 to return to the Active Camera view. While you're keeping an eye on **Camera 1**'s Position property in the Timeline window, use the Track Camera tools to change the Comp window. Notice that in this case, the Position of the camera *does* change. The same will be true in the Camera 1 view. Tap C to toggle between the different tools, and practice using each one – the Orbit Camera tool is particularly fun and very useful for manipulating the Custom Views as well.

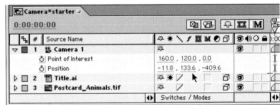

The Track Camera tools have different functions in different views – it's important to remember which view you are in and what you are trying to do before using them.

Another option for manipulating views is the Zoom tool: Press Z to select it, and click in the Comp window in the middle of the area you wish to zoom closer to. Hold the spacebar down and drag to pan around with the Hand tool. Option+click (Alt+click) to zoom out.

16 If you use the Track Camera tools in a Camera view (left), the camera's Position values will change (right).

STEP 17: When you're done experimenting, position the camera at an angle to the existing layers, so you can see a little perspective (something like our first camera position, as seen in Step 16's figure.) Set the Comp window to Active Camera view, and 100% zoom. In the next section you will add more layers and animate the camera around them.

Save your project. If you are already familiar with manipulating the camera and views and therefore skipped this Part, duplicate our comp [**Camera_after Step 17**] *to use from here forward.*

Part 3: A Moving Experience

You should now feel more comfortable manipulating the camera and the different views. With that under your belt, it's time to have some fun continuing to build this project. You will add additional layers and cameras, plus animate the cameras.

STEP 18: In the Project window, locate the **MySources** folder and twirl it open. Select **MapBackground.tif** and drag it to the Timeline window, placing it at the bottom of the layer stack and starting at time 00:00.

Notice that the layer is rendered behind the other layers; a 2D layer at the bottom of the Timeline is rendered first. You can set it to Best Quality if you like, although this will slow down your previews slightly.

Press F10 and F11 to check the Left and Top views. In version 5.0, 2D layers keep the same placement in the Comp window regardless of what view you are using. Press F12 to switch back to the Active Camera view.

STEP 19: With **MapBackground.tif** still selected, hit P to reveal its Position property. Note that there are only two values – X and Y – because new layers default to 2D.

Turn on the 3D Layer switch for **MapBackground.tif**. You will notice in the Comp window that it jumps to the same perspective as the other 3D layers.

It also renders in front of the **Postcard_Animals.tif** layer: This is because its Z Position defaults to 0 – the same as the **Title.ai** layer – so it is technically in front of the **Postcard_Animals.tif** layer placed at Z = 100, regardless of where they are in the layer stack.

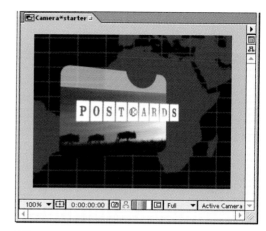

18 Add the source **MapBackground.tif** to the bottom of the layer stack (above). In version 5.0, 2D layers look the same in every view (below).

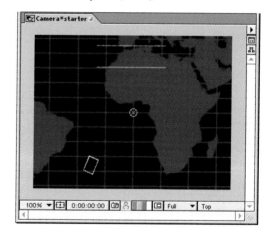

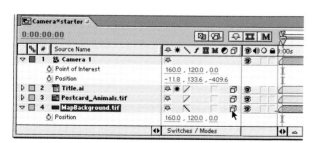

19 Turn on the background's 3D Layer switch (above), and it will be shown in the same perspective as the other layers (right). Since it is located at Z = 0, it renders in front of the **Postcard_Animals.tif** layer.

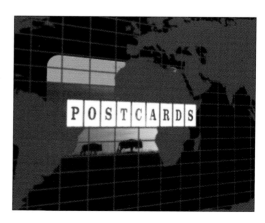

19 *complete:* **MapBackground.tif** is placed at Z = 200. Here, we are dragging its Z axis arrow; it's alright if black shows around the map's edges.

As you remember from Part 1, there are several ways you can edit the Z Position of **MapBackground.tif**:

- If the Selection tool is not already active, press V. You can select the layer and move your cursor into the Comp window, positioning it over the blue Z axis arrow until the cursor shows a small Z next to it. Drag your mouse right and left to see how the layer can easily be positioned in front of the title (negative Z) and behind the other two layers (positive Z values larger than 100).

- Scrub its Z Position value in the Timeline.

- Enter an exact value in the Z Position field.

We settled on a the value of Z = 200, which leaves us some room to later position more postcard layers inbetween the title and background.

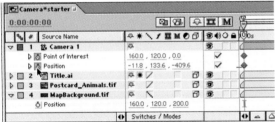

20 Set comp marker 0 at 00:00, and enable keyframing for both Position and Point of Interest.

Animating Cameras

STEP 20: With the time marker at 00:00, press Shift+0 to set a comp marker – it will give you another way to jump back to the start of the comp. Then enable the keyframe animation stopwatch for **Camera 1**'s Position *and* Point of Interest properties. You can tweak the camera's pose if you like.

STEP 21: Press Command+G (Control+G) to open the Go To Time dialog, type "**300**" and click OK. The time marker will jump to 03:00. Verify that the work area ends at this time (hit N if it doesn't), then press Shift+3 to set a comp marker at this point in time.

Move **Camera 1** to a new position by selecting the Orbit Camera tool (shortcut: C until it cycles to it), and dragging in the Comp window; note how only the Position of the camera has changed, not the Point of Interest. (The Track Z and Track XY tools change both values.) Feel free to use alternate views to move the camera and Point of Interest; our animation move is shown below in Top view. Hit F12 to jump back to the Active Camera to see what the camera sees. Press 0 and 3 to jump between 00:00 and 03:00 to check your beginning and ending poses, then RAM Preview to see the animation you created.

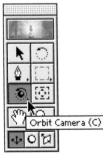

21 The default motion path is linear (right). This often causes the camera to pass closer to the layers than you intended in the middle of its move. Use the motion path's Bezier handles to create a smoother arc for its path (far right).

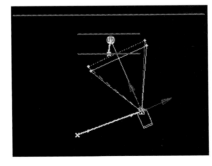
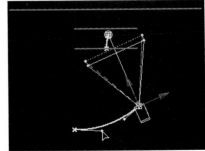

The camera's Position and Point of Interest have Bezier motion paths, just like Position or the Anchor Point for any other keyframed layer. The default motion path is linear, which often does not work well for camera motion – especially if you are trying to get it to swing in an arc. (This is true even if you used the Orbit Camera tool to swivel around your pose.) The result can be that the camera passes closer to the layers than you intended in the middle of the move, then pulls back as it reaches its second Position keyframe. Press V to return to the Selection tool, and practice using the Bezier handles on at least the Camera's Position path to create a more artistic swoop for your animation. RAM Preview until you're happy with the move.

Make sure the handles are not tugged in the opposite direction you want to move; this will result in some strange "loops" to your animation near the keyframes – especially if your Bezier handles are very short. Use the trick of pressing Z to select the Zoom tool and clicking on the keyframe points in the Comp window to get a close look at your handles and path. Option+click (Alt+click) to zoom back out, then press V to return to the Selection tool.

Twirl up the Camera layer when you're done.

Hidden Handles

If you can't see the ends of the motion path handle to grab, Command+drag (Control+drag) out of the "X" keyframe icon to pull out a new handle. It's best to move to a point in time where the camera back is clear of the keyframe icon.

Viewing a Second Opinion

Switching between the Active Camera and the various orthographic views can be cumbersome. However, there is a way in After Effects 5.0 to get two views of the same comp. In the Project window, drag the comp you are working on – **[Camera*starter]**, in this case – onto the Create New Composition icon at the bottom of the Project window. This will create a second comp with the same dimensions, frame rate, and duration as your first comp; it also has your first comp nested inside of it. Rename the new comp "**Viewer**" and check that its magnification is set to 100% and the background color is black. Drag its tab outside its current Comp window so that it sits alongside the Comp window of your working comp. Make sure Edit>Preferences>General>Synchronize Time of All Related Items is on. You can then change views and move your camera or layers in the first comp, and after you release the mouse, the Active Camera view will render in the second comp.

Note that changing the Resolution of the **[Viewer]** comp also sets the nested **[Camera*starter]** comp to the same Resolution. Hold down Control (Command) as you change the Resolution to not have it affect nested comps.

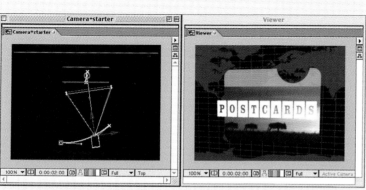

Nest your working comp into a second comp, and arrange them side by side. After you edit the first comp in any view, the second comp will update and display the Active Camera's view. Feel free to use this setup for the rest of the tutorial.

Zoom ≠ Move

There are two ways to zoom or push in on a layer: move the camera closer (which will give a new visual relationship between layers), or change its Zoom property (which scales the image as viewed by the camera as it changes the Angle of View).

Handheld Camera

Next you will create a second camera, and animate it using a different technique. Compositions in After Effects can have multiple cameras. If the Comp window is set to Active Camera, the camera that is nearest the top in the layer stack at the current time, with its Video switch turned on, is the one that renders. You can also select specific cameras from the Comp window's View popup.

STEP 22: Press 3 to locate to comp marker 3 at 03:00. Then select Layer>New>Camera. You can try out a different preset if you like; we chose 50mm. Keep the default name – **Camera 2** – and click OK.

- Press F10 or F11 to switch to the Top or Left view. You will see two camera icons. The currently selected camera will also display its Point of Interest, Angle of View, and axes arrows. If you need to, use the Camera Track tools to see both in the Comp window at the same time.

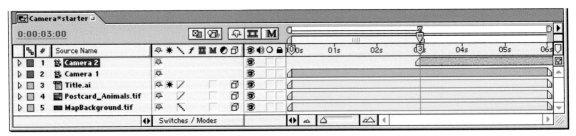

22 Move to 03:00 and add a Layer>New>Camera. It will automatically be placed at the top of the Timeline (above). In Top or Left view, you should see both cameras at the same time (right).

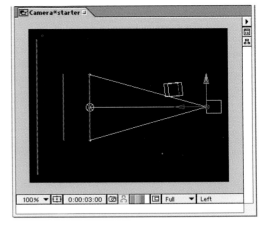

Invisible Camera

Turning off the Video switch for inactive cameras hides them in the Comp window, which can be less distracting while you're animating the active camera. Don't forget to switch them back on before you render!

- Press F12 to return to the Active Camera view. If the time marker is at 03:00, you will see the view from your new camera, **Camera 2**. Press Page Up to back up in time to 02:29. The Comp window will jump to **Camera 1**'s view: Since **Camera 2** has not started yet at this time, **Camera 1** is the Active Camera.

- Press Page Down to step back to 03:00, where **Camera 2** is active again. Turn off **Camera 2**'s Video switch in the Timeline window. Since this makes **Camera 2** inactive, **Camera 1** underneath takes over.

• Switch **Camera 2** back on, then experiment with the View popup in the Comp window, switching between **Camera 1** and **Camera 2**. This allows you to directly pick which camera to use, regardless of which one is on top in the Timeline, or whether or not their Video switches are on. *This is for previewing only – when you render, the Active Camera is used,* ***regardless*** *of which view you have chosen with this popup.*

• Press F12 to return to the Active Camera view.

You cannot set Opacity keyframes to crossfade between different cameras; they simply switch at their in and out points. If you want to crossfade between cameras, they will need to be in their own compositions; you can then fade between these comps as if they were normal layers. You could also render a single comp in sections, with different cameras active for each render, then crossfade the overlapping frames in your video editing application (or do a final edit in After Effects).

STEP 23: With **Camera 2** selected, press P to reveal its Position, then Shift+A to reveal its Point of Interest.

Type Command+Option+O (Control+Alt+O) to open the camera's Auto-Orientation dialog. The default is for the camera to point (orient) to its Point of Interest. Select Off, and click on OK. (We'll discuss the middle option – Orient Along Path – in the next tutorial, *The Planets.*)

Notice in the Timeline window that the Point of Interest property disappears. With **Camera 2** still selected, press F10 or F11 to view the Top or Left views. You will still see the camera as well as the cone that indicates its Angle of View, but you will no longer see the anchor point-style icon for its Point of Interest, or a line connecting the camera to this point.

STEP 24: Press F10 to switch to Top view, then Shift+R to reveal **Camera 2**'s Orientation and Rotation properties. 3D objects have two different ways to rotate them; we'll use just Orientation for now.

Scrub Orientation's X, Y, and Z values (which default to 0, 0, 0), and note how the camera reacts in the Comp window. If you are having trouble corresponding the two, remember that the RGB arrows relate to the XYZ axes: For example, scrubbing the X Orientation value has the same effect as twirling the Red arrow along its axis. (If you make a mess, return the Orientation property to 0, 0, 0, and start over.)

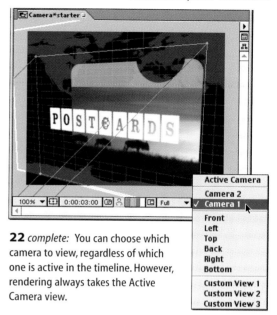

22 *complete:* You can choose which camera to view, regardless of which one is active in the timeline. However, rendering always takes the Active Camera view.

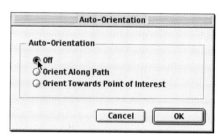

23 Switch the Auto-Orientation option for **Camera 2** to Off. This will make the camera react more like a handheld camera, in which you point it just by moving the camera's body.

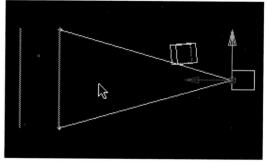

23 *complete:* When the camera's Auto-Orientation is turned Off, the Point of Interest as well as the line connecting it to the camera disappear (shown here in Left view).

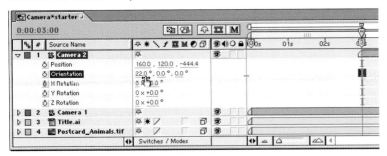

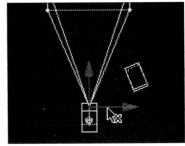

24 Scrubbing Orientation's values (left) twirls the camera around its corresponding axes (right).

Several 3D programs use this "one-point" camera model, and you may be more comfortable with it. Without the Point of Interest, however, it can be harder to visualize what a camera is looking at in the alternate views; read the sidebar *Viewing a Second Opinion* for a trick to see the Active Camera's result while you're in one of these other views.

STEP 25: Press 3 to make sure the time marker is at 03:00, and B to start the work area at this point. Then enable keyframing for **Camera 2**'s Position and Orientation. Play around and choose a placement you like that is different from **Camera 1**'s final keyframes, employing the tools you've learned.

Press End to locate to the end of the comp (05:29). Press Shift+6 to set a comp marker here, and N to extend the work area to this point.

Edit **Camera 2** again for a different framing of your scene. RAM Preview to see your new move. Remember that the Position path is a Bezier curve; if your animation wobbles a bit around the keyframes, your path handles are probably pointing at angles that don't describe a smooth path.

When you have a second camera animation that you like, double-click the ribbed area of the work area bar along the top of the timeline. This resets the work area to the entire length of the comp. Press F12 to switch back to the Active Camera view and RAM Preview, noting the switch when **Camera 2** starts in the timeline. If you don't see a switch, make sure the Video switches for both cameras are turned on.

Twirl up **Camera 2**'s properties when you're done.

25 Set up an animation for your second camera. Don't forget to smooth its motion by tweaking its path between keyframes (below).

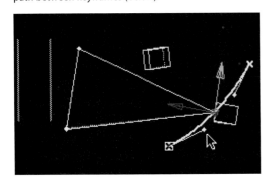

We encourage you to practice and create your own camera animations. If you become frustrated, check our prebuilt comp [Camera_after Step 25] for ideas, but remember that your animation doesn't have to be the same as ours. And don't forget to save your project.

Orbiting Camera

It can be difficult to craft a Bezier motion path for the camera that creates a perfectly smooth "orbit" animation. You can use Parenting (covered in *RoboTV*, *Piccadilly Circus*, and *Flamingo 4*) and a null object (also covered in *Piccadilly Circus*) to help execute this move:

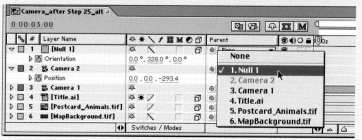

• Create a new camera, and set its Auto-Orientation to Off. Position it so that it is pointing along the Z axis at the point you want it to orbit around, with no Rotation or Orientation offset.

• Create a Layer>New>Null Object, make it a 3D layer, and place it at the point you want to orbit around. It should have the same X and Y coordinates as your camera.

• Parent the camera to the null object.

For perfectly smooth orbits and zooms (top sequence), parent a camera to a null (above). Rotate the null, and animate the Z Position of the camera for the zoom.

• To orbit the camera, rotate the null object, not the camera – the camera will be swung around by the null.

• To zoom the camera in and out, change just the camera's Z Position in the Timeline window.

This technique is used for **Camera 2** in **[Camera_after Step 25_alt]**.

Part 4: Rotation Reorientation

In this section, you will experiment with rotating layers in 3D space, adding more 2D and 3D layers, and precompose some of them into their own comp. Precomposing is as useful at grouping together 3D layers as it is 2D layers – especially since you can still Collapse Transformations and have their 3D positions ripple into your final composition.

Throughout this book we've encouraged you on occasion to vary from our choices when you're building your comp. This is even more true for the next two sections: Have fun, compose an elegant frame, make a mess, whatever; the main point is to learn the tools. In the last section and corresponding PDF on the CD, we will walk through a more carefully thought-out project in detail.

Work Area = Comp

Double-click the ribbed area of the work area bar to reset it to the length of the comp.

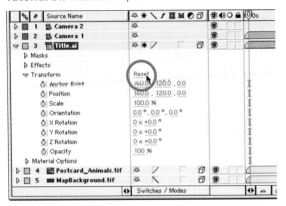

🔲	#	Source Name	⚒ ✳ ➲ ∫ ▦ M ⊘ ⌗	◉ ◐ ○ 🔒	00s
▷ ■	1	🎥 Camera 2	⚒	◉	
▷ ■	2	🎥 Camera 1	⚒	◉	
▽ 🔲	3	🔳 **Title.ai**	⚒ ✳ ∕	⌗	◉	

- ▷ Masks
- ▷ Effects
- ▽ Transform   *Reset*
  - ⏱ Anchor Point   160.0 , 120.0 , 0.0
  - ⏱ Position   160.0 , 120.0 , 0.0
  - ⏱ Scale   100.0 %
  - ⏱ Orientation   0.0 °, 0.0 °, 0.0 °
  - ⏱ X Rotation   0 x +0.0 °
  - ⏱ Y Rotation   0 x +0.0 °
  - ⏱ Z Rotation   0 x +0.0 °
  - ⏱ Opacity   100 %
- ▷ Material Options

▷ ■	4	🖼 Postcard_Animals.tif	⚒ ∕	⌗	◉	
▷ ■	5	▬ MapBackground.tif	⚒ ➲	⌗	◉	
		◀▶ Switches / Modes	◀▶ ⌂

26 Reveal **Title.ai**'s Transform properties in the Timeline window, and click on the word "Reset" (circled in red) to make sure it is at its default location.

🔲	#	Source Name	⚒ ✳ ➲ ∫ ▦ M ⊘ ⌗	◉ ◐ ○ 🔒	00s
▷ ■	1	🎥 Camera 2	⚒	◉	
▷ ■	2	🎥 Camera 1	⚒	◉	
▽ 🔲	3	🔳 **Title.ai**	⚒ ✳ ∕	⌗	◉	
		⏱ Orientation	0.0 °, 0.0 °, 0.0 °		
		⏱ X Rotation	0 x +0.0 °		
		⏱ Y Rotation	0 x +0.0 °		
		⏱ Z Rotation	0 x +0.0 °		

27 3D layers have two sets of rotation properties: Orientation, which sets an XYZ rotational pose, and individual Rotation values for the X, Y, and Z axes.

27 *complete:* Practice animating the three Rotation properties; feel free to have a bit of fun. **Title.ai**'s axes arrows in the Comp window help show which way it is pointing.

Rotation versus Orientation

STEP 26: To start fresh, make sure all the properties of **Title.ai** are twirled up in the Timeline window, and twirl it down again. The subsection Transform should also be twirled down at this point. Click on the word "Reset" next to the word "Transform": All the values for Anchor Point, Position, Scale, Orientation, Rotation, and Opacity will return to their defaults. (This is probably where the values already are, but we're just being safe.) The **Title.ai** layer will deselect automatically when you click reset – who knows why.

STEP 27: Make sure the Comp window is set to Active Camera view. Select the **Title.ai** layer again, and press R. When a layer is 2D, R will twirl down a single property: Rotation. When a layer is 3D, as in this case, Rotation consists of four properties that you can edit: Orientation, plus individual X, Y, and Z Rotations.

The Orientation values consists of X, Y, and Z values, so a keyframe set for Orientation will remember a "pose" (more on this in the next Step). The Rotation values are used for rotating, rather than posing, a layer. Unlike Orientation, you can set Rotation values for multiple full rotations – not just an angle from 0 to 360.

Turn on the stopwatches for X, Y, and Z rotation and set up some keyframing over a second or so so you can see how this works. Have fun rotating around all three axes, and don't worry about making a creative mess – we will Reset these values in a moment. Make sure you animate at least one axis through a full rotation.

When you've set some keyframes, RAM Preview and see how it looks. (You can also turn on Motion Blur for this layer if you like.) Rotation and Scale occur around the Anchor Point, which is currently in the center of the **Title.ai** layer; leave it here, as it works fine in this case.

Step 28: After you've had some fun with Rotation, reset **Title.ai**'s Transform properties again: In the Timeline window, twirl up the **Title.ai** layer, twirl it down again, and click on the word "Reset" – all the Rotation values will return to their defaults. If you have set any keyframes, turn off keyframing for these values. Then press R to show just the Orientation and Rotation properties.

At the risk of repeating ourselves, Orientation should be thought of more as a "pose" than a way to rotate a layer. If you try to keyframe a rotation animation using Orientation, you will be disappointed:

• Change the Comp window to Front view to remove any perspective distortion and ignore the camera's animation.

• At time 00:00, turn on the stopwatch for Orientation to set a first keyframe with a value of 0,0,0. Press B to start the work area here.

• Move to 01:00, and press N to end the work area here.

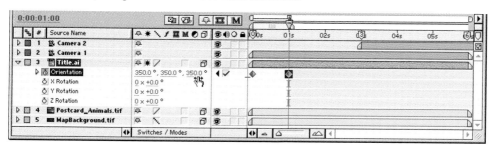

• Scrub Orientation's X value – the first of the three numbers – around almost a full rotation to about 350° (be sure to scrub, don't just type in numbers). You will see **Title.ai** flip around in the Comp window.

• Do the same for Orientation's Y and Z values, scrubbing their values to about 350°. The title should end up facing the front again, albeit at a slight angle.

• Press 0 on the extended keypad to RAM Preview your animation. You might expect, after rotating in all three axes and seeing these exciting flips and tumbles happen as you scrubbed their values, that you had created a wildly flipping animation. Instead, you're greeted with a very sedate move of 10° in the opposite direction.

What happened? Orientation takes the shortest path to move from one keyframe to the next – it feels no obligation to carry every twist and turn that the Rotation properties do. Keep this in mind when you're deciding which property to use when you're animating a layer.

28 Even though you keyframed a 350° move for each axis of Orientation (above), the resulting animation (below) moves only 10° in the opposite direction. Unlike Rotation, Orientation takes the shortest path between keyframes.

If your Orientation animation did not turn out as we described, compare your version against [**Camera_after Step 28**]. *Feel free to continue with this prebuilt comp if you prefer. Save your project; you'll be adding more layers in the following Part.*

Intersection Dissection

Let's take a moment to talk about intersections between layers – or the lack of them, as is often the case. The **Title.ai** layer is 320 pixels wide, which means that if you rotate this layer's Y value to +90° or –90°, it should intersect the **Postcard_Animals.tif** layer positioned only 100 pixels behind it in Z space.

Open **[Camera_for intersections]** in this project's **MyComps** folder, and try the following steps:

- Press F12 to use the Active Camera view. If the Rotation properties for **Title.ai** are not already exposed, select this layer and press R.

- Scrub the degrees portion of **Title.ai**'s Y Rotation value from 0 to 300, and watch it swivel around in the Comp window. It does not appear to collide with the **Postcard_Animals.tif** layer.

- Set the Y Rotation value to 90°, and press F11 to change to Left view. In this view, you can see that the P on the left side of the title is crossing over the line where the layer **Postcard_Animals.tif** sits.

- Return to Active Camera view (F12). Because we're using the Standard 3D rendering plug-in, which doesn't allow for layers to intersect, the Active Camera view ignores this incursion and doesn't render the intersection. This speeds up rendering, and allows you to be less precise with your arrangement and animation of layers in 3D space.

- That said, there are certainly times when you *do* want to see these intersections. At the time this book was being written, Adobe had released a public beta

For layers to intersect (above), use the Advanced 3D plug-in from the Composition Settings>Advanced tab (below).

version of an Advanced 3D rendering plug-in. If you don't have it installed, look for it on Adobe's Web site under Downloads>After Effects; Save and Quit the program, install it, and reopen this project.

- Select Composition Settings for **[Camera_for intersections]** and click on the Advanced tab. In the Rendering Plug-in popup, select Advanced 3D, and click OK.

- In the Comp window, you will now see the P in **Title.ai** cut off by the **Postcard_Animals.tif** layer it is intersecting with.

Why not use the Advanced 3D plug-in all the time? For one, it renders more slowly than the Standard 3D plug-in. Also, at the time of this writing, Advanced 3D disabled some functions such as the Stencil transfer mode that are available when using Standard 3D. However, it is a great option to have around. Adobe plans to eventually include the Advanced 3D plug-in with After Effects, and we hope to see third-party rendering engines appear as well.

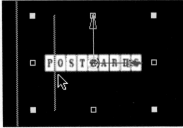

Using the Standard 3D rendering plug-in, layers never seem to intersect (left), even though alternate views (such as Left view) show they do in certain poses (right).

Part 5: Adding and Collapsing

We'll wrap up this portion of the tutorial by adding more 2D and 3D layers, plus a light. To make the final composite easier to manage, you will group some of your layers into a precomp. It is possible to have 3D layers in a precomp and still manipulate them in 3D space in the comp they are then nested in; you can also collapse transformations for nested 3D comps with interesting results.

Again, the point of this section is to have fun while you're mastering a few additional concepts – so we're going to give you looser instructions than normal. However, you will also find we've saved prebuilt comps of most of these steps showing our own ideas, if you want to just poke around or compare your results with ours.

Step 29: Press Home to return the time marker to 00:00, and F12 to return the Comp window to Active Camera view.

Reset the **Title.ai** layer to its original placement. This includes turning off any animation keyframes for its Rotation or Orientation properties and zeroing out these values. Twirl up its properties to create more room in the Timeline window.

Step 30: In the Project window's **MySources** folder, we've already imported some additional "postcards" for you to play with. Drag one or more into [**Camera * starter**]. Set them to Best Quality so they will render more cleanly.

Dynamic Resolution

Manipulating 3D layers and lights can be slow. You can use Dynamic Resolution to render at a lower resolution while you are manipulating objects, until After Effects has time to catch up. It can be toggled on/off from the Comp window's wing menu, or in Preferences>Previews.

30 We've provided three more postcards for you to play with. The images inside are from the Artbeats volumes Penguins, Timelapse Plants, and Under The Sea.

Turn their 3D Layer switches on, and array them as you please in 3D space. The only suggestions we'll make are to keep them in front of **MapBackground.tif**, and to not obscure **Title.ai**. If you are having trouble fitting them in, you don't need to rely on their Z Position to make them smaller; go ahead and reduce their Scale as well.

For our own version, we brought in two more layers, placed them to the left and right of the **Postcard_Animals.tif**, and scaled all three postcards to 80%.

> Rather than pose multiple layers in 3D space, you could set up one layer, duplicate it, and replace the duplicate layer's source by Option+dragging (Alt+dragging) a new layer from the Project window to the comp. The new layer will have identical attributes (3D switch, scale amount, and so on) – you need to reposition only the duplicate in 3D space.

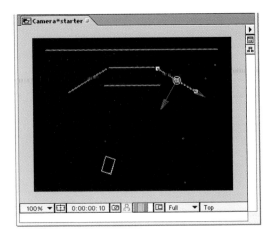

31 Practice using the Orientation and Rotation properties to add interest to the arrangement of your layers (left). Remember that alternate views, such as Top view (right), can help you better visualize what is happening.

STEP 31: Experiment with the Orientation and Rotation properties of the postcard layers – make them seem more like elements of a mobile hanging in space, or pose them to give the appearance they are facing the main title. This may require some tweaking of their Position properties as well.

We chose to orient the two cards on the sides in toward the title. Remember that alternate views such as Top come in very handy for arranging layers in 3D space. If you're using the optional [**Viewer**] comp, you'll see the active camera's output in this comp.

Precomposing 3D Layers

Layers in 3D have more properties to keep track of. It is not unusual to reach a point where you think "This idea looks good – but now I need to scale them all down and rotate them a bit. What a pain." Fortunately, there are a couple of tools in After Effects that make it possible to act on a group of layers as if they were one object: the new-to-version 5.0 feature Parenting (discussed in the *RoboTV, Piccadilly Circus,* and *Flamingo 4* tutorials), and good ol' fashioned Layer>Pre-compose, which we will use here.

32 Select your postcard layers in their current arrangement (above), and Layer> Pre-compose them. Unfortunately, the result is the postcards jumping to new positions (below). Don't panic…

STEP 32: Set your Comp window to Active Camera view. Select all the postcard layers, and select Layer>Pre-compose, or use the shortcut Command+Shift+C (Control+Shift+C). The Pre-compose dialog will open; give this new comp a useful name such as "**Postcards_precomp**" and click OK.

When you precompose 2D layers, you are used to the Comp window not changing; the only action happens in the Timeline window, where the previously selected layers are replaced with a precomp. However, in this case the Comp window may have changed considerably: The postcards act like they are being seen in Front view, while the rest of the layers appear in their normal Active Camera view poses.

The problem is related to After Effects not knowing whether or not you also wanted to pre-compose the cameras as well, and how to treat this precomp in the main composition. The pre-composed layers are now using the default camera in [**Postcards_precomp**], with the result appearing as a 2D layer in [**Camera * starter**].

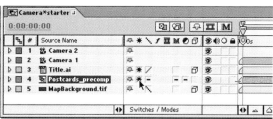

This can be remedied with a single click of the mouse: In the Timeline window for [**Camera * starter**], turn on the Collapse Transformations switch for the layer **Postcards_precomp**. This will instruct the 3D layers in the comp [**Postcards_precomp**] to ignore their own camera (and any lights), and to use the camera in [**Camera * starter**]. The Comp window should return to displaying the same poses as before you precomposed.

32 complete: Turn on Collapse Transformations for your nested precomp. This will instruct the 3D layers in the precomp to use the cameras in this higher-level comp.

> Note that merely turning on the 3D switch for the precomp layer is not the solution – this just sets the precomp's 2D composite output as a 3D layer in the main comp, where it reacts to the camera in a different way. You need to also Collapse Transformations.

STEP 33: As with any precomp, you can further transform this layer in the current comp:

• Turn on the 3D Layer switch for **Postcards_precomp**. You need to do this to manipulate this precomp in 3D space. Since you've collapsed this precomp's transformations, all 3D transforms performed here will be factored into the 3D transforms for each individual layer in the precomp.

• With **Postcards_precomp** still selected, press R to reveal its Orientation and Rotation properties. Experiment with scrubbing their different parameters – especially Y. Your entire set of postcards will rotate around **Title.ai**, *in 3D space.*

33 Scrub the Y Orientation parameter for **Postcards_precomp**. Although it may seem you should just be twirling this layer around its center (below left), since it has been collapsed you are also swinging all of the nested layers, with their 3D offsets taken into account (below right). The Advanced 3D plug-in was used for these illustrations, allowing intersections between the layers.

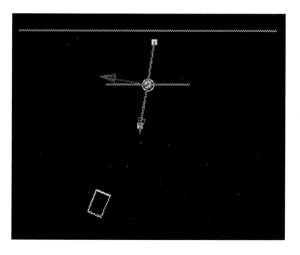

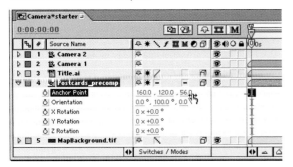

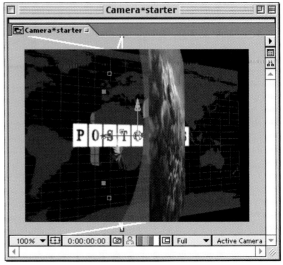

33 *complete:* Scrubbing the Z value of the precomp's Anchor Point (above) moves the entire group in relation to their center (right). This also changes the arc they will rotate in.

Effecting 3D

Trying to apply effects to a group of 3D layers is a frustrating experience. An advantage of precomposing (see Step 32) is that normally, you can apply an effect to the precomp and have it treat all the grouped layers at once. However, collapsing a precomp's transformations removes the ability to add effects – and if you try using an Adjustment Layer instead, it will break the 2D/3D rendering order, as Adjustment Layers must be in 2D. Even Parenting is no use here, as it controls transformations only, not effects.

There is one workaround: After you Precompose, Copy the Camera layer from the current comp and Paste it into the precomp. As a result, you won't have to collapse the nested precomp layer to borrow the camera's move, and you can apply effects to this precomp normally. Drawbacks include keeping two cameras in sync (Expressions can handle that pretty easily), and the fact that the precomp layer must be 2D (if you turn on the 3D switch it will react to the main comp's camera as well). You also can't interact with other 3D layers, such as casting or receiving shadows.

Okay, that was kind of freaky; what's going on? 3D layers – including precomps – have 3D Anchor Points, as well. If a layer's Anchor Point is set to be forward of the surface of the layer, rotating or orienting it will swing it around as if it was on a stick attached to that anchor in 3D space. A precomp defaults to having its Position and Anchor Point at Z = 0, which is the same location as **Title.ai**. However, since some of your postcards are probably set back at a different Z value, rotating their collapsed precomp swings the nested postcards around the precomp's anchor.

If you want to get a better handle on this, press Shift+A to also reveal **Postcards_precomp**'s Anchor Point, and scrub its Z value. You will see the entire group of postcards move closer to and farther away from the center of the comp where **Title.ai** is. Then continue to scrub the Orientation and Rotation properties, noting how the postcards swing in different arcs depending on the anchor's position.

Step 34: Feel free to experiment with the other Transform properties of **Postcards_precomp**, such as Position, Scale, and Opacity. These should all work as you would expect. Finish by placing this precomp in a pose you like. We personally settled on our arrangement at the time we precomposed. When you're done, twirl up all layer outlines to tidy up your Timeline window.

Stationary Bugs

As mentioned earlier, After Effects allows 2D and 3D layers to be mixed in the same comp. This comes in handy if you have an object that needs to stay in the same place in a frame, regardless of what the camera is doing.

STEP 35: With the time at 00:00, press the apostrophe key (') to toggle on the Title-Action Safe grid in the Comp window.

Then locate the **EarthBug.tif** in the **MySources** folder, and drag it to the lower right corner of the Comp window, near the Title Safe lines. You are going to be using this as a "bug" to overlay on top of your composition. Scale it down (shortcut: S) to an appropriate size – around 15% to 25% is good – and tweak its Position. Toggle the title safe guides back off.

Jump around to different points in time in the comp. Note that the bug stays in the same position regardless of the camera move. This is because new layers default to being 2D, which aren't affected by the camera. If you place this layer on top of the stack in the Timeline window, it will also render on top of all the other layers, regardless of their Z Positions.

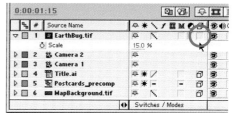

35 The earth "bug" in the lower right corner (top) is not affected by the camera's animation, because it is a 2D layer (above).

A Light Touch

The final optional element you might add is a spotlight to further enhance the feeling of depth, and to add a vignette effect to the edges of the frame. Lights were covered in more detail in the tutorial *Piccadilly Circus*; if you are not familiar with them, you might want to come back to these final steps after you have worked through that tutorial. Here we will remind you of a few general tips.

STEP 36: Return the time marker to 00:00, and twirl up all layers. Select Layer>New>Light. The Light Settings default to the last light you created; use a Type of Spot and enable Casts Shadows. We used the values shown in the figure to the right, but you can always tweak all of these parameters later.

New lights also tend to be positioned too close to layers that are near Z = 0; move the light's Z Position to at least –300 to illuminate more of the scene.

Layers default to *receiving* shadows, but not *casting* shadows. You want the main title to cast shadows on the postcards behind. Select the layer **Title.ai**, and type AA to reveal its Material Options. Toggle the Casts Shadows option from Off to On.

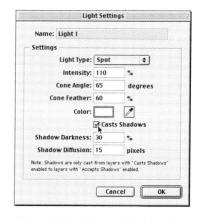

36 At 00:00, add a spotlight (above). For shadows to work, they need to be enabled both for the light, and for a forward layer to cast them (below). New lights may not fully illuminate layers that are near 0 on the Z axis (left).

37 The light will initially be too close to the layers, so only a small area will be illuminated, until you move it back in Z.

Draft 3D

Lights and shadows require a lot of extra rendering time. To speed up previews, turn on the Draft 3D switch in the Timeline to temporarily disable the effect of lights and the camera's optional Depth of Field.

38 Frames from the final animation. Note the shadow cast by the title, and how the 2D earth bug in the lower right corner is not affected by animating the light and cameras.

STEP 37: Since you want the light to focus on the main title, check the Position of **Title.ai** (it should be 160,120,0) and check that these values are also being used for the Point of Interest of your light. The same shortcut – A – reveals the Point of Interest for both cameras and lights.

With the light selected, type Shift+P to reveal its Position property, and enable it for animation. Since we have not animated the layers, animate the light to perform a mild sweep during the length of the comp so the result does not appear static. Everything you've learned about moving the camera applies to lights, including taking advantage of the different views, and making sure your motion path is smooth.

STEP 38: RAM Preview or jump around to different points in time, and see if you are happy with your light and animation. If not, feel free to tweak away. Here are a few tips to keep in mind when you're working with lights and shadows:

• A light's falloff darkens an image, as it is no longer fully illuminated. Increase the light's Intensity past 100% if needed – there is no penalty.

• If the light is closer to the layer casting shadows than the camera is, the resulting shadow will be larger than the layer casting it. The farther away the light, the tighter the shadow.

• In order to see a shadow, there needs to be some separation in space between layers casting shadows and those receiving them. You might need to move **Postcards_precomp** farther away from the title to better see the shadows they are receiving.

• In After Effects version 5.0, soft shadows tend to be a bit blocky, which can look messy – particularly if the layer casting the shadow has details you want to see, like the characters of a word. Try lower Shadow Diffusion values for the **Light** layer. We find that 5 to 15 pixels work well for a 320×240 pixel comp. Once you reduce the Shadow Diffusion amount, your shadow may now appear too dark. Reduce the Shadow Darkness amount to get a less heavy-handed shadow effect.

When you're finished, set all the layers to Best Quality, and either RAM Preview or render your final composition. Our favorite features in After Effects are those that give us "looks" we could not get in prior versions; 3D space certainly qualifies for this award.

Part 6: Postcards from Earth

The techniques you've learned in this tutorial are easily extended to more complex projects. Go back and play the file **Postcards.mov** in this tutorial's **Final Movies** folder. The project that created this movie – **Postcards_5.aep** – is broken down in detail in the document **08B_Postcards_Bonus.pdf** on your disk. In the meantime, here are the highlights:

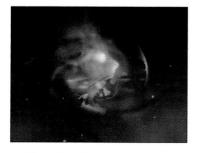

The project **Postcards_5.aep** extends the techniques learned in this tutorial. The earth is created with the FE Sphere effect (included free on your CD) and expressions make it follow the camera creating the illusion of real 3D. The opening movie (left) is from the Artbeats CD Space and Planets; the gradient wipe is from Pixelan's Video SpiceRack.

- 2D and 3D layers are interwoven throughout the spot. The opening space flythrough is 2D footage, which dissolves away with a gradient wipe to reveal a 3D world behind. A pair of 2D layers provide a steady backdrop throughout. The main title is also in 2D, composited over the 3D world. The postcard precomps are used both in 3D space in the middle of the spot and as 2D elements in the main title at the end.

- Four different 3D cameras are used to view the same world from different angles. The cameras are trimmed to cut on musical beats.

- The "hero" of the 3D scenes – a stylized earth floating in the middle of the frame – is created using the classic effect plug-in FE Sphere (included free on your CD courtesy of Media 100). We will detail how we created the texture map for this translucent globe, and a series of relatively simple expressions which keep FE Sphere's 2D layer always oriented towards the currently active camera, creating the illusion that it has true 3D depth.

- The postcards were built using a series of template precomps for their shapes and the circular cutout animation. Different footage was then used inside these templates. This means changes made in one composition – such as altering the basic postcard shape – automatically ripples through to all of the postcard precomps. Expressions also allow us to control the opacity of the solid-colored frames for all the postcards from one slider in the final composition.

- Notice how the background flashes in time with the soundtrack? We'll walk you through how to use Time Remapping to force the pace of one clip to follow another.

The new 3D space features introduced in After Effects 5.0 have opened up new worlds for graphical design. Have fun exploring them!

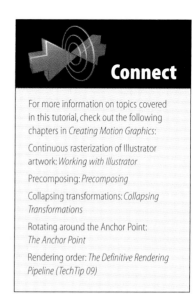

Connect

For more information on topics covered in this tutorial, check out the following chapters in *Creating Motion Graphics*:

Continuous rasterization of Illustrator artwork: *Working with Illustrator*

Precomposing: *Precomposing*

Collapsing transformations: *Collapsing Transformations*

Rotating around the Anchor Point: *The Anchor Point*

Rendering order: *The Definitive Rendering Pipeline (TechTip 09)*

The Planets

Swooping through a universe of 2D layers that auto-orient toward the camera.

This tutorial serves two purposes: to teach some additional tricks that help manage layers in 3D space, and to prepare elements that will be used in the next tutorial. You will animate a 3D camera through a number of objects – flat art of fanciful planets – arranged at varying distances in Z space. The camera and light will both auto-orient along the path they're traveling, and the flat objects will auto-orient toward the camera as it flies past to help maintain the illusion that they have depth. You will then prerender this action as separate color and matte layers to use as part of an opening title sequence.

OVERVIEW

Main Concepts:

These are the features and concepts we will be focusing on in this project:

- Auto-Orient Camera along Path
- Expressing the Light Position
- Auto-Orient Light along Path
- Multiple view windows
- Pixel Aspect Ratio correction
- Auto-Orient layers toward Camera
- Creating a 3D layer
- Adding camera roll
- Depth of Field & Focus Distance
- Field rendering
- Adding Output Modules
- Rendering a separate fill and matte
- Rendering with straight alpha

Requirements:

After Effects 5.0 or later standard version.

(Rendering techniques in Part 4 are applicable to all versions.)

Getting Started:

Inside the **Tutorials** master folder on the accompanying CD, locate and copy the folder **09_Planets** to your hard drive.

In the folder **Final Movie** inside this main folder, double-click on and play **Planets.mov**.

Inside the **Project** folder you'll find the finished After Effects project file **Planets_5.aep**. Open the project file – this is your starting point; we suggest you save under a new name after each major section.

Much of the tedious work of arranging the camera and the faux planets in Z space has already been done. This will allow you to focus on the core of this tutorial: using tools in After Effects to orient the camera, light, and objects for you. Afterward, you will position one remaining planet, tweak the position of another, and swap out other planets to taste. On the technical side, you will also be working in a D1 NTSC composition with non-square pixels which you will need to field render for the next tutorial.

We're going to assume you already have some experience working in 3D comps, or have already completed the previous tutorial *Postcards in Space*. If not, work through at least enough of that tutorial to familiarize yourself with navigating After Effects' 3D toolset.

A frame from the final *Planets* fly-through. Depth of field is turned on which renders the planets in the foreground and background out of focus.

The Tasks

This is what you will be doing in the various parts of this tutorial:

PART 1: Use Auto-Orientation to automatically point the camera and light along their paths and the planets at the camera, express the light to follow the camera, and create a second viewer comp.

PART 2: Add another planet and place it in 3D space, tweak the positions of some of the planets, and swap out planet layers with alternate planets.

PART 3: Improve the camera's motion by adding an ease out and banking rotation, plus use Depth of Field for selective focusing.

PART 4: Learn how to render a composition as separate RGB and alpha channel movies.

Draft vs. Best

To speed up previews, we have left the planet layers in Draft Quality. They will shimmer more, but the time savings is worth it. You will render them at Best Quality at the end.

Part 1: The Orient Express

Previous to version 5.0, After Effects had the ability to automatically orient layers so they would point along a 2D animation path. With the addition of 3D space in version 5.0, Auto-Orientation has been expanded to include auto-orienting cameras and lights as well as layers along a 3D path. Layers can also be set to automatically orient themselves toward the camera so you can always catch their good side.

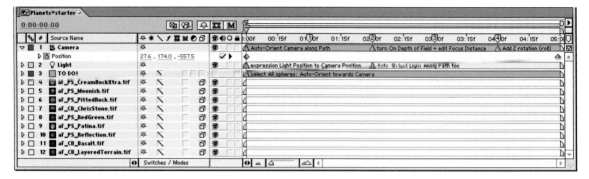

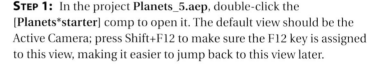

1–2 In the starter comp, only the camera's Position property is animating. The layer comments applied to **Camera** and **Light** spell out what else you will be doing to these layers; we also added a solid with its Video switch turned off to give more room for comments.

Pasteboard Zoom

To zoom the Comp window down and see more of the pasteboard, use the shortcut , (comma key). Use . (period key) to zoom back up.

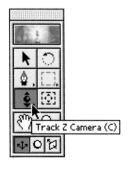

4 To zoom the 3D views in to fit inside the Comp window, first select the Track Z Camera tool.

STEP 1: In the project **Planets_5.aep**, double-click the [**Planets*starter**] comp to open it. The default view should be the Active Camera; press Shift+F12 to make sure the F12 key is assigned to this view, making it easier to jump back to this view later.

STEP 2: Use Command+A on Mac (Control+A on Windows) to select all the layers, press U to reveal any animation keyframes that have already been applied, then press F2 to deselect the layers. You will notice that only the Camera is animating, with two Position keyframes.

STEP 3: Select the Camera layer, then select the Left view from the View popup at the bottom of the Comp window. Press Shift+F11 to ensure that F11 has been assigned to this view. This will make switching views easier as you proceed.

From this angle, you should see the camera and a portion of its motion path, but you might be zoomed in too close to see its full path and all the layers. You can either enlarge the Comp window and/or reduce the comp's magnification until you see the entire path, or use the Track Camera tools:

STEP 4: To quickly resize the Left view, follow these steps:

• Make sure the Tools window is open; if not, press Command+1 (Control+1) to open it.

• Press C until the Track Z Camera tool is selected.

• Click in the Comp window and drag either left or down to zoom out until you can see all of the layers and the entire length of the camera's motion path.

> When you're in any of the orthogonal views (Top, Left, Right, and so on), the Camera Track tools can be used to zoom in and recenter your view of the world – without affecting the X, Y, and Z values of your camera layers. These tools only affect values in Active Camera view.

To get another perspective on the camera's path, select the Top view, and press Shift+F10 to make sure this shortcut key has been assigned. With the Track Z Camera tool still selected, click and drag in the Comp

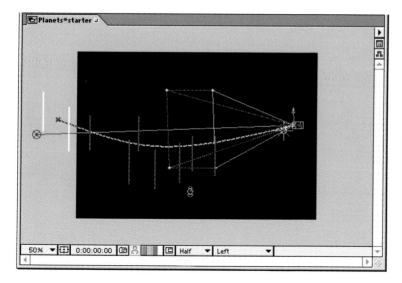

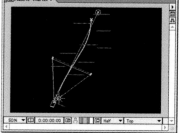

4 *continued:* In the Left view, zoom the 3D views in to fit inside the Comp window (left) by clicking and dragging in the Comp window with the Track Z Camera tool until the camera path and all of the layers fit.

window to zoom back as necessary to see the entire path. If the layers are a bit off center in the Comp window, press C twice to toggle around to the Track X/Y Camera tool, then drag them inside the Comp window until they are centered to your taste. When you're satisfied with your views, press V to return to the Selection tool.

STEP 5: Drag the time marker in the Timeline window and watch the camera move along its path. Note that only the "back" of the camera is moving, with its Point of Interest remaining behind the farthest layer.

Orienting the Camera along its Path

The current camera animation just pushes forward past the planets, rather than swooping between the planets as you might hope. You could try animating the camera's Point of Interest to change the direction the camera is looking as it sweeps along its curved path, but the effort will soon feel like you're trying to steer both the front and back wheels of a car independently from each other. In other words, it's tricky. Using the Auto-Orient option tells After Effects to do the steering for you.

STEP 6: Select the **Camera** layer, twirl up its properties to hide the Position keyframes, and twirl the layer down again to reveal all of its Transform properties.

STEP 7: With the **Camera** layer selected, press Command+Option+O (Control+Alt+O), or use the menu command Layer>Transform>Auto-Orient. A dialog will appear with a set of choices of how you want the object to orient. Choose Orient Along Path and click OK.

Out of the corner of your eye, you may have caught that the Timeline display changed. Look closely, and you will notice that the Point of Interest parameter has disappeared, since it is no longer being used.

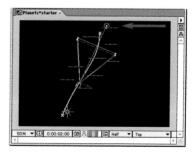

4 *complete:* The Top view gives a different perspective on the camera's path. Use the Track Camera tools to alter this view to taste.

5 As the camera moves along its path, the Point of Interest (where arrow is pointing) remains stationery.

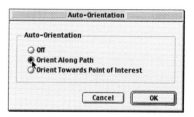

7 Select Layer>Transform>Auto-Orient for the **Camera**. Select the option Orient Along Path.

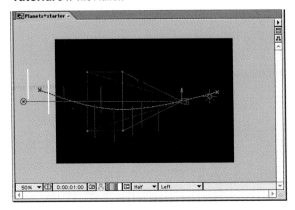
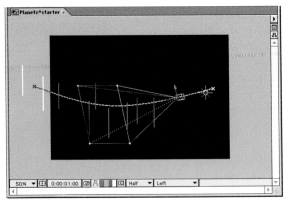

8 The camera defaults to orienting toward its Point of Interest (left). When Auto-Orientation is set to Path, it points along a tangent to its Position path (right).

Step 8: Still in the Top view (shortcut: F10), scrub the time marker and observe the camera's path now. Notice it now points at a tangent to its current position on its Position path, rather than at its Point of Interest (which is now gone). Press F11 to switch to Left view, and scrub the timeline here also. If you want to compare the difference, just bring up the Auto-Orientation dialog and set the option back to Orient Towards Point of Interest and notice the difference. Be sure to set it back to Orient Along Path when you're done.

> The third Auto-Orientation choice – Off – also disables the Point of Interest, but it does not force the camera to look along its path either. In this mode, you use Rotation and Orientation to point the camera, which mimics the way some 3D programs work.

If you need to compare your work so far, we've saved a comp in your project with the camera already oriented correctly, under the name [Planets_after Step 08]. *You can find it in the* **Planets * prebuilt> compare comps_after Step ## *folder. Don't forget to save your project.***

The Collapse of Auto-Orient

If you precompose a group of 3D layers that are set to Orient Towards Camera, and then Collapse Transformations, you might expect the layers from the precomp to continue to auto-orient toward the camera. But they won't.

Expressive Lighting

To illuminate your way as you travel among the planets, it would be handy if the light always pointed the same way as the camera. This is very easy to set up with expressions (refer to figures on the next page).

Step 9: Select both the **Camera** and **Light** layers. Type P to reveal both of their Position properties. Note that they are currently different from each other.

Step 10: Option+click (Alt+click) on the **Light** layer's Position animation stopwatch. This will enable expressions for this property and write a default expression that means "Position = position."

Drag the pick whip tool for the **Light** layer to point at the word Position for the **Camera** layer. Release the mouse, and hit Enter to accept the new expression. Look at their Position properties, and note that they are now the same.

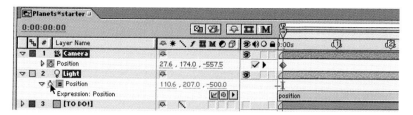

10 Option+click (Alt+click) on the stopwatch to enable Expressions for the **Light** layer's Position property.

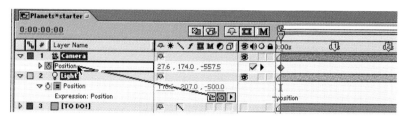

Once the Expression is enabled, drag its pick whip to the Position property for Camera.

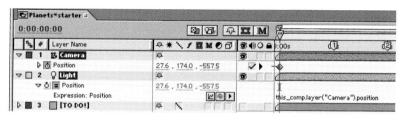

Release the mouse, and hit Enter to accept the new Expression.

Step 11: With both the **Light** and **Camera** layers still selected, press F11 to recall the Left view, and scrub the time marker along the length of the timeline. The **Light** layer does indeed stay attached to the **Camera** layer...but it doesn't point in the same direction; it's still pointing at its own Point of Interest. Use the same cure as you did for **Camera**:

- Make sure **Light** is the only layer selected.

- Press Command+Option+O (Control+Alt+O) to bring up its Auto-Orientation dialog.

- Select Orient Along Path, and click OK.

11 The light has been expressed to have the same position as the camera, but it's still aimed at its own Point of Interest (below left). It needs its Auto-Orientation also set to Orient Along Path (below right).

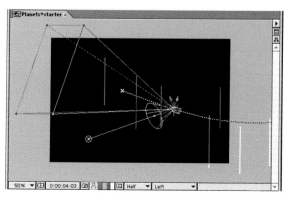

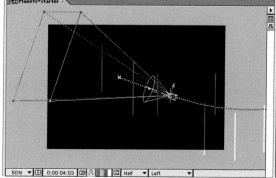

Time Lock

In Edit>Preferences>General, make sure the option to Synchronize Time of All Related Items is enabled. When you move the time marker in either the precomp or viewer comp, the other will update to the same time.

The **Light** layer will lose its Point of Interest, and instead snap to point in the same direction as the **Camera** layer. You'll notice that the Light has no visible motion path, since it's following the Camera's path via the expression. You can scrub the time marker and check out the different views to verify this, if you wish. Twirl up their Position properties when you're done.

> You could have achieved a similar result by Parenting the light to the camera, but both would need to have been set to the exact same position and orientation at the moment you parented. On the other hand, if you wanted the light to be offset from the camera's positioning, it would be easier to set up this offset and then parent, rather than use an expression.

We've saved a version with the light already expressed and oriented under the name [**Planets_after Step 11**], *if you need to compare your version with ours.*

Second Sight

Use F12 to switch [**Planets*starter**] to the Active Camera view, and RAM Preview the comp. The **Camera** and **Light** layers now are flying nicely along their paths, but the overall scene just doesn't look that good – the planets are darkly lit, and something funny is going on with their aspect ratios (they should all be perfect spheres). To get further insight to what's going on, we'll create a viewer comp to give you a second window on your edits to [**Planets*starter**].

12 Drag [**Planets*starter**] to the New Composition button at the bottom of the Project window to create your viewer comp.

STEP 12: In the Project window, drag [**Planets*starter**] to the New Composition icon at the bottom of the window. This will create a new comp called Comp 1. Press Command+K (Control+K) and give it the new name "**My_Viewer**".

13 By nesting [**Planets*starter**] into another comp, you can look at alternate views in the first comp (below left) and see the result of the Active Camera in the second comp (below right).

STEP 13: If your new comp opened in the same set of windows as [**Planets*starter**], drag its tab in the Comp window outside the boundaries of that window, and release – a new Comp window will be created for it. Resize and position both windows so you can see them at the same time. On a 1024×768 or similar monitor size, setting both to 50% Zoom and Half Resolution works well.

Back in [**Planets*starter**], use F10 or F11 to change the view mode to Top or Left, respectively. Note that [**My_Viewer**] continues to show you the equivalent of the Active Camera view. This saves some extra clicking around when you're trying to compare your edits with their results.

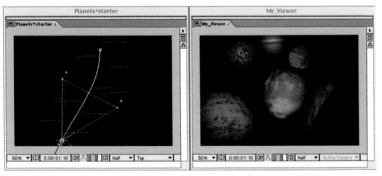

Step 14: Select [**My_Viewer**] and use Command+K (Control+K) to open its Composition Settings. Its Pixel Aspect Ratio is set to D1/DV NTSC. This setting tells After Effects that when it's played back on a real video monitor, the final image will be scaled horizontally by about 90%. In the meantime, the comp you are viewing on your computer monitor looks about 111% as wide as it will on playback.

There are two ways to compensate for this while you work. One is to change the Preset for [**My_Viewer**] to NTSC, 648×486. This will change the Pixel Aspect Ratio to Square Pixels – what your computer monitor displays. Instead, let's exploit a new feature introduced in After Effects 5.0 to give us a temporary square pixel view.

Click on Cancel to get out of the Composition Settings dialog, and instead click on the wing menu icon at the upper right edge of the Comp window for [**My_Viewer**]. Enable the option Pixel Aspect Correction. The display in the Comp window will now shrink horizontally about 10%, to give you a more accurate view. This scaling is done using the equivalent of Draft Quality (no antialiasing), and is only for preview; the comp would not be rendered this way. After Effects will warn you of these consequences – but this mode is still good for a quick check.

> For more details on managing D1/DV NTSC non-square sources, check out the tutorial *AutoTracker* earlier in this book, and the chapter *Working with D1/DV NTSC* in *Creating Motion Graphics*.

Angling for Attention

Set the time marker to around 01:10, and stare at the spheres in [**My_Viewer**]. The spheres roughly in the center of the window look taller than they should; the sphere in the lower left corner looks wider than it should. These distortions are not caused by their pixel aspect ratio, but by the fact that they do not face the camera head-on. Instead, you are viewing them at a slant, which is causing this perspective distortion.

Fortunately, just as you can orient cameras and lights along a path, you can orient other layers to face the camera.

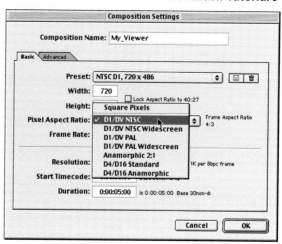

14 Both of your comps use D1/DV NTSC aspect pixels, which means their images display about 10% wider on your computer monitor than they will during final video playback.

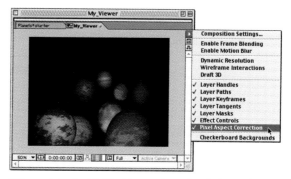

14 *complete:* Enable Pixel Aspect Correction for [**My_Viewer**] to preview this comp using a square pixel aspect ratio.

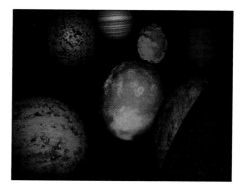

15 If the planets do not face the camera, the resulting perspective distortion makes them look like out-of-round spheres.

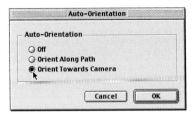

15 *continued:* Set all the planets to Orient Towards Camera.

STEP 15: Bring the [**Planets*starter**] comp forward, and set its view to Top. Then select all the planet layers (select layer 4 then Shift+click layer 12), and press Command+Option+O (Control+Alt+O) to open the Auto-Orientation dialog. Pick the option Orient Towards Camera, and click OK. You will notice three things happen:

• In the Comp window for [**Planets*starter**], all of the planet layers will snap to new orientations, pointing at the camera. While they are still selected, note their axis orientation arrows – their blue Z arrows are all pointed straight at the camera.

• All of the planets in [**My_Viewer**] suddenly look a lot more like spheres.

• All of the planets in [**My_Viewer**] are also brighter. Not only are they facing the camera, they're facing the light you expressed to the camera back in Step 10. This light is now getting bounced straight back at the camera, resulting in better illumination.

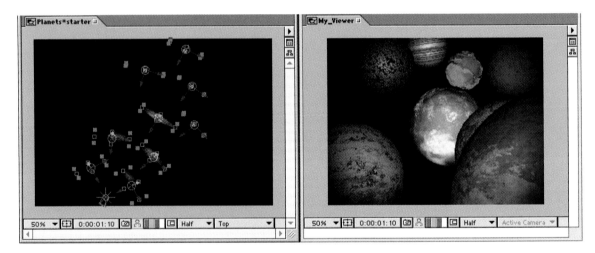

15 *complete:* After you set the planets to orient toward the camera, notice how their blue Z axis arrows now all point at the camera (left). The result the camera sees (right) is less perspective distortion, and better illumination. Compare this with the otherwise identical figure for Step 15 on the previous page.

Still in the Top view, scrub the time marker in [**Planets*starter**] and watch how the planets continue to rotate to face the camera as it travels along its path. Whenever you stop and release the mouse, [**My_Viewer**] will update to show you what the camera sees. RAM Preview [**My_Viewer**] (or switch [**Planets*starter**] back to Active Camera view using F12 and RAM Preview it), and observe that you don't really notice these planets rotating around as the camera flies by them – the result looks surprisingly natural, and helps sell the illusion that they are 3D spheres, rather than cardboard cutouts of spheres.

• Deselect All (F2) when you're through exploring.

Now would be a good time to Save your project. If you want to make sure the light, camera, and planets in your comp are behaving correctly, compare it with our version [**Planets_after Step 15**].

Virtual Planets

All of the "planets" in this project are simple spheres created in and rendered from the 3D program Electric Image (www.electricimage.com). The camera and light were aimed straight toward their centers, to remove any sense of directional lighting that would have caused perspective problems later in After Effects. Their surfaces were created using a procedural shader called aFraktal, distributed by Triple D Tools (www.tripledtools.com). Virtually all of the planets use presets provided with aFraktal; the second pair of letters in their names denote who created the preset:

CB = *Chris Bernardi*

ML = *Mark Lewno*

PS = *Paul Sherstobitoff*

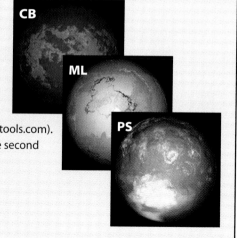

Part 2: Building a Better Universe

The basic flythrough is working well now. In this part, you will enhance it further by adding one more planet and tweaking the positions of others or swapping them out.

The Final Sphere

We purposely left out a planet so you could get a little practice adding and positioning a 3D layer.

STEP 16: With the [**Planets*starter**] comp forward, press Home to return its time marker to 00:00, and press F10 to switch to the Top view. Turn on the Draft 3D switch in the Timeline window to speed up interactions; this has the side benefit of making all the planets appear evenly lit regardless of where the **Light** layer is pointing.

    If you can't see all the planets in the Comp window, press C until the Track Z Camera tool is selected, and zoom the display back a little. Keep [**My_Viewer**] open and visible elsewhere on your screen; you will be using it to help you place the final planet.

STEP 17: In the Project window, open the _**Planets * prebuilt> Sources** folder. Select the footage item **aF_PS_CreamRock.tif** and press Command+/ (Control+/) to add it to [**Planets*starter**].

STEP 18: From the Top view, all of the other planets are being viewed from above, meaning they appear as thin slivers. However, as soon as you add **aF_PS_CreamRock.tif** to the comp, you'll notice that it's quite large and that it's facing directly at you. If you were to switch to the Left view (press F11), it would still be facing you. This is because it

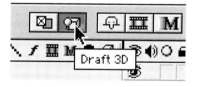

16 Enable Draft 3D to speed up interactions during the next few steps.

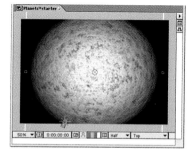

17 When you add the **aF_PS_CreamRock.tif** to your comp, it will dominate the frame because it is still a 2D layer.

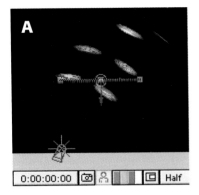

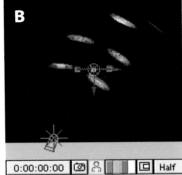

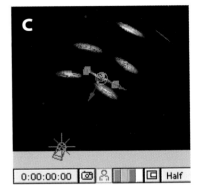

18 Set the new planet's 3D Layer switch (A), scale it to roughly 40% (B), and set it to auto-orient toward the camera (C). The timeline reflects the changes so far (right).

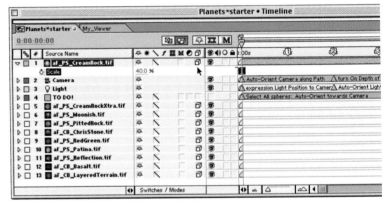

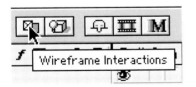

Wily Wireframes

Wireframe Interactions makes After Effects faster to use by turning off realtime previews while editing a layer's properties or scrubbing the Timeline. It is equivalent to holding down the Option (Alt) key while editing (see also Preferences>Previews).

defaults to being a 2D layer, ignoring these 3D perspective changes. To put it in its place, from the Top view:

• Enable its 3D Layer switch in the Timeline. It will now shift in perspective to match the other planets, but it's still larger than they are.

• With the layer selected in the Timeline, press S to reveal its Scale property, and enter 40% to start with – roughly the same value as used by the other spheres. It will now match the other planets in size. But if you look at [**My_Viewer**], you will note it looks oblong instead of round – because it isn't oriented toward the camera like all the other planets are.

• Press Command+U (Control+U) to turn on Best Quality.

• With this layer still selected, press Command+Option+O (Control+Alt+O) to bring up its Auto-Orientation dialog. Select Orient Towards Camera, and click OK. It will now face the camera just as all the planets do.

STEP 19: We felt this new planet should go just forward, to the left, and slightly above the nice blue-gold planet (**aF_PS_Patina.tif**) that's roughly in the center of the arrangement. Practice using some of After Effects' different tools while you're placing it to your taste:

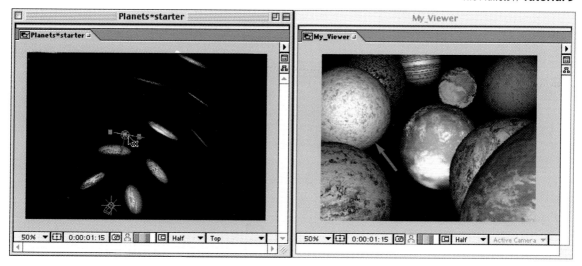

• With **aF_PS_CreamRock.tif** still selected, press P to reveal its Position property. Scrub the X, Y, and Z parameters in the Timeline to position it. When you release the mouse, [**My_Viewer**] will update to show you the Active Camera's view.

• Still in the [**Planets*starter**] comp, press V to make sure the Selection tool is active. Directly click on **aF_PS_CreamRock.tif** in the Comp window and move it. You may want to zoom into the comp 200% (press the period key on the keyboard) in order to see the object clearly. If the characters X, Y, or Z appear near your cursor as you are about to click, your movements will be constrained to just this axis. A cursor with no characters means you can move it freely, though clicking outside the object will deselect it. Try clicking on the left side where there is no axis if you want to move the layer freely.

• Enable Wireframe Interactions in the Timeline window, then again try moving the planet directly in the Comp window – notice how much faster the window updates as you move it around.

• Disable Wireframe Interactions, and move the time marker to see how the planet interacts as the camera gets closer – it will swivel away slightly as it tries to stay oriented toward the camera. This might change your opinion on where to place the planet, and how large you want to scale it.

We decided on a Scale of 33% and Position of X330, Y300, Z360. If you would like to place it somewhere else, feel free to do so – just make sure the camera doesn't crash into it during its flythrough! When you're done, drag **aF_PS_CreamRock.tif** down the layer stack in the Timeline so that it sits between other planets near it in the Top view, to help keep things organized.

3D layers do not need to be sorted in the Timeline, as the render order is based on their position in space (layers farthest away from the camera are rendered first).

19 Place your new planet along the camera's flight path. Here, we are parked at 01:15; we're using the Top view of [**Planets*starter**] (left) to position it and [**My_Viewer**] (right) to check the result. The X by the cursor means that if we were to click and drag now, movement would be restricted to the X axis.

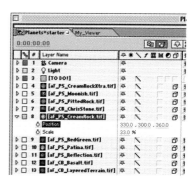

19 *complete:* After you've set the Position and Scale of the final planet, drag it down the layer stack until it rests between adjacent planets in the comp.

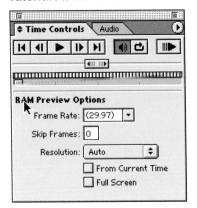

20 Toggle between "RAM Preview Options" and "Shift+RAM Preview Options" by clicking on their names.

21 Move **aF_CB_Basalt.tif** closer to the camera as it flies by to create more excitement.

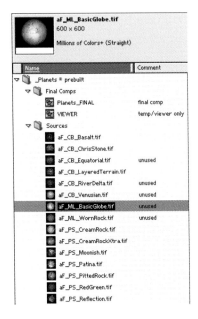

Planet Tweaks

All of the planets are now in place so now is a good time to Save. The next steps will fine-tune their positions and replace some of the planets.

STEP 20: In [**Planets*starter**], press F12 to set the view back to Active Camera. Press 0 on the keypad to perform a RAM Preview. If it is taking too long to render, stop the preview, and hold down Shift when you press 0 – this calls up an alternate set of preview parameters. The default is to preview every other frame, but you can adjust these settings in the Time Controls window. If you can't see the Time Controls, press Command+3 (Control+3) to open its window.

STEP 21: As we mentioned earlier, one of the side effects of using Auto-Orientation is that the planets tend to swivel aside as the camera gets close to them. This reduces the excitement of some of the closer encounters you might have noticed back before Step 12 – especially as

you pass by the second-to-last planet **aF_CB_Basalt.tif** at around time 04:00. Feel free to alter the Position or Scale of some of the planets to increase the fear factor. We nudged **aF_CB_Basalt.tif** over to X540, for example.

STEP 22: We supplied you more planets than we used in the final comp. Feel free to swap out some of the planets for ones you like better.

In the Timeline, twirl up all layers. In the Project window, look at the **_Planets * prebuilt>Sources** folder. Resize the window, or reduce the size of the Name panel along the top, until you can see the Comments panel – note that we have entered "unused" in the Comment field for some (see figure on left). You can also select one of these footage items, and look at the top of the Project window to see if they are already used in compositions. Press the up and down arrows to scroll through them.

To see what a planet looks like, double-click it to open its Footage window. To swap it in for another planet in [**Planets*starter**]:

• In [**Planets*starter**], select the planet layer you wish to replace.

• In the Project window, select the planet you wish to use instead.

• Press Command+Option+/ (Control+Alt+/) to swap in the new planet for the old, keeping the old planet's Scale and Position values as well as its Auto-Orientation options. You can also Option+drag (Alt+drag) the replacement to either the Comp or Timeline windows.

Feel free to customize your universe to your own tastes. If you want to compare the results with ours, check out our prebuilt comp, [**Planets_after Step 22**]. *Don't forget to Save your project file.*

Part 3: A Classier Camera

In this section of the tutorial, you will refine the camera move in three ways: making it pick up speed at the start of the composition, adding a bit of banking as it swerves between the planets, and enabling its Depth of Field to automatically vary the focus depending on how close the camera is to each planet at any point in time.

Go ahead and close the comp [**My_Viewer**]; you can rely on the single view in [**Planets*starter**] for the remaining steps. If your screen updates are still a bit slow, you can leave the Draft 3D switch On for now to speed them up.

Easing Out

As useful as it is, the Easy Ease keyframe assistant is not the answer for every situation in which you want an animation to speed up or slow down. In this case, we just want a small speed-up at the start of the camera's animation, rather than the full ease-out from a standstill that Easy Ease would create.

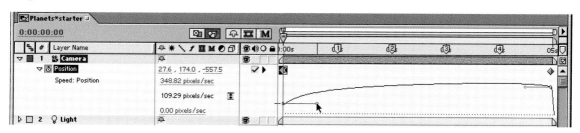

Step 23: In [**Planets*starter**], select the layer **Camera**. Press P to reveal its Position property in the Timeline, then twirl down the arrow next to the word Position to reveal its velocity graph. Press Home to return the time marker to 00:00, and select the Position keyframe at this time.

Step 24: When you select this keyframe, a handle will appear on the velocity graph line right underneath it. Drag this handle down about two-thirds of the way, until the pixels/sec readout to its left is just above 100 pixels per second. Also extend the handle's length until it's about two-thirds of the way to the first comp marker, at 01:00.

Step 25: If you look at the right end of the velocity graph, you will notice that it dips slightly before the last keyframe. Since you slowed down the initial velocity, After Effects had to make up time by speeding up the animation later in the timeline – but it was bound by the second keyframe, which forced this slight slowdown at the end. Drag this second handle up slightly until you have a flat line entering the second keyframe.

24 Pull the velocity handle for the camera's first Position keyframe down about two-thirds, to give a slight ease-out from its initial position.

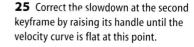

25 Correct the slowdown at the second keyframe by raising its handle until the velocity curve is flat at this point.

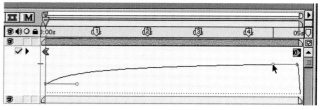

Rotation vs. Orientation

3D layers have two different ways to rotate them: normal Rotation and Orientation. As a general rule, use Rotation when you want to animate the rotation of an object and ensure that just that axis will rotate. Use Orientation when you are trying to pose an object, rather than animate it. You can animate the Orientation property, but After Effects will take shortcuts to get from one orientation to the next, which might not be what you want. A good analogy is to think of a spinning top: Animate the Y Rotation parameter for the spin, and animate Orientation to make it wobble about as it spins.

RAM Preview this new animation – the result should be subtle compared with a full Easy Ease, but it still adds interest as it builds up speed toward the end. If you like, tweak these velocity handles further to get the speed change you want.

Since you attached the light to the camera back in Step 10, there is no need to redo its Position velocity as well. The advantage of applying the expression to the light instead of simply copying and pasting the keyframes is that any change you make to the camera path or speed will automatically be reflected by the **Light** layer.

Bank 'n' Roll

The partial ease-out was a nice addition, but we want to add more drama to the animation and make it appear as if the viewer is really swooping around these planets:

STEP 26: With the **Camera** layer still selected, press R. This will twirl up the Position property and velocity graph, and twirl down its Rotation and Orientation values. Press Home to go to time 00:00, and enable the animation stopwatch for Z Rotation.

STEP 27: The goal is to make the camera bank into and out of its turns, as you would expect a plane to. We looked at the Top view and scrubbed through the timeline, looking at how much the camera's path was curving at different points in time as an indication of how much banking to include. Go to the following times, and enter the corresponding Z Rotation values:

00:00	Z Rotation 0°
01:15	Z Rotation +5°
04:00	Z Rotation −10°
04:29	Z Rotation −5°

STEP 28: Click on the words "Z Rotation" in the Timeline to select all of these Z Rotation keyframes, and use the menu command Animation> Keyframe Assistant>Easy Ease, or use the shortcut: F9. (Okay, we just told you Easy Ease wasn't the answer to every animation problem. That doesn't mean it isn't the perfect solution to some problems…)

RAM Preview again to check the results. If you start to feel a little seasick, reduce the Z Rotation amounts slightly, or if you'd like a wild ride, double the values. When you are satisfied, select the **Camera** layer, and press R again to twirl up the Rotation and Orientation properties.

28 Add some Z Rotation keyframes to simulate banking. Instead of just flying on a flat path between the planets, you will swoop between them. Select all the Rotation keyframes and apply Ease Ease (shortcut: F9) to smooth them out.

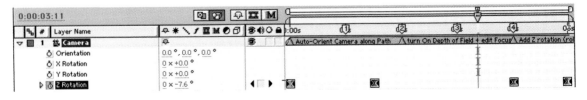

Save your project. You can compare your modified camera animation with our prebuilt comp [**Planets_after Step 28**].

Camera Depth of Field

After adding drama, now you're going to add some depth of character to your final piece. To do this, you will be using an option where only objects a certain distance from the camera are in sharp focus, while others closer or farther away are progressively out of focus.

STEP 29: *Turn the Draft 3D switch Off* – you cannot see the results of the Depth of Field parameters with it on. Press 2 to jump to 02:00 in the timeline, where you have planets both near and far to better see the effects of the following adjustments.

STEP 30: Hit Command+A (Control+A) to Select All, and press P to reveal the Position properties for all the layers. Scan down the list of layers, paying attention to the third Position parameter: their Z position. The planets are arrayed from about –100 to +900. The Depth of Field parameter uses distance from the camera to decide who is in focus and who isn't; looking at these numbers will give us a clue as to a good starting value. Press P to twirl up Position, and press F2 to Deselect All.

STEP 31: Twirl down the properties for the **Camera** layer, and twirl down the Options section (you can twirl up Transform as you don't need it). Click on the word Off to the right of the Depth of Field property; this will toggle it On. Increase the Blur Level to 300% so you can better see what effect changing the Focus Distance has. Experiment with the Focus Distance until you get a look you like; lower values bring the foreground objects into focus, while larger values bring background objects into focus. We used a Focus Distance of 500 (roughly the middle of our planet array, from front to back), and left the Blur Level at 300%.

If you have a little time to wait for the render, RAM Preview again to see how the objects that are in focus change throughout the flythrough. If you're impatient, initiate a Shift+RAM Preview, or simply check out the Comp window at a few different times along the Timeline.

Save your project. If you are completely lost, open our prebuilt [**Planets_FINAL**] *comp to compare your results.*

Aperture

The Aperture parameter in After Effects determines how many pixels in Z depth stay in focus, centered around Depth of Field. Objects outside this zone get progressively blurrier.

Delay of Field

Depth of Field adds a significant render hit. This is another reason the Draft 3D switch – which temporarily disables the Depth of Field effect – is a handy tool.

31 The difference between Depth of Field switched Off (far left) and On (left). Feel free to experiment with the Focus Distance and Blur Level parameters (above).

Alpha Panic

Most editing systems require a straight alpha. The edges around objects in the RGB movie will be expanded – often in ugly ways – to provide additional information for the alpha channel to fade away. This occasionally causes panic in editors who receive your footage; tell them to apply the alpha matte before they freak out…

Adding Modules

An additional Output Module was added by selecting the original render queue item and selecting Composition>Add Output Module. You can add as many Output Modules as you need.

In the Render Queue, you will find one composition to render, with two Output Modules: one for RGB, one for alpha.

Part 4: The Render Queue Tour

The planets flythrough animation is finished. We've already rendered the [**Planets_FINAL**] version to use in the next tutorial: an opening title for a mythical show called *Cosmopolis*. The render was created in two pieces – one movie with the RGB color information, and one with an alpha matte – which requires two Output Modules. If you want to learn how we set this up, read the following section.

Many editing systems can import movies rendered from After Effects with the alpha already embedded in the movie, in which case you would need only one Output Module. In it, set the Channels to RGB+Alpha, and Depth to Millions of Colors+ (the plus symbol indicates an alpha channel will be included). It's still safest to set the Color to Straight (Unmatted) for best results.

If your editing system has a codec that supports an embedded alpha, choose it under the Format Options button in the Output Module. We prefer the QuickTime Animation codec, set to Millions of Colors+, with the Quality slider set to 100%: This makes it lossless. This is our codec of choice when we're prerendering elements to be reused in After Effects. (Do not use the None codec: Contrary to a popular myth, its quality is no better, and it creates unnecessarily large files.)

Two Paths, One Goal

The title designer has been looking over your shoulder while you've been working on this animation, and says that she has an idea for making the title appear from behind the planets. This means you will need to deliver this render with an alpha channel, to ease compositing later. Some editing systems (such as the Avid) are also happier if you deliver separate color and alpha/matte movies; that's what we're going to do in this case.

Open the Render Queue window (under the menu item Window> Render Queue). We have already queued up [**Planets_FINAL**] (our version of this project), with two Output Modules: one for the RGB information, and one for the alpha channel matte.

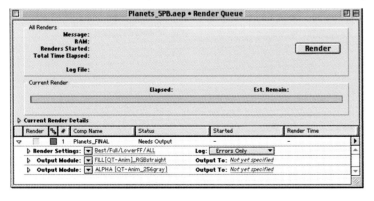

Click on "Best/Full/LowerFF/ALL" to the right of Render Settings to open the dialog. This is a template we have created for typical NTSC output: After Effects will render each frame of the animation at the comp's rate of 29.97 frames per second (fps), at Best Quality, with Full Resolution, Lower Field First, and the entire length of the composition. Click OK or Cancel when you're done reviewing its settings.

As After Effects renders each frame to these specs, it holds in memory an RGB image and its associated alpha channel. This frame is then passed to the Output Modules, which performs further processing on it before saving it to disk. In this case, we need two Output Modules: one to save the RGB information, and one to save the alpha.

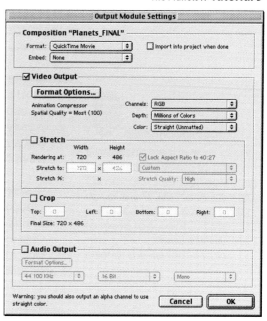

Click on the text "FILL[QT-Anim]_RGBstraight" for the first Output Module (shown at right). In the Video Output section, note that the Channels popup is set to RGB, with a Depth of Millions of Colors. What is slightly unusual is the Color setting: Straight (Unmatted). If you glance at the bottom of the dialog, you will also see the message "Warning: you should also output an alpha channel to use straight color."

Most editing systems require a Straight, rather than Premultiplied, alpha. Ironically, the alpha channel is identical between these two settings – it's the color channels that differ. For Premultiplied, the color channels look exactly like the final result. For Straight, the

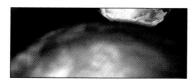  

Premultiplied color channels (left) look exactly like the final result. Straight color channels (middle) have extra pixels that are faded later by the alpha channel (right): Look closely at the curvature along the top left of the blue planet.

The second Output Module saves the alpha as a grayscale movie.

color channels have additional pixels spreading past the edges of the alpha channel, which will be faded later by the alpha. This looks strange in isolation, but it gives a slightly better result.

The second Output Module – ALPHA [QT-Anim_256gray] – makes use of just the alpha channel from the 32-bit image created during the render, and saves it as a 256-gray-level movie (some editing systems may require Millions of Colors even for the alpha). This is later used as a luma matte for the color channels saved by the first output module.

*If you want to use your own version of the Planets flythrough in the next tutorial, add **[Planets*starter]** to the Render Queue and duplicate the settings above. Set the Output To destinations and name the fill and matte movies appropriately. Save, and click the Render button.*

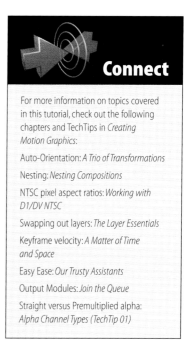

Connect

For more information on topics covered in this tutorial, check out the following chapters and TechTips in *Creating Motion Graphics*:

Auto-Orientation: *A Trio of Transformations*

Nesting: *Nesting Compositions*

NTSC pixel aspect ratios: *Working with D1/DV NTSC*

Swapping out layers: *The Layer Essentials*

Keyframe velocity: *A Matter of Time and Space*

Easy Ease: *Our Trusty Assistants*

Output Modules: *Join the Queue*

Straight versus Premultiplied alpha: *Alpha Channel Types (TechTip 01)*

Cosmopolis

An effects and transition workout to create a spacey show title at D1 NTSC resolution.

In this project, you will create a D1-resolution opening title sequence for a show called *Cosmopolis: Planet of the Cosanauts*. To do so, you will use the planet flythrough you created in the previous tutorial, combining separate color and matte movies to reconstruct the main footage element with an alpha channel. You will then employ a combination of Illustrator files and clever effects to create the text treatments.

To save time (and in case you don't have After Effects 5.0 or later, which the previous tutorial requires), we've prerendered the planet flythrough; you can swap in your own version if you like. We've also saved

OVERVIEW

Main Concepts:

These are the features and concepts we will be focusing on in this project:

- Separating interlaced footage
- Combining fill and matte movies
- Nesting compositions
- Choosing a title font
- Importing an Illustrator file as Comp
- Applying effects and Effect Favorites
- Gradient Wipe effect
- Displacement Map effect [PB]
- Block Dissolve effect
- Adjustment Layers
- Knoll Light Factory EZ effect*
- Velocity controls for effects
- Using modes to enhance footage
- Snapshots for comparing effects
- Field rendering for D1 and DV

Requirements:

After Effects 4.1 or later; Production Bundle recommended for Displacement Map effect, but this effect is optional.

Third-party effects: Knoll Light Factory LE and Tinderbox T_LensBlur (both included on this book's CD in the **Free Plug-ins** folder).

Getting Started:

* Be sure to install the Knoll Light Factory LE effect from Pinnacle Systems (www.pinnaclesys.com) and the Tinderbox T_LensBlur effect from The Foundry (www.thefoundry.co.uk) included in the accompanying CD's **Free Plug-ins** folder.

Inside the **Tutorials** master folder on the accompanying CD, locate and copy the folder **10_Cosmopolis** to your hard drive.

In the folder **Final Movie** inside this folder, double-click on and play **Cosmopolis.mov**.

Inside the **Project** folder you'll find the finished After Effects project file **Cosmopolis.aep**. Open the project file that is appropriate for your version: **_4** for 4.1, or **_5** for 5.0. If you have the Production Bundle, open the file ending in **PB**. This is your starting point; we suggest you save after each major section.

most of the effects settings used here as Favorites if you want to skip the keyframing and parameter entry we'll be leading you through. One step calls for the Displacement Map effect, which is available only in the Production Bundle; you can skip it without compromising the final result.

The Tasks

This is what you will be doing in the various parts of this tutorial:

PART 1: Import your sources, check field separation of the prerenders, use track mattes to recombine matte and fill movies in a nested comp, and start building the main composition including background and soundtrack.

A frame from the final *Cosmopolis* title sequence.

PART 2: Bring in the Illustrator artwork for the main title, apply a variety of transition and displacement effects to build them on in an interesting manner, and tweak their timing.

PART 3: Nest the title into the main composition, scale it over time, and use an Adjustment Layer to tint the title and background.

PART 4: Animate a lens flare along a Bezier path, with additional tweaks to its parameters and velocity. This part includes the concepts of applying an effect to a solid, and using transfer modes to blend it on top of other layers.

PART 5: Use snapshots and the Instant Sex technique to further enhance the planets.

PART 6: Take a guided tour through the opening and closing transitions, and field render your final movie.

Matching Pair

Command+– (the minus key) on Mac (or Control+– on Windows) will zoom down and resize the Comp window; use the shortcut Command+= (Control+=) to zoom up and resize. Match resolution to magnification: Full Resolution at 100%, Half Resolution at 50%.

Part 1: Music of the Spheres

In this section, you will import your source material, recombine the separate RGB and alpha layers of the planets flythrough sequence, and add a soundtrack. Open the version of the **Cosmopolis.aep** project that matches the version of After Effects you own. The **Cosmopolis * prebuilt** folder contains both the final version and partial comps saved after various crucial steps; feel free to explore them before you start, but close all extraneous windows before diving in below.

1 After Effects 5.0 added a feature that allows you to import the varied contents of an entire folder in one click.

1 *complete:* You now have all the sources you will need for this project, including the two layers that make up the planet flythrough.

STEP 1: In version 5.0 or later, type Command+I on Mac (Control+I on Windows) to open the Import dialog. Inside this tutorial's folder, open the **Project** folder, then select – but do not open – the **Sources** folder. To import all the sources at once, click the new Import Folder button in this dialog.

(In version 4.1, the only way to import a folder is to use a drag-and-drop technique. First arrange your screen so you can see both the Project window and this tutorial's **Project>Sources** folder on your drive. Select the **Sources** folder but keep the mouse depressed; add the Option (Alt) key, then drag this folder into the Project window.)

One of the items you are importing is an Illustrator file. After Effects will present you with a dialog asking how you want to handle the layers inside it. Use the default Merged Layers option and click OK.

Select this **Sources** folder in your Project window, and hit Return to highlight its name. Type "**My_Sources**" and hit Return again. Click on the arrow next to it to twirl it open, then twirl open the **Planets_render** folder inside of it to see all the items you just imported.

> If you rendered your own version of the planets flythrough in the previous tutorial, you can easily replace the sources: Select **Planets_fill.mov** in the Project window, type Command+H (Control+H), navigate to and select your own RGB render, and click Import (Open). Do the same for **Planets_matte.mov**.

Interlacing and Edges

Individually select **Planets_fill.mov** and **Planets_matte.mov** in the Project window, and note the information displayed at the top. After Effects automatically detects movies with a size of 720×486 pixels as having a D1/DV NTSC pixel aspect ratio. It also detects these movies as being lower field first, because After Effects placed a tag in their files when they were rendered. Verify that this separation is taking place:

STEP 2: Double-click on **Planets_fill.mov**. It will open in a QuickTime player. Move the time marker to about one-third of the way into the movie, then use the left and right arrow keys to step through individual frames. The "comb teeth" effect you see on some of the faster moving planets is the result of two interlaced fields, from different points in time, being drawn in the same frame. Close the player window.

2–3 The QuickTime window (left) will show both interlaced fields in the same frame. After Effects' Footage window (right) shows each field after it has been separated.

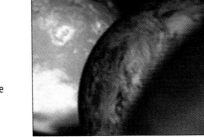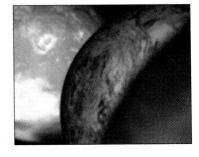

Step 3: Option+double-click (Alt+double-click) the same movie in the Project window to open it in After Effects' Footage window. Make sure Magnification is set to 100%, and move the time marker to about the same point in the file. Use the Page Up and Page Down keys to step through the movie; you shouldn't see any interlacing teeth as you did in the QuickTime viewer. This is because the Footage window displays files after they have been processed by the Interpret Footage settings, so you're stepping through the already separated fields.

If you are seeing interlacing lines in version 4.1, then the footage has not been separated; if the motion seems to jerk back and forth as you step through the fields, they have been separated incorrectly. Select the footage, press Command+F (Control+F) to open the Interpret Footage window, and set Separate Fields to Lower Field First.

Check the field separation for both **Planets_fill.mov** and **Planets_matte.mov**. Close their Footage and QuickTime windows when you're done.

> More information on interlaced fields is contained in Part 1 of the *AutoTracker* tutorial earlier in this book, as well as in the chapter *Playing the Field* in *Creating Motion Graphics*.

Planets Track Matte

The planets flythrough was rendered as separate RGB (fill) and alpha channel (matte) movies. Some stock footage CDs deliver their content as separate color and matte files; it allows them to compress the fill movie to take up less space on the CD. (This is also a popular way to import footage with an alpha channel into some editing systems). You will build a precomp that recombines these two pieces.

Step 4: Select **Planets_fill.mov** and drag it to the New Composition icon at the bottom of the Project window. This will create a composition that is the same size, duration, and frame rate as the source footage. This comp will be named **Planets_fill.mov Comp 1** and will appear in the **Planets_render** folder in the Project window in version 5 (or loose in the Project window in version 4.1). Rename it "**My_Planets_precomp**" (either by selecting it in the Project window and hitting Return, or by editing it in Composition>Composition Settings). In the Project window, drag the renamed comp to the **My_Comps** folder.

Step 5: [My_Planets_precomp] should be the only open composition. Select the footage item **Planets_matte.mov** in the Project window, and type Command+/ (Control+/) to add it to [**My_Planets_precomp**]. It will appear above **Planets_fill.mov** in the Timeline window, which is exactly what you want.

3 *complete:* If the fields are not separated correctly for **Planets_fill.mov** or **Planets_matte.mov**, use the Interpret Footage dialog to choose Lower Field First.

New Comp from Multiple Sources

In After Effects 5.0, you can drag multiple sources to the New Composition icon and have them all added at the same time.

4–5 Drag the **Planets_fill.mov** to the New Composition icon (above), and rename the resulting new comp "**My_Planets_precomp**". Then add the **Planets_matte.mov** to the comp.

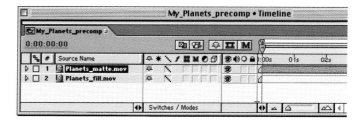

STEP 6: When separated layers are viewed in Draft Quality, their lines are doubled to cover for the separated fields. If you'd rather see interpolated images, and your computer is fairly fast, type Command+A (Control+A) to Select All, Command+U (Control+U) to set the layers to Best Quality, then F2 to Deselect All layers.

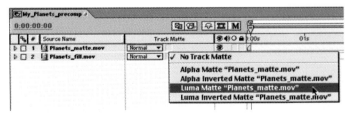

7 Press F4 to reveal the Modes panel, and set **Planets_matte.mov** to be a luminance matte for **Planets_fill.mov**.

STEP 7: Bring [**My_Planets_precomp**]'s Timeline window forward, and press F4 to reveal the Modes panel (if it's not already visible). Under the TrkMat (Track Matte) heading, click on the popup menu for **Planets_fill.mov** and select Luma Matte "Planets_matte.mov". This will use the luminance of the matte movie as an alpha channel for the fill movie. The Video switch (the "eyeball") for **Planets_matte.mov** will automatically turn off (otherwise you would see the matte movie).

STEP 8: To verify that the matte is doing its job, click on the Show only Alpha channel button (the white swatch) along the bottom of the Comp window – the result should look a lot like the **Planets_matte.mov** did. Turn this button off, and the comp's background color will now show between the planets. This color isn't important here, but setting it to black will more closely match the night sky it will be composited against later. (If you need to change the background color to black, go to Composition>Background Color.)

8 After the matte has been applied, the edges of the planets will be clean.

STEP 9: If you want to save screen real estate, or if your computer is short on memory or CPU power, feel free to reduce the Magnification to 50% and Resolution to Half. Press 0 on the keypad to RAM Preview the matted movie.

For those who have not done the *Planets* tutorial, the camera flies in 3D space between flat 2D layers of planets that auto-orient toward the camera, so you never see them on edge (which would otherwise give the illusion away).

Digital Night

The movie **xTB_Nightsky.mov** was created using the Tinderbox T_NightSky effect from The Foundry's Tinderbox 2 set (www.thefoundry.co.uk).

Planets in the Cosmos

The last steps in this section include creating what will be your main comp, and adding the background, planets, and soundtrack to it.

STEP 10: Select the **My_Comps** folder in the Project window. Then either click on the New Composition button at the bottom of the Project window, or type Command+N (Control+N) to make a new composition. Pick the D1 NTSC 720×486 preset, verify that the frame rate is 29.97 frames per second (fps), and set its duration to 08:01.

Give it the name "**My_Cosmopolis**" and click OK. (In version 4.1, drag this new comp to the **My_Comps** folder to keep things organized.)

STEP 11: In the **My_Sources** folder in the Project window, select **CM_CosmoMusic.mov**, then Command+click (Control+click) on **xTB_Nightsky.mov** – both will now be selected. Press Command+/ (Control+/) to add them to the [**My_Cosmopolis**] comp. They should both start at 00:00, with **xTB_Nightsky.mov** centered in the Comp window.

STEP 12: Drag the [**My_Planets_precomp**] into the [**My_Cosmopolis**] comp. If you are using version 5.0 or later, drag it inbetween the **CM_CosmoMusic.mov** and **xTB_Nightsky.mov** layers, and After Effects will automatically place it there in the layer stack for you. (In version 4.1, manually drag it to this position after it has been added to the comp.)

Hit 0 on the keypad to RAM Preview this composite with the soundtrack. Between 04:00 and 05:00, pay attention to the way the last two planets part, revealing the starfield background. You will use this in the next section to help reveal the show's title.

Because you composited the fill with the matte in a precomp, you can easily transform or add effects to this composite in [**My_Cosmopolis**] as it is now a single layer. In the precomp, you can also apply effects to either the fill or matte individually, while still dealing with just one layer in your final comp. Prudent use of precomps often yields a nice combination of flexibility and convenience.

Save your project before diving into the next part. If you want to make sure you got this far intact, compare your comp with our [**Cosmo_after Step 12**] *in the* **Cosmopolis ** **prebuilt>_compare comps_after Step ## ** *folder.*

At the end of this section, you have the planets composited in front of a night sky, with the soundtrack in place (right and below).

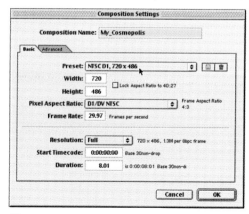

10 Create a new comp using these settings. This will be your main composition.

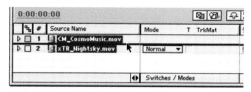

12 In version 5.0, drag [**My_Planets_precomp**] into [**My_Cosmopolis**]'s Timeline window, carefully positioning it until you see a bar between the two other layers. When you release the mouse, it will be placed here in the layer stack (above).

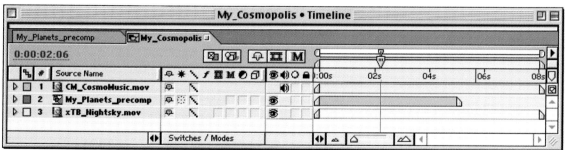

Part 2: Title Effects

This is the main section of this tutorial, where you will be treating the show title with a variety of transition effects.

STEP 13: When we told you in the first step to go ahead and import the Illustrator file with the title as Merged Layers, we got a bit ahead of ourselves.

In 5.0 and later, under Edit>Preference>Import you can set Photoshop and Illustrator files to automatically import as Compositions when you drag them from the Finder to the Project window, or when they are included in a folder of sources imported at once. We're assuming this preference has not been set.

13 The merged Illustrator file contains both the main and subtitles in the same footage item, but later you will be treating them separately. The fonts used are Mason Alternate and Mason Sans Regular from Emigre (www.emigre.com).

In the Project window, look in the **My_Sources** folder for the file **CosmopolisTitles.ai**, and double-click it to open it in its Footage window. You will see a main title and a subtitle, created with white type and saved as outlines from Illustrator (converting to outlines is not necessary, but it allows us to use any font we want without assuming you'll also have it installed). You need to re-import this file so that the two titles are on separate layers. Close this window, and delete this file (make sure it is still selected in the Project window, and hit Delete).

After Effects 5.0 or later:
• Select the folder **My_Sources** in the Project window, and press Command+I (Control+I) or select File>Import>File. Locate the layered Illustrator file **CosmopolisTitles.ai** from the **Project>Sources** folder on your disk. In the lower left portion of this dialog, select the option Import As: Composition. Click Import (Open).

• After Effects will create a folder and a composition, both named **CosmopolisTitles.ai**. Drag the comp [**CosmopolisTitles.ai**] into the **My_Comps** folder.

13 *continued:* When you reimport **CosmopolisTitles.ai** in After Effects 5, be sure to use the Import As: Composition option in the dialog.

After Effects 4.1:
• Select File>Import>Illustrator as Comp and locate the file **CosmopolisTitles.ai** from the **Project>Sources** folder. Click Open.

• After Effects will create a folder and composition, both named **CosmopolisTitles.ai**. Drag the folder into the **My_Sources** folder in the Project window, and the comp into **My_Comps**.

Music Credits

The soundtrack **CM_CosmoMusic.mov** was arranged by Chris Meyer of CyberMotion. The rhythm track is from the sampling library *Metamorphosis*, and the echoed guitar stabs (played by Peter Maunu) are from the library *Bizarre Guitar*. Both libraries are from Spectrasonics (www.spectrasonics.net), and are distributed in the United States by Ilio Entertainment (www.ilio.com).

STEP 14: Double-click the comp [**CosmopolisTitles.ai**] to open it. Press Command+K (Control+K) to open Composition Settings, verify that its duration is at least 05:00, and rename it "**My_Titles_precomp**". Its size and pixel aspect ratio are copied from the original Illustrator file. We created this file at a size of 720×540 pixels so we could work in square pixels and not lose any resolution when we later fit it into a 720×486 non-square pixel NTSC D1 composition. Click OK to close the dialog.

STEP 15: Some final housekeeping before applying effects to the title layers:

• Select the **guides** layer in the Timeline window, and Delete it (it's a carryover from Illustrator).

• Make sure the Switches/Modes panel is set to Switches (press F4 or click at the bottom of this panel to toggle its state), and drag your mouse down the Quality switches to set the two remaining layers to Best.

• Turn off the **POTC_Subtitle** layer's Video switch – we'll work on applying effects to the **Cosmopolis** title first.

This would be a good time to Save your project. We suggest you save frequently, but we wouldn't want to nag…

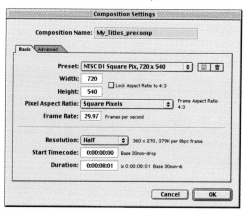

14 The title was built in Illustrator at 720×540 pixels.

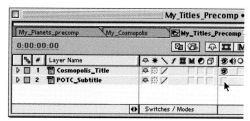

15 Delete the **guides** layer, set the remaining layers to Best Quality, and turn off **POTC_Subtitle** for now.

Choices, Choices…

How do we decide what font to use for a title? First we consider a few different stylistic directions – for this job, computerish, Egyptian, or '60s kitsch. We then hunt through our font libraries, looking for fonts that match our themes or otherwise catch our eye. We'll then build a page in Illustrator, repeating the words we will be typesetting with our different font choices applied. It's important to use the actual words instead of gibberish or a series of letters so you can see how the specific characters work – sometimes a font will have some characters you really like or dislike. Finally, we eliminate the fonts we don't like until a winner emerges, bouncing our "short list" off each other or the client to help break ties.

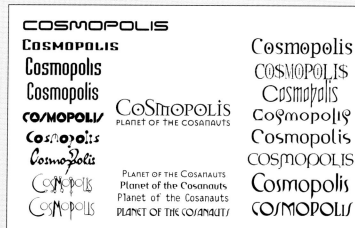

Some of the fonts we auditioned in Illustrator for the Cosmopolis opening title. The winner, Mason from Emigre, is shown in the center.

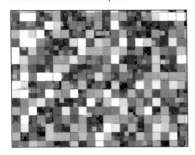

16 Gradient maps don't need to have any color, but they should have good black-to-white contrast with lots of intermediate gray values.

Gradient Wipe

For your first effect, you will use the Gradient Wipe effect to bring on the title "Cosmopolis" in an interesting way:

STEP 16: In the **My_Sources** folder in the Project window, select **FractalNoiseMap.tif** and press Command+/ (Control+/) to add it to [My_Titles_Precomp]. Make sure it starts at 00:00, and after checking it out, drag it to the bottom of the layer stack. Turn off its Video switch – you will not see this layer in the final composite; it will only be used by the Gradient Wipe effect to modify the main title layer.

FractalNoiseMap.tif was created in After Effects 5.0 using the Fractal Noise effect that comes with the Production Bundle. If you have this version, the project used to create it is included in the **FractalNoiseMap_5PB** folder inside the **10-Cosmopolis** folder.

STEP 17: In [My_Titles_Precomp], select **Cosmopolis_Title** and apply Effect>Transition>**Gradient Wipe**. This will automatically open the Effect Controls window for Gradient Wipe. This effect looks to a second layer to determine the pattern used to reveal the layer it is applied to. In this window, click on the popup menu for Gradient Layer, and select **FractalNoiseMap.tif**.

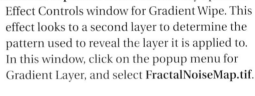

17 Add the Gradient Wipe effect to **Cosmopolis_Title**, and pick **FractalNoiseMap.tif** to be the Gradient Layer.

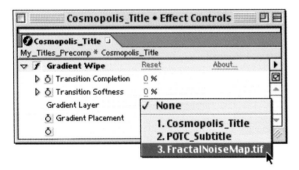

18 The result is an interesting, fractured effect as the title transitions on (above). Soften the "popping" of the chunks by setting the Transition Softness to around 15% (below).

STEP 18: Transition effects can be used to transition a layer on or off; here you will be using it to transition the main title on. Scrub the Transition Completion slider to preview the way you want it to animate. In this case, it will become obvious that you need to animate from 100% to 0% to wipe your layer on. Set the slider to 100%, where the title has completely disappeared.

• If you are using version 5.0 or later, in the Effect Controls window turn on the animation stopwatch for Transition Completion. (In 4.1, you can Option+click (Alt+click) on the words Transition Completion in the Effect Controls window to turn on the stopwatch.) This sets the first keyframe to 100% at time 00:00.

• Press U to reveal this now-animated property in the Timeline window.

• Move to 01:10 in the timeline. Set the Transition Completion value to 0%; a new keyframe will automatically be created at this time.

• Set the work area to end at this frame by pressing N (for eNd work area), and RAM Preview.

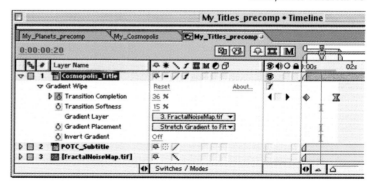

• Remembering what the **FractalNoiseMap.tif** looked like, note how the title appears in fractured chunks. However, the way entire chunks of the title pop is a little abrupt. Go to some time in the middle of the transition (such as 00:20) and scrub the Transition Softness parameter – this will make the chunks fade instead of pop. Set it to 15% or so, and RAM Preview again.

• The nature of this gradient wipe map is that the title initially seems to be reluctant to transition on, but it speeds up near the end. Smooth this out by context-clicking on the second Transition Completion keyframe in the Timeline window and selecting Layer>Keyframe Assistant>Easy Ease (or select the keyframe and press F9). RAM Preview again; the transition should have an interesting pace.

Save! If you had trouble setting up this compound effect, compare your [My_Titles_Precomp] *with* [Titles_Precomp_after Step 18].

 Displacing Cosmopolis

The next step calls for using the Production Bundle's Displacement Map effect to further fracture the word Cosmopolis. If you don't have this effect, ignore this step and skip ahead to **Step 21**.

STEP 19: In [My_Titles_Precomp], move the time marker to around 00:20, so you can see it partway through its transition. Select the **Cosmopolis_Title** layer, and apply Effect>Distort>**Displacement Map**. This should bring the Effect Controls window back to the foreground. Change the following settings:

• Set the Displacement Map Layer popup to the **FractalNoiseMap.tif** layer.

• Set Max Horizontal Displacement to 0 – we will not be displacing the title to the left and right.

• Set Use for Vertical Displacement to Luminance (the Red, Green, or Blue channels will also work; with grayscale maps, the luminance information is the same for each of the RGB channels).

• Scrub the Max Vertical Displacement parameter and notice how the title takes on a broken mirror effect. Set it to 75.

18 *complete:* The Gradient Wipe effect transitions over 01:10, easing into the second keyframe, with a Transition Softness of 15%.

 **Scrubbing in Steps**

To edit values in the Effect Controls window by integer increments, hold down the Shift key while dragging their sliders.

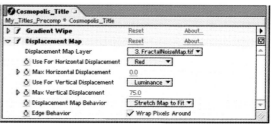

19 Set the Displacement Map effect (above) to displace in just the vertical direction by 75 pixels, using **FractalNoiseMap.tif** as the Displacement Map Layer. The result (below) is an unusual, broken mirror echo.

Spicy Gradients

For the ultimate in gradient fun, check out SpiceRack Pro and OrganicFX from Pixélan Software (www.pixelan.com). (Free samples are included in the **Goodies** folder on the CD that came with *Creating Motion Graphics*.)

STEP 20: Hit Home to return to 00:00. You won't see anything, because the Gradient Wipe is completely faded out at this point – but you're going to start the Displacement Map animation at the same time as the transition.

> The order you apply effects is important. Here, you are displacing the wiped pieces, so they stay aligned. If Displacement Map was placed before Gradient Wipe, the wipe would not be aligned with the displaced pieces.

• If you are using version 5.0 or later, turn on the animation stopwatch for Max Vertical Displacement in the Effect Controls window. (In 4.1, Option+click (Alt+click) on the words "Max Vertical Displacement" in the Effect Controls window.) This sets the first keyframe to 75.0 pixels at time 00:00.

• Press U twice to reveal the animated parameters for **Cosmopolis_Title** in the Timeline window. You should see keyframes for Transition Completion and Max Vertical Displacement.

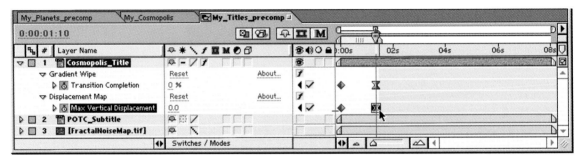

20 Keyframe the displacement animation to occur over the same time as the gradient transition, also easing into the last keyframe. (Use the keyframe navigation arrows to make sure new keyframes you create line up with ones you've already set.)

• In the Timeline window, click on the arrow to the right of the keyframe checkbox for Transition Completion. This will forward the time marker to 01:10, the time the transition finishes.

• Enter a value of 0.0 for Max Vertical Displacement to create a new keyframe, which will also be selected. Press F9 to apply Keyframe Assistant>Easy Ease to it.

Your work area should still be set to extend from 00:00 to 01:10. RAM Preview the composition to see how the Gradient Wipe and Displacement Map effects work in tandem.

20 *complete:* The Gradient Wipe and Displacement Map transitions combine to enhance the fractured effect.

Save your project and twirl up all layers. If you need to, compare your result to our prebuilt comp [**Titles_Precomp_after Step 20**].

Favorite Route

We also saved the stack of effects for the **Cosmopolis_Title** layer as a Favorite. If you'd rather use the preset, select the layer and choose Effect>Remove All Effects. At time 00:00, select Effect>Apply Favorite. Navigate to the **_Favorites** folder inside the **Cosmopolis** main folder on your disk. If you're using the Standard version, apply the favorite **CosmopolisTitle_S.ffx**; if you have the

Production Bundle, apply the favorite **CosmopolisTitle_PB.ffx** which will also apply Displacement Map. Note that favorites also apply all the keyframes added including the Easy Ease!

One problem with Favorites is that they don't apply the map layer in a compound effect, but default to None. For both the Gradient Wipe and Displacement Map effects, you'll need to reset the map layer popups to the **FractalNoiseMap.tif** layer.

Effecting the Subtitle

That finishes the main title; next is using a different type of transition plus a track matte to reveal the subtitle.

STEP 21: Set [**My_Titles_Precomp**] to 100% Magnification and Full Resolution. Turn off the Video switch (the "eyeball") for the **Cosmopolis_Title** layer for now, and turn on the Video switch for **POTC_Subtitle**. With **POTC_Subtitle** selected, move to time 01:00, and hit [(the left square bracket key) to start the layer at this time.

STEP 22: Type Command+Y (Control+Y) to create a new Solid layer. Name it "**Block Dissolve solid**," make it 720×200 pixels in size, and set its color to white. Click OK, and drag this new layer down the Timeline window stack so that it sits directly above the **POTC_Subtitle** layer – mattes need to sit above the layer they reveal.

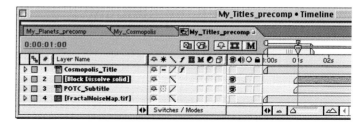

22 Create a 720×200 pixel solid, and place it just above **POTC_Subtitle** – you will be using it as a track matte for the subtitle layer.

STEP 23: With **Block Dissolve solid** still selected, apply Effect> Transition>**Block Dissolve**. Scrub the Transition Completion slider from 0 to 100% and see how the white solid dissolves. The default for this transition is to use one-pixel blocks. Change this to use very wide blocks, and animate the block height as the transition plays out:

• Leave the Transition Completion slider at around 50% so you can see how changes to the other parameters will affect the block style.

• Set the Block Width to 120, resulting in six horizontal divisions (720÷6=120).

• At time 01:00, set the Block Height to 10, and enable keyframe animation for this parameter as you did in Steps 18 or 20 above.

23 At 01:00, the Block Width is set to 120 and the Block Height to 10; enable keyframing for Block Height.

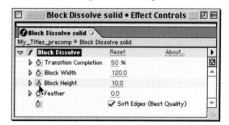

23 *complete:* In Draft quality (above left), Block Dissolve renders with hard edges. In Best Quality (above right), you can see that the blocks in reality are soft. If you prefer the hard look, disable its Soft Edges option (below).

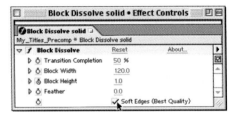

• Press Shift+1 (on the keyboard, not the keypad) to create comp marker #1 at this frame. You can hit 1 whenever you need to return to this point. Press B to set the work area to also start here.

• Move to 02:00, and change the Block Height value to 1.

• Press Shift+2 (on the keyboard) to create comp marker #2 at this frame. Press N to extend the work area to end at this time.

• Turn on Best Quality and notice how the edges get very soft. This is controlled by the Soft Edges (Best Quality) checkbox in the Effect Controls window. Click on this checkbox to turn this option off. We'll use the harder version, but if you prefer soft edges, leave this option on.

STEP 24: Now let's animate the transition so that the solid changes from completely black to completely white, which will serve as a matte to transition on the subtitle.

Comp Marker to Layer Markers

When you nest a composition, its comp markers become layer markers in the master comp.

• Hit 1 (on the keyboard, not the numeric keypad) to jump back to 01:00. Enable keyframe animation for the Transition Completion parameter, and set its value to 100%. The solid should be invisible.

• Hit 2 to move to 02:00, and set the Transition Completion slider to 0% – the solid will now be all white.

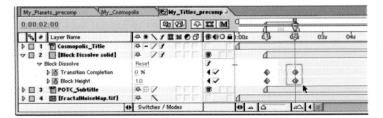

• Hit U to see your Block Dissolve keyframes in the Timeline window. Drag a marquee selection around the two keyframes at 02:00, and hit F9 to apply Easy Ease to them. If you like, RAM Preview to get a feel for the matte's animation.

24 After keyframing the Block Dissolve, select the last two keyframes, and hit F9 to apply Easy Ease.

STEP 25: If the Modes panel is not currently revealed in the Timeline window, press F4 to toggle it on. In the Modes panel, set the Track Matte popup for **POTC_Subtitle** to Alpha Matte "[**Block Dissolve solid**]". This will take the transparency of the layer above (**Block Dissolve solid**) and use it as a matte, creating transparency for the subtitle. Since you made the solid white, you could also apply it as a Luma Matte.

You may be wondering why we didn't just apply the Block Dissolve effect directly to the text layer. While this will work, it's difficult to tell exactly what is going on since the blocks are seen only inside the shape of the text. If the layer was a full-frame video layer, we would have elected to apply it directly; in this case, we felt for illustrative purposes that it was better to use it as a matte layer.

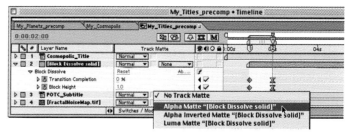

Save your project. Twirl up the **Block Dissolve solid** layer and turn the Video switch for **CosmopolisTitle** back on. Set the work area to start at 00:00, and RAM Preview your final title transitions.

25 Set the Track Matte popup for **POTC_Subtitle** to use the alpha of the **Block Dissolve solid** layer as a matte.

*If you got lost, we saved an Effect Favorite with these parameters and keyframes in this tutorial's **Projects>_Favorites** folder on your disk. Delete the Block Dissolve effect you added in Step 23 but keep the solid selected, go to 01:00, and select Effect> Apply Favorite>**BlockDissolve_subtitle.ffx**. We also saved the entire comp at this point in the **_compare comps…** folder as [**Titles_Precomp_after Step 25**].*

25 *complete:* The subtitle is now revealed through a flickering series of progressively thinner bars.

Part 3: Reveal, Scale, and Tint

You now have your precomps in order; the following sections will focus on combining them and adding some overall effects. First up is adding a scale animation to the title, followed by using an adjustment layer to tint the titles and stars to work better with the planets.

Step 26: To reduce clutter, close the comps [**My_Planets_precomp**] and [**My_Titles_precomp**], leaving just the comp [**My_Cosmopolis**] open. Locate to 04:00 in this comp. Hit Shift+4 to create a comp marker at this time.

Step 27: In the **My_Comps** folder in the Project window, locate [**My_Titles_precomp**] and drag it to [**My_Cosmopolis**] comp in that same window. This will add the first comp to

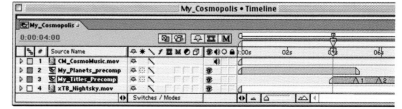

the second, centered and at the current time. In the Timeline window for [**My_Cosmopolis**], drag **My_Titles_precomp** down the layer stack until it is between **My_Planets_precomp** and **xTB_Nightsky.mov**. Press Command+U (Control+U) to set the title layer to Best Quality.

Scrub the time marker from 04:00 onward. Note that as the planets part, the titles are revealed – this is because the titles are underneath the planets in the layer stack.

27 Nest [**My_Titles_precomp**] in [**My_Cosmopolis**], and place it above **xTB_Nightsky.mov** in the layer stack. Note the comp markers in the titles precomp came in as layer markers here – we'll use those to aid navigation.

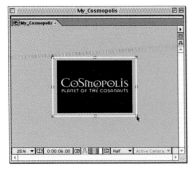

28 Zoom down the Comp window and note that the **My_Titles_precomp** layer is larger than the composition (above). Scale it to 90% to fit the comp window (below).

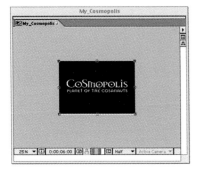

Realtime Previews

In 4.1, hold down the Option (Alt) key when you're editing effect parameters for a realtime preview. In 5.0, the Option (Alt) key toggles realtime previews off (or on, depending on how Preferences are set).

STEP 28: Shift+drag the time marker along the timeline to 06:00 – it should snap to layer marker 2 in **My_Titles_precomp** (this is comp marker #2 in the precomp, where both titles are fully on). Press Shift+6 to set a new comp marker for this time.

Press , (the comma key) to zoom the Comp window down and see more of the gray pasteboard around it. The white outline you see is the outer edges of the **My_Titles_precomp** layer – it's larger than the comp. This title was created at a size of 720×540 with square pixels, and has been nested in a 720×486 comp with NTSC-spec non-square pixels. The pixel aspect ratio correction automatically scales up the width of the title layer to adjust for this, resulting in a "fatter" image (720 × 10 ÷ 9 = 800 pixels wide). However, we want these 720 pixels to map across the width of the comp on a 1:1 basis, and for the 540 pixels in the height to be scaled down to 486. This will convert the square pixels to the D1 pixel aspect ratio at the highest quality possible.

With **My_Titles_precomp** selected, press S to reveal its Scale property in the Timeline window. Note that its current value is 100%. Then press Command+Option+F (Control+Alt+F), which will fit the selected layer to the size of the comp. The scale value should now read 90%, and the layer will fit the comp window perfectly. Turn on Best Quality, and reset the Comp window's Magnification back to where it was by pressing the period key (on the keyboard, not the keypad).

STEP 29: To add interest to the title as it becomes the center of attention, increase its size over time:

• Move to 07:00, and turn on the animation stopwatch for **My_Titles_precomp**'s Scale property to create a keyframe of 90%.

• Press F9 to add an Easy Ease interpolation to this keyframe.

• Press N to set the end of the work area here.

• Hit 4 to jump to the comp marker you set at 04:00, and change the scale value to 70%, which will create a second keyframe. (If it didn't, you forgot to enable the animation stopwatch above.)

• Press B to set the beginning of the work area here and RAM Preview.

STEP 30: After Effects helpfully created this new keyframe with the same interpolation method as your first keyframe. Twirl down the arrow next to the word Scale in the Timeline window to see Scale's velocity graphs. Unfortunately, we don't want an Easy Ease on this first keyframe; we feel the animation works better if the title is scaling steadily as it is revealed behind the planets. That's easy enough to fix by holding down the Command (Control) key and clicking on the first Scale keyframe until it reverts to the Linear keyframe's diamond icon. Note the change in the velocity graph, and twirl it up when you're done. Press S to twirl up the Scale property.

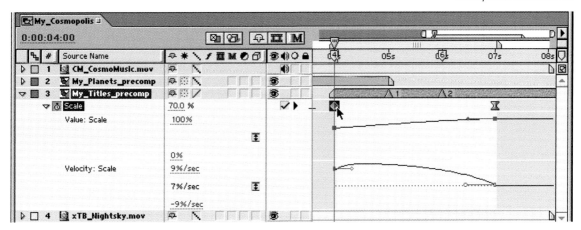

STEP 31: Last in this section is using an Adjustment Layer to tint the white title and stars to a beige color that better matches the warm brown colors in the planets.

- Hit Home to return to 00:00. The Adjustment Layer will need to start from the beginning to tint the entire duration of the **xTB_Nightsky.mov** layer.

- Select Layer>New>Adjustment Layer (in version 4.1, select Layer>New Adjustment Layer).

  Adjustment Layers are borrowed from Photoshop. They apply effects to the composite of all layers below the Adjustment Layer in the Timeline window's layer stack.

- You want to tint only the background layers; not the planets. Therefore, drag this new layer in the Timeline window above the **My_Titles_precomp** and **xTB_Nightsky.mov** layers, and below the **My_Planets_precomp** layer.

- With the Adjustment Layer still selected, apply Effect>Image Control>**Tint**. This will open its Effect Controls window; set the Amount to Tint parameter to 100% so you can see the results of your color choices.

- Go to somewhere between 04:15 and 04:20 in the timeline where you can see both the title and the planets. Set Tint's Map White To color to a pale, warm beige or straw. (Either pick a color by eye, or eyedrop the planets to get a good starting point.) We used HLS colorspace settings of Hue 45, Saturation 100, Lightness 85 on Mac (try RGB 255/236/179 on Windows). Then hit 6 to jump to comp marker 6, and see how the title looks on its own in this color. (This Tint color is saved as a favorite as **Tint_beige.ffx** in the **10_Cosmopolis>_Favorites** folder on disk.)

- With the Adjustment Layer still selected, type Command+Shift+Y (Control+Shift+Y), rename it to "**AL/Tint**," and click OK.

30 The **My_Titles_precomp** layer scales from 70% to 90%, starting linear and easing into the last keyframe.

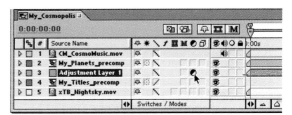

31 Create a new Adjustment Layer, and drag it down the layer stack to be just above the title and nightsky layers.

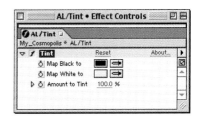

31 *complete:* Use the Tint effect (above) to more closely match the title and stars to the planets (bottom).

This completes Part 3, so it's a good time to Save your project. If you think you might have missed a step, compare your comp with [Cosmo_after Step 31]. And don't forget to save your project!

Light Factory on AE5 and Windows

If you're using Windows and version 5 and are experiencing redraw problems with Light Factory LE, Pinnacle is aware of the problem. Please visit their website to check for an updated demo of Knoll Light Factory for Windows: <www.commotionpro.com/products/demos/demos_area.html>

Part 4: Lens Flare Arc

Lens flares can be an overused cliché, but they're a great way to add light sources to the frame – just avoid the temptation to get too carried away (you know who you are). In this project, we were inspired by the star shapes in the center of the O characters in the main title, and decided to animate a flare between them to better tie the word together. (If you want to refresh your memory, play the final movie **Cosmopolis.mov**.)

In this section, you will animate the effect point for the flare along a Bezier path. Make sure you have installed the free copy of Light Factory LE provided by Pinnacle Systems (www.pinnaclesys.com) before proceeding.

34 The black solid initially shows just the flare, and nothing behind (top). Set its Mode to Add to drop out the black areas and mix the flare with the background (above).

STEP 32: Go to 05:20, and press Command+Y (Control+Y) to create a New Solid. Click on the Make Comp Size button to make it full frame, and select black as its color. Name it "**Lens Flare Solid**" and click OK.

STEP 33: With this solid still selected, apply Effect>Knoll Light Factory>**Light Factory LE**. We'll use the default Flare Type of Warm Sun Flare, since it already has yellow and orange tones that match the rest of our layers.

STEP 34: In the Timeline window, make sure the Modes panel is visible (press F4 if it isn't), and set the Mode for **Lens Flare Solid** to Add. Since the solid is black, it doesn't "add" any color to the layers behind, so the black areas will disappear, revealing just the flare while adding its brightness to the image underneath.

For the next step, we suggest you view the comp at 100% Magnification, and set it to Full Resolution by pressing Command+J (Control+J). If you're short on monitor space, resize the window vertically to crop the top and bottom; you need to see only the Cosmopolis title.

STEP 35: Now you will animate the flare's center. Check the Comp window's wing menu to make sure Effect Controls is enabled. This will allow you to position the flare's center while you're seeing the title, rather than working in the Layer window.

• In the Effect Controls window, context-click on the parameter named Light Source Location, and select Add Keyframe (in version 5.0,

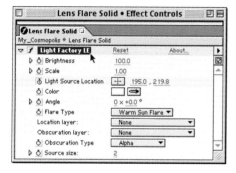

you can also directly enable the animation stop-watch for this parameter in the Effect Controls window). Hit U to twirl down animated properties in the Timeline window, and check that all is well.

• Make sure the name of the effect is highlighted in the Effect Controls window. In the Comp window, you should see a circle with a cross in its middle located where the flare's light source seems to be. Drag this point so it's on top of the dot in the first O (in the "Cos" of Cosmopolis).

• Move to 06:20, and drag the center of the flare so that it's on top of the dot in the last O (in the "pol" of Cosmopolis). This should add a second keyframe for Light Source Location.

• With the **Lens Flare Solid** still selected, press Option+] (Alt+]) to trim out the layer at 06:20, for a one-second duration.

• Set the work area to the exact length of **Lens Flare Solid** by pressing Command+Option+B (Control+Alt+B). RAM Preview (0 on the keypad) to see what you have so far.

35 Enable keyframing for the Light Source Location, and make sure the effect's name is selected in the Effect Controls window (left). Then in the Comp window, move the effect control point for the Light Source Location until it sits in the center of the first O (right).

35 *complete:* Set the second keyframe for the Light Source Location to be the center of the last O (above). Trim the layer to end after this second keyframe, then set the work area to equal the length of this layer (below).

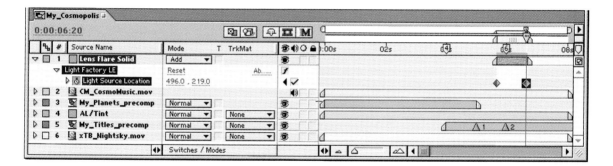

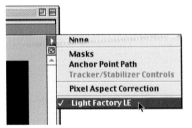

36 Open **Lens Flare solid**'s Layer window, and enable viewing of light Factory LE's motion path.

STEP 36: There are a few problems with our initial lens flare animation. The first one to solve is its motion: Currently, it moves in a straight line from the first O to the last. We want a nice arc that rises above the title in the middle. Fortunately, you can create Bezier paths for effect control points; you just need to do it in the Layer window (this is because the X, Y coordinate values are in relation to the layer, not the comp).

• Double-click **Lens Flare Solid** to open its Layer window. Go to this window's wing menu (look for the arrow in the upper right corner), and select Light Factory LE – this allows you to see its motion path in the Layer window.

• The motion path should default to using Auto Bezier spatial keyframes, in which case you should see a dot indicating the position of the handle at each keyframe. Right now, this dot is in line with the motion path, making it harder to see (look for the slightly larger dot). Selecting the Light Source Location parameter in the Timeline window will also make it easier to see.

If the handles are hard to find, hold down the Command (Control) key and drag a new handle out of the keyframe icon.

• Select one dot and drag the handle upward, then repeat for the other dot. Tweak their positions until you have a gentle arc. Be sure not to reposition the keyframe icons by accident – just move their handles. If you like, you can bring the Comp window back forward and RAM Preview to check out the path. When you're happy with the shape, close the Layer window.

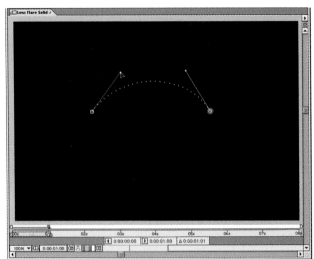

36 *complete:* In the Layer window, pull the effect path's handles upward to form an arc.

STEP 37: Now let's animate the lens flare so it grows from nothing at the start, to a larger size in the middle, then dies away at the end.

• Move the time marker to 06:05 – the center of the lens flare section – and enable keyframing for the Brightness parameter. This sets a keyframe in the middle of the layer's animation at its default value of 100. Press U to reveal this newly animated parameter in the Timeline.

• With the flare layer still selected, hit I to return to the layer's in point at 05:20. Enter a Brightness value of 0. This will create a second keyframe at the beginning of the layer, which will also be selected in the Timeline window.

• Select the Timeline window to bring it forward. With the first keyframe above still selected, choose Edit>Copy or press Command+C (Control+C) to copy its current value.

• Hit O to jump to the layer's out point at 06:20, and choose Edit> Paste or Command+V (Control+V) to paste a new Brightness keyframe with a value of 0. RAM Preview and observe how the lens flare now acts more like a signal flare shot across the sky.

Step 38: The lens flare animation is getting there, but it's moving a bit fast. Let's try extending it to last 40 frames, instead of 30. Fortunately, After Effects makes it easy to redistribute keyframes across time:

• Make sure the **Lens Flare Solid** layer is still selected, with the Brightness and Light Source Location parameters revealed in the Timeline window.

37 Make the flare animation more interesting by having it grow and recede in brightness as it flies across the sky.

• Move the Time Marker to 07:00 – the new target for when the animation is supposed to end. Press Option+] (Alt+]) to trim **Lens Flare Solid** to this new duration.

• Click on the word Brightness in the Timeline window to select this parameter's keyframes. Then Shift+click on the parameter name Light Source Location to add this second row of keyframes to the selection.

• To expand the keyframes, hold down the Option (Alt) key, and drag one of the keyframes currently at 06:20 to the right. After you start dragging the keyframes, also hold down the Shift key. When you get close to the time marker at 07:00, holding down Shift will make the cursor snap to this time. Notice that the keyframe in the middle is also moving, maintaining the relationship it has as the "middle" keyframe.

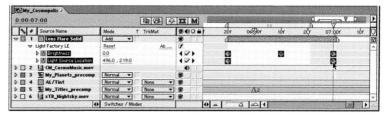

38 Select all of **Lens Flare Solid**'s keyframes, and hold down the Option (Alt) key while you're dragging the last one. The timing for all the keyframes will expand or contract to match.

> Summary: Whenever you need to expand and contract a set of keyframes, select them first, hold down the Option (Alt) key, and drag either the first or last keyframe(s) in the set. This feature works across multiple layers as well!

• Press N to trim the work area to end at this new time (07:00), and RAM Preview to see if you like the slower animation. We think this pace matches the music better as well: The flare dies away with the last guitar sting. When you're done, press F2 to deselect the keyframes to make sure you don't accidentally edit them.

Refinements

Some animators would stop here and move on to the next effect. However, we believe that spending the extra time to refine an animation is worth the resulting polish. When you're animating effects, it's often the subtle timing differences that make the effect really work.

When you want to tweak the speed of a parameter or movement, it's tempting to add additional keyframes. However, with some judicious velocity curve editing, you can add subtle interpolation while still using a minimum number of keyframes.

Selective Deselection

In version 5.0 or later, press Shift+F2 to deselect all keyframes, without losing any layer selections. F2 by itself deselects all layers and all keyframes.

STEP 39: One concern we have after RAM Previewing is that the flare still moves so fast that the viewer might not pick up its exact start and stop points. With **Lens Flare Solid** selected, press I to jump to its in point (05:20), and press Page Down and Up to play the frames at the beginning of the layer. Notice that the Light Source moves away from the dot in the first O before the viewer has a chance to notice it in the frame. Let's make it linger a bit longer before taking off:

- Twirl down the velocity graph for the Light Source Location. It is currently a flat line, indicating constant speed.

39 With linear velocity, by 05:24 the flare has moved well beyond the O (above left), making it hard to spots its origin. By applying Easy Ease to the movement, the flare lingers closer to the center of the O before it takes off (above right). These speed changes are visible in the Timeline's velocity graph (right).

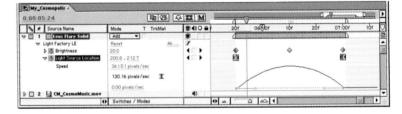

- Click on the parameter name Light Source Location in the Timeline window to select both of its keyframes, and hit F9 to apply Keyframe Assistant>Easy Ease. Now the velocity graph is an arc, indicating it moves more slowly at the start and end points.

- Page Down again from 05:20 to 05:25 and notice how much slower the light leaves the dot location. This gives the viewer enough time to register that the dot in the O was the origin of the light.

- Move to 06:25 and Page Down frame by frame into the last keyframe. Notice that the ease into the last O is also slower.

• RAM Preview again and see if you agree that the origin of the light source is better defined, and that its exit into the second dot is better explained.

• Twirl up the velocity graph for the Light Source Location.

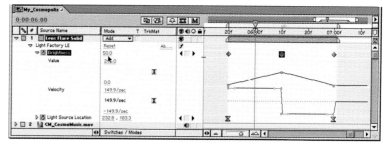

Step 40: We have the opposite concern with the Brightness animation: We wish it built up to maximum brightness more quickly, and lingered at this value in the center of the animation. Fortunately, there's a keyframe in the middle of the animation, which will make controlling its speed easier:

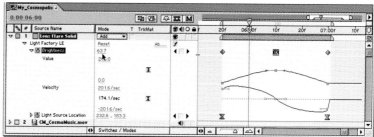

• Twirl down the velocity graph for the Brightness control. Notice how the Linear keyframes ramp the value from 0 at the in point to 100 at 06:10, then sharply down to 0 again at the layer's out point.

• Press 6 to move to 06:00 (between the first and second Brightness keyframes) and see how small the lens flare appears in the Comp window. The numbers in the Timeline window tell you it has a Brightness value of 50 at this point in its interpolation.

40 The initial Brightness animation has a linear rise and fall, resulting in a value of 50 at 06:00 (top). Applying Easy Ease to the middle keyframe adds some roundness to this curve, resulting in a value near 64 at 06:00 (above).

• Select the middle keyframe, and hit F9 to apply Easy Ease keyframe assistant. Notice how the curves change in the velocity graph, and that the value of Brightness at 06:00 has changed to almost 64%.

RAM Preview and see if you like this animation better. To tweak how long this brightness peak lasts, Option+double-click (Alt+double-click) the middle keyframe to open its Keyframe Velocity dialog, and change its influence numbers: Larger influence percentages mean a longer time spent near the maximum value at this keyframe. If you don't like the extended brightness, Command+click (Control+click) on the middle keyframe to return its interpolation method to linear. When you're done, twirl up the Brightness velocity graph and the layer.

40 *complete:* You can increase the influence this keyframe has in its Keyframe Velocity dialog. (As a guide, the Easy Ease keyframe assistant uses a 33.33% influence value.)

Save your project. If you had trouble getting a handle on interpolation amounts, compare your lens flare effect with our [**Cosmo_after Step 40**] *comp. The Light Factory LE effect is also saved as a favorite – to use it, remove your copy of the effect from the* **Lens Flare Solid** *layer, hit I to jump to the in point, mouse to Effect>Apply Favorite, and select* **LightFactoryLE_cosmo.ffx** *from the* **10_Cosmopolis>_Favorites** *folder.*

Part 5: Sex in Space

Self-contained FX

Some third-party blur effects –
such as in the Boris AE set and
The Foundry's Tinderbox 1 –
include transfer modes and
composite-on-original features
inside the plug-in. This means
you can perform Instant Sex
with one layer, instead of
requiring a duplicate.

In our experience, many 3D renders tend to have a flatter look (no pun
intended) than often desired for hot, sexy motion graphic design. A
good technique to enhance them is to duplicate a render, and mix in
the one on top using transfer modes. You can extend this trick by applying a blur to the version on top, which adds a filmic, blown-out look.
Multiple duplicates can be used with different modes to fine-tune the
effect. We dubbed this technique "Instant Sex", and it's what you will
use to improve the planet render we provided.

STEP 41: Move the time marker to a place where you can see a lot of
planets onscreen at once, such as around 02:00. Make sure the Modes
panel is still visible in the Timeline window (press F4 if it isn't).

Select the **My_Planets_precomp** layer, and type Command+D
(Control+D) to duplicate it. Rename this duplicate layer so you can
keep track of it: Hit Return, name it "**Planets+Overlay**" and hit Return
again to accept the new name.

Set the Mode for **Planets+
Overlay** to Overlay. This really
pumps up the saturation and
contrast on the planets – perhaps
too much. Hit T to twirl down
the Opacity property for
Planets+Overlay, and scrub its
value until you see a blend you
like. We set our layer to 40%.

41 The planets before (left) and after
(right) adding a copy in Overlay mode
on top.

In After Effects 4.1, you can scrub values by Option+clicking (Alt+clicking) on the word
Opacity and using the magic popup slider.

42 Adding another copy of the
planets layer, blurred and in Screen
mode, brightens the image and blows
out the highlights slightly.

STEP 42: With **Planets+Overlay** still selected, type Command+D
(Control+D) to duplicate it again; this second duplicate will be above
the other two planet layers. Hit Return to enable editing, rename it
"**Planets+Blur/Screen,**" and hit Return again. Press T to reveal its
Opacity property.

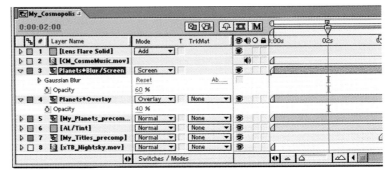

Change the Mode for this layer to Screen – notice how the image now brightens and even blows out slightly. With this topmost copy still selected, apply Effect>Blur & Sharpen>**Gaussian Blur** (if you have a slower computer, Fast Blur will do). Set its Blurriness slider to a small value, such as 5. Then scrub its Opacity value until you get a blend you like; we used 60%.

Experiment with turning the duplicated layers on and off to get a feel for what they are adding to the original image – in general, the Overlay layer is adding contrast and saturation, and the Screen layer is enhancing the highlights.

Snap Comparisons

There are numerous third-party blurs to choose from. If you have already installed the Tinderbox T_LensBlur effect included free on this book's CD, let's use After Effects' snapshot feature to compare some different looks.

To best see what's going on, hit Home to return the time marker to 00:00, set the Comp window to 100% Magnification and Full Resolution (space permitting), and set all three planet layers to Best Quality by selecting them and hitting Command+U (Control+U).

Step 43: Select just the **Planets+Blur/Screen** layer. If its Effect Controls window is not already open, press F3 to reveal it. You might want to close the effect tabs for other layers, to reduce clutter and potential confusion.

• Click the Take Snapshot icon at the bottom of the Comp window (the camera icon), or use the shortcut: Shift+F5. This saves a copy of the image currently in the Comp window to memory for later recall. This will be your reference of what the Gaussian Blur effect looks like.

• In the Effect Controls window, turn off the Gaussian Blur effect by clicking on the stylized "f" to the left of its name.

• Apply Effects>Tinderbox – Blurs>**T_LensBlur** to **Planets+Blur/Screen**. Its default settings are a bit enthusiastic. In the Effect Controls window, twirl down its Controls, and set the Radius to about 8. Also set the Process Alpha popup to Yes.

• To compare these two effects, recall the snapshot by pressing F5, or click on the Show last Snapshot icon (the one that looks like a little man) along the bottom of the Comp window. As long as you are holding down this button (or F5), After Effects will display the previous snapshot you stored to memory – in this case, of the Gaussian Blur effect. Note that the T_LensBlur effect yields a brighter center to the planets, and gives a softer look overall.

• Press and release this switch to decide which you prefer. Make sure the effect you choose is turned on, and the other turned off, in the

Snapshots times 4

There are four snapshots available: Press Shift+F5, F6, F7, and F8 to take a snapshot in the Comp, Layer, or Footage windows. Press F5, F6, F7, and F8 to display a snapshot in the active window (which means you can take a snapshot in one window and display it in another).

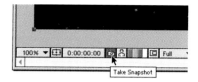

43 The Take Snapshot button is along the bottom of the Comp window. It will store a copy of the image in the Comp window for later recall.

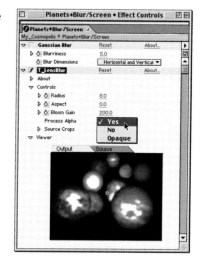

43 *continued:* Tone down T_LensBlur's defaults by reducing Radius to about 8. Be sure to set Process Alpha to Yes so that the blur is applied to RGB+Alpha.

43 *complete:* The Comp window normally shows the current state of the composition – in this case, with the T_LensBlur effect applied. Click on the Show last Snapshot icon (where the cursor is pointing) to compare it with the last snapshot you created.

Slider Range

When you're editing effects sliders in 4.1, it can be helpful to reset the slider range: Click on the value of the slider to open a dialog box and set the Slider Range to a smaller or larger range.

Effect Controls window. (For a cleaner project, it's best to delete unused effects once you're sure you won't be needing them again. We left both of them in our comparison versions of this comp, in case you wanted to compare them later.)

Snapshots are useful for comparing different values in effects. For instance, you could set the T_LensBlur to different Radius and Bloom Gain values and toggle back and forth to see which one you liked best. However, there is no way to "return to the snapshot values" – you need to be aware of what values were used to create a snapshot, and use Undo (if possible) to revert back to that state.

Save your project before going to the next section and twirl up all layers. You can compare your version of the planets with ours in [**Cosmo_after Step 43**]. *We chose the Gaussian Blur for a harder look; feel free to use T_LensBlur.*

Part 6: Transitions Tour

This final part consists of combinations of effects and techniques covered earlier, so we'll just give you a guided tour of how we finished off the tutorial. To check out these effects, in the Project window open the comp **Cosmopolis * prebuilt>Final Comps>Cosmopolis_FINAL** and poke around the upper layers as noted below. If you want to finish off your [**My_Cosmopolis**] comp, there should be enough information in the steps below to do so now that you have the basics down (or you could cheat and apply the Effect Favorites to Adjustment Layers as noted below).

STEP 44: In our final comp, select the **AL/Wipe Off** layer, and type Command+Option+B (Control+Alt+B) to set the work area to equal it. If its animated properties are not already revealed, hit U to twirl them down, and then F3 to reveal its Effect Controls window. RAM Preview to see this transition in action.

• At time 07:00, we created a new Adjustment Layer and renamed it **AL/Wipe Off**. Of course, naming it "Wipe Off" doesn't mean it will do anything – so don't forget to apply the effect!

• We applied the Gradient Wipe effect to this Adjustment Layer. We then added the **FractalNoiseMap.tif** to the comp and turned off its Video switch. (This layer is 720×540, but there's no need to prescale it, as the Gradient Wipe effect will automatically stretch the gradient to fit the 720×486 layer size.)

• In the Gradient Wipe effect, we set the Gradient Layer to the **FractalNoiseMap.tif** layer.

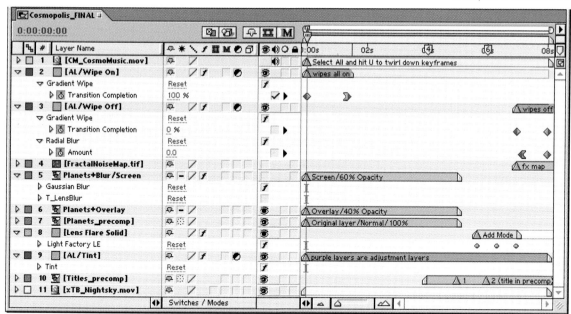

• We animated the Transition Completion from 0% at 07:00 to 100% at 08:00. This will wipe off all layers below, revealing the Background color (which should be black).

• We set the Transition Softness to 25% to soften the transition of the individual pixels so that they fade as they transition off.

Step 45: We also added the Radial Blur effect, using the default Spin blur setting. The Radial Blur Amount ramps up in intensity as the gradient wipe is transitioning off.

When you first apply Radial Blur it will look quite grainy. Radial Blur is a slow effect to render, so its antialiasing is set to Low while the layer is in Draft Quality, and High when the layer is in Best Quality. In order for this to occur, you must change its Antialiasing (Best Quality) popup in the Effect Controls window from Low to High. This will ensure that when you render using Best Quality for all layers, Radial Blur will appear smooth. If you have a fast computer, set the layer to Best Quality while you work. You can always revert the layer back to Draft Quality if the render hit is killing you – but don't change the Antialiasing popup to Low, or your final render will also look grainy.

The final Timeline window. Note the Adjustment Layers added near the top – these create transitions for all of the layers underneath.

44–45 The ending transition is a combination of Gradient Wipe using the now-familiar **FractalNoiseMap.tif** map, and a Radial Blur effect.

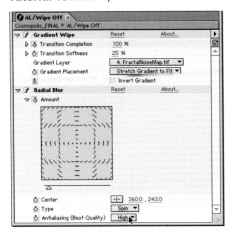

45 *complete:* The Effect Controls window for the transition effects. The cursor is pointing at the Antialiasing popup for Radial Blur, which is important for managing quality versus render times.

Layer, Go Home

Need a layer to start at 00:00? In After Effects 5.0 or later, select it, and type Option+ Home (Alt+Home) to quickly snap it back to zero.

46 The opening also includes a Gradient Wipe effect, this time using the planets as the gradient layer.

• The Radial Blur defaults to applying a blur Amount of 10, although the value of blur doesn't appear in the Effect Controls window (go figure). However, if you hit E to twirl down Effects in the Timeline window, and twirl down the Radial Blur effect, you can see the value for Amount. We originally animated the Amount from 0 at time 07:00 to 8 at 08:00.

• We also added an Easy Ease to the first Amount keyframe, so the blur ramps up slower, and then moved this keyframe to 07:05 by dragging it along the timeline, biasing the Radial Blur effect to come on even more toward the end.

This stack of effects is also saved as a favorite. To use it, go to 07:00, add the **FractalNoiseMap.tif** *layer to your comp, and turn off its Video switch. Make a new Adjustment Layer, and apply Effect>Apply Favorite>***GradWipeOff.ffx.** *Reset the Gradient Layer popup in the Effect Controls window to* **FractalNoiseMap.tif.**

STEP 46: The transition at the beginning is a variation of the transition used to wipe everything off at the end. Select **AL/Wipe On**, hit F3 to reveal its Effect Controls window, set the work area to equal this layer's duration, and RAM Preview to see this effect.

• At time 00:00, we created a new Adjustment Layer and renamed it **AL/Wipe On**.

• We applied the Gradient Wipe again, but this time we set the Gradient Layer to the **Planets_precomp** layer. This will wipe on the animation based on the luminance values of the planets.

• We animated the Transition Completion from 100% at 00:00 to 0% at 01:10. This will wipe on all layers below over 40 frames, using the luminance of the planets as a guide. Notice how the **xTB_Nightsky.mov** layer appears only toward the end of the transition, after 01:00; we set the second keyframe to Easy Ease In to lengthen this final fade.

• We set the Transition Softness to 25% to soften the transition of the individual pixels; this is especially important when the gradient layer was not designed to be a map for a gradient wipe effect and the values don't smoothly step between the 0–255 gray levels.

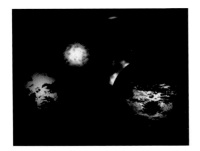

- We trimmed the adjustment layer's out point to 01:10, so it will not be sampled after this point (although it won't have any effect, it will add a little rendering time each frame as After Effects looks at it).

*This stack of effects is also saved as a favorite. To use it, make a new Adjustment Layer at 00:00. Load the effects by applying Effect>Apply Favorite>**GradWipeOn.ffx**. Be sure to reset the Gradient Layer popup to the **Planets_precomp** layer (any one of the three **Planets_precomp** layers will do; compound effects refer to the source of the layer only, before effects and modes are applied).*

Rendering with interlaced sources

If you'd like to render your finished Cosmopolis comp, remember that it included field-rendered, interlaced sources (**Planets_fill.mov** and **Planets_matte.mov** are separated as Lower Field First). In order to output both fields, you must turn on Field Rendering in your Render Settings. If you have a 720×486 Lower Field first hardware system (the most common in NTSC land), select your hardware compressor in the Output Module and render away.

If you are using DV, then render to the DV codec of your choice, still remembering to Field Render with Lower Field First. NTSC DV has a frame size of 720×480, not 720×486, so you will need to compensate for this. In the Output Module, use the Crop section to trim two pixels off the Top, and four off the Bottom, which will convert the 720×486 D1 Lower Field First output to a 720×480 DV movie and maintain the field order.

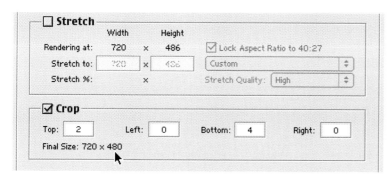

If you just want to save a small test movie to playback on a computer monitor, then render with Best Quality and Full Resolution, but turn Field Rendering *off* – there is no interlacing on computers. In the Output Module, pick a codec of your choice, and Stretch the final output to any small size (240×180, 320×240, and so on). Be sure to use a 4:3 aspect ratio so that you end up with a square pixel movie for playback on a computer – don't simply divide the 720×486 size – and keep in mind that some codecs are optimized for multiples of 8- or 16-pixel blocks in each dimension. We rendered the version in the **Final Movie** folder at a size of 384×288 (which we hope will play well from most hard drives).

Saving Favorites

You can save your own favorite stack of effects, including keyframes, by selecting the effects in the Effect Controls window and choosing Effect>Save Favorite. We recommend you create a central folder on the desktop for your favorites.

Connect

For more information on topics covered in this tutorial, check out the following chapters in *Creating Motion Graphics*:

Importing footage, folders, and separating fields: *Customs and Immigration*

Combining RGB and alpha elements: *All About Track Mattes*

Comp window Magnification, Zoom, and Resolution: *Creating a Composition*

Nesting compositions: *Nesting Compositions*

Editing and animating effects, including Effect Favorites: *Applying Effects*

Easy Ease: *Our Trusty Assistants*

Transition effects, including Gradient Wipe and Block Dissolve: *Standard Effects Round-Up*

Compound effects, including Displacement Map: *Compound Interest*

Adjustment layers: *Adjustment Layers*

Applying effects to solids: *That Ol' Black Solid*

Transfer modes: *Transfer Modes*

Snapshots: *The Layer Essentials*

Field rendering: *Playing the Field*

Just an Expression

A gentle introduction to creating and modifying several common, useful types of expressions, including synchronizing them to music.

Expressions are one of the most powerful additions to After Effects version 5.0. They let you automate a great number of tedious animation tasks, causing layers and their properties to react to other layers in ways that would otherwise be difficult to keyframe. To use this tool at an advanced level, however, you must not have too strong a fear of math or of reading JavaScript code. Because of this, learning how to manage expressions is a daunting task for many artists. However, learning just a little lets you do a *lot*.

Other tutorials in this book, such as *Piccadilly Circus* and *The Planets*, have already introduced simple forms of expressions that require a single "pick whip" move to tie one layer's properties to another. In this tutorial, we will introduce a series of slightly more advanced – but still easy to master – expressions that are useful for a number of common

OVERVIEW

Main Concepts:

These are the features and concepts we will be focusing on in this project:

- Expressions
- Effect Favorites
- Swedish plug-ins*
- 3D animation
- Orientation
- Bevel Alpha effect
- Texturize effect
- Tint and Fill effects
- Transfer modes
- Path Text effect
- Set Matte effect

Requirements:

After Effects 5.0 or later standard version

Third-party effects: Trapcode Swedish Plug-ins (included free on this book's CD)

Getting Started:

* *Be sure to install the Swedish plug-ins from Trapcode (www.trapcode.com) included on the accompanying CD in the **Free Plug-ins** folder.*

Inside the master **Tutorials** folder on the accompanying CD, locate and copy the folder **11_Expressions** to your hard drive.

In the folder **Final Movie** inside the project's folder, double-click on and play **Expressions.mov**. (This movie was built with the **MusicalExpression_5.aep** project which is described in the file **11B_Expressions_bonus.pdf**; you will learn the concepts behind it here and then explore the more complex bonus project later.)

Inside the **Project** folder you'll find the finished After Effects project file **Expressions_5.aep**. Open this project; this is your starting point.

animation tasks. While we're building those expressions, we will also try to expose the most common trip-ups, and how to solve them. In the process, you will gain a fundamental understanding of how expressions work and how to manage them in your own projects.

The final movie demonstrates what might look like a rather complex project. However, the underlying concepts are easy to master. In the following pages, rather than construct this complex project, we will discuss these concepts using simple shapes. This tutorial then continues on the CD with a bonus PDF tutorial, **11B_Expressions_Bonus.pdf**. This document covers in detail how we constructed the project that created the final animation you see in **Expressions.mov**.

A frame from the *Musical Expression* bonus project in which a series of rings, text-based dots, and volume bargraphs jump in time to the music while the text and edges of the frame react to the camera and another 3D layer.

Surface elements include footage from the Bestshot/ColorFlow CD and the EyeWire/Pop Psychedelia CD; background from the Bestshot/Upbeat CD.

The Tasks

This is what you will be doing in the various parts of this tutorial:

PART 1: Learn how to create, modify, and disable simple expressions, including how to match parameters with different value ranges or number of dimensions.

PART 2: Scale a layer to create a bargraph animation by borrowing keyframed values from another layer or effect.

PART 3: Employ an alternate method to animate the volume bargraph by having one layer's position follow another.

PART 4: Learn an expression modifier that allows one layer to borrow another layer's animation, offset in time.

PART 5: Make one layer point at another in 3D space.

PART 6: Coax 2D effect parameters to react to the 3D position of a camera or light.

PART 7: Take a quick tour of the **MusicalExpression_5.aep** project where a variety of objects and effects react to the soundtrack or each other, employing simple expressions that build on the above concepts.

CD BONUS TUTORIAL: An indepth PDF guided tour of the more complex *Musical Expression* project which employs techniques covered here, plus others. See the file **11B_Expressions_Bonus.pdf**.

Hold That Thought

To save a library of expressions, copy and paste them into a text file or virtual scrapbook. Later on, you can copy and paste them into the expression text field in new animations. You may need to re-edit them to change the names of layers or parameters they point to.

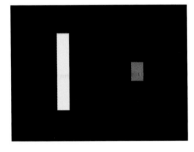

Part 1: A Gentle Introduction

If you're new to expressions, this section will lead you through the easiest way to create expressions: using the pick whip tool to tie one property to another. A large number of useful expressions can be created using this simple tool. If you've already mastered this much, jump ahead to Step 5 to learn how to link dissimilar parameters together, or skip to Part 2 to start exploring more advanced techniques.

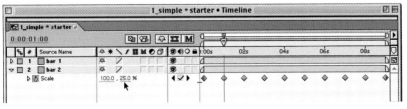

1 The comp [**1_simple * starter**] contains two bars, one of which already has its Scale property animating.

STEP 1: In the Project window, locate and double-click the comp [**1_simple * starter**] to open it. It contains two bars made from solids. Note the Scale keyframes applied to the **bar 2** layer (if the Scale property is not already visible, select the **bar 2** layer and type S). We've already created some simple Scale keyframes for it; press 0 on the numeric keypad to RAM Preview this animation.

STEP 2: The easiest expression to create is one in which a property of one layer exactly mimics what a similar property of another layer is doing. Follow these steps to make the Scale property of the **bar 1** layer animate exactly the same as the Scale of the **bar 2** layer:

• Select the **bar 1** layer and type S to reveal its Scale property.

• Click on the word Scale to select it, and use the menu option Animation>Add Expression to enable expressions for this property.
    Scale will twirl itself open in the Timeline window, and reveal a line that says Expression: Scale. To the right will be the word **scale**, currently highlighted. This preliminary expression says "Scale equals scale." Simple, but boring…

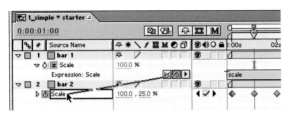

2 Use the pick whip tool to tie the Scale of the **bar 1** layer to the Scale of the **bar 2** layer.

• Click on the pick whip tool, the one that looks like a small spiral. With the mouse held down, drag this tool to the word Scale under the layer **bar 2**.

• After you release the mouse, After Effects will write a more useful expression for you:

this_comp.layer("bar 2").scale

The language this expression is written in is called JavaScript. The secret to reading JavaScript is that the periods give you clues on how to break up the expression. This expression says that for the property you've applied it to (**bar 1**'s Scale), After Effects is going to:

look inside this comp:	**this_comp**
for a layer called "bar 2":	**.layer("bar 2")**
and use its Scale property:	**.scale**

- To finish off the expression, either hit the Enter key on the numeric keypad (not the Return key – this will just start another line of text) or click somewhere else in the Timeline window. After

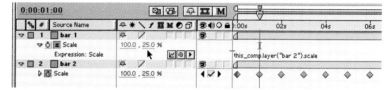

Effects will check to see if you wrote a valid expression – if not, you'll get an error message, and the expression will be disabled. Since After Effects wrote this expression, there shouldn't be any problems.

- RAM Preview and observe that **bar 1** and **bar 2** both scale together.

STEP 3: An important feature of expressions is that they are always "live" – if you edit a parameter that is being looked at for an expression, the "expressed" layer will automatically update and follow along. You can test this by editing one of the Scale keyframes for the **bar 2** layer. Or select all of the Scale keyframes for **bar 2**, and change their interpolation method: Either Command+click on Mac (Control+click on Windows) on one of the keyframes to change them all to the Auto Bezier interpolation method, or press F9 to set them all to Easy Ease. RAM Preview, and note that the two bars still animate exactly the same without having to rewrite the Expression.

STEP 4: Expressions are easy to turn off. In the Timeline window, click on the = sign to the left of the word Scale for **bar 1**. This will change it to a ≠ symbol. You'll notice that its value jumps back to its original 100%, and the bar will return to its full height in the Comp window. Leave the expression disabled for now.

STEP 5: Expressions can be created to link dissimilar properties – it just takes a little extra care. For example, Rotation can be linked to Scale. The potential problem is that for 2D layers, Rotation has one parameter, whereas Scale has two parameters: X and Y. The pick whip tool often allows you to make this distinction:

- If not already disabled, disable **bar 1**'s Scale expression by clicking on the = sign to the left of the word Scale.

- Select **bar 1**, and press R to reveal its Rotation property.

- Enable expressions for Rotation using a shortcut: Hold down the Option (Alt) key, and click on the stopwatch to the left of the property's name. This will twirl down the Expression line; you'll see the word **rotation** which is a basic expression that means **Rotation = rotation**.

- If you were to drag Rotation's pick whip tool directly to **bar 2**'s Scale property, After Effects wouldn't know which dimension of Scale you wanted – so it would assume the first dimension, which is X. But you want Y because it is the value that's animating (X's value is 100%

2 *complete:* After hitting Enter to accept the expression, the Scale value for the **bar 1** layer (where the cursor is pointing) equals **bar 2**'s Scale. Note that "expressed" values appear in red in the Timeline window.

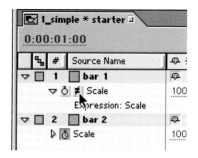

4 To disable an expression, click on its = symbol to the left of the parameter's name. It will change to a ≠ symbol as confirmation. (To re-enable the expression, click on it again.)

Deleting Expressions

To remove an expression, select the parameter in the Timeline window and use the menu command Animation>Remove Expression. You can also Option+click (Alt+click) on the animation stopwatch.

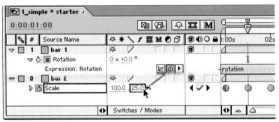

5 Rotation has one dimension, while Scale has two dimensions: X and Y. To express Rotation to Scale, drag the pick whip to the specific Scale dimension you want.

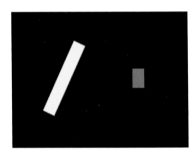

5 *complete:* The result is that **bar 1**'s Rotation follows **bar 2**'s Y Scale. When you want to access just one dimension of an overall value, JavaScript requires an additional designation inside brackets to know which one to use.

throughout). So click on Rotation's pick whip tool, and carefully drag it just to **bar 2**'s Y Scale parameter (the right-most one of the pair).

• When you release the mouse, the following expression will be written for you:

this_comp.layer("bar 2").scale[1]

This is very similar to the expression you created in Step 2, except the word "**scale**" is now followed with the designation [1]. This is JavaScript's way of noting which dimension of a property to use. The designation [0] means use the first dimension – X, in this case – and the designation [1] says use the second dimension, Y.

• Hit Enter to accept this expression, and note how **bar 1**'s Rotation value now matches **bar 2**'s Y Scale value. RAM Preview to see the result.

STEP 6: Not only do Scale and Rotation have a different number of dimensions, they have different value ranges as well: Whereas Scale goes from 0% to 100%, Rotation goes from 0° to 360° to define one full rotation. If you want 100% of scale to equal 360° of rotation, you will need to make a simple modification to the expression:

• Calculate how much you need to modify the Scale parameter to get the desired Rotation result. In this case, you want 100% to equal 360°, so you need to modify it by a factor of $360 \div 100 = 3.6$. You can add this modification to the beginning or end of the value you want to modify – if you're at the front, you would say **3.6 *** ; at the end you would say *** 3.6**. (You could also enter *** 360 / 100** for the same result.)

• In the Timeline window, click somewhere in the expression's text field to select it. Move your cursor to the front of the expression; pressing the left cursor arrow should do the trick.

• Type **3.6 *** at the beginning of this expression. The asterisk says multiply the expression's result by 3.6.

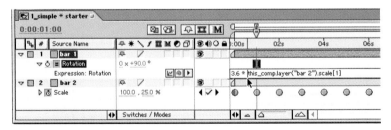

• Hit Enter, and either scrub the time marker or RAM Preview to see your new result. Feel free to try different values to get different relationships between Scale and Rotation – for example, if you want 100% to equal 180°, change **3.6** to **1.8**.

6 You can use simple math to modify how an expression responds. Here, the Y Scale for the **bar 2** layer is being multiplied by 3.6 to produce **bar 1**'s Rotation amount.

Save your project. To check whether you created these two expressions properly, compare your comps with [**1_simple_after Step 02**] *and* [**1_simple_after Step 06**]. *They are saved in the Project window's* **_Expressions * prebuilt>_compare comps_after Step ##** *folder.*

Part 2: Scaling New Heights

These next two Parts will explore using expressions linked to other parameters to alter the scale or position of a layer. The task you will be working on is animating bargraph-style volume indicators in sync to music, similar to what you saw in **Expressions.mov**. Of course, these techniques are easily applied to other animations.

STEP 7: Close any extraneous comps that may be open, then open comp [**2_bargraph * starter**]. It also contains two bars filled with audio icons using the Image Club font Mini Pics Digidings.

STEP 8: In the Project window, twirl open the **Sources** folder. Locate the file **CM_Express_music.mov**, and drag it on top of the [**2_bargraph * starter**] icon in the Project window. This will add it to that comp, starting at 00:00. Bring the Comp or Timeline window back forward, and RAM Preview to get a feel for the music.

STEP 9: We have already created a set of keyframes that follow the volume of a few of the musical parts in the soundtrack and that have value ranges of roughly 0 to 100. Previously, you would do this by using the Production Bundle's Motion Math scripts Layer Audio or Comp Audio; for this project we used a new plug-in from Trapcode that does a better job (see the sidebar *Sound Keys and Swedish Plug-ins* later in this chapter for more information). These keyframes have been applied to a custom effect – Swedish Sliders – and saved as an Effect Favorite.

• Select the layer **bar 1**.

• Select the menu item Effect>Apply Favorite. Navigate to the **_Favorites** folder inside this tutorial's folder on your disk, open it, and select the file **2_SoundKeys.ffx**. Click Open.

• The Effect Controls window will open, showing an effect called Swedish Sliders, with three parameters: Slider 1, 2, and 3. (If you got an error instead, you haven't installed the Swedish Plug-ins yet from the Free Plug-ins folder: Save your project, quit After Effects, install them into the After Effect Plug-ins folder, and relaunch the program.)

• In the Effect Controls window, select the effect's name, and hit Return to enable it for editing. Type in **"audio 1-3"** and hit Return again. It can be useful to rename effects to keep better track of what they do.

• Slider 1 holds keyframes representing the loudness of a combination of the bass drum and the guitar line; Slider 2 and 3 represent two different percussion instruments. With **bar 1** still selected, press U to reveal these keyframes in the Timeline window. Twirl open the arrow next to

Music Credits

The soundtrack for this tutorial was arranged by Chris Meyer of CyberMotion. The ethnic drums and bells came from the sample library *Ethno Techno* by Bashiri Johnson (distributed by Ilio Entertainment – www.ilio.com). The guitar and fast pop drums are from Zero-G's library *Total Drums and Bass* (www.zero-g.co.uk). The whoosh sound came from an "Acidized" version of Bill Laswell's *Sample Material* (www.sonicfoundry.com).

Arrays and Dimensions

When a property has more than one dimension, its overall value is referred to in JavaScript as an *array*. For 2D scale, its value is an array with the dimensional parameters X and Y.

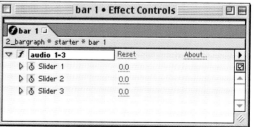

9 To rename an effect name, select it in the Effect Controls window, hit Return, type a new name, and hit Return again.

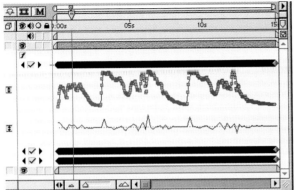

each Slider to see the value graphs for these keyframes. Twirl up the value graphs when you're done, but keep the Slider parameters exposed.

Step 10: You want to adjust the height of **bar 1** using one of these sets of keyframes. Since we already adjusted the keyframe value ranges to be 0 to 100, this would seem like a simple task:

• With the layer **bar 1** still selected and the sound keyframes revealed, type Shift+S to also reveal its Scale property.

• In the Timeline, Option+click (Alt+click) on the animation stopwatch for Scale to enable expressions.

9 *complete:* We saved an Effect Favorite with keyframe data for three different musical lines, applied to dummy effects. Their value graphs give you an idea of how they fluctuate over time.

• Drag the Scale's pick whip to Slider 1. Release the mouse, and hit Enter to accept the expression.

The result is a long expression – so long, you will probably need to resize the Timeline window to read it all. If you look at it carefully, you will see it repeats itself; it contains two copies of the phrase:

effect("audio 1-3").param("Slider 1")

Now glance at the Comp window, or RAM Preview. Oops; the bar is scaled both horizontally and vertically. The pick whip was an overachiever: Since Scale has two dimensions – X and Y – it assigned the parameter Slider 1 of the effect audio 1-3 to both of these dimensions.

10 Dragging the pick whip from Scale to Slider 1 results in its values being used twice – for the X and Y dimensions of Scale.

STEP 11: You want to affect only the Y dimension of Scale. However, the expression language requires you to provide an answer for both the X and Y dimensions. *These two values must be stored inside a pair of brackets separated by a comma* – for example [X, Y].

You want to use Slider 1 for Y; you also need to tell After Effects to use the previous X scale value for X. This latter parameter goes by the name **scale[0]** (the [0] says use the first dimension – X – of Scale).

• Click on the expression's text field to select it, then hit Delete to erase it.

• To fill in the answer for X, carefully type:

[scale[0],

• Now use the pick whip to drag to the parameter name Slider 1 (or one of the other Sliders, if you want to try out different audio data) in the Timeline window. After Effects will automatically type in the correct effect and parameter name.

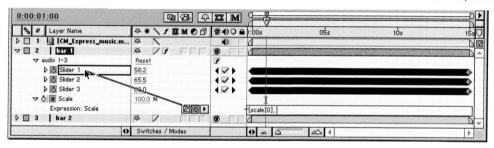

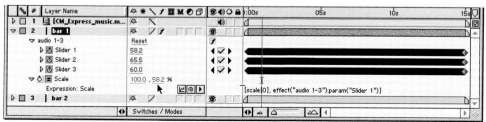

• In an expression, every open bracket or parenthesis needs a matching close bracket or parenthesis. Finish off the expression by typing] and hit Enter. RAM Preview; now only the height should be animated.

STEP 12: The height of **bar 1** now scales in time with the music, but it's scaling from its center. A bar graph should scale up from its bottom. Fortunately, this does not require an expression to solve:

• Double-click on **bar 1** to open its Layer window.

• Check the Layer window's wing menu to make sure Anchor Point is selected.

• Click on the Anchor Point icon – the circle with the X in the middle – and with the mouse button still held down, hold down the Shift key. This will constrain your movements to just the X or Y axis. Then drag the Anchor Point down until its crosshairs center on the bottom of the layer. If you have the Info window open, it will tell you how far you've dragged; 50 pixels is correct. Press Shift+A to twirl down Anchor Point in the Timeline; its value should now read X10, Y100.

• Close the Layer window, and RAM Preview: **bar 1**'s height should scale correctly now. Drag **bar 1** to line up with the bottom of the Comp window (Y Position = 240), and it will behave just like a bargraph meter.

If you had trouble creating this expression, study the prebuilt comp **[2_bargraph_after Step 12]** *to make sure you entered it correctly. Save your project before moving onto the next section.*

11 To alter just the Y dimension, tell After Effects to use its previous X scale value for X and then use the pick whip to assign Slider 1 to Y (top), and finish off the expression with a close bracket. Notice how the Scale property now uses Slider 1's value for just the Y dimension (above), which makes the bar's height jump in response to the loudness of the bass drum followed by the guitar line.

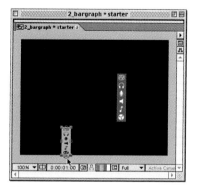

12 Align **bar 1** with the bottom of the comp, and now it will behave like a bargraph volume meter.

Part 3: Raising the Bar

Although scaling is a versatile way to animate a layer, there are times when it's a bad solution – such as when the layer contains an image you don't want to squish and stretch. An alternative approach is to use expressions to animate the Position of a layer. This is not much more difficult than animating its Scale.

For this part, continue using the comp you created in Steps 7 through 12. If you are jumping straight into this Part and have skipped the previous one, open the comp [3_**bargraph_2** * **starter**].

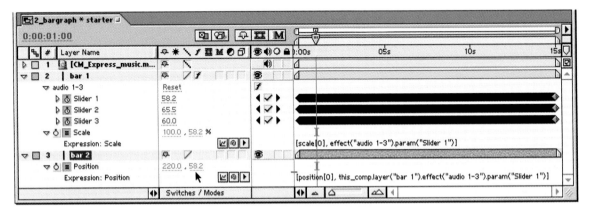

13 The expression to make **bar 2**'s Y position follow **bar 1**'s Slider 1 is not much different from the Scale expression you created in Step 11 (above). However, the animation is in the wrong place (below)…

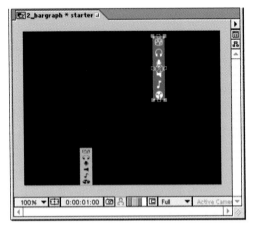

STEP 13: You want to animate the position for **bar 2** to make it jump up from the bottom of the comp like **bar 1** does, just without the stretching effect that scaling creates. Like Scale, 2D Position has two dimensions: X and Y. Again, *these two values must be stored inside a pair of brackets separated by a comma* – for example [**X, Y**]. You want to animate only the Y dimension, and leave the X dimension alone. Fortunately, this is a problem you already know how to solve:

• Make sure **bar 1**'s effect parameters are exposed in the Timeline window (if not, press E to twirl them down).

• Select **bar 2**, and type P to reveal its Position property.

• Option+click (Alt+click) on Position's animation stopwatch in the Timeline window to enable expressions.

• To tell After Effects to leave the X position alone, type:

[**position[0]**,

• Drag Position's pick whip up to **bar 1**'s effect parameter Slider 1. Note that the expression fragment After Effects writes for you is a little longer than before, because it's pointing to a property in another layer.

- Type] to close off the brackets, and hit Enter to enter the expression.

RAM Preview and notice that **bar 2** hops in a similar manner as **bar 1**. However, there are some problems: **bar 2**'s location in the Comp window is all wrong, and it moves in the opposite direction. These take a little thought to fix, but the concepts are easy.

STEP 14: The sound keyframes we saved in Slider 1 increase in value as the sound gets louder. However, to make an object move "up" in After Effects, you need to *decrease* its Y position value. This contradiction is easy to solve with a minus symbol:

- In the Timeline, click on **bar 2**'s expression field to highlight it.

- Click again just after **[position[0]**, to place the cursor in front of the statement for the Y position.

- Type − (a minus symbol on the keypad, or hyphen on your keyboard). This says use the negative of the value for **bar 1**'s Slider 1. Press Enter to accept your edit.

If you RAM Preview now, you will notice that the two bars now move in the same direction – but **bar 2** is hanging off the top of the Comp window, not the bottom like **bar 1** is.

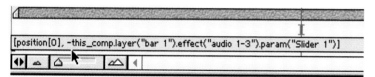

14 To make the bar rise in the frame as the sound gets louder, you need the negative of Slider 1's value.

STEP 15: The layer **bar 2** is now correctly bouncing up in time with the music. But where should it be bouncing up from? The bottom of the composition. This comp is 240 pixels high, so fixing this is a simple matter starting with 240, then subtract Slider 1's value from it. If you were to type **240** in front of the minus sign you added in Step 14, you would have this result. But there is a more clever trick you can use, which makes After Effects do some of the work for you:

- Select the expression, and place your cursor just before the minus symbol you entered above. Carefully type:

this_comp.height

This expression fragment is what it says: After Effects will automatically figure out this comp's height in pixels, so you don't have to remember its size. If you were to resize this comp later, After Effects would automatically take this new size into account, keeping the bar at the bottom.

- Hit Enter and RAM Preview again: The motion is correct; **bar 2** just starts higher than it should. We'll fix that problem shortly.

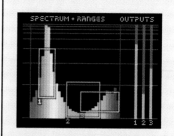

Sound Keys and Swedish Plug-ins

We created the keyframe data used in this project with a preliminary version of a new plug-in from Trapcode (www.trapcode.com) called **Sound Keys**. Sound Keys is able to analyze individual frequency bands and loudness ranges of audio, and to create streams of keyframes from this data (the graphical portion of the user interface is shown above). Sound Keys has a lot more control than the Motion Math audio scripts, and is capable of creating keyframe data with more fluid motion.

Trapcode also created a series of "dummy" effects called Swedish Plug-ins (Trapcode is based in Sweden). These include four effects: **Color**, **Dial**, **Point**, and **Sliders**. They have no effect on a layer, but they are great tools to hold keyframes and control expressions. They are included free, courtesy of Trapcode, on this book's CD. We used Swedish Sliders to store the keyframes that were generated by Sound Keys for this tutorial.

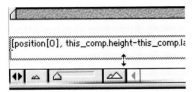

16 You can increase or decrease the height of the area where you read an expression by click+dragging on the line just below it.

STEP 16: If you can't read the entire expression at this point, make the Timeline window wider. This already-long expression is also about to get longer, so open up more height for it in the Timeline window. Place your cursor just underneath the expression field, until a double-arrow icon appears. Click and drag downward to open up a larger expression window.

• Clean up the expression to make it more readable: add spaces on either side of the minus sign. Place the cursor just before the long fragment created by the pick whip tool in Step 13 (just after the minus symbol), and hit Return to move it down to another line. Expressions ignore space and most returns, so these edits won't alter what the expression does.

• Hit Enter to accept the modified expression. It should now read:

[position[0], this_comp.height -

this_comp.layer("bar 1").effect("audio 1-3").param("Slider 1")]

16 *complete:* Your modified expression now takes the height of this comp and subtracts from it the value of **bar 1**'s Slider 1. This will give you the jump-up motion you want.

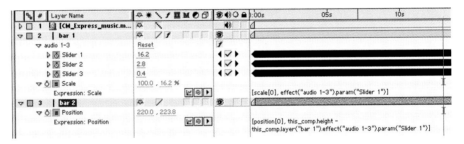

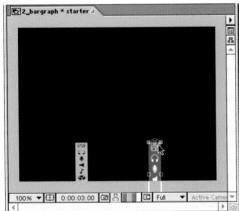

17 Set **bar 2**'s Anchor Point to its top. That way, the layer will extend off the bottom of the comp.

STEP 17: The motion is correct but **bar 2** starts higher than it should. As in Step 12, we can fix this easily by moving the Anchor Point (since the value of Position used by the expression is the value of the Anchor Point in the Comp window):

• Double-click **bar 2** to open its Layer window.

• Check the wing menu to ensure Anchor Point is selected.

• Drag the Anchor Point to the top, not the bottom, of the layer – when at rest, you want it to extend off the bottom of the comp. Remember that you can hold the Shift key while you're dragging to constrain your movement. When you're done, close the Layer window.

• RAM Preview for the final time. The two bars are now jumping in unison – but since we used Position rather than Scale to accomplish this with **bar 2**, you don't have to worry about the image inside this bar getting squished.

Save your project. We've saved prebuilt comps for most of the steps in this section for you to compare your results with.

Part 4: Shifting Time

The next trick is using a simple expression to make one layer's animation follow another, but shifted in time. The example we'll use here is creating a "wave" type animation, but this technique has many uses – such as setting up a transition animation for one layer, and having all other similar layers use the same animation at different points in time.

STEP 18: Close any extraneous compositions, and open the comp [4_time delay * starter]. It contains three bars made from simple solids. The first one (which appears left-most in the Comp window) already has an expression assigned to it similar to the ones you created earlier: its Y Scale follows the values stored for Slider 2 in an effect that has already been applied.

STEP 19: Make sure the Scale property for **bar 1** is visible in the Timeline window. Then select **bar 2**, and type S to reveal its Scale property. Create an expression for its Scale to follow **bar 1**'s Scale using the pick whip:

- In the Timeline window, Option+click (Alt+click) on the animation stopwatch next to **bar 2**'s Scale property to enable expressions.

- Drag the pick whip for **bar 2**'s Scale to point at the word Scale for **bar 1**. Make sure you drag the pick whip to the word next to the animation stopwatch, and not the next line down that says Expression: Scale.

- Hit Enter, and RAM Preview – the two bars animate together.

STEP 20: The expression for **bar 2** should say:

this_comp.layer("bar 1").scale

To make it look at a different point in time to borrow **bar 1**'s Scale property, do the following:

- Select the expression field for **bar 2**, and move your cursor to the end of the line.

- Type the following immediately after the word **scale** at the end of the expression:

.value_at_time(time - 0.05)

The *method* (a command to calculate something) **value_at_time** says "When looking at that other layer's Scale property, check out what its value would be at the time detailed in the following set of parentheses." In this case, that value is the current time minus 0.05 seconds. Press Enter.

Methods of Madness

A parameter value of a property such as Scale or Position is referred to as an *attribute*. A command to calculate something – such as **value_at_time** – is called a *method*.

19 Use the pick whip to make **bar 2**'s Scale follow **bar 1**'s Scale.

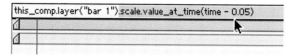

20 The highlighted area shows the attribute that tells an expression to look at a different point in time when it's borrowing another parameter's value.

One Frame Offset

To calculate one frame of delay, you can divide one second by the comp's frame rate, or have After Effects calculate it for you by using the attribute **this_comp.frame_duration** in place of a specific number. For two frames, add *** 2**, and so on.

22 Copy **bar 2**'s expression and paste it into the expression field for **bar 3**. Modify it so that it looks at **"bar 2"** instead of **"bar 1"** so it will follow one more frame behind.

• RAM Preview and note how **bar 2**'s movement now lags slightly behind **bar 1**.

• You can enter any amount of delay you want in place of the 0.05 we had you type in. For example, replace 0.05 with **0.033**, which works out to one frame of delay at 30 frames per second (fps). RAM Preview, and notice how **bar 2**'s movement seems to follow **bar 1** more closely.

STEP 21: Now make **bar 3** follow behind **bar 2**. You can do this by copying and pasting the expression from **bar 2** to **bar 3**, changing just one number:

• Select the Scale expression for **bar 2**, and Edit>Copy it.

• Select the layer **bar 3** and type S to reveal its Scale property.

• Option+click (Alt+click) on its animation stopwatch, and Edit>Paste the expression you copied.

• Hit Enter, and RAM Preview. The layers **bar 2** and **bar 3** move together. This is because **bar 3** is also looking at **bar 1**'s animation, not **bar 2**.

STEP 22: Highlight the expression text for **bar 3**. Modify the phrase "**bar 1**" to say "**bar 2**" so it will look at the next layer in line.

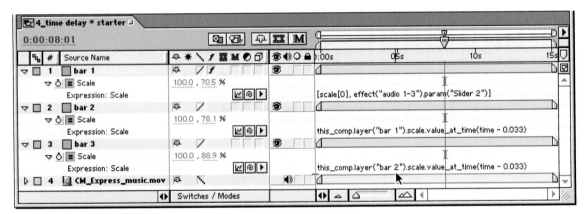

• Hit Enter, and RAM Preview. The three bars will now follow each other, delayed by one frame each.

The entire chain of expressions remains live: Any changes to **bar 1**'s animation will ripple through to the other bars. For example, edit **bar 1**'s expression to look at **"Slider 1"** instead of **"Slider 2"** – all of the bars will now follow this alternate set of keyframes (which follow different instruments in the music), each still delayed by the same amount of time.

Save your project. As with the previous example, prebuilt comps have been saved for most of the steps in this section. Compare your final result with [**3_time delay_after Step 22**].

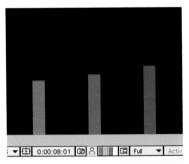

Part 5: Here's Looking at You

These next two parts will extend expressions into the realm of 3D space. Part 6 will show a trick to make certain 2D effects appear to be tracking a 3D object, such as a camera or light. Here we will demonstrate a simple expression that makes a layer track another object: the **look_at** method.

STEP 23: Close any extraneous comps, and open [**5_lookat * starter**]. It contains two layers: a stylized profile of an eye (**CM_eye.tif**), and a sphere from Tutorial 9: *The Planets* (**aF_CB_Venusian.tif**).

> **CM_eye.tif** was created using masks paths and the Stroke effect. The comp it was made in is stored in the **Expressions * prebuilt** folder in the Project window.

STEP 24: This expression requires the objects to be in 3D space. In the Timeline window, make sure the Switches panel is visible – press F4 if it isn't – and enable the 3D Layer switch (the checkboxes under the wireframe cube) for both of the layers.

STEP 25: The **look_at** expression method compares the position of two layers, and re-orients the layer it is applied to so that it faces the second layer. To use the pick whip tool to create this expression, you need to reveal the Position property of both layers – so select them both and press P.

You will apply this expression to the Orientation property of the **CM_eye.tif** layer, so select it by itself, and type Shift+R to reveal this property.

STEP 26: You're going to build this expression using a combination of typing, popup menus, and the pick whip tool. The format to keep in mind when you're working with expression methods – commands to calculate new values – is *the name of the method, followed by a set of parentheses that contains the parameter they are operating on.* If there is more than one parameter, these parameters are separated by commas. For example:

> method_name(parameter1, parameter2)

• Option+click (Alt+click) on the animation stop-watch next to Orientation to enable the expression.

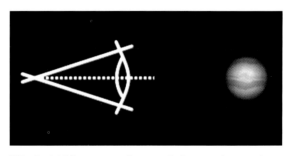

23 The initial comp contains a small planet, and an eye that will look at it using an expression.

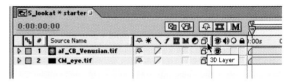

24 This expression requires that both layers be in 3D space.

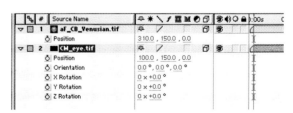

25 Reveal the Position property for both layers, and the Orientation/Rotation properties for **CM_eye.tif**.

Revealing Expressions

To reveal all expressions used for a layer, select that layer and type EE (two Es in quick succession). Typing U reveals all properties that have keyframes or expressions attached, but it does not reveal the expressions themselves; twirl these properties open to read their expressions.

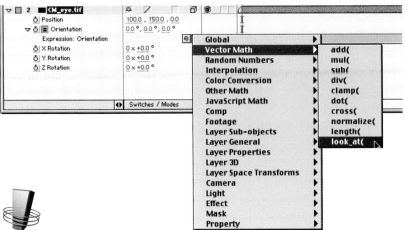

26 If you can't remember the exact wording for an attribute or method, After Effects has an extensive popup menu that will type the correct letters for you.

Turn Your Back

The After Effects manual says the order of the parameters for **look_at** are the "from point" followed by the "to point." This is incorrect, and should read "to point" followed by the "from point." However, the example shown later in the same paragraph of the manual is correct.

• Click on the arrow to the right of the pick whip tool. A large menu will appear; it contains a library of pretyped expression attributes and methods. Mouse over to the one called Vector Math (the second from the top), then mouse over and down to the one that says **look_at(** and release the mouse. After Effects will automatically type this method for you (with no typos), as well as the first part of the parentheses you need for its parameters.

• The first parameter you need is the position of the layer you will be looking at (also known as the "at point"). Use the pick whip and drag it up to the Position property of **aF_CB_Venusian.tif**. Release the mouse, and After Effects will add to the expression the phrase **this_comp.layer ("aF_CB_Venusian.tif").position** – the position of the layer you want to look at.

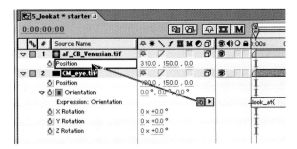

26 *continued:* The first parameter is the position of the layer you want to look at. Use the pick whip tool to point to it.

• Before entering the second parameter, you need to type a comma after the first one – where your cursor should be right now – to separate them. You can also add a space to improve readability; After Effects will ignore it.

• The second parameter is the Position of the layer doing the looking (the "from point"). Use the pick whip again, this time dragging it to the word Position for the **CM_eye.tif** layer. Release the mouse, and After Effects will add the word **position**.

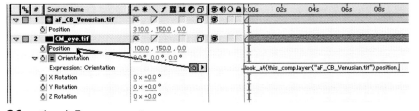

26 *continued:* Type a comma to separate your parameters, then use the pick whip to point to the position of the layer doing the looking.

	#	Source Name						:00s	02s	04s	06s	08s	10s	12s	14s	
▽ □	1	aF_CB_Venusian.tif														
		Ŏ Position	310.0 , 150.0 , 0.0													
▽ □	2	CM_eye.tif														
		Ŏ Position	100.0 , 150.0 , 0.0													
	▽ Ŏ	Orientation	0.0 ° , 270.0 ° , 0.0 °													
		Expression: Orientation					look_at(this_comp.layer("aF_CB_Venusian.tif").position,position)									
		Ŏ X Rotation	0 x +0.0 °													
		Ŏ Y Rotation	0 x +0.0 °													
		Ŏ Z Rotation	0 x +0.0 °													

- Finish this expression by typing a close parenthesis, and hit Enter. Your final expression should read:

    look_at(this_comp.layer("aF_CB_Venusian.tif").position,position)

26 *complete:* Type a final close parenthesis, hit Enter, and your **look_at** expression is done.

STEP 27: Now turn your attention to the Composition window. The **CM_eye.tif** layer has turned sideways in relation to the **aF_CB_Venusian.tif** layer so that its Z axis points at the planet. This is easier to see if you use a different camera position; to get a better perspective, try selecting Custom View 1 from the View popup at the bottom of the Comp window.

Select the **CM_eye.tif** layer and note how the eye's blue Z axis coordinate arrow points directly at the planet (to be exact, the planet's anchor point).

Experiment with moving the **aF_CB_Venusian.tif** layer, either directly in the Comp window or by scrubbing its Position coordinates in the Timeline window. The eye will continue to face the planet. Now change the **CM_eye.tif** layer's Position, and notice that it continues to re-orient itself toward the planet. This will also be true if you keyframed an animation path for either layer.

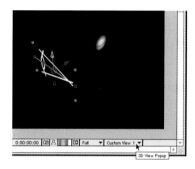

27 After this expression has been applied, the eye layer faces toward the planet along its Z axis (the blue arrow) as viewed in Custom View 1.

STEP 28: A design issue with the current arrangement is that **CM_eye.tif** was drawn to *point* at another layer, not face it. This is where having two different sets of Rotation properties for a layer comes in handy.

The eye needs to be rotated on its vertical – or Y – axis to change where it points. Watching the Comp window, scrub the Y Rotation property in the Timeline until the **CM_eye.tif** (and its red Y axis arrow) points toward the planet. This might be easier to see from the Top view; the correct value is 90°. To verify that this works, move either layer around and observe that the eye continues to point at the planet.

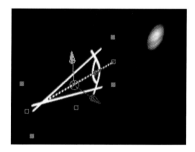

28 Entering a Y Rotation value of 90° redirects the eye to point at the planet along the correct axis.

If your pointer layer was originally drawn pointing up or down, modify its Z Rotation to aim it in the direction you want. If you need to also animate the layer's rotation, you could apply this expression to a null object, and parent your animating layer to the null. (Parenting a layer to a null object is covered in Tutorial 6, *Piccadilly Circus*.)

Save your project. This finished expression, with Y Rotation offset, is saved as prebuilt comp [5_lookat_after Step 28].

Part 6: 2D Meets 3D

Even though After Effects 5.0 introduced the concept of 3D space, all of the individual objects in this space are still flat 2D layers with no depth. Several effects, such as Bevel Alpha and Texturize, fake 3D depth by changing the apparent light levels across a layer's surface. Expressions can be employed to make this fakery appear to track a 3D camera or light (or other layer). This expression can be applied to any effect that has a rotational parameter – such as Directional Blur, Twirl, Wave Warp, or even the normal 2D Drop Shadow effect (if you want to avoid the render hit 3D lights and shadows incur). It does contain some more complex math than what we've dealt with so far, but fortunately, it's a standard formula that you can use as-is.

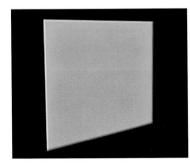

30 The Bevel Alpha effect creates the illusion that a layer is being lit from a certain angle (above). However, this angle does not automatically track objects such as a 3D camera (below).

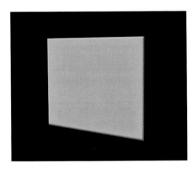

STEP 29: Close any extraneous comps, and open [6_faux 3D * starter]. It contains a solid called **Gold Slab** enabled for 3D, and an animating camera. RAM Preview and note how the camera's perspective changes.

STEP 30: Select **Gold Slab**, and apply Effect>Perspective>**Bevel Alpha**. Its edges will now appear to be affected by a light that's where the camera starts. (In the next step we'll build on this idea by using a Light layer.) In its Effect Controls window, increase the Edge Thickness parameter to 4.00 so you can see this more clearly.

RAM Preview again, and the illusion breaks down: Even though the camera moves, the lighting on the beveled edge does not. You could try to hand animate Light Angle's value to keep the illusion alive, but there's a better way…

STEP 31: Delete the Bevel Alpha effect (select it in the Effect Controls and hit the Delete key). Make sure **Gold Slab** is still selected, then go to Effect>Apply Favorite. Navigate to the _Favorites folder inside this tutorial's folder on your drive, select 6_CameraBevel.ffx, and click Open. This favorite applies the Bevel Alpha effect, with an expression already written.

With **Gold Slab** still selected, type EE to reveal the expression applied to the Light Angle parameter. You will probably need to drag

31 Applying this expression to Bevel Alpha's Light Angle parameter causes it to track the camera's relative position (sequence below).

the thin white line below the expression text field downward to see the entire expression; it is four lines long:

```
angle_offset = 90 + rotation;
target_layer = this_comp.layer("Camera 1");
rel_pos = sub(position, target_layer.position);
(Math.atan2(rel_pos[1], rel_pos[0])*180/Math.PI) - angle_offset;
```

This could have been written in one long line, but we broke it up into more easily digestible pieces. This required naming some "variables" to equal intermediate values along the way.

The first line helps compensate for the way different effect parameters behave. You need to determine by observation what value works for each effect. An offset of 90° works for the Light Angle parameter; Drop Shadow's Direction parameter would require you to replace the **90** with **270**.

We also considered that the layer might be rotating as well by adding its Rotation property to **angle_offset** in the first line. To try this out, type Shift+R to also reveal this layer's Rotation property, and scrub the Z Rotation parameter – note how the light still appears to come from the camera's position.

The second line indicates which object you want to track. If you wanted to track a different layer instead, select the phrase **this_comp.layer("Camera 1")** and pick whip to the name of the layer you wish to track.

The third line finds the difference in positions between the layer the expression is being used on and the object you're tracking. The fourth line uses the math function arc tangent (**atan2**) to calculate the rotational angle between these two layers, including an offset you can adjust in the first line.

*A finished version of this comp is saved in the _Expressions * prebuilt>_compare comps_after Step ## folder as [6_faux 3D_after Step 31].*

STEP 32: Open comp [**6_faux 3D_light**]. This is a prebuilt variation of [**6_faux 3D * starter**], with a stationary camera and an animating light. The expression has been modified to track the light instead of the camera (drag the expression field taller so you can read the entire four lines of code).

Select the **Light 1** layer and scrub the Timeline to see how the bevel edges appear to follow the light's direction. (To see the motion path for the light, with the light still selected, set the Comp's View popup to Top view or Custom View 2.)

There are several ways to trick this expression into not working, such as placing the camera or light at the same position or on the same plane as the object – after all, 2D effects don't understand "in front" or "behind"; just left, right, up, or down. But overall, this expression has many applications in making the layer it is applied to appear to react to other 3D objects.

Further Reading

Two additional documents with more information on expressions are included in the **Further Reading** folder inside the **Goodies** folder on your disk. **DV_Expressions.pdf** is a PDF file of a column we wrote on Expressions for *DV* magazine (www.dv.com). The other is an archive of a Web site fellow artist JJ Gifford created, based on a presentation he gave on Expressions at the first After Effects West conference (www.aftereffectswest.com). Open the file **JJ_Expressions.html** in your Web browser (Java plug-in required).

There are numerous books on the JavaScript language. You can ignore the chapters on Web programming – the bulk of most books – and focus on the language itself. The After Effects manual also has an excellent chapter on expressions.

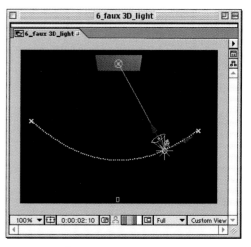

32 A simple variation of this expression can track an animating light.

Part 7: Musical Expression Project

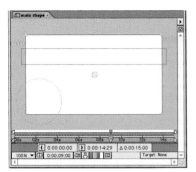

33 The overall shape was created by masking a solid.

Go back and play **Expressions.mov** from the **11_Expressions>Final Movie** folder on disk. All of the expressions used to create this movie are derived from those you learned in the previous sections. The individual pieces have been broken down into their own precomps; we'll give a brief overview of those here. For more detail, read the file **11B_Expressions_Bonus.pdf** in the **11_Expressions** folder on your disk.

STEP 33: Open the **MusicalExpression_5.aep** project; you'll find it in the **11_Expressions>Project** folder. Then open the composition **[ME_1 shape build]**. RAM Preview it and watch how the black bars along the lower right side jump in time with the music.

The overall shape was built by masking a white solid. The six bars are black solids that knock holes out of the overall shape. The three on the left are animated using the Scale trick demonstrated in Part 2; the three on the right are animated using the Position trick demonstrated in Part 3.

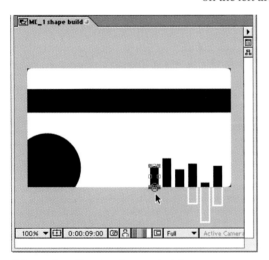

33 *complete:* The three bars on the left are animated with an expression attached to their Y Scale; the three on the right have their Y Position animated.

34 The dots and outmost ring have their Z Position animated in the same way as the bargraph's Y Position in the previous comp. The other rings follow the first one, delayed in time by one frame each. The dots are created with Path Text, their Left Margin and Tracking expressed to follow along with the music as they flow around a Loop path. The Hue of the rings is also offset using a simple expression.

STEP 34: Open the comp [ME_2 ring/dot bounce]. It has a lot of keyframes; if your screen is redrawing too slowly, twirl up the **SoundKeys** layer. It is easier to see what is going on if you view these 3D layers at an angle, such as with Custom View 1. Locate to 03:00 to see the animation at its peak, then RAM Preview.

The outermost ring has its Z Position animated with an expression similar to that used to move the bar graphs up and down. The other rings have their Z Position tied to the first ring, but are delayed in time one frame each using the same method discussed in Part 4.

Each of these rings has the Fill effect applied. The first ring is having its hue value shifted by scaling down the values of one of the **SoundKeys** keyframe sets. The other rings again just follow the first, delayed in time.

The characters (bullets on Mac, Yen symbols on Windows!) are created using the Path Text effect applied to the layer **Path Text dots**. The path is set to Loop, causing them to zoom around the outermost ring and continue on in a straight line. The Left Margin parameter is offset in much the same way that you learned to offset Position in Part 4; the Tracking is adjusted similar to the way you manipulated Scale in Part 3. This layer also has its Z Position animated in the same way as the outermost ring.

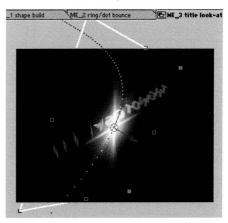

STEP 35: Open the comp [ME_3 title look-at] and RAM Preview it. Each of the individual characters of the title use the **look_at** expression you learned in Part 5 to follow the flare layer (prerendered using Knoll Light Factory) as it flies through the scene in 3D.

All of the characters were created in white with black outlines. The Tint effect was applied to each of them. These in turn were expressed to the layer **master tint**: Change the colors in its Tint effect, and watch all of the characters follow. Additional simple expressions were used to blink the Opacity of each character in time with the music, including a trick in which all of the layers are faded to full opacity using a separate dummy slider. This trick is explained in detail in the companion PDF file, **11B_Expressions_Bonus.pdf**.

35 Each of the characters are individually expressed to look at the flare layer as it flies by (above).

STEP 36: Open the comp [ME Final Build]: This is where it all comes together. Select layer 4 – **ME_1.1 surface precomp** – and type EE to reveal its expressions. Both the Bevel Alpha and Texturize effects use the same angle expression discussed in Part 6.

36 The main surface (left) has the Texturize and Bevel Alpha effects applied, expressed to follow the camera's position.

Although this is not expression related, you might also note that the precomps [ME_2 ring/dot bounce] and [ME_3 title look-at] have their Collapse Transformations switches turned on. You can collapse 3D compositions; they will then use the camera and lights of the comp they are nested into. This is how we could build 3D elements in precomps and have them integrate with the camera animation in our final scene.

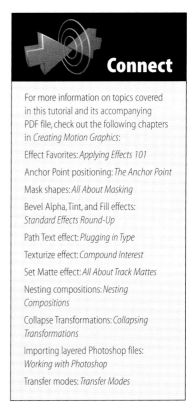

Connect

For more information on topics covered in this tutorial and its accompanying PDF file, check out the following chapters in *Creating Motion Graphics*:

Effect Favorites: *Applying Effects 101*

Anchor Point positioning: *The Anchor Point*

Mask shapes: *All About Masking*

Bevel Alpha, Tint, and Fill effects: *Standard Effects Round-Up*

Path Text effect: *Plugging in Type*

Texturize effect: *Compound Interest*

Set Matte effect: *All About Track Mattes*

Nesting compositions: *Nesting Compositions*

Collapse Transformations: *Collapsing Transformations*

Importing layered Photoshop files: *Working with Photoshop*

Transfer modes: *Transfer Modes*

36 *complete:* The final comp. Note that some of the precomps have their Collapse Transformations switch enabled; even 3D layers and comps may be collapsed.

Thanks to Michael Natkin – Adobe's expression wizard – for his support and advice, and to fellow user JJ Gifford whose use of expressions inspired some of the ideas in this tutorial.

Flamingo 4

Using Illustrator artwork and other vector-based elements to create an animation for the Macromedia Flash file format (SWF).

The artistic brief behind this tutorial is creating Web animations to teach kids about numbers. Today's number is 4, and you've enlisted a flamingo to help illustrate this. You'll import a flamingo and a background already created in Illustrator, adding water to the background and text on a curve in the foreground. To animate the flamingo, you will need to set up anchor points and a Parenting relationship (new to After Effects 5) for its layers. Since you want to export the final animation as a Macromedia Flash format file (SWF) – another new feature in After Effects 5 – you will need to take care to keep all the elements as vector art throughout. After the hard work is done, you can have fun making the flamingo dance to the accompanying music.

OVERVIEW

Main Concepts:

These are the features and concepts we will be focusing on in this project:

- Importing Illustrator files as Comp
- Anchor Points
- Parenting
- Spotting music
- Path Text on a curve
- Keyframe interpolation
- Masking a solid shape
- Exporting as SWF

Requirements:

After Effects 5.0 or later Standard version

Getting Started:

Inside the **Tutorials** master folder on the accompanying CD, locate and copy the folder **12_Flamingo** to your hard drive. In the folder **Final Movies** inside this project, double-click on and play **Flamingo.mov**. Alternatively, you can open and play the file **FlamingoR.htm** or **Flamingo.swf** in your Web browser.

Open the file **Flamingo_5.aep** inside the **Project** folder – this is your starting point; we suggest you save under a new name after each major section.

Windows users: Ignore the error message that the Sand font was not found – you can replace it later with a font of your choice.

Credits:

The concept and artwork for this project were created by Kristin Harris Design (www.kristinharrisdesign.com). Music by Carolyn West.

The Tasks

This is what you will be doing in the various parts of this tutorial:

PART 1: Import the layered Illustrator file that contains the flamingo, set anchor points, and build a parent/child hierarchy for its body parts.

PART 2: Resize the flamingo, add a layered Illustrator file which contains most of the background elements, and animate its clouds.

PART 3: Add the soundtrack and spot the beats in it for animation cues, and animate the legs of the flamingo to form the number "4".

PART 4: Create a water element by masking a solid, animate a bouncing title using Path Text, and add your own dance moves for the flamingo.

PART 5: Rendering for SWF (pronounced "swiff") output.

The flamingo in its final pose. Artwork © 2001 Kristin Harris Design, Inc. Music © 2001 Carolyn West.

Part 1: First Steps

The folder **Flamingo * prebuilt comps** in the accompanying project contains a number of compositions saved after various pivotal steps below, so you can check your own work if you go astray. Feel free to explore these comps before you get started, but be sure to Close All (Windows>Close All) when you're done peeking so you can start with a clean workspace. Also in the Project window, we've created two folders called **My_Comps** and **My_Sources** for you to put your own work into and keep it separate from the prebuilt versions. Select the appropriate folder before creating a new composition or importing a file; After Effects 5 will automatically sort it into that folder for you!

Import the Flamingo

STEP 1: First, you need to get a flamingo into your project. Guest artist Kristin Harris has already created one in Illustrator, so select the **My_Sources** folder in the Project window, and use File>Import File> File to locate the layered Illustrator file **Flamingo4.ai** from the **12_Flamingo>Project>Sources** folder on your drive. In the Import As popup, select Composition to make After Effects build a starter comp for you out of the file's layers, and click Open. The result is a folder with the individual layers, and a comp with a size of 370×530 pixels.

Bound by the Box

When you import an Illustrator file as a Composition, the comp will be created at a size just large enough to include all the elements. To predetermine the comp size, draw a rectangle in Illustrator around the elements and convert it to crop marks (Object>Crop Marks>Make).

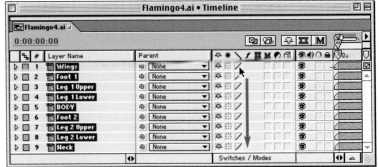

2–3 Change the comp's background color to white, and set all the layers to Best Quality (above and right).

4 Move the anchor point for the **Wing** layer from its center to a more natural position. The Pan Behind tool edits both the Position and Anchor Point values together, so the layer remains stationary in the comp.

STEP 2: In the Project window, double-click the comp [**Flamingo4.ai**] to open it, and make sure it's set to Full Resolution. The flamingo has an alpha channel, which means the comp's black background color will be visible around it. This background color is usually irrelevant to the final render, but it may appear when you render to SWF. Change Composition>Background Color to white for this tutorial.

STEP 3: The outlines of the flamingo look a bit jagged; that's because After Effects defaults to Draft Quality when layers are added to a comp. Change all the layers to Best Quality to have them antialiased properly. You can do this by dragging the mouse down the row of Quality switches in the Timeline window, or Edit>Select All and change just one to Best by clicking on its switch or pressing Command+U (on Mac) or Control+U (on Windows). When you're done, Deselect the layers (shortcut: F2); this will make it easier to focus on individual layers.

Setting the Anchor Points

STEP 4: When you import a layered Illustrator file, all the layers are the same size as their comp, with all their anchor points in the center of each layer. However, when the flamingo animates, each part needs to rotate around an anchor point that makes sense for that part: for example, the upper legs should rotate from the hip, and the lower legs should rotate from the knee.

To change the anchor point for the layers, select the Pan Behind tool from the Tools palette (shortcut: Y) and start by selecting the top layer, **Wings**. Its anchor point is visible in the center of the comp. Click directly on it and drag it to the left side of the **Wings** layer, about where the wings would naturally rise if they were flapping.

The Pan Behind tool is also referred to as the "Anchor Point" tool. With it you can move the anchor point directly in the Comp window. If you were to change the Anchor Point in the Layer window, it would move in the Comp window to reflect this new center – meaning you would then have to reposition the layer in the Comp window to get back to where you started. Moving the Anchor Point with the Pan Behind tool automatically changes the Anchor Point and Position values in concert with one another so the layer keeps its same relative position in the comp. Very handy!

Step 5: Continue moving the anchor points for all the other layers to positions that make sense for each body part. Keep in mind that some of the layers are partially hidden by other layers: for example, **Leg 2** (the leftmost one) is tucked partially behind the body. Feel free to turn layers off or solo layers to see the layer you're working on more clearly.

As this illustration has a loose, fun style, you don't have to place your new anchors exactly at the right pixel, but here are some guides:

• **Foot 1 & Foot 2:** Move these anchors near the top of the feet, where the ankle would hinge, but still inside the foot.

• **Legs Upper:** Move their anchors to the top of the upper leg (the hip).

• **Legs Lower:** Move their anchors to the top of the lower leg (the knee).

• **Body:** Move the anchor to the center of body.

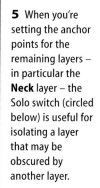

5 When you're setting the anchor points for the remaining layers – in particular the **Neck** layer – the Solo switch (circled below) is useful for isolating a layer that may be obscured by another layer.

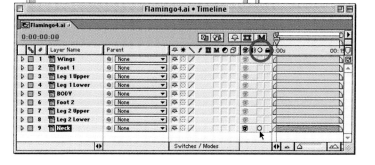

• **Neck:** Move the anchor point to the bottom end of the neck – you will probably want to solo this layer to see it more clearly.

To test that parts such as the **Wings** or **Neck** will rotate correctly, select a layer, hit R for Rotation, and scrub its value. Or, select the Rotation tool (shortcut: W for "wotate") and drag around the layer's anchor. Tweak the anchor points using the Pan Behind tool until you're happy. Be sure to use Undo (or otherwise return all rotations to 0°) and revert to the Selection tool (shortcut: V) before the next step.

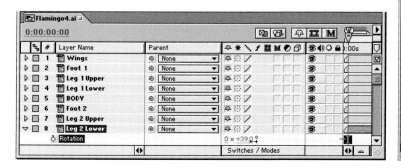

5 *complete:* To make sure your new anchor points work as expected, scrub a layer's Rotation property while checking how the corresponding body part moves, or use the Rotation tool and drag the layer clockwise in the Comp window.

We interrupt this tutorial to note that if you are completely lost, open our [**Flamingo_after Step 05**] *comp to compare your results; you will find it in the* **Flamingo * prebuilt>_compare comps_after Step ##** *folder. You can also use this comp to continue with the tutorial.*

Parenting

You've probably heard the children's song "the leg bone's connected to the hip bone, the…" These connections are a good thing, because you wouldn't want to move your hip, and not have your leg follow along with it – like the flamingo's foot in the illustration on the previous page.

This concept is supported by a new feature in After Effects 5 known as Parenting. You can now connect layers to each other, so as you move, rotate, or scale the parent, all the connected children will follow. This is an exceptionally handy way to group together layers, and in many cases replaces the need for nesting layers together in subcomps. But Parenting goes beyond grouping, allowing you to set up "kinematic" chains of layers which are useful for character animation and other similar techniques.

Step 6: The **BODY** layer is the centerpiece of the flamingo, and therefore will be the center of our parenting. Now consider how the body parts connect to this: the wings, neck, and both upper legs would be direct children of the body; the lower legs would be children of the upper legs; the feet would be children of the lower legs. Now let's go hook up the body parts of your flamingo in the same way.

Be sure the selection tool is active and make sure the Parent panel is visible in the Timeline window. If it isn't, press Shift+F4, or context-click on the top of one of the other panels to reveal the Panels popup menu, and select Parent. You can slide most panels left and right to re-arrange them; we prefer it near the layer's name.

Start with the **Wings** layer. You can either click on the popup menu for this layer under the Parent panel and select the **BODY** layer, or use the pick whip tool: Click on the pick whip (the symbol that looks like a tiny spiral), and drag it to the layer you wish to be the parent.

When you know that more than one layer will have the same parent, you can assign them all at the same time. Select the layers **Leg 1 Upper**, **Leg 2 Upper**, and **Neck**. Remember that you need to Command+click (Control+click) to select multiple layers that are not right next to each other in the Timeline window. Now use the popup menu or pick whip for any one of the selected layers to choose the **BODY** layer, and the rest of the selected layers will get the same parent.

Solo Selecting

You can view each layer separately by clicking the layer's Solo switch. You can solo more than one layer at once; Option+clicking (Alt+clicking) on a Solo switch will turn off any other solo layers. Remember to turn off (not on!) all solo switches to view all the layers again.

🏳	#	Layer Name		Parent	
▷ ☐	1	🎬 **Wings**	🌀	None	▼
▷ ☐	2	🎬 Foot 1	🌀	None	▼
▷ ☐	3	🎬 Leg 1 Upper	🌀	None	▼
▷ ☐	4	🎬 Leg 1 Lower	🌀	None	▼
▷ ☐	5	🎬 BODY	🌀	None	▼
▷ ☐	6	🎬 Foot 2	🌀	None	▼
▷ ☐	7	🎬 Leg 2 Upper	🌀	None	▼
▷ ☐	8	🎬 Leg 2 Lower	🌀	None	▼
▷ ☐	9	🎬 Neck	🌀	None	▼

6 The pick whip tool makes it easy to set up child/parent relationships.

A child can have only one parent. However, a child can act as a parent for another layer, which is exactly what we need to finish hooking up the rest of our body parts. You're probably already ahead of us:

- Connect **Leg 1 Lower** to **Leg 1 Upper**
- Connect **Foot 1** to **Leg 1 Lower**
- Connect **Leg 2 Lower** to **Leg 2 Upper**
- Connect **Foot 2** to **Leg 2 Lower**

Save your project. If you're lost, open our [**Flamingo_after Step 6**] *comp to compare your results.*

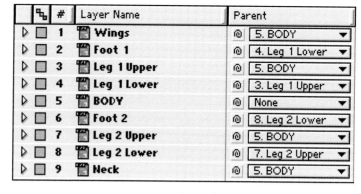

		#	Layer Name		Parent
▷	☐	1	Wings	ⓐ	5. BODY ▼
▷	☐	2	Foot 1	ⓐ	4. Leg 1 Lower ▼
▷	☐	3	Leg 1 Upper	ⓐ	5. BODY ▼
▷	☐	4	Leg 1 Lower	ⓐ	3. Leg 1 Upper ▼
▷	☐	5	BODY	ⓐ	None ▼
▷	☐	6	Foot 2	ⓐ	8. Leg 2 Lower ▼
▷	☐	7	Leg 2 Upper	ⓐ	5. BODY ▼
▷	☐	8	Leg 2 Lower	ⓐ	7. Leg 2 Upper ▼
▷	☐	9	Neck	ⓐ	5. BODY ▼

6 *complete:* Our final parenting hierarchy for the flamingo. Note the **BODY** layer's parent is set to None; it's the master of the entire chain.

Part 2: Composing the Frame

In this part, you will scale down the flamingo to its final size, and add a multilayered background behind it. You will make the background elements semi-transparent, to get a more interesting visual mix.

Comp Size and Scaling

The flamingo is larger than you will need in the final composition. To reduce it and the comp down to their final sizes, you'll take advantage of the Parenting feature:

STEP 7: When you imported the flamingo's layered Illustrator file as a composition, the resulting comp received the same name and size as the Illustrator file. Type Command+K (Control+K) to open Composition Settings, and make the following changes:

- Change the Composition Name to "**MyFlamingo**" (all together now: "My, my, mmyyyyy flamingo!").

- Set the comp Width to 400 and Height to 300. If one number changes when you type in the other, verify that the Lock Aspect Ratio checkbox is turned off. Make sure the Pixel Aspect Ratio is still set to Square Pixels.

- Change the Frame Rate to 12 frames per second (fps) – this is the same as most cartoon animation.

- Set the Duration to 15:00, and click OK.

The following step will scale and position the flamingo character in the resized composition.

Counting Off Base

Since After Effects can't count in the timeline at 12 fps, the File>Project Settings have been saved at 24 fps (the best choice as it's a simple duplicate).

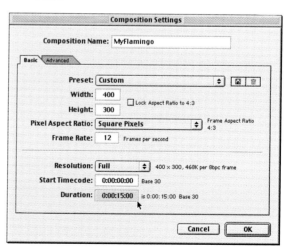

7 Edit the comp's settings from their imported defaults to something that will fit the final animation better.

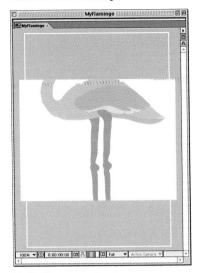

7–8 After you resize the comp, the flamingo will appear cropped top and bottom (above).

If your comp's duration was originally less than 15 seconds, you might notice that your layers appear trimmed in the Timeline window to prematurely stop at the old duration's time. There's a sequence of keyboard shortcuts that can quickly fix this:

- Press the – (minus) key on the keyboard to zoom the timeline out to its full duration.
- Hit the End key to locate to the end of the comp.
- Use Command+A (Control+A) to select all of the layers.
- Press Option+] (Alt+]) to trim the out point of all selected layers to the current time.
- Hit F2 or Command+Shift+A (Control+Shift+A) to Deselect All layers.
- Hit the Home key to locate back to the beginning of the comp.

Step 8: The flamingo now appears larger than the comp. To scale the entire character, all you need to do is scale the master parent – and the children will follow along. Select the **BODY** layer, hit S for Scale, click on the Scale value and enter a value of 50%.

If you've executed all the steps to this point correctly, the entire flamingo will now be 50% of its original size – and floating a bit too high in the frame. With the **BODY** layer still selected, drag it down until it is roughly centered in the frame. Again, the body pieces followed because of the parenting chain you set up in Step 6.

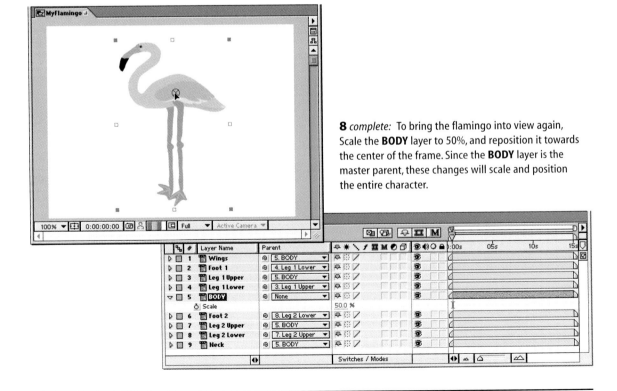

8 *complete:* To bring the flamingo into view again, Scale the **BODY** layer to 50%, and reposition it towards the center of the frame. Since the **BODY** layer is the master parent, these changes will scale and position the entire character.

Twirl up all layers and Save your project. If you think you missed something, open our comp **[Flamingo_after Step 08]** *to compare your results, or use this comp to continue with the tutorial.*

Adding the Background

STEP 9: The background was also created in Illustrator 9, at the intended final size of 400×300. Import it as a composition, just as you did with the flamingo in Step 1: Select the **My_Sources** folder in the Project window, then File>Import>File the **Background.ai** from the **Project>Sources** folder. Remember to select Composition from the Import As popup near the bottom of the import dialog, and click Open.

9 The **Background.ai** file Kristin Harris created consists of three layers: the palm trees, the clouds, and the beach.

STEP 10: You'll now have a composition and a folder of sources, both called [**Background.ai**]. Double-click the comp to open it, and explore the three layers inside: **BG_Palm Trees**, **BG_Clouds**, and **BG_Beach**. The fourth layer contains just the Illustrator guides and can be ignored. Turn on Best Quality for all layers so they antialias.

STEP 11: Deselect All (F2), then select layers 1, 2, and 3. Command+C (Control+C) to copy these layers and press Command+W (Control+W) to close the comp windows.

If you've been exploring different layers and properties, it's best to Deselect All (F2) or Deselect All Keyframes (Shift+F2) before Copying and Pasting layers. If you don't, After Effects defaults to copying any selected keyframe or property value rather than copying the layer itself. For instance: If you select the **BG_Clouds** layer and move it to see what it might look like when it's animated, the Position property is selected along with the layer. If you now Copy, you're actually copying the Position value, not the layer. When you then try to Paste this layer into another comp, either nothing will happen, or you'll paste a new Position value to another (unsuspecting) selected layer. So if you've ever pasted a layer and nothing happened, you know you're not going crazy…

Just to make life more confusing: In this example, if you used Cut instead of Copy, the layer will disappear, but only the Position keyframes – not the cut layer – can be pasted. Although you can Undo when you realize that Paste isn't working, play it safe and Copy – don't Cut – layers when pasting from one comp to another.

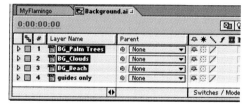

10 Open the comp [**Background.ai**], select the top three layers and Copy. You can then close this composition.

11 Paste the layers into [**MyFlamingo**] and drag them to the bottom of the stack.

STEP 12: The [**MyFlamingo**] comp should now be forward. Paste the three background layers. While they are still selected, drag them to the bottom of the layer stack and check that they appear in the same order as before (top to bottom): **BG_Palm Trees**, **BG_Clouds,** and **BG_Beach**.

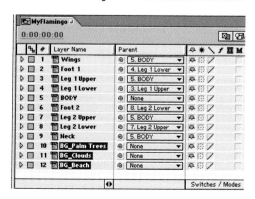

Since your final output will be SWF, you must place all the vector artwork in one composition. This is why you can't simply nest the [**Background.ai**] comp into the [**MyFlamingo**] comp. If you did, the background layers would render out as pixels, not vectors, making your SWF unnecessarily large.

STEP 13: Finish off the background layers by setting all three layers to 35% Opacity (shortcut: T to twirl down Opacity). This will appear to lighten the background layers, since earlier the comp's background color was set to white. The less saturated background should also make the flamingo stand out more.

13 At this point, the background layers are behind the flamingo, and made partially transparent to create more contrast and interest.

Note how the semi-transparent background layers appear: Even the tree trunks in the **BG_Palm Trees** layer are see-through. When you later export this comp as a SWF, you can also choose to have each vector shape in a layer be individually semi-transparent rather than the entire layer looking like one semi-transparent image. This creates yet a different look, as even the individual leaves on the trees will be semi-transparent, overlapping in interesting ways.

We're using transparency here because we want to show off these features of the SWF file export; if your only goal was to make the background lighter, you could just change the colors in Illustrator. Note that, when you're planning on using SWF export, you shouldn't use a plug-in effect to adjust their color in After Effects: Most plug-ins convert vector art layers to pixels, which will greatly reduce the efficiency of a SWF file.

STEP 14: To create additional interest, animate the clouds from right to left. At time 00:00, select the **BG_Clouds** layer, hit P for Position, and turn on its keyframing stopwatch in the Timeline window. Set the first keyframe by dragging the layer in the Comp window to the right, or scrubbing the value for X position in the Timeline window. A Position of roughly

14 As you drag the **BG_Clouds** layer in the Comp window at 14:22, the white outline in the pasteboard shows the edges of the layer; the gray line in the middle of the Comp window shows the motion path.

If you don't see both keyframes of the motion path, set Edit>Preferences>Display>Motion Path to "All Keyframes". The default is to show only 15 seconds worth, which means that long animations will have truncated motion paths.

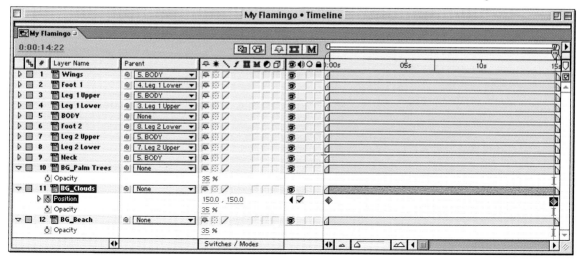

X250, Y150 should be good. Hit the End key to go to the last frame (14:22), and move the clouds to the left to roughly X150, Y150. You can RAM Preview this if you like by hitting 0 on the keypad.

14 *complete:* Animate the **BG_Clouds** layer to drift from right to left by setting keyframes for Position.

Twirl up all layers and Save your project. If you had trouble following along, open our [**Flamingo_after Step 14**] *comp to compare your results. You can also use this comp to continue with the tutorial.*

Part 3: Let's Dance

We like to coordinate our animation to audio whenever we can, as this often increases the combined impact. Since you're ready to start making the flamingo move, now would be a good time to import the music track that goes along with this piece, and "spot" some beats or other key moments to suggest good points in time to place the keyframes.

Parent Panel Toggle

You can toggle the Parent panel open and closed by pressing Shift+F4. Close it anytime after Part 2 to save screen real estate.

Motivating Music

STEP 15: If you want to get some practice spotting the music yourself, select the **My_Sources** folder in the Project window (to help keep your own files sorted), and import the music track **Come_to_the_Island.aif** by Carolyn West – it's in the same **Sources** folder on the disk where you found the Illustrator files. Drag it into the [**MyFlamingo**] comp, making sure it starts at time 00:00. Reveal its audio waveform by twirling down the corresponding property in the Timeline window, or use the short-cut LL (two L's in quick succession).

You can either RAM Preview the work area of the comp by hitting 0 on the keypad, or audition just the audio from the current time forward by hitting the . (period) key on the keypad. The duration of the audio-only preview is determined by Preferences>Previews>Audio Preview. We suggest you set it to 15:00, since that's the length of this project.

Audio Shortcuts

Hit L to twirl down audio Levels, and LL (two L's in quick succession) to twirl down the audio waveform.

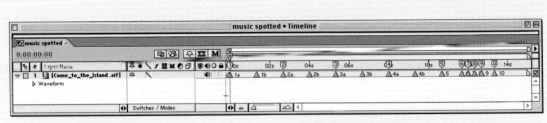

Marking Time

You can add layer markers to any layer by selecting it and hitting the * (asterisk) key on the keypad. This creates a layer marker at the current time.

Option+* (Alt+*) will let you name layer markers as you add them; you can also double-click them later to add or edit a name.

Note that you can add layer markers while previewing audio; this allows you to tap along to the music. When the preview is done, the layer markers will appear along the selected layer.

You also have ten Composition markers, which you can set by pressing Shift+# (number from 0–9 from the keyboard, not the keypad). Press the number alone to jump to that point in time.

New to After Effects 5, you can also create Web Links and add URLs to any Layer Marker (which can tell your Web browser to switch pages as the file plays), and export these with the SWF file. These options are covered in the Help>After Effects Help menu under *Creating Web links from markers* and *Including Web links in a SWF file*.

Music Spotting

Spotting the music in a separate project file is a great way for a team to share the music on a large job. The artist with the best sense of time can annotate the music with layer markers, and everyone else can import this project into his or her own animations. Plus, everyone will agree where the beats fall!

Make a note of where the major beats seem to fall – we counted four measures and an ending. Now add layer markers to the music track at these points (see *Marking Time*) to mark the major beats so that you can close the waveform display, which slows down timeline redraws and takes up a lot of screen space.

If that sounds like more work than you're up for right this moment, we've prepared an After Effects project file which you can merge with your current project. To do this, select the **My Sources** folder in the Project window, go File>Import>File, select the _music_spotted.aep project file which is loose in the **Project** folder, and click Import. A folder will be created, holding the audio layer and a comp named **[Music Spotted]**. Open this comp and check out the audio: On average, we've marked only every other beat; we know from listening to the music that there is an additional beat inbetween most of our markers – and we'll actually spot to some of those in the animation later on.

Select the audio layer, and Copy. Now Paste this layer into your **[MyFlamingo]** comp. (Don't delete the _music_spotted.aep project folder, as it holds the source for this audio layer.)

If that still seems like too much work, you can always cheat by opening our finished composition **[Flamingo_Final]**. Select the audio layer (Layer 1), Copy, and Paste it into your own composition. Our

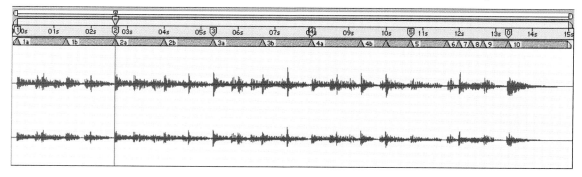

layer is already annotated with layer markers. But where's your sense of adventure and accomplishment?!

Animating the Legs

It's time to make your flamingo dance. We'll start by animating the grand finale: where the Leg 2 chain rotates to form the number 4. You can return later and add more animation to the wings, neck, and legs.

STEP 16: Go to time 08:00 – where music measure 4 begins – and select three layers: **Foot 2**, **Leg 2 Upper**, and **Leg 2 Lower**. Hit R to twirl down their Rotation properties, and click+drag across these stopwatches to turn on keyframing for all three layers. This will create the first set of Rotation keyframes at the current time.

• Go to time 08:16, which is about one beat after the start of this musical measure, and rotate **Leg 2 Upper** to +45°. Notice how the lower leg and foot follow, as they are children of the upper leg. (If they don't, go back to Step 6 and double-check your work.)

• Go to time 10:00 – about three beats into this measure – and rotate **Leg 2 Upper** to +35°. Why back up from the previous keyframe's value? Because a regular component of character animation includes overshooting the mark, especially if you then need to fold other limbs into position.

• Also at 10:00, rotate **Leg 2 Lower** to –125°. This should form the number 4 and leave the foot visible behind the other leg.

• Still at 10:00, rotate the **Foot 2** layer to –100°, so that its lower-most toe is pointing horizontally.

• Move to time 11:16, right before the music's final statement, and rotate **Foot 2** to –65°. This will move the foot slowly as the music dies down. Like over-shooting, relaxing is another technique you can use to add interest to character animation.

15 Spot the beats in the music as a guide to help time your animation. We like to use layer markers for individual beats and events in the music, and comp markers for overall sections.

Color Coding

When animating a character with many parts, color code the different layer groups. To do this, select the layers you want to be part of a particular group and context+click on the color swatch in the Timeline window to pick another color.

16 Through the use of Parenting, the flamingo's leg can be folded up into the number 4 using just Rotation keyframes, without having to animate the position of the limbs as well.

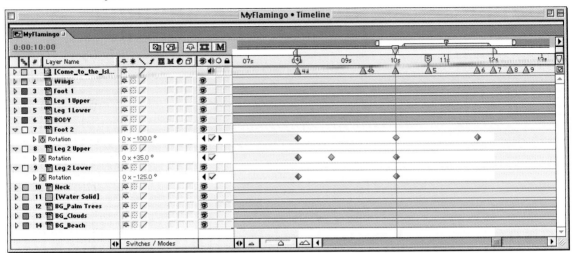

17 The linear rotation keyframes are set with the work area encompassing them for RAM Preview purposes. Zoom into the timeline to see the keyframes more clearly by using the + and – keys on the keyboard. (You can also center the view around the time marker by pressing D.)

STEP 17: Set the work area to encompass this section of your animation (08:00 to 12:00), and render a RAM Preview (0 on the keypad). Notice how jerky the animation is: This is because all the Rotation keyframes are Linear, with no ease in and outs added.

STEP 18: Select all the Rotation keyframes by dragging a marquee around them in the Timeline window. (You can also select them by clicking on the word Rotation in the Timeline window for **Foot 2**, which selects all Rotation keyframes for this layer, and then Shift+clicking on Rotation for **Leg 2 Upper** and **Leg 2 Lower**.)

Once all the Rotation keyframes are selected, context-click on any keyframe and select Keyframe Assistant>Easy Ease. RAM Preview again and see if you like the smoother animation.

For the most part Easy Ease works well – especially when the music softens toward the end. However, the first move for the upper leg hits on quite a sharp musical beat, which asks for a sharper animation move. Therefore, try changing **Leg 2 Upper**'s middle keyframe to an Auto Bezier (or "smooth") keyframe. To do this, be sure to Deselect All (F2) and then Command+click (Control+click) on the middle keyframe for **Leg 2 Upper**. This will revert it to Linear interpolation (denoted by a diamond icon). Now Command+click (Control+click) a *second* time to change its interpolation method to Auto Bezier (circle icon). RAM Preview again, and see if you like the result better.

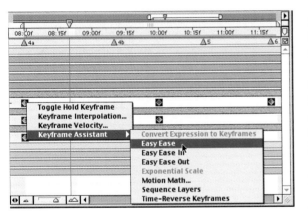

18 To alter a bunch of keyframes at the same time, drag a marquee around them and pick a new interpolation method. Easy Ease is a good start for a less robotic animation, but is not always the right fix…

If the flamingo kicked you in the head instead of posing for the number 4, compare your result with our comp [**Flamingo_after Step 18**]. *Then twirl up all layer outlines and Save your project.*

Graphical Speed

To get a better idea how the keyframe interpolation types are affecting the Rotation, twirl down the Rotation velocity graph for **Leg 2 Upper** and zoom into the timeline. Repeat Step 18, changing the middle keyframe from Easy Ease to Linear and back to Auto Bezier, and observe how the velocity graph changes. Notice how the Auto Bezier method even includes a little "overshooting" for a few frames after the middle keyframe: Although the middle keyframe has a value of 45° and is interpolating to 35° at the third keyframe, it rotates a little more than 45° as it moves through the middle keyframe. Auto Bezier is a good option for middle keyframes where you don't want a full ease in/out feel, but where a linear move is too bumpy.

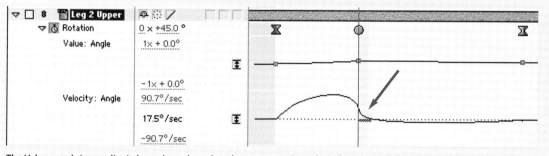

The Value graph (upper line) shows how the value changes over time; the Velocity graph (lower line) shows changes in speed over time. The small gray bar (where the arrow is pointing) indicates an overshoot in the velocity. (Overshooting means that the velocity is interpolating in the opposite direction than the keyframe values would lead you to believe.)

Part 4: Final Touches

Time to add the final strokes. This will include adding a water layer to the background and animating the title text across the screen using additional tools in After Effects that will render as vectors. You will then finish off the flamingo's animation by improvising your own moves.

Just Add Water

After Effects can also export shapes created using masks and solids as SWF vector shapes. We're going to add some water to the background using this technique. (Note that you can't feather the mask without the shape being converted to space-consuming pixels on output.)

STEP 19: With the **MyFlamingo** comp forward and the current time marker at 00:00, make a new solid (Layer>New> Solid), name it "**Water Solid**", pick a nice blue color using the color swatch in the Solid Settings dialog, and click on Make Comp Size to make sure it's big enough to fill the frame. Click OK, set the resulting layer to Best Quality, and move the new solid down the layer stack in the Timeline window so that it's below the flamingo but above the three background layers.

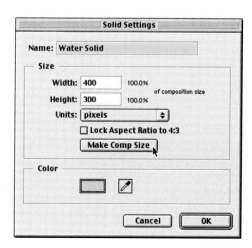

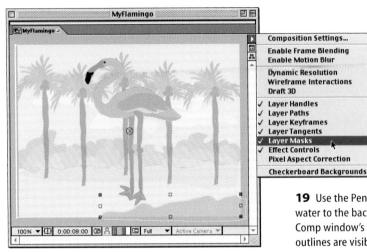

19 Use the Pen tool to mask a solid, adding SWF-friendly water to the background. The Layer Masks option in the Comp window's wing menu determines whether mask outlines are visible or hidden in the Comp window.

Select the Bezier pen tool (shortcut: G) and draw a funky wavy shape at the bottom right corner of the beach to make it look like the water is about to wash up on the flamingo's toes. Don't forget to click on the first mask point again to close your mask shape – open mask shapes won't mask out any of the layer.

Open our comp [**Flamingo_after Step 19**] *to check how we arranged the water layer, or use this comp to continue from this point.*

Text Along a Curve

In addition to Illustrator artwork and masked solids, you can use the standard effect Path Text to create words that will render as SWF-friendly vectors. If you're not yet fluent with using Path Text, this next step will give you a nice little workout. If you are, you can jump ahead to Step 20 Alternate and apply a previously created Effect Favorite.

Step 20: To create some animated text for your piece, move the time marker to 10:00 and create a Layer>New>Solid that is 400 pixels wide by 300 high (or click the Make Comp Size button). Name your solid something useful, such as "**PT/flamingo**". Any color will do, as the text effect will replace it anyway. Click OK.

Apply Effect>Text>**Path Text**, enter "flamingo" in the text entry dialog, and pick a fun font from your library – for example Sand, which comes bundled with the MacOS. (Windows users: pick any fun font that works for you.) Click OK. The Effect Controls palette will open, and you will see your type applied in the Comp window with the default settings: namely bright-red and left justified on a simple Bezier path.

To create the final title, there are a few settings you'll need to tweak. Your goal is to have the text slide in from the right side, across the sand, in front of the flamingo, and stop in the middle of the frame, jiggling in a fun manner.

Masking Mischief

Masks applied to solids are supported as vectors provided you don't use a feather or mask expansion value other than zero. But if you animate this mask shape, a new object will be added to the SWF file on each frame the layer appears!

The Work Area

To start the work area at the current time, hit B (for Begin work area). To end the work area at the current time, hit N (for eNd work area!). You can also slide the ends of the Work Area bar independently, or drag it by its ribbed center.

• Turn on Best Quality for the layer so the text is antialiased.

• Move the control points for Vertex 1 and 2 – the crosshairs inside the larger circles, at the ends of the curved line the text is resting on (see the figure to the right) – until they are pushed out to the edges of the solid with the path between running across the sand and the flamingo's legs. (If you can't see the control points in the Comp window, select the name of the effect again in the Effect Controls window.)

• Move the control point tangent handles – the ones pointing up from the vertexes – until you create a curved line for the text to follow. (If you prefer to enter numerical values, Shape Type and Control Points are grouped under Path Options in the Effect Controls window.) You can tweak the Bezier handles to improve the curve anytime you like, so just make your best guess for now.

• Twirl down the Paragraph section in the Effect Controls window, and change the Alignment to Center. This isn't entirely necessary, but it makes a few things easier such as keeping your type centered in the frame when you resize it.

• Twirl down the Character section in the Effect Controls window, and set an appropriate point size for your title. We happened to choose 48 points for the Sand font.

Next, we're going to set up our animation move. Sometimes it's easier to work backward: So we'll first create a nice end frame, set keyframes at the point in time the animation is supposed to stop, then back up and build the start of the animation.

• Go to time 12:16 – a nice beat before the ending flourish in the music – and turn on the animation stopwatch for Left Margin.

• With your time marker still at 12:16, tweak the Left Margin parameter under Paragraph in the Effect Controls window until you feel the word "flamingo" is nicely centered in the frame. As you can see, the Left Margin is the parameter for moving text along the curve.

• Now move back to 10:00 (pressing I for in point is a good shortcut), and while scrubbing the Left Margin's parameter, watch the Comp window until the text slides off the right side of the frame. (If the Comp

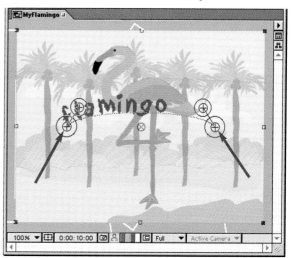

20 The beginnings of your title, using Path Text's defaults. The arrows are pointing to the control points for Vertex 1 and 2, which you will move out to the edges of the solid. The path and control points are only visible when the effect is selected.

20 *continued:* Partway through your tweaks. Best Quality has been turned on; we've made a first pass at the path the text will follow and increased its size. We moved in time to 12:16, the title's final resting position, and turned on the stopwatch for Left Margin.

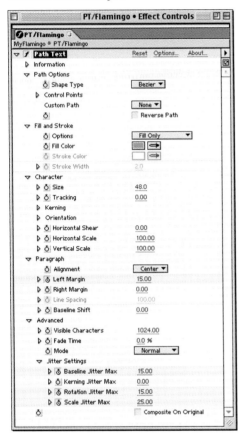

The Effects Control window for Path Text at 12:16 (above) and the final Timeline window (below).

window is not updating while you're dragging, either hold down the Option (Alt) key while dragging, or go to Edit> Preferences>Previews and set Interactive Previews for Wireframe Interactions while the Option Key is Down.)

• RAM Preview. If you'd like a smoother stop, reveal your keyframes in the Timeline window by pressing U, and apply Animation>Keyframe Assistant>Easy Ease In to this last keyframe in time (the one at 12:16).

• Twirl down the Fill and Stroke section and pick a nice Fill color for your text. Kristin's design called for a shade of purple, and who can argue with purple…

That's the basics of the text animation. RAM Preview it to see what it looks like: Set the beginning of the Work Area to 10:00 and the end to 12:16 or later, and hit 0 on the keypad. To finish up, we're going to take advantage of one of Path Text's special features: the ability to automatically jiggle and jitter the type, without having to enter a lot of keyframes.

• Go back to where your last Left Margin keyframe is, at 12:16 in the timeline. In the Effect Controls window, twirl down the Advanced section, and then the Jitter Settings sub-section hidden underneath. (You might need to scroll down to see it; your list of parameters is pretty long at this point.) Turn on the stopwatches for Baseline Jitter Max, Rotation Jitter Max, and Scale Jitter Max. Set these parameters to taste, RAM previewing to see what they look like. We chose settings of 15, 15, and 25 respectively, but experiment a bit before taking our word for it (the amount of caffeine consumed can influence your judgement…).

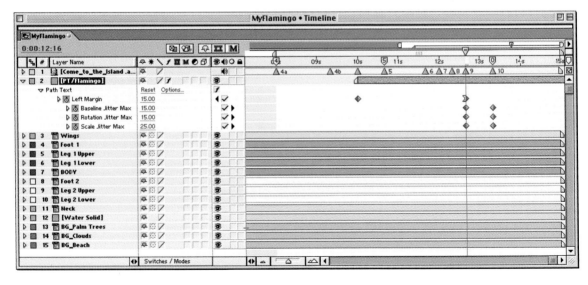

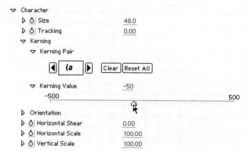

- Move to 13:00 (just before the last musical flourish) and change all three jitter values back to 0 so that the title stops moving. Make sure your Work Area ends at 13:00 or later, and RAM Preview. You'll see lots of jitter as the title moves along the curve, but as soon as it reaches its resting place, the jitter will ramp down to zero. (If you feel like having even more fun, you could keyframe these values back up and down again during the last jangle of the steel drums starting at 13:08…)

- Depending on your typeface, you may need to track or kern your title. Tracking and Kerning are both found under the Character section. Tracking will affect the entire title, while kerning will fix problems between specific character pairs. You'll want to adjust these at some point where the type is no longer jittering, such as at 13:00.

To kern pairs, twirl down the Kern section, and use the arrows to the left and right of the character display to navigate to the problem pair. The Kerning Value is used to close up the pair (negative values) or to add space (positive values). With After Effects 5, you now have an interactive slider to alter this value, instead of increment/decrement arrows. Don't track or kern too tightly if you have a lot of Rotation or Scale Jitter, as the letters will crash into each other.

- If you want to try a different font or change the words, click on Options at the top of Effect Controls to return to the entry dialog box where we started.

STEP 20 ALTERNATE: If you don't need the Path Text practice, we've included an Effect Favorite with all the appropriate settings and keyframes already applied.

- Move to 10:00 in the timeline, and create a New Solid at 400×300 (Comp Size), name it "**PT/flamingo**", select any color, and click OK.

- Select Effect>Apply Favorite and navigate to this tutorial's **12_Flamingo>_Favorites** folder. Select the file **PT_flamingo.ffx** and click Open. Path Text will be applied including all the keyframes (hit U to twirl open just the keyframes for this layer). You won't see anything right away, as the title starts out off the right side. Play the comp and you'll see the text slide into the frame along the curve. If you don't have the Sand font installed, the title should default to something basic, like Arial. Click on the Options at the top of the Effect Controls window to replace the font.

- Turn on Best Quality for this layer to enable antialiasing.

Twirl up all layers and Save your project. Open our [**Flamingo_after Step 20**] *comp to compare your results. You can also use this comp to pick up the animation another day if you want to experiment further.*

20 *complete:* To add professional polish, kern the spacing between letter pairs so the overall spacing looks nice and even. In the Sand font, the spaces before and after the "a" could use closing up.

Jitter +/–

Path Text Jitter animations are smooth if you use positive values and very jerky if you use negative ones. At 12 fps you could get away with jerky jitter, but avoid it if your project is going to be field rendered – text jumping at 60 times a second is hard on the eyes!

Don't Hit that M switch…

Normally you might turn on Motion Blur for a text layer that's moving along a curve and jittering, as it would reduce any strobing artifacts. However, motion blur will force Path Text to render as pixels when it's exporting to SWF.

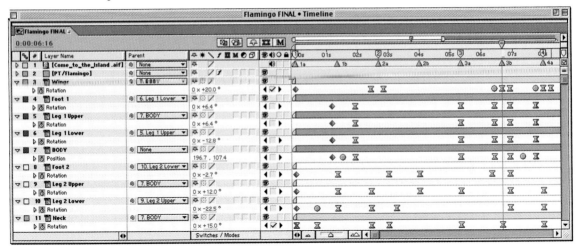

21 Help the flamingo strut its stuff by animating the neck, wing, and legs according to your own tastes for the first eight seconds of the comp.

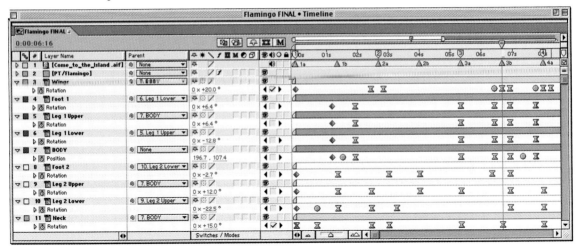

22 The SWF Settings dialog helps After Effects decide what to do with layers it cannot convert into vectors. Don't forget to enable Audio so you can hear the accompanying music; Flatten Illustrator Artwork affects layers with multiple shapes that are semi-transparent.

Flamingo Antics

Step 21: Okay, now it's your turn to have some fun without having us telling you everything to do. We left 00:00 through 08:00 for you to add your own animation to the flamingo character. Have fun rotating the wings up and down, as well as rotating the legs and neck – all in time to the music, if you can. You could even add a simple walk cycle if you're feeling empowered! Check out the prebuilt comp [**Flamingo_Final**] to compare approaches.

Part 5: A SWF Resolution

Step 22: Once you're happy with your animation, you can export the animation to SWF by selecting File>Export>Macromedia Flash (SWF). Be aware that exporting defaults to outputting the *work area only*, so set the work area to the full comp if you want to export the entire animation.

The Save File As dialog will prompt you to name your file – call it "**MyFlamingo.swf**". Make a note of where it's being saved to so you can play it back later. Clicking Save then opens the SWF Settings dialog. All of the options presented herein are explained in the online Help file, but here are a few particulars to be aware of:

- Not everything After Effects can do can be converted to efficient vectors for a SWF file; in fact, we've already covered most of what you can do. If you're trying to export an animation that has

Export Exceptions

When you're creating compositions for output to the SWF format, it's best to avoid features and effects that cannot be represented as vectors. Maintaining vectors throughout means working with a limited feature set, and avoiding such After Effects standards as multiple effects per layer, nested comps, transfer modes, and track mattes. Of course, you can use all these features if you must – but any such layers will be JPEG'd on export to SWF. And that sort of defeats the whole purpose of creating SWF (small files, fast downloads, scalable art).

To see a full list of supported features, we encourage you to pull up Help>After Effects Help and search for "SWF". This should turn up a few pages worth reading carefully, including *Exporting to Macromedia Flash (SWF) format*, and *Supported features for SWF export*. Don't worry; we won't tell anyone you've actually read the manual.

Be sure to also check out the Read Me file that is installed in the After Effects 5 application folder. It includes some important news under *SWF Export Documentation Updates* that are not covered in the manual or Help files.

Symbols and Meaning

There are two main approaches to helping After Effects create an efficient SWF file. One is using only layers or effects that generate vectors; otherwise, those pieces of artwork will be rasterized into far less efficient JPEG images. That has been the focus of this tutorial. The other is minimizing the number of "symbols" After Effects creates.

A symbol is one instance of an object in a SWF. The SWF format is smart enough to re-use symbols where possible – such as realizing one symbol is animating in different places in the frame, or that ten identical objects are actually just copies of the same symbol. However, the SWF file has to be told this.

As of version 5.0, After Effects manages Illustrator artwork best: If you duplicate the same Illustrator layer in an animation, After Effects will save the symbol for that layer only once. However, if you duplicate a masked solid, After Effects will save a symbol for every duplicate of that solid – so use Illustrator artwork where possible for repetitive shapes.

We mention elsewhere not to use the Fill Over Stroke option in Path Text. If you do, After Effects will save a JPEG symbol for every frame – a double whammy.

If you want to better understand how After Effects converts your layers into SWF, it is worth investing in a copy of the Macromedia Flash authoring tool to peer inside the result. Many have also reported that re-saving an After Effects generated SWF through Flash further decreases its size.

Special thanks to Jim Tierney of Digital Anarchy (www.digitalanarchy.com) for the information on symbols.

---

components that cannot be converted to vectors – known as Unsupported Features – you can use options here to Ignore them, or to Rasterize them to less efficient pixels. In this animation it's irrelevant, since we were careful not to add any unsupported features (like a Drop Shadow or Motion Blur on the title). If you are creating what should be a pure vector-based animation, the Ignore option is a handy way to check that layers are indeed all outputting as vectors (any missing layers in your SWF file indicate an unsupported feature is being used and is thus easier to track down).

• Turn on the Audio checkbox to also export the audio. The soundtrack Carolyn West provided is CD quality, at 44.1 kHz and in stereo; if you need to keep the file size small, you can get away with a lower

Fill and Stroke

If you want to retain vectors instead of pixels in Path Text, SWF export supports only the Fill Only, Stroke Only, and the Stroke Over Fill Character options. Avoid the Fill Over Stroke option as it saves a JPEG on every frame.

Roll your own curve

If you'd rather create a more complex curve for Path Text to follow, you can tell it to follow a mask shape on the same layer. With the solid selected, use the Pen tool to draw a curved line in the Comp window in version 5 (or in the Layer window in 4.1). There's no need to close the shape. In the Path Text>Path Options, set the Custom Path to Mask 1. This is demonstrated in the prebuilt composition **[Flamingo_text along a mask]**.

Vector Synthesis

The Audio Waveform and Audio Spectrum effects also export as vectors when exporting to SWF. Open the prebuilt comp **[Flamingo_audio waveform]**, preview it, and feel free to poke around to check this out.

To create this effect, Effect>Render>Audio Waveform was applied to a New Solid layer, and the layer was set to Best Quality. The Audio Layer popup was set to the music layer, **Come to the Island.aif**. We also created a mask directly in the Comp window with the Pen tool and made the waveform follow this curve by setting the effect's Path popup to Mask 1. The Maximum Height and Thickness settings were set to taste. Try the Display Options popup set to Analog Dots for another fun effect!

The Read Me file in the After Effects 5 application folder includes rules for using these plug-ins with SWF export and covers a few unsupported features (Outside color, Softness, and Composite on Original for starters).

Connect

For more information on topics covered in this tutorial, check out the following chapters in *Creating Motion Graphics:*

Setting anchor points before parenting: *The Anchor Point*

Frame rates, displaying time and the work area: *Creating a Composition*

Spotting music: *Audio Basics and Effects*

Comp and Layer Markers, Color Coding: *The Layer Essentials*

Keyframe animation and velocity graphs: *A Matter of Time and Space*

The work area: *Creating a Composition*

Illustrator artwork: *Inside Illustrator, Working with Illustrator*

Masking the water: *All About Masking*

Path Text effect: *Plugging In Type*

Easy Ease keyframe assistants: *Our Trusty Assistants*

Sample Rate and even Mono. Leave the Bit Rate set to Auto to choose the most appropriate bit rate given the Sample Rate/Channels options you've selected.

• The only Option box that you'll want to check for the Flamingo animation is Flatten Illustrator Artwork. This will take all the individual shapes on each of the layers and flatten them so that the final animation will look like it does in After Effects.

If all the layers were set to 100% opacity, it may not matter much whether or not you flatten. However, since the three background layers are set to 35% opacity, if you don't flatten the artwork, each shape (not just layer) will *individually* render as 35% transparent. Export both ways and check out the difference, particularly in the palm tree leaves and shrubs. You might even prefer the effect created by not flattening the artwork.

When you're done with the SWF Settings, click OK, and the comp will be exported post haste as both a SWF and an HTML file. Save your After Effects project at this point before exiting the program.

Find the file **MyFlamingoR.htm** and open it in your favorite Web browser. When the browser window opens, the animation will play back automatically; scroll down to see a report of the settings used. If you click on the name of the SWF file underneath the image, it will open the animation in a second window. Note that you can resize this browser window and the animation will resize – this is the beauty and power of creating vector-only SWF animations. You can also open **MyFlamingo.swf** directly in your browser or in Macromedia Flash.

Guest Artist: Kristin Harris

The concept and artwork for this tutorial were created by Kristin Harris Design. Harris's clients include HBO, Discovery Communications, PBS, Children's Hospital, Marriott, Verizon, Department of Agriculture, United States Postal Service, Red Cross, National Institutes of Health, and International Bureau of Broadcasting.

Harris splits her time between being a fine artist, animator, and educator. She specializes in animation for children. She recently completed a thirty-part series of preschool science interstitials for HBO Family. Her bold, colorful style is especially appropriate for the preschool age group, but it speaks to all ages. Harris is currently producing a five-minute animated video project to help young children learn about skin cancer. She is also developing interactive Web-based programs to help young students learn math, science, art, and reading.

In the fine arts side of her career, Harris has exhibited her paintings and drawings in both individual and group shows in galleries and museums all over the United States. Her work hangs in major corporate collections, including Mobil Oil, Texas Instruments, The George Washington University, and the California College of Arts and Crafts.

About the Musician

To create music for this tutorial, Harris enlisted composer Carolyn West. After earning her Master of Music in Studio Composition and Production at The University of Miami in 1983, she has gone on to produce original music for film, TV, video, and electronic multimedia, with extensive experience scoring and conducting orchestral sessions with live players as well as making the most of her MIDI-based home studio. West has earned a reputation of musical inventiveness and detail in music scoring, with sensitivity to style and appropriateness. Some of her clients include the A&E *Biography* series, more than 200 segments of *America's Most Wanted*, The National Park Service, Bell Atlantic, The Smithsonian Institution, Fox Television, Marriott International, and Narada Productions.

Contact:

Kristin Harris Design, Inc.
3035 Hazelton Street
Falls Church, VA 22044
Tel: (703) 536-9594
Fax: (703) 241-7463
www.kristinharrisdesign.com

Carolyn West
1761 Honey Trail
Annapolis, MD 21401
Tel: (410) 849-2511
Email: cwestmusic@aol.com

The Diecks Group : ESPNDeportes.com

Swarming boxes chase and frame video clips plus Web pages in this high-energy spot.

The Diecks Group in New York were approached by ESPN International to help it launch ESPNDeportes.com: a new Spanish-language Web site targeted to the Hispanic/Latin American market in the United States. ESPNDeportes.com is a separate entity from ESPN.com, with original content, original artwork, original events, and original programming. The challenge was to convey the appropriate "Latin flavor" while avoiding both Web commercial and Latin clichés.

One of the most popular sports for this market is soccer. A desire to abstract the organized chaos of soccer players running up and down the playing field led to a concept of colored boxes blinking, dashing, darting, and sliding rhythmically to a high-energy music track. These boxes frame images of sports and of the Web site content.

An ever-changing window, bordered by a complement of constantly morphing boxes, reveals Web pages and sports videos while the logo peeks from behind.

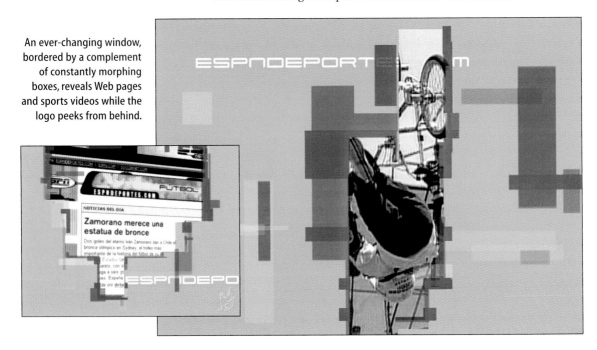

Exploring the Spot

Copy the folder for The Diecks Group case study from the accompanying CD to your hard drive. Inside the **Final Movie** folder, open **Diecks_ESPNDeportes.mov** in the QuickTime Player and preview it. This is a special version of the spot using ESPN X Games footage, as it was impractical to clear all the original sports teams' rights for this book. Then open the project **Diecks_ESPNDeportes_ref.aep**, and look at the composition [**01_Diecks_ESPNDeportes**] where you can RAM Preview or single-step through the commercial. Here are some details to note as you use the comp markers in After Effects:

1 ESPN has a very strong brand, so The Diecks Group sprinkled the text ESPNDEPORTES.COM throughout the spot. They chose the typeface Xenotron because they felt it had an international quality.

2 At this marker, the flowing matte opens up to reveal sports footage behind. This matte was created and animated using a clever arrangement of mask shapes timed to the music. The frame around it is derived from multiple variations on this central shape.

3 Web pages were sprinkled between the video clips, tilted in 3D to add excitement to what would otherwise be a still image.

Marking Time

Comp markers are used to mark specific frames in the animation. Press the numbers 0–9 on your keyboard (not the keypad) to jump to these marked frames.

   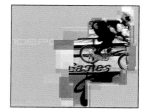

4 & **5** Over thirty sports clips and Web pages appear inside of twenty-five seconds. In some cases – such as between these two markers – clips are stutter-cut to create more excitement.

Some clips were stutter-cut to create additional excitement from an otherwise linear piece of action.

6 The video was originally cut as a full-frame sequence, then adjusted to taste on a shot-by-shot basis to better fit inside the framing presented by the animated matte. The process of editing and treating the video is one of the subjects we will cover in detail later.

7 In addition to the swarming boxes derived from the original animated matte, additional colored boxes were added to help fill the frame – especially at the conclusion of the commercial, when the video closes to make room for the ending tags.

8 The commercial ends with the ESPN logo partially hidden by animating boxes, and a list of sports. Notice how this list accordions together, then continues to scroll up the screen.

The commercial ends with the name of the Web site, the ESPN logo, and a scrolling list of featured sports.

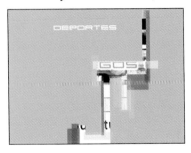

Style frames The Diecks Group created for the ESPNDeportes spot.

Footage Licensing

The original broadcast version of this spot featured many sports, including baseball, football, motorcycle racing, and of course, lots of soccer. ESPN was not able to provide clearance to use all this footage in this book; instead, they graciously provided the X Games footage you see here. Therefore, the voiceover will not precisely match the images – but we're sure you'll get the idea.

Artistic Overview

How do you avoid the pitfall of promoting a sports entertainment and news Web site through the use of the television media, without resorting to showing full-frame views of Web pages? To The Diecks Group, it seemed natural to profile the sports that the Web site would be built upon. These sports would then provide the paint for the canvas that was the Web pages. This decision led to an approach of intertwining sports footage with these pages.

The Diecks Group decided early on that the music and color palette would dictate the spirit and energy of the spots. As noted earlier, they wanted to appropriately reflect the target Hispanic/Latin American market, but not fall back on clichés. For example, it would be typical for the chosen music to head off in a fiery salsa direction. Instead, Diecks chose a hyperkinetic "drums and bass" style soundtrack from the Gravity library, represented by Who Did That Music. The upfront percussion and exhausting tempo was intended to reflect the energy of soccer players running up and down the playing field, reacting to sudden changes in the direction of the ball and game.

This tempo and its analogy of soccer players running up and down the playing field then led to the concept of the boxes that appear in the final spot blinking, dashing, darting, and sliding rhythmically to the drum beats. This in turn allowed them to maintain a fast and furious visual pace, even if the image being shown is that of a relatively static Web page.

Latin America has a color palette that tends to be hotter and more vibrant than what is commonly seen in North America or Europe. Members of The Diecks Group drew on their previous visits to Mexico City, from which they remembered colors such as fiery brick red, plum purple, electric blue, sunflower yellow, pumpkin orange, hot pink, and ochre green. With this in mind, they started pulling color swatches from Pantone books and spreading them out on their conference room table until they could begin to visualize the spirit they were after. These colors were then re-created by eye on the computer.

Execution

The centerpieces of the ESPNDeportes spot are the dashing, darting boxes, and the imagery they frame. These are the two main areas we will discuss, as they illustrate a great example of creative problem-solving when you're faced with an otherwise extremely labor-intensive task. Other items worth noting are the Web pages, and the scrolling list of sports that end the spot.

Swarming Boxes

The video segments are revealed through a track matte that was originally constructed out of five white solids. To make this "window" constantly evolve, each solid had its own animated mask that changed

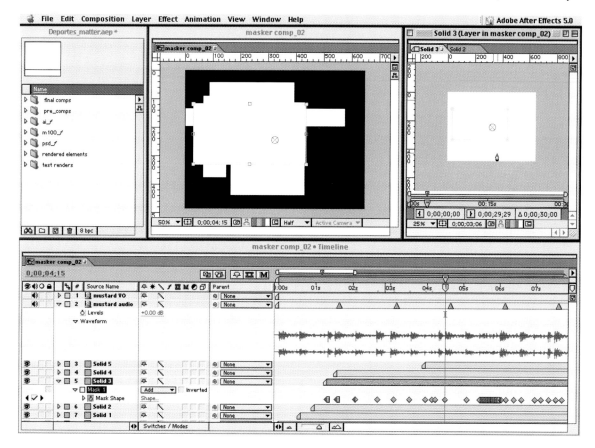

shape in time with the music. A mixture of linear and hold keyframes were used, which allow the shape to stutter and turn on a dime.

To see this matte in action, open the composition [**02_box examples**] in the accompanying project. You can either Option+double-click on Mac (Alt+double-click on Windows) the layer **DG_videomatte.mov** and play it back, or RAM Preview the comp, making sure only the third and fourth layers (**DG_videomatte.mov** and the audio portion of **Diecks_ESPNDeportes.mov**) are enabled.

When the original style frames were presented to Erik van der Wilden, the Director of Editorial and Animation at The Diecks Group, the element that concerned him most was the colored boxes that surrounded the video. The style frames contained an average of 100 boxes that were supposed to change constantly. Given the tight deadline he was working under, it would not be feasible to realize this by animating 100 solids over 900 frames (30 seconds) conventionally.

His first thoughts were to create an enlarged outline shape from the video matte with a plug-in such as Matte Tools>Simple Choker or Channel>Minimax, then find a way to hollow out the center. In the end, van der Wilden used two copies of the video matte layer – one

The video matte was a composite of five white solids. Each solid had an animated mask that changed shape in time to the soundtrack.

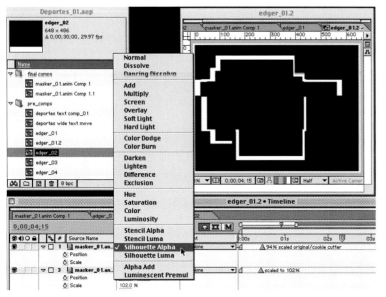

scaled slightly larger than normal, and one slightly smaller – and the transfer mode Silhouette Alpha so the smaller one would cut a hole out of the larger.

The next trick was finding a way to animate the shape of this frame so that it constantly evolved. The solution van der Wilden hit upon was to offset the copies of the matte from each other, both in time and position. By doing this, the portion being cut out would have a different form than the outside shape, but the two would always be related, as they came from the same source. The result was a swarming, chasing effect that's very engaging.

A smaller version of the video matte, in Silhouette Alpha mode, cuts the center out of a larger version of the matte.

Ten variations of this animated mask frame were rendered, each using a different combination of offsets in scale, position, and time. To see one of these frames in action, in the comp [**02_box examples**] turn on the layer **DG_boxbase.mov**. Move the time marker to different points in the timeline, and turn this layer on and off to compare it with the underlying **DG_videomatte.mov** it came from.

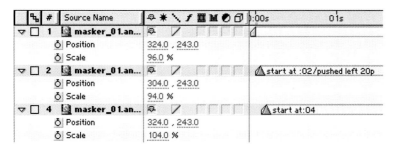

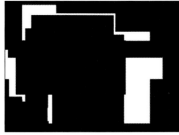

The layers that make up the frame are offset in time and position from each other (left), resulting in a broken shape (right) that evolves over time as it chases the video matte.

The original video matte layer was used to mask the edited video. However, the frame still looked somewhat whole, if slightly fractured. In contrast, the style frames employed a large number of smaller boxes and fragments that made up the overall frame shape.

To create smaller boxes from the larger frames, multiple rectangular masks were created at random. The result was that only fragments of each remained; these more closely resembled a series of overlapping, animating boxes than a carefully constructed frame. To observe this, turn on the layer **DG_boxresult.mov** in comp [**02_box examples**]. Again, move to different points along the timeline and audition the various layers to see how the matte (layer 3) became the frame (layer 2), which in turn became a set of fragmented boxes (layer 1).

The animated, fragmented frame that remained was then tinted a color from the target palette. A transfer mode was applied to make it blend on top of the video and solid-colored background in a more interesting, semi-transparent fashion. Several more of the variation frames were layered on top of this, adding more boxes and interest. Between ten and twenty-five of these layers could appear at any one time. If the final image became unbalanced, additional tinted solids were created to fill the blank areas.

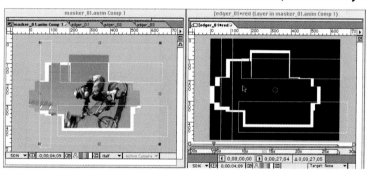

Open the comp [**03.1_videomatte example**] to see a simple version of this stack. In this example, **DG_videomatte.mov** is used as a matte for an edited video subcomp. Instances of **DG_boxbase.mov** and **DG_boxresult.mov** are used as mattes for color layers, which are then applied with modes. These layers were also offset in time and position. RAM Preview the section between markers 1 and 4 to see the result.

A series of random rectangular masks over the animated frame creates a fragmented series of shapes (above). The final stack (below) included several variations of the masked animating frames, plus additional color solids to help fill excessive open areas. Different modes and opacity settings create a semi-transparent, overlapping mix.

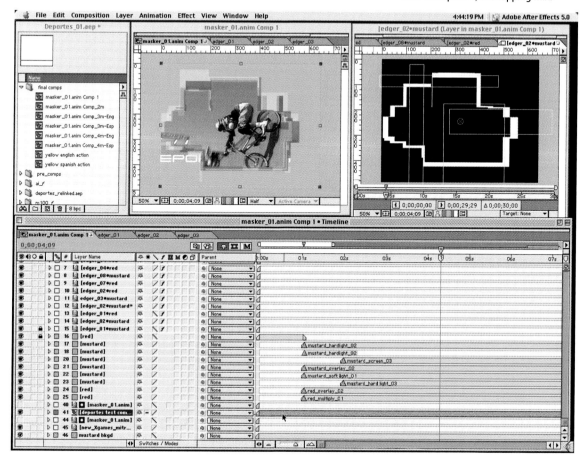

Close to the Edit

Another strong feature of this commercial is the way the video fits so well inside the evolving matte. This is a result of both planning ahead and of making adjustments after the fact.

The first pass at the video edit was executed before the boxes were created. It was executed with a Media 100 nonlinear editing system,

using the soundtrack and a working copy of the voice-over as guides. The voiceover gave a general idea of which visual subject should be presented when in the original multisport version of thi s spot; the soundtrack suggested where to place specific cuts. A secondary edit of alternate clips was created to allow more flexibility during the times the video matte would close down and re-open. This second edit wasn't as sport-specific; instead, it was intended to provide interesting fills when only a small portion of the frame would be revealed.

These Media 100 projects were then imported into After Effects as compositions. The advantage to this approach, rather than rendering out the Media 100's

Much of the original video source material was provided on VHS, and would require enhancing to bring up to typical "sexy-looking commercial" standards.

timeline and importing it as a single linear clip, is that the resulting compositions contained the entire original clips with their handles. This allowed The Diecks Group to tweak the edits inside After Effects without having to make a trip back to the Media 100.

When the animated matte was created, some consideration was given to the video content, but the greater focus was on how it articulated to the music. The video clips were then scaled and repositioned as needed to better fit into the matte's openings. A simple form of this is demonstrated in [**03.2_video edit precomp**], particularly in the way the position of the second video clip animates across the frame to better align the skateboarder with the matte opening (turn layer 1 on and off to compare).

The comp [**03.2_video edit precomp**] gives a simple example of how individual video clips can be repositioned to better fit the matte openings. Skateboarding footage courtesy of Creative License.

The next task involved enhancing the source footage. Many of the clips provided came from VHS dubs of live sporting events – not exactly your ideal shot-for-commercials footage. Raw Media 100 clips also exist in the 16–235 luminance range, compared with the 0–255

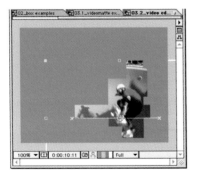

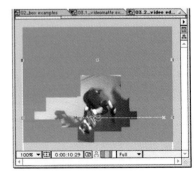

luminance range After Effects works in. The result was a lot of washed-out imagery.

Each clip was duplicated, with a transfer mode such as Overlay applied to the copy on top. Opacity was varied to control the blend. This is a great technique to increase the apparent richness of an image. Effects such as Adjust>Levels and Adjust>Curves were also applied to bend the color closer to the vibrant, Latin palette desired for the spots.

Text Elements

Although most of our focus in this case study has been on the video and the colored boxes that swarm around it, text elements also play important roles in this spot. In addition to the Web site address mentioned earlier, there are sample Web pages throughout, and the spot ends with a list of some of the sports to be covered (reinforcing that soccer would not be the only sport covered).

The Web pages were not frame-grabbed from the site, but instead painstakingly re-created, then imported into After Effects. To create a tilting 3D camera move, the pages were animated using the Atomic Power Evolution Shatter plug-in inside After Effects 4.1. (This project was executed in version 4.1; Shatter is now built into version 5.0, which also allows layers to be placed directly in 3D space.) As you probably noticed, these layers did not shatter apart in the final spot; however, The Diecks Group found the 3D positioning controls in this plug-in more responsive than the other 3D effects available to them.

These tilted pages were then masked by the animated matte, just as the video clips were. Since these were stills being animated inside After Effects rather than having preordained

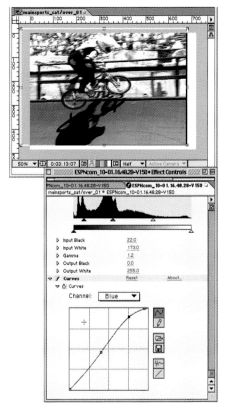

The Comp window shows how individual clips were animated to center inside the animated matte. Clips were duplicated with the top layer transfer moded on top; Levels and Curves were applied for additional color correction.

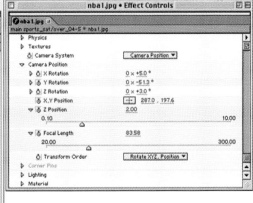

Web pages were re-created, then tilted using the 3D controls in the Shatter effect. (The image in this window was blurred for rights clearance reasons.)

These animated pages were then treated the same as the other video elements, masked and ringed with the swarming boxes.

motion, it was easier to choreograph their movements to better fit the music and matte. A good example of this is after comp marker 3 in [**01_Diecks_ESPNDeportes**], where two of these pages appear back to back, tilted at different angles.

While still in the comp [**01_Diecks_ESPNDeportes**], go to comp marker 8 and step or RAM Preview from here to the end, keeping an eye on the list of sports in the upper right corner. Notice that it "accordions" together, while continuing to scroll off the top of the frame – a trick that is hard to accomplish with the typical Adobe Illustrator file often used for text elements in After Effects.

This list was created in the plug-in Text>Basic Text using the font Helvetica Neue 43 Light Extended. The accordion effect was created by animating Basic Text's Line Spacing parameter; normal Position was animated to continue the scrolling action. A gradient was then created using the Render>Ramp plug-in applied to a solid. This in turn was used as a luminance matte for the Basic Text layer to create the fade at the bottom of the list.

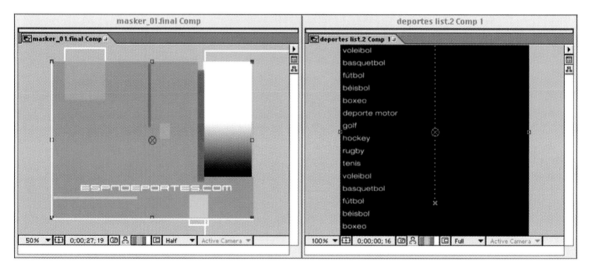

The text list at the end was made to accordion together by animating the Line Spacing parameter in Basic Text, then scrolled by animating its position (right). A gradient created with Ramp was then used as a luminance matte to fade it off at the bottom (left).

Postscript

Three different voiceovers were created for each of these spots: in Spanish, Portuguese, and English. In the original composition [**01_Diecks_ESPNDeportes**], turn off the Audio switch for the layer **Diecks_ESPNDeportes.mov**, turn on this switch for the layer **DG_voiceover_english.mov**, and preview the comp again.

Creative Director Brian Diecks notes "Spanish and Portuguese have so much more spirit and zest than English. In my opinion, the English version of the spots is weaker than the other versions – the tonality in the English version is all 'used car salesman' where the Spanish and Portuguese are full of life, energy, and excitement."

The Diecks Group, Inc.

Opened in 1993, The Diecks Group is a creative development and branding agency for the entertainment industry. The multi-disciplinary firm offers marketing, strategy, and brand building as well as design, editorial, live action production, and visual effects for clients involved in various media: broadcast, advertising, interactive and convergent media, and print.

The Diecks Group has won numerous awards from organizations such as AIGA, International Monitor Awards, New York Festivals, Promax/BDA, and the Type Directors Club. Cofounder and President/Creative Director Brian Diecks currently sits on the board of the Type Directors Club and teaches Broadcast Design at Parsons School of Design.

The Diecks Group's extensive client list includes: ABC, Discovery Kids, ESPN, Fox Cable Networks, HBO, The Independent Film Channel, Leo Burnett/USA, Lifetime, McCann Erikson/Detroit, Media 100, Mullen Advertising, National Hockey League, PentaMark, Sci-Fi Channel, Showtime, Tribeca Films, Turner Network Television, and Young & Rubicam.

Contact:

The Diecks Group, Inc.
530 Broadway, 9th Floor
New York, NY 10012
Tel: (212) 226-7336
www.diecksgroup.com

Belief : Alive

Crafting a flexible, international image using fluids and silhouettes.

Belief is developing a name for itself in branding multinational, multinational networks. Their success is partly due to their ability to cross cultures with suggestive yet abstract imagery. For the Hong Kong-based Alive travel network, Belief used water to depict landscapes, and silhouettes to depict people of many nations enjoying themselves. In addition to creating beautiful designs, Belief also created projects that would be easy for affiliates to localize and personalize.

In this case study, we'll look at how the human and liquid elements were captured, processed, and blended into final frames. Equally important, we'll discuss some of Belief's concepts behind creating a look that translates across cultures and languages, and projects that local affiliates can further customize to their needs.

Common themes throughout the Alive package include silhouettes of people, water movements as landscapes, 3D universal travel icons, graphical sunbursts of rays, and curves everywhere.

Exploring the Spot

Open the project **Belief_Alive_ref.aep**, locate the **Sources** folder, and play back the three **Belief_Alive** movies by double-clicking them in the Project window; you can also locate these movies on the CD and open them using QuickTime Player.

Now open the comp [**03_Belief_Alive_3**] and RAM Preview it (hit 0 on the keypad). Note the constant use of curves, including animated strokes that snake throughout the frames. Also note the gentle use of 3D. We'll be taking a look at several of these details later. Referring to the comp markers, here are a few of the highlights:

1 Curves are used to mark borders between graphical elements, to give the action something to follow, and to create a sensuous feeling overall.

1 Note the use of curved lines, as well as curved matte shapes that keep the elements separated. These shapes also give the action something to follow, such as the skier in this open.

2 Although most of the look is graphical 2D, there are subtle 3D touches that create a more tactile look. Press the spacebar to play or use Page Down to single-step forward from this marker, and note the horizontal icon bar that forms on the right.

Also note the stroked line that snakes from right to left across the screen. You can create a simple version of this using the Stylize> Write-On effect; to have it travel along a path, Belief had a custom plug-in written.

Marking Time

Comp markers are used to mark specific frames in the animation. Press the numbers 0–9 on your keyboard (not the keypad) to jump to these marked frames.

3 The ghosting of the water skiers, as well as other silhouettes, was the result of slowing down the original footage and using Frame Blending. You'll also note very subtle, diffuse hazes or drop shadows around many of the elements; these were created using ICE'd Drop Shadow from Media 100 by setting the distance parameter to 0 and increasing the softness to very high values.

A graphical design element you will notice throughout is a series of rays that might remind you of a sunburst or spikes on a lens flare. They were created a number of ways, including starting with Illustrator artwork and using the third-party plug-in Hall of Mirrors from Pinnacle Systems Image Lounge package to repeat the patterns and give animated control.

3 Other common design elements are graphical flares or rays.

4 Notice the color change from blue to orange. Belief color-coded different themes of activities for Alive: blue is "traveling," orange is "learning about," and green is "learning to do."

As you step or play forward from here, you will notice that another 3D icon bar appears. Watch how the moving colors in the bar are a reflected wash of those in the frame; we'll discuss how Belief created this later on.

5 Liquids are used throughout as stand-ins for landscapes. Here, the mountain range in the background is actually an upside-down

Real footage can be too literal. By converting scenes with people to silhouettes with abstract backgrounds, viewers can more easily project themselves into a scene, at any locale.

version of viscous fluid dripping. We'll reveal the original elements of the landscape as well.

This scene includes another instance of the 3D icon bars. Note how they usually have additional small figures inside them. This sense of big and small helps add depth to the scene. We'll also be looking in more detail at the large version of the mountain climber that appears inside this particular bar.

6 The ending wipes in with a splash, which gives way to the final logo and the ink element drifting much more slowly in the background.

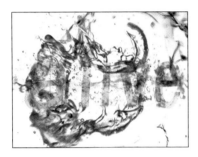

6 A splash wipes into the end logo for Alive, where graphic lines create the outlines of slow-moving waves.

By the way, as you step frame by frame through these movies, you may have noticed a pattern of five unique frames, with the fifth frame repeating for the sixth frame of the sequence. The Alive project was originally created at PAL frame rate and resolution, full frame without interlaced fields. These renders were then merely scaled to fit in an NTSC-size comp running at 29.97 frames per second (fps), resulting in this 5:6 sequence (same as the ratio between 25 and 30 fps).

Artistic Overview

Just before the Alive project, Belief completed a branding campaign for Columbia-Tristar's AXN Action Network. The Singapore-based AXN airs in six languages across 42 countries. Alive saw Belief give a presentation on AXN at the Promax Asia conference in late 2000, and was interested.

Alive was based out of Hong Kong, serving the Asian region including India, Singapore, and Australia. Alive's plan was to focus on the moderate-income travel market: the large middle ground between youth hostels and four-star hotels. In addition to cable channels, Alive intended to move into physical stores, books, and electronic versions of information for Web-access phones (WAPs) and personal digital assistants (PDAs). Belief worked closely with Alive to develop an overall brand for the entire cable network, while also taking into account how it would translate into other media.

Being Suggestive

Your first thoughts of a travel channel might be footage of exotic locations with people enjoying interesting activities such as skiing, climbing, or spending a night on the town. But aside from being too obvious, this path can also be too literal – especially when you want your brand to extend across multiple countries and cultures. The scenery you choose may not be representative of the affiliate country you're in; the ethnicity or manner of dress might not match that of your viewer. Belief was also interested in capturing the essence of travel: the sensations of relaxation and relief, the seductive quality of exotic locales, the feeling of immersing yourself in another culture.

One solution Belief came up with was using liquids. For example, the outline of water cascading can easily form the image of a cliff that's not a specific cliff. Water flowing and bubbling also has the sensuous quality Belief was looking for. To test that this idea would work, Belief shot quick tests with a still camera, and incorporated them into early storyboards.

A second solution was representing all the people in silhouette. This solved the problem of nationality, and in some cases, even masked the manner of dress, gender, or the activity. Aside from being more flexible, silhouettes let viewers more easily project themselves into the activity portrayed. It also contains a bit of a voyeuristic quality, furthering the sensuous feeling Belief wanted to promote.

Separating the people from their locations also provided more flexibility. For example, a silhouette of a water skier gliding across a graphical landscape eliminates problems such as "but wait – our lakes don't have sandy shores; they're supposed to have mountains in the background."

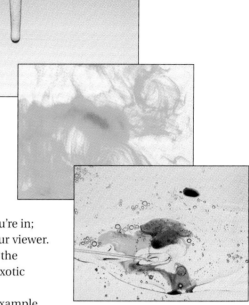

To see if the idea of using liquids would work, Belief shot quick tests with a still camera and incorporated them into early storyboards.

Shooting various activities on a greenscreen stage, rather than on location, allows them to be relocated into an entirely graphical scene that could be anywhere. The result is that the viewer focuses on the activity, instead of the person or location.

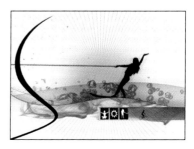

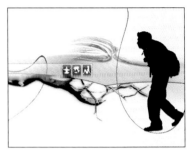

Style frames Belief presented to Alive two weeks into the project. At this stage, ideas other than fluids – such as a tree branch (far right) – were still being considered as stand-ins for landscapes.

Phasing In

Belief is a strong believer in creating storyboards and style frames at early stages in a project, and in testing design and production theories at this early point. Rather than use the computer to generate stand-ins, Belief will shoot preliminary versions of ideas to make sure they will work, and to see if any unexpected results shake out before a design has already been committed to. In the case of Alive, Belief used a still-image camera to shoot a first pass at the fluids. They also shot other ideas for textures such as branches or crystals.

The graphics were created in three phases, which in many ways were three complete iterations of the entire design. The first phase consisted of basic elements: end pages, IDs, transitions. They were considered placeholders while Belief developed more complex portions of the design.

Phase 2 introduced more liquid and silhouette elements. All of these elements were custom-shot for this project on 35mm film. Alive used these earlier phases for fund-raising, as well as for internal testing: it ran the network live for three weeks before it went on the air, to work out any kinks.

Phase 3 brought a further evolution in design, elegance, and complexity. As you look at some of the examples on these pages, you will notice some of these refinements, such as the use of more gradients, more curviness (further enhancing the sensuous, rather than technical, feel), fewer of the murkier desaturated colors, and simplifying some elements while adding others such as more bursts of graphical rays.

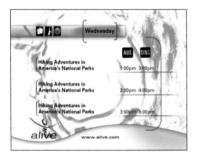
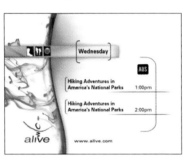

Examples of how the design evolved from Phase 2 (top) to Phase 3 (bottom). Note in particular the increase in readability, including fluid elements that are less distracting from the text. Sunburst rays are also used more to fill in areas that might have been too empty otherwise.

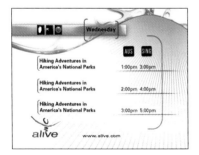

Whereas it might seem more work to do everything three times, Belief welcomed the chance to go back and revisit the designs. All too often, you have time to do everything only once. Although the schedule was very tight, Belief felt that working in phases allowed them to refine and further evolve the look they had developed.

Execution

We've hinted above how Belief created many of the elements used in the Alive spots. Shooting preliminary ideas at the storyboard stage helped Belief focus refining techniques during production, rather than scramble to see if an idea would even work.

Fluid Motion

Although it's tempting to refer to the "water elements" Belief used throughout the Alive spots, in truth the water is usually what you *don't* see. Instead, a variety of fluids – typically ink, food coloring, methycellulose, oil, and mixtures of these, as well as ice and dry ice – are dropped into water, with the results being what was captured on film. Different techniques were also used to physically animate the results, such as feeding fluids down a clear tube (which needed to be rotoscoped out later), or using a jet of compressed air.

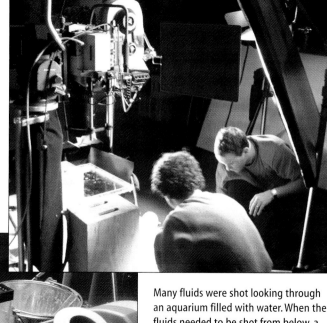

Many fluids were shot looking through an aquarium filled with water. When the fluids needed to be shot from below, a mirror underneath reflected the image back up to the camera. For shots from above, the camera was mounted on a post, looking down, and lit from below. A video tap previewed what the camera saw. Pictured above are Mike Goedecke, Belief's creative director and live action director/cinematographer (right), and Maziar Majd, the lead designer/animator on Alive (left).

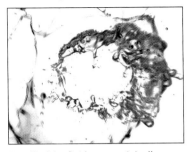

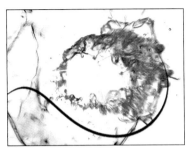

Not all of the fluids were originally colored – many of the images started essentially as grayscale (left), then had color added during transfer or in post production and composited with other elements (right).

Many of the fluid elements were shot at high speed (100 fps on up). Even with a video tap on the camera to preview what it was seeing, the short duration of the events resulted in a certain chance element: you would get the camera up to speed, drop the fluids into the water tank, and let it rip – hoping you had captured something in those brief few seconds.

Not all of the elements had color in them when they were shot; color was added to the resulting grayscales either in the film to video transfer at Company 3 in Los Angeles, or in After Effects using the Digital Film Tools Composite Suite plug-ins.

Belief prefers to shoot elements on 35mm film for several reasons. Besides the usual advantages of resolution, texture, and natural motion blur, film's large dynamic range of luminance and color provide the additional visual information needed to perform more extreme color corrections without yielding posterized images. This additional color information is often missing from video, especially if it has already been compressed either by the VTR or during capture into a nonlinear editing system. That said, there were still occasions when Belief needed to go back and shoot additional elements on video in the name of expediency as the deadline approached.

Dripping Spires

But Belief didn't stop at capturing and colorizing various liquids. Many of the liquid elements were inverted, masked, and warped to create more curvaceous, landscape-like shapes.

For example, look again at comp [**03_Belief_Alive_3**], previewing between comp markers 5 and 6. Notice how the tips of the mountains in the background seem to break off and float upward. In reality, this is a highly viscous fluid dripping downward.

Look again, and you'll notice that the mountain range has an undulating, rather than level, base. To create this, Belief took the dripping footage and fed it through a wave warp effect. After colorization, plus masking to create a clean horizon line, Belief had a fluid mountain range.

To create a mountain range, Belief filmed a highly viscous fluid dripping. They then inverted it to get the shape of mountain peaks, and warped it to create an undulating horizon. Belief then masked and colorized it for the final composite.

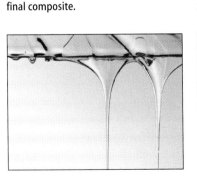

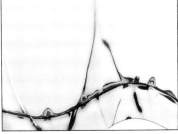

Hot Winds and Cool Ice

As you may have noticed in several of the illustrations, the liquid elements had a lot of grayscales and gradients which give them more character than simple shapes would. Belief wanted the same look for their silhouettes, to give them more depth and dimension. At one point, they even experimented with painting a person head to toe in black body makeup, hoping this would allow them to capture some lighting falloff around the body's contours.

However, this approach proved impractical, and Belief resorted to a normal greenscreen shoot. They used a large stage, with props such as walls, wind fans, and stand-off boxes as needed. Even though they planned to keep only the outlines of the people in the end, they still shot on film, liking the graininess of motion blur and its edges.

In the name of speed, Belief attempted to key the actors in realtime during the telecine transfer process using a hardware Ultimatte system. Unfortunately, many shots needed to be redone; Belief used the software version of Ultimatte running on ICE hardware accelerators as needed. Belief also used Pinnacle Systems' essential Composite Wizard plug-in package to help with automatic matte cleanup.

Various actions were shot on a large greenscreen stage, with props such as fans. These were then keyed using hardware and software Ultimatte® systems to create the silhouettes. Ice dropped into water, inverted, slightly warped, and colorized creates a nice abstract glacier/mountain range to composite the silhouetted dancer against.

Ropes and Curves

Sometimes, merely keying an actor wasn't enough to create the desired final look. For example, while the rope a climber hangs onto is taut, the remaining length that falls behind is usually limp – and not aesthetically pleasing (see figures on the next page). In cases like this, Belief would hand-mask or rotoscope the undesirable elements out of a scene, then either leave a clean white plate, or replace them with stroked lines or whatever other graphical elements were appropriate.

To see the results of just such a correction, open the composition [02_Belief_Alive_2], and play or preview the frames between comp

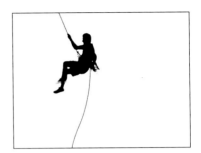

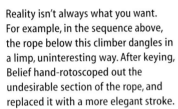

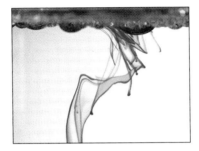

Reality isn't always what you want. For example, in the sequence above, the rope below this climber dangles in a limp, uninteresting way. After keying, Belief hand-rotoscoped out the undesirable section of the rope, and replaced it with a more elegant stroke.

To create the cliff the climber is descending (far right), another water element (right) is positioned and non-uniformly scaled to create a thinner, taller shape. It is then warped, masked, and colorized to suit.

markers 1 and 2. Notice too that the cliff the climber is on has been created out of another water element, this time turned on its side, masked, and wave warped.

This climber element also appears in the vertical icon bar in comp [**03_Belief_Alive_3**] between comp markers 5 and 6. Repurposing elements in this way helped tie the look of all the promos together, without a variation seeming to be an outright copy of another version.

Bars and Cubes

The silhouettes at different sizes help give the Alive spots a sense of dimension. This is further enhanced by the subtle use of 3D in the icon bars that appear throughout.

The icon cubes were rendered in 3D Studio MAX. Although they are simple black-with-white icons, notice how they have rounded bevels and specular hot spots as they rotate – this continues the "shades of black" idea that tempted Belief to try to shoot the silhouettes as real people in black body makeup.

These elements proved to be time consuming to create, as the icons (some of which animate) were created on the Mac, turned into texture maps for MAX running on a pair of Windows machines, rendered, and transferred back to the Mac. Only when it was too late to turn back did Belief get the idea of rendering just one set of blank cubes, then match-moving the icons onto them using an After Effects plug-in such as Boris Cube. Next time…

As you play the various movies, notice how the colors in the glass bars that hold these icons react to the overall frame. You would expect this reflected and refracted look to be the result of a render inside a ray-tracing 3D program. In fact, they were created inside After Effects

by taking the background composition, blurring it, color correcting it, and processing it through Panopticum's third-party Lens effect. Remember, in motion graphics we are often creating impressions, not realities; giving the viewer the impression of a more complex reality is often enough to really lift a design.

Designing for Change

Unlike some cable networks that deliver 24 hours of full programming, Alive's concept was closer to a network/affiliate model, in which the main network has a core of programs, but the local affiliates that carry it fill a substantial amount of the day with their own programming. In the United States, many local stations develop their own look for their own programming.

The challenge for Belief was delivering a package of graphics that the local affiliates could easily slip their own programs into and customize as needed, without losing Alive's overall look. Beyond just swapping out layers, Belief took the approach of enabling the affiliates to swap out concepts to better tune the package to their own markets. This extended to colors (so affiliates could color-code their own programming blocks) and even speed of cuts.

The icon bars subtly enhance the sense of dimension. Note the beveled edges and specular hot spots on the black cubes as they rotate. Also note how the colors change over time in the glasslike bars: rather than 3D renders, they are actually copies of the background composition inside After Effects, blurred, color corrected, and fed through Panopticum's Lens effect.

Examples of some of the lower thirds Belief created for Alive. Since Belief delivered entire After Effects projects, it would be easier for Alive's affiliates to customize these elements for their own programming.

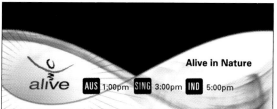

To accomplish this, Belief actually delivered a toolkit of QuickTime movies, image elements, and After Effects projects, with a guide on how to use and customize them. Belief specified the hardware and software required, so Alive could open the projects with no problems

After Effects has several features that make delivering a project in this manner easier. For example, sources and compositions could be organized into logical folders in the Project window. Nesting compositions also make it possible to build processing chains so that an edit in one comp – say, just a text element – could then ripple through to several different final spots.

Postscript

Belief and Alive met in November of 2000; the network planned to go on the air by the end of February 2001. Since Belief traditionally takes a companywide vacation between Christmas and New Year's, they essentially had two months to design, film, and deliver the package. As we mentioned earlier, working in phases allowed Alive to approve the elements and execute its off-air test while Belief refined their designs and created additional elements. The time difference between Hong Kong and California also worked to an advantage: Belief worked while Alive slept; Alive approved elements while Belief slept.

The final elements were first delivered via Internet. Belief had their own server on site, making it easier to load or change elements. Although it took all weekend for Alive to download, this was still faster than any express delivery service because packages would get held up in customs in Hong Kong. Backups on FireWire drives and videotape followed later.

The Alive job also represents a bit of a visual departure for Belief. Many of their prior designs were based on light sources – glows, neons, and so on – against a black background, with many, many layers. Alive isn't nearly as dense or layered. Belief feels the design has a softness and maturity to it that they probably wouldn't have conceived even a year earlier.

Alas, the Internet business development slowdown during 2000 and 2001 caught up with Alive, as diversifying into online services was one of the keys to its business plan. As of the time this book was written, the fate of Alive was in limbo. However, that does not detract from the clever solutions to various problems Belief devised for this project.

Best of Belief

Belief plans to release two titles of backgrounds and elements through the Bestshot.com stock footage library. Tentatively titled Belief Organics 01: Liquids and 02: Light, they will include layered After Effects files and suggestions on how to best use the movies creatively.

Water, silhouettes, subtle 3D, and key colors add up to a clear, elegant, flexible design.

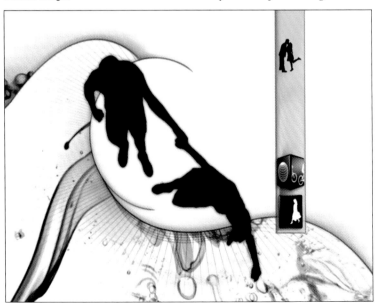

Belief

Founded in 1997, Belief is a design and production studio based out of a 9,000-square-foot artist's loft in Santa Monica, California. They view modern motion graphics as a new visual language, which they harness to help deliver messages and branding for their clients.

Belief has an unusual structure: rather than run an assembly line, in which a project gets passed from specialist to specialist inside the company, virtually all of Belief's employees are multidiscipline designers. When a designer is assigned a job, he or she oversees (and often executes) every aspect of it from concept to delivery. Another important concept of Belief's is its reliance on desktop tools. This allows them to put more money "on the screen" – for example, by shooting custom film, rather than relying on video stock footage – instead of in the pockets of lease companies.

Belief has been recognized for its world-class design and production for clients including Columbia-Tristar, USA Networks, TVS Superstation, New Line Cinema, The Food Network, Universal Pictures, The Discovery Channel, The Disney Channel, Mattel, and many others. The company has designed and produced an extensive list of image campaigns, show opens, originally produced content, and stylized graphics for commercials and on-air promotions.

Belief also founded an experimental content division in 1999, known as Belief EXP. It exists to stretch the talents of its in-house designers in the arena of experimental media, fine art, and non-commercial creative content. Belief EXP projects have been showcased extensively at film festivals, museums, and galleries including The Sundance Film Festival, The Museum of Modern Art San Francisco, The Museum of Contemporary Art Los Angeles, New York VideoFest Lincoln Center, and Resfest.

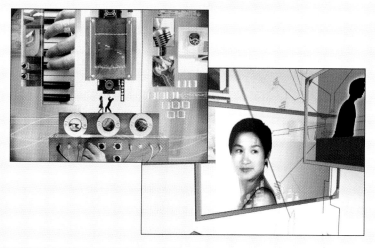

Contact:

Belief
1832 Franklin Street
Santa Monica, CA 90404
Tel: (310) 998-0099
Fax: (310) 998-0066
www.belief.com

ATTIK : Adidas Performance

A dense collage of graphical layers and treated live-action footage.

Performance was originally projected at the Adidas global marketing meeting at the Sydney Opera House in March 1999. Later that year it appeared in Adidas stores in Europe and eventually as television commercials in the United States. This high-energy video quickly intercuts between highly processed images of athletes melded with graphical backgrounds and provocative type.

The creation of this spot wound a path from After Effects to 16mm film to the discreet inferno* to the Quantel Henry and back to the inferno*. By combining systems, and pushing each to their limit, directors Monica Perez and Simon Dixon of ATTIK felt they were able to achieve a spontaneous energy that would not otherwise be attainable through careful planning. We'll step through some of the individual frames, explaining some of the techniques used.

The Adidas Performance video combines filmed athletes, abstract backgrounds, heavily treated text, and other graphic elements to create a tightly wound, high-energy collage.

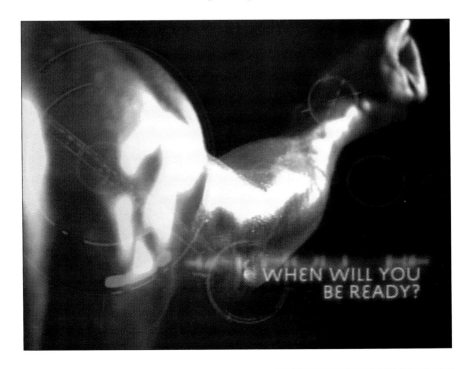

Exploring the Spot

Open the project **ATTIK_Adidas_ref.aep** on the CD that came with this book. Play back the entire clip, **ATTIK_Adidas_Perf.mov**, by double-clicking on it in the Project window's Sources folder, or locating it on the CD and using QuickTime Player. Now open the comp [**01_ATTIK_Adidas_final**]. We'll be referring to different sections of the finished piece by using composition markers – just hit the corresponding number to jump to that point. If you have a *lot* of RAM installed (Performance is one minute long), you can RAM preview the entire piece by hitting 0 on the extended keypad or using the Composition> Preview>RAM Preview menu option. You can preview just sections of the comp – such as between two markers – by setting the comp's work area.

Got all that?! Good. Now, referring to the comp markers in [**01_ATTIK_Adidas_final**]:

Marking Time

Comp markers are used to mark specific frames in the animation. Press the numbers 0–9 on your keyboard (not the keypad) to jump to these marked frames.

1 A large amount of the tension in this spot is created by the way the images of the athletes flicker from frame to frame. Step forward from this marker (use the Page Down key) to get an idea for how fast these flickers occur.

2 A female athlete slowly comes into focus as graphics flicker on top.

2 Another technique is to blur the athletes in and out of focus. A lot of this was done "in camera" using manual defocusing. As you step (press page down repeatedly) or play (hit the spacebar) from here, note how the female athlete slowly comes into focus while the graphics flicker at a much faster rate on top. The combination of skittering elements with slower or more linear layers is used throughout.

3 Lending to the concept that athletic performance is a science – an appropriate message for a sporting goods company – is the regular use of technical graphics such as circles, graphs, and connecting lines over muscles and bodies. This marker shows the scene from the first image (opposite page) of circles over a well-developed arm.

4 A variety of graphic elements were constructed to overlay the live action and backgrounds, such as the modern update on DaVinci.

4 Continuing the theme, this scene plots an athlete stretching over a grid. The organic-looking background was a real backdrop that was shot at the same time as the action; the more technical elements were

overlaid later. Overall, note the cinematic switching between close-up, medium, and wide shots, such as between this full-body image and the close-up on the arm in the previous scene.

5 Another good example of the "flickering" technique is the female athlete running. This is one of the sequences we'll step through later. Note the slow motion nature of this shot as well as others; many scenes were filmed at 48 or 72 frames per second (fps), then played back at normal speed.

6 An additional example of technical overlays combined with live footage. In this scene with the basketball player, note the spinning arrow – another apt metaphor for an athlete focused on attaining a goal.

7 Distorted type is used to great effect throughout the piece to echo the main message. Also note the honeycomb pattern in the background, mimicking the pattern on a real soccer ball.

7 A recurring image is the circular icon, this time over a soccer ball. Also note the use of distorted type here and throughout the entire spot.

8 One of the "clearest" (pun intended) examples of distorted type elements. We will go into this technique in more detail later.

9 In addition to blurring and applying lighting tricks to the athletes, ATTIK also plays with sudden jumps in time, such as this extended scene of an athlete straightening to stare at the camera.

0 The spot ends with a flickering Adidas logo, an echo of which zooms toward the viewer as the final athlete walks away.

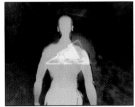

Artistic Overview

ATTIK has a reputation for having a ball-of-electricity style that pushes through conventional boundaries. Adidas knew this full well going in, and gave ATTIK a lot of free reign, simply asking ATTIK to focus on the themes of "performance" and "never accepting second best." Their main concern was that ATTIK capture the energy and intensity of the athletes. This led ATTIK to interpret the athlete's motion and the passion behind their drive as a series of short, inspirational visual bursts.

These bursts contained frozen and active live-action shots of pivotal moments in an athlete's actions. ATTIK wanted the live action, animation, graphics, and spirit of the piece to be a natural and fluid extension of an athlete's explosive, yet controlled, inner strength.

The live-action was shot with a very textural feel, often against graphical backdrops rather than the traditional blue or green screens. This raw material provided an organic bed for ATTIK to begin building on. Using the live action as a template, typography, graphic elements, and lighting techniques were then layered and blended above the live action. Part of this layering included processing elements multiple times then re-compositing – usually pairing unlikely source footage to result in another level of texture.

Execution

The production flow for Performance more closely resembled a jam session than a carefully orchestrated symphony. ATTIK likes using this method because they are more likely to come up with fresh ideas when they spontaneously react to the different inputs than when they try to plan everything out in advance.

The general overview went this way: The live action was shot on both 16mm and 35mm film stock and transferred using several different colorization techniques such as color casting, solarization, negative transfers, and inverting certain color plates during the telecine process. Realtime in San Francisco then edited together a template for the spot with varying cuts, scenes, and transitions from this footage on a Quantel Henry.

Meanwhile, the typographical elements were created in After Effects, printed out, and reshot on film (a process we'll cover in more detail below). Radium in San Francisco then scanned in and further manipulated the typographic treatments in 3D and with Sparks plug-ins on a discreet inferno*. ATTIK's directors chose Radium because they liked working with Radium's inferno* operator, Alaina Goetz.

These treated layers of text were then transferred back to the Henry to color correct and blend with the live action. This blend of footage and typography was then re-transferred back to the inferno*. This second inferno* session saw further visual effects, dimensional manipulation, color treatments, and blending.

"Overall, this produced a system of design that would've been hard to create on an individual

The live action was shot with rich lighting and projected backgrounds, rather than on an evenly lit greenscreen stage.

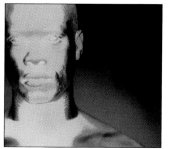

After the footage was shot, it was transferred using a number of colorization techniques.

Color-treated live footage layered with organically distorted type – the result of multiple processing passes on multiple systems.

Typographic elements were printed on clear acetate, then projected on a warped reflective Mylar background, creating a multilayered effect. You can see the cameraperson reflected in the first frame of this sequence.

system," notes ATTIK. "By leveraging two post facilities working at once, we were able to create an organic way of compositing all the info, with the two styles coming together. We were reacting to each progressing pass of footage or animation, enhancing it, re-compositing, and then returning it to the original source."

Type, Project, and Capture

As mentioned above, ATTIK built the typographic elements in After Effects, with help from Photoshop and Illustrator. Stills were printed to clear acetate. A layer of reflective Mylar film was then placed behind and manipulated by hand. In some cases, different words or symbols were printed on different layers of acetate, allowing interaction such as the different elements coming in and out of focus. Additional animations were projected directly onto the Mylar. The result was a seriously warped echo of the original type.

Text elements were shot on 16mm film, resulting in a grainy, organic look (right) from the previously laser-sharp type (above).

These constructs were then shot in house on 16mm film, which resulted in a grainy, slightly blurred version of the original – "Anything we can gain in camera when mixed with After Effects to create a more fluid and organic result." ATTIK also performed exposure grade changes to the footage, enhancing the depth and blackness of the film. You can see in the before and after images how this process really softened up the normally clean type.

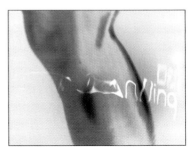

These filmed text layers were further color-treated and processed, and blended with the live action. This particular sequence starts at comp marker 8 in the comp **[01_ATTIK_Adidas_final]**.

"The typographic elements work so well because of the combination of real and virtual elements – things shot and things created on the fly," ATTIK suggests. The spontaneity goes well beyond what most could animate with keyframes and a plug-in. To a degree this means that you have to live with what you shot and find a way to make it work, rather than composing and balancing a frame like a carefully considered painting. However, the result practically crackles with energy.

disContinuity

The energy projected in Performance is not restricted to the warping of typographic elements. ATTIK employed several techniques to make the live action flicker and jump in unexpected ways, all serving to keep the viewer's attention. Several of these sequences are illustrated below; also make sure you check out the comp [**01_ATTIK_Adidas_final**] in the project **ATTIK_Adidas_ref.aep** on the enclosed CD to get a better idea of how these techniques work at full speed.

One is through lighting and color. A good example starts at comp marker 1, flickering the first athlete with yellow hot spots over a basic blue tonality as he slowly walks toward the camera. As you look at the sequence above, keep in mind that this does not happen as a slow crossfade; these are subsequent frames at 29.97 fps. In addition to lighting tricks and colorizations during the telecine process, ATTIK also employed several custom Sparks (inferno*-speak for plug-ins) to achieve lighting and texture effects.

Another way this energy is projected is through cuts between different versions of the same footage, varying levels of blur, colorization, even points in time. Overall, this is a linear shot, which gives continuity, but these jumps catch the eye before it has a chance to become too familiar (and therefore bored) with the shot. The images below are taken from the sequence that occurs from comp marker 5 forward,

One of the graphical text elements used in Performance. This grid-like theme appears in several scenes composited with the live action.

with the main jumpiness occurring near the beginning and end of the overall scene as bookends. Step through it to see the variety of lighting and blurs.

Jumping in time is another way to introduce these breaks. You've undoubtedly seen the technique of running footage fast, then slow (made easy with After Effects' Time Remapping feature); when pure jumps in time are applied to an otherwise slow action shot, you get this effect at its extreme – with a much more nervous result. Look closely at the sequence above (which starts after comp marker 8 in the final spot) stepping just a few frames per image: you'll also note some double exposures resulting in layering the footage with itself, offset in time.

Postscript

"There is really no specific recipe to achieve this specific look; merely excellent work flow and experimentation – pushing the box to break and crash by combining things that are not supposed to work," notes ATTIK. "Key to the process is a creative director willing to take chances and trust the process. It is only through experimentation that you can transform expectations into creative vision."

"It is a natural process for us to mix our media. We work in several different disciplines – live-action, 3D, and animation – which gave us a broad perspective upon which to draw. Flexibility and a more lateral approach open doors that ordinarily remain closed."

Another series of treated text elements used in this spot. Note how the word "enough" and the question mark are on different layers, allowing them to alternate which one is in focus.

ATTIK

ATTIK was founded in 1986 by James Sommerville and Simon Needham in Huddersfield, England. They have since grown to a network of offices in Huddersfield, London, New York, San Francisco, and Sydney.

The company will frequently use the skill sets of one office to complement another. This ensures that the right people work on the right project. For example, filming could take place in Australia, with final graphics and production taking place in London. If a Web designer is free in Huddersfield, he or she might work on a project for San Francisco. If appropriate, the New York office will collaborate on a pitch with an office in England. By sharing skill sets across the offices and keeping constant communication, the staff shares common values. This keeps consistency in the quality of design across the network.

When ATTIK evolved from a design company to a brand communications group, along with it came a shift of thinking: "Amazing images are fine, but unless they work within the constraints of a client's brand, they won't pass the Creative Director's eye." This doesn't necessarily mean

restraint, ATTIK notes, but "truly crawling inside a brand and designing your way out. Design isn't enough. The design has to do something. Make you feel something. This Adidas spot is an example of that."

ATTIK tries to pick global brands that can benefit from having a globally wired agency. They might determine the brand for a client, then roll it out across the world. Some of ATTIK's clients include Ford, Nike, and Microsoft.

Contact:

Tracey Tannenbaum
Group Marketing Director
ATTIK
3rd Floor
Elsley Court
20–22 Great Titchfield Street
London W1W 8BE
England
Tel: +44 (0) 207 674-3000
Fax: +44 (0)207 674-3100
Email: TraceyT@ATTIK.com

Christine Esposito
Marketing Manager
ATTIK
520 Broadway, 4th Floor
New York, NY 10012
USA
Tel: (212) 334-6401
Fax: (212) 334-6279
Email: Christine@ATTIK.com
www.ATTIK.com

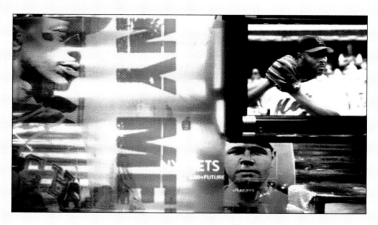

Curious Pictures : Sol

Electric pixels and wooden puppets combine to create a quirky set of beer commercials.

Ever since *The Simpsons*, animated characters have been more popular than ever. But how do you take advantage of this trend while still looking fresh and interesting? For the Mexican beer company Sol, Curious Pictures tapped the tradition of Mexican puppetry to create Woodmation: a graphical blend of physical animation and digital compositing.

In this case study, we'll trace how these puppets were hand drawn, scanned, distressed, printed on wood veneer, filmed individually, and re-composited in a manner that makes it look like all the action took place on a puppet stage – but with the flexibility and control of digital compositing.

Exploring the Spot

Open the project **Curious_Sol_ref.aep**, locate the **Sources** folder, and play back the entire clip, **Curious_Sol_Farmer.mov** by double-clicking

For the Sol commercials, Curious Pictures constructed and filmed wooden puppets, and re-composited them in After Effects in a process they refer to as Woodmation. The result is graphical, but with textures of realism.

on it in the Project window; you can also locate it on the CD and open it using QuickTime Player. Now open the comp [**01_Curious_Sol_final**] and hit RAM preview (0 on the keypad). Listen closely to the soundtrack; it's a pretty twisted little tale. Here are a few of the graphic highlights (numbers relate to Comp markers along the Timeline):

1 There are a few things to pay attention to as the beer bottle flies toward you. First is the textured flickering in the overall frame, which simulates an old-film feel; second is that the sun rays on the bottle's label are actually animating.

2 The original bottle was shot under smooth motion control; the camera shake was faked in After Effects. A clue to this is the cropped-off top of the bottle on some frames from this marker forward; this is buried outside the action safe area and is not visible during normal playback. (To check this, press the apostrophe key (') to turn the Safe Areas guides on and off.)

3 As you step forward and back between this frame and the next, notice the jump from the animated label to the puppet set with the same sun and clouds. At full speed, this is covered by the logo flying at you. The faux label was re-created in layers and matched to the real bottle inside After Effects using a combination of the Final Effects Cylinder and Advanced 3D plug-ins (now distributed by Media 100). This allowed the logo to fly out separately from the rest of the label.

4 Notice the use of multiplaning as the virtual camera pans over to the farmer: the foreground elements move faster than the background

1 The flickering lighting at the start of the commercial is the result of transfer-moding a sequence of paper textures over the entire frame.

Marking Time

Comp markers are used to mark specific frames in the animation. Press the numbers 0–9 on your keyboard (not the keypad) to jump to these marked frames.

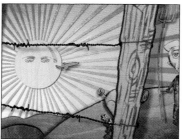

ones. This is how we perceive objects at different distances in the real world. Since this puppet set was assembled inside After Effects 4 in layers, Curious made sure they re-created this phenomenon in their animation.

5 To keep the commercial visually interesting while the pig tries to talk the farmer into becoming a dot-com millionaire, blinks are animated for the farmer.

4 A good example of multiplaning: the fence, which is closest, pans by more quickly than the hill with the farmer and pig on it; the sun (which is supposed to be much farther away) remains stationary.

6 In this close-up scene, the farmer's eyebrows are animated along with the blink, adding another little "surprise" element to keep the viewer's attention. To make the original puppet easier to manage, the eyebrows were animated as separate elements in After Effects.

6 The farmer's eyebrows were animated separately in After Effects to coincide with the blink, adding more interest.

7 All of the puppets were made out of wood. This is particularly apparent in this scene, where you get a chance to study the pig and the scenery behind it.

8 The signature image for Sol is the sun with its rays. The thinking-while-drinking scene transitions to the sun, which is a common thread in all the commercials Curious created.

9 Curious animated an entire supporting cast for this party scene. Note the sparkles on the bottles: rather than use a plug-in, Curious shot glitter and rhinestones on a black card through a star filter with a miniDV camera. The best flares were then composited over the bottle using transfer modes in After Effects.

7 All of the puppets were really made of wood. This can be seen more clearly in the objects that are closer to wood in natural color, such as the pig.

0 The spot ends with the reverse of how it began: the set switches back to the bottle's label, which flies back into place for the final tag line.

Artistic Overview

These spots originated as a pitch by the Kirchenbaum and Bond ad agency to win Sol's North American advertising account. Curious Pictures was asked to make a 30- to 50-second animatic featuring crude, Mexican folk art-inspired characters that told a story written by Kirchenbaum and Bond.

David Kelley of Curious turned to an illustrator he had worked with for some time – Jeff Quinn – to make crude drawings in black and white. These were colored in, creating a paper cutout version of what would become the Farmer and Pig spot presented here. Sol chose this approach from a wide assortment of creative ideas pitched to the company; Kirchenbaum and Bond went back to Curious to animate three spots, refining the character's look and implementing the animation in a "wooden" style. The goal was to bring a series of twisted little fairytales to life, without looking too commercial.

The agency wanted to create a look for Sol that suggested the "roots" of being a good Mexican beer, without looking too foreign. The look decided upon was a melding of Mexican influences: Day of the Dead folk art and José Guadalupe Posada's wood-cut artwork "meets modern comic book strangeness" as Curious notes. As you look at the spots, you will notice it didn't stereotype Mexican culture using tired icons such as big sombreros. The resulting approach is more universal and current.

Execution

As Curious Pictures notes, "The beauty of After Effects is that it allows one to create animations that are a combination of animation disciplines – for example, stop motion, cel, live action, 3D computer animation, and 2D animation. When these disciplines are mixed, the results can be exhilarating. Even though some of these disciplines are mimicked in style, the final goal is to make the combinations of technique appear seamless, real, and believable."

Since Curious had to composite wooden puppets into an artificial scene in a way that made the viewers think they were witnessing a real puppet show, Curious had to be mindful to avoid smooth, computer-animated looks. "Crudeness in animation is harder to mimic than one might think," notes Kelley of Curious. "There is a sort of charm in how to animate more with less; the stuttery, accidental moves; the dropped frames; sometimes a strange cut; and otherwise attempting to introduce imperfections and spontaneity."

Sol Timeline

1 week	Approval of character designs.
2 to 3 weeks	Approval of wood texture from color drawings on wood in color, and of prototype puppet design. Puppets plus some set pieces were constructed and presented at preproduction meetings with the ad firm and clients. All aspects of the script were discussed, as well as how the animation will look. Basic concerns were addressed.
3 days	All shooting was completed with the client present, including puppet elements, set pieces, backplates, secondary plates, and motion control move on the product.
2 days	Telecine transfer including color correction, and digitizing into an Avid.
2 days	Scratch voiceover and music supplied by the client were cut, and rough cuts and animatics were edited to these on the Avid.
5 weeks	Selects were digitized uncompressed with Digital Voodoo D1 Desktop on a Mac and transferred to FireWire drives. Production workflow was put into place, including naming conventions, backup protocol, deadlines, and shot priorities. Two animators did rig removal and greenscreen cleanup while another two did the compositing and animation. One animator was also assigned initially to just the product label zoom, as it required blending the live shoot with computer elements.
1 week	Client revisions, voiceover rerecorded.

The puppet sketches were printed onto wood veneer, which in turn was glued to 1/8-inch plywood and cut out.

Puppets were shot against blue or green screens. The large green stick attached the farmer's head can be keyed out; the wire riggings attached to his hands would need to be hand-rotoscoped.

When a character would appear small in a scene, a special "small" version with thicker outlines was created (right) so these lines would not vibrate on video when they were scaled down in the final composite (far right).

Puppet Making

The characters and set pieces were first sketched in pencil, then drawn in ball point on white paper. These sketches were scanned into the computer. To give the objects more of labored folk-art look, each of these lines was then hatched and otherwise dirtied up in Photoshop to look more like wood cuts. The outlines were also made a dark brown instead of pure black.

Areas of the puppets were filled on separate layers from a pre-approved palette of fifteen colors. The outlines were then layered on top using Multiply mode in Photoshop. By keeping the fills and outlines separate, it was relatively easy to tweak or change them if Curious or the client wasn't happy with how they printed.

These drawings were then printed directly on wood veneer using an Iris inkjet printer. This veneer was glued to a plywood backing, and the pieces cut out using a bandsaw and a jeweler's saw. Each puppet was then assembled using wire connectors the way a traditional Mexican puppet maker would have made them. They were mounted and rigged with long thin poles, and shot in front of either blue or green screens depending on the character's colors.

Capture

Most of the puppets and major set pieces were shot solo, to be composited together later. Aside from giving total flexibility, shooting solo was physically more practical. For example, if the puppets were 15 inches tall but had to appear less than full frame, the sets would have needed to be 10 to 30 feet in size. Instead, each was shot full frame, and later sized proportionally in After Effects. Exceptions included cases in which a puppet would be very small in the frame, such as the pig and farmer standing on the earth; special versions with thicker outlines were made so the lines would not become too thin and vibrate on video when they were reduced later.

The puppeteer's actions were filed on 35mm stock at 30 frames per second (fps), so they could be transferred frame for frame to NTSC video with no interlacing. All of the shots were then color-corrected at Manhattan Transfer in New York. Curious brought the physical product plus style frames to the session for reference. The colorist paid special attention to product color matching, like the color of the label and the beer in the bottle; the bluescreens and greenscreens were also enhanced to make them easier to key later.

Curious suggests asking for an important option during a transfer session: digital pin registration. It stabilizes any jitter or gate weave introduced by the camera – which would have made the following rotoscoping stages painful.

The puppet and product colors were checked on an NTSC monitor to make sure they would translate correctly at the final stage. This also lessened some of the worry about them during the animation stages. Everything, including some alternate color passes, was then transferred to Digital Betacam, plus a 3/4-inch or 1/2-inch viewing copy with burned-in timecode. This allowed Curious to view the dubs at home or in the office in order to start building a list of selected shots. Other elements were scanned, silhouetted, and animated inside After Effects to mimic the spontaneous movements of the live-action puppetry.

Key and Roto

All of the animation in the Sol commercials was done "on 2s" – at 15 fps. This adds a stop-motion feeling; it also halves the number of frames requiring rig removal and greenscreen cleanup.

To create alpha channels, in most cases the puppets were masked rather than keyed out of their bluescreen backgrounds. Since their limbs and outlines didn't change shape, Curious found it was easier to create a mask in After Effects for each limb and just track the puppet's movements. The result was very clean, without the edge chatter you sometimes get from keying.

Color or difference keying was used to drop out areas too difficult to mask, such as little holes or complex shapes. The final edge cleanup was applied using the Production Bundle's Matte Tools>Matte Choker. If too much edging was lost, Matte Choker was used in reverse to grow the alpha channel and reveal more edge. Another trick involved using a small amount of Perspective>Bevel Alpha to artificially reintroduce more of an edge.

Spill suppression was used to remove some of the reflections from the green or blue backgrounds. To reduce the color contamination problems resulting from natural motion blur or focus problems (blurry edges often have some of the background color mixed in), Curious tends toward camera choices that will reduce motion blur, including shooting at 30 fps instead of 24 fps. They will then fake depth of field or motion blur in After Effects.

Still Curious?

To see two other commercials Curious created for Sol, in the project **Curious_Sol_ref.aep** open the folder **Other Spots**, double-click on each movie, and play.

Since they were cut from wood, some of the puppets had rough edges and small burrs. In many cases, the puppets were masked rather than keyed to create alpha channels, since an advantage of wood is that it rarely changes shape as the puppets move.

Look closely and locate the dark spots that indicate the pivot points for the puppets' limbs, such as the farmer's arms, neck, and head, and the pig's feet and head. This is where you would place anchor points in After Effects to animate these limbs in post production.

The airplane flying was re-animated in After Effects by taking a still of the model (above), using Motion Sketch to trace out its movements, then adding or deleting keyframes to tweak the stop-motion look Curious was after (below).

Character Animation

Many of the puppet moves were executed by a puppeteer who was listening to a scratch voiceover on the set for timing. If you look closely at some of the images of the more involved puppets, you can see the swivel points for the various joints, even though the wire rigging has been rotoscoped out. Still, about 70% of the moves were modified or animated in After Effects.

There were instances when the live action footage of the puppets wasn't quite right, or when elements were added to a scene later that needed to be animated in a similar style. Simple linear keyframes for the movements would be too computer-perfect; instead, Curious used the Motion Sketch assistant in After Effects to draw out the motion it wanted.

One example of this is the airplane that flies by in the background. It was originally shot dangling from a springy wire rig over a greenscreen. The puppeteer first moved the airplane horizontally across the screen from left to right while adding bumpy movements. However, the springiness of the wire made the movement too chaotic, potentially taking your focus away from the farmer and pig in the foreground.

Instead, Curious took a still image of the airplane, and set Motion Sketch to record on 2s or 3s (15 fps or 10 fps). They then moved it via the mouse while previewing the background. Afterward, they deleted keyframes that made it look too bumpy, or added new keyframes for steppiness to maintain the stop-motion flavor.

Shadowplay

Because most of the puppets and other foreground objects were shot individually, the interplay of the shadows between the layers had to be re-created inside After Effects.

For simpler shadows, Curious used the Perspective>Drop Shadow effect, set to a dark brown shadow color, 10% to 30% transparency, and high softness settings. When shadows fell on layers at different distances, which required different shadow sizes per object to enhance the sense of depth, Curious created their own shadows by duplicating the layers, filling them with a dark brown or maroon color, blurring them with Blur & Sharpen>Fast Blur, reducing their transparency, and compositing them using the Multiply transfer mode. The combination of colored shadows and transfer modes gives richer color variations inside the shadowed areas.

These shadow layers were then offset in position depending on how far (in virtual space) the shadow was to be cast onto a receiving layer behind. Layers that received shadows were then duplicated and used as track mattes for the shadow-casting layers. In this way, the shadows

Parents of Characters

To perform the kind of linked character animation described in this case study, the first step is to create a layer for each limb to animate, such as hand, forearm, upper arm, and torso. You then need to align each layer's Anchor Point with the point where you want its pivot to be – the pivots on the assembled puppet are a good guide.

Before After Effects version 5 came along, at this point you would have needed to dedicate a composition to each link in the chain of building a limb. For example, you would first have a comp with the hand and forearm properly aligned (this is the comp where you would animate the hand). Then you would need to create a new comp for the upper arm, and nest into it the hand/forearm comp, setting the anchor point for this nested comp to the pivot point where the forearm would attach to the upper arm. This new comp is where you would animate the forearm. This would continue up the chain. As you can imagine, it's a bit of a nightmare to manage.

After Effects 5 has added a new feature – Parenting – which makes this much easier. You no longer need to nest compositions; instead, you just build a chain of child-parent relationships. In the example here, the hand would be parented to the forearm, which in turn would be parented to the upper arm, which in turn would be parented to the torso. This keeps all the animation inside one comp. For more on this technique, make sure you check out the *RoboTV* or the *Flamingo 4* tutorials elsewhere in this book.

---

were automatically masked to appear just on specific layers. This procedure was repeated per layer every time a shadow needed to be cast at a different "distance" onto another layer.

This technique, combined with the multiplaning discussed earlier, allowed Curious to re-assemble a world with an interplay of light and movement that could fool the viewer into thinking all the action took place on one physical set – without the headache of trying to coordinate and shoot all the movements in one pass.

Finally, Curious created lighting mattes for the overall scene, which give the impression of a light focused on the middle of the scene, getting darker in the corners as the light's cone of illumination falls off. To do this, they masked Solids with very large feather settings (about 200 pixels or so), reduced their transparency, and used the Multiply transfer mode on top. Remember that multiplying a dark object on top of another layer will darken the underlying layer.

Lighting and multiplaning are also techniques that After Effects 5 makes easier: since it introduces a concept of depth and 3D space, with its own camera and lights, you can now let After Effects do the work in creating true parallax and shadows that fall correctly across multiple objects. However, there will always be times when you want to create these phenomena by hand to more precisely control the look you're after – even if it's not mathematically "correct."

Notice how the shadow from the bird and branch fall clearly on the pig, but are much reduced against the background. To create more realistic multidimensional shadows, Curious created multiple shadow layers, matted by the layers they would fall on. Also notice how the edges of the scene are a little darker than the center; Curious faked this lighting fall-off effect inside After Effects.

By capturing puppets and stage pieces separately so they could be animated and effected individually, Curious had more control to re-create a sense of depth inside After Effects through multiplaning and shadowplay.

The After Effects comp for the final scene. Notice in the Timeline window how many of the elements have been grouped into precomps, such as the balloons and other party revellers. The hash marks on the topmost layer means it is playing backward; this is a great shortcut to create symmetrical animation, such as a toast in which the arm rises and then falls.

Postscript

The farmer was originally shot holding an electric carving knife. The client felt this didn't make too much sense given the otherwise rustic nature of the character. Curious made a wooden butcher knife and fork as potential alternates so they could decide later on taste and violence potential (as you can see in the finished spot, the winner was the fork). The farmer's arm was also scanned and the fork appropriately positioned. Curious then had to rotoscope out the old arm and replace it with the new arm and carving utensil, animated in After Effects to match the live action.

Overall, Curious recommends trying to edit spots like these cinematically, varying the use of wide, medium, and close-up shots as well as cutaways. They like cut edits because they feel they add dimension to a story line, as well as reduce the amount of animation that needs to be created for each scene (since there is no need to animate overlapping handles as well). And don't be afraid to put in the work necessary to make a scene look better or more believable. As Kelley of Curious notes, "Like a painting that has been refined and retouched and polished, the hard work shows. The love and spirit comes through in unusual surprises, serendipity, and happy accidents, which all make a project all the more interesting to watch."

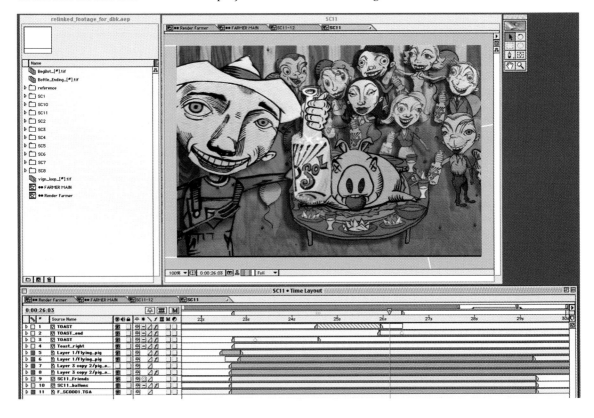

Curious Pictures

Curious Pictures creates comedy, graphically inspired live action, special effects, graphics, and animation of all types for film and television, including full-length programs such as *Avenue Amy* for the Oxygen Network. In particular, Curious is developing a reputation for creating innovative animation styles. Their 30,000-square-foot facility in lower Manhattan contains both a cel and a computer animation department, a shooting stage with two motion control camera systems, a prop and model shop, and digital editing rooms.

Curious's digital division uses a combination of Mac, NT, and SGI workstations, employing After Effects for 2D compositing and graphics, and Maya plus 3D Studio MAX for 3D animation. Digital Ink & Paint of cel animation is performed with Softimage Toonz.

Clients include numerous major global advertising agencies, Nickelodeon, Cartoon Network, and VH-1. Recent clients have included AT&T, Kraft, Wendy's, Nike, Miller, Levi's, Reebok, Sony, PBS, HBO, Mercedes, Cartoon Network, and Oxygen Network.

Credits for Sol "Farmer and Fisherman" and "Hatmaker":

Agency: Kirshenbaum Bond & Partners
Producer: Sharon Harte
Creatives: Sean LaBounty and Doug Darnell ("Farmer and Fisherman"); Megan Skelley and Chad Walker ("Hatmaker").
Creative Director: Bill Oberlander ("Farmer and Fisherman"); Stuart D'Rozario ("Hatmaker")

Production Company: Curious Pictures
Director: David Kelley
Producer: Nancy Giandomenico

Music: Gomez (original track)

Contact:

Curious Pictures
440 Lafayette Street
New York, NY 10003
Tel: (212) 674-1400
Fax: (212) 674-0081
www.curiouspictures.com

Fido : Boxman

Creating a hybrid 2D/3D cel animation Tina Turner music video with After Effects and Softimage.

Stockholm-based Fido created this series of promo spots for Swedish Internet CD outlet Boxman at the end of 1999. Each spot focused on a different artist, such as Elvis, Tina Turner, or Tom Jones, and humorously portrayed them singing a hit song by using a combination of 2D and 3D to create a final cel animation-style look.

Exploring the Spot

In this case study, we'll analyze several of the animation tricks Fido employed in After Effects and Softimage to create the different scenes. Open the project **Fido_Boxman_ref.aep** and RAM preview the comp **[01_Fido_Boxman_TinaT]** (or play the movie **Fido_Boxman_TinaT.mov** from the **Sources** folder on the CD). This spot appears to move seamlessly between 2D and 3D realms. Fido employed some nice sleight-of-hand tricks to accomplish this, such as swapping out images on musical downbeats to cover these transitions. Referring to the comp markers, here are a few highlights to look for:

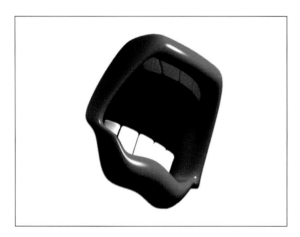

Two recurring themes are hearts and Tina Turner's memorable lips in Fido's commercial for Boxman.

1 The O logo first morphs to a heart, then veins grow inside the heart-like vines.

2 Note the change from the 2D to 3D heart on a musical downbeat – you probably didn't notice it in realtime as it was masked by the musical event, but it's really obvious when you single-frame through.

3 Blood spurts as the arrows pierce the heart. Also notice how the heart reacts in shape whenever an arrow pierces it.

4 The heart cracks apart and falls.

5 Tina's face, fit inside the logo's O, bobs around the frame and sings.

6 The scene cuts on a musical downbeat to the

Tina-face floating among 3D balloons. Note you can see her face reflected in the left-most balloon before she even appears onscreen.

7 A balloon explodes to reveal a giant set of 3D lips singing. This sudden change masks the Tina-face slipping out of the frame on the right.

8 The lips morph back into the O logo, which later morphs back into the heart. The slogan appears inside the O heart, reinforced by the voiceover.

9 This final heart explodes, revealing the full logo.

0 Hidden again by a musical downbeat, the logo quickly cuts to an O morphing into the final CD case.

We'll discuss in more detail the veins, blood, heart cracking, singing face and lips, balloons, and final CD scenes.

Artistic Overview

Boxman hired the Bacon Advertising Agency in Stockholm to help establish its brand identity. Bacon in turn hired Fido to design and animate the spots, with the main concept of having the musical artists morph in and out of the O in Boxman's graphical red, black, and white logo.

Originally, the spots were intended only to build the brand, with broader themes such as "The Best of Rock: Elvis Presley" or "The Best of Soul: James Brown." However, there was trouble clearing songs for this broad approach; the only music they were allowed to use were songs from new releases. That meant the spots now had two jobs: to sell the brand, and to sell a specific CD.

The framework that was decided upon was to start with the O and return to it 20 seconds into each spot, add appropriate text, resolve to the full logo, then finish with a shot of the specific CD being sold.

Bacon's art director Walter Kalmaru provided Fido with the songs to use plus photos of the artists to be featured. Fido took these, watched the supporting videos (if they existed), and brainstormed a visual story to support a 20- to 30-second snippet of each song. Fido decided to capitalize on the O, using it as a common visual theme throughout to get them into and out of the scenes inspired by the song, and to tie together the various images and caricatures of the artists featured.

For Tina Turner, the song selected was "When the Heartache Is Over"; the only visual guide they had were a few photos and their imaginations. They developed a list of ideas which could be used to represent the signature O in various forms, such as a heart, balloons, and Tina's famous mouth.

Fido's chief designer/director Pontus Wahlstrom drew storyboards, while the animators worked on models and motion tests. The storyboard drawings were scanned, cut up in Photoshop, and sequenced in After Effects to create a roughly timed "animatic" (animated storyboard) of the final. From here, they could divide the commercial into scenes, and decide which parts to execute in 2D versus 3D.

The O of the Boxman logo is a central graphical theme the spots keep coming back to.

Marking Time

Comp markers are used to mark specific frames in the animation. Press the numbers 0–9 on your keyboard (not the keypad) to jump to these marked frames.

The only source materials Fido started with were a song, a few photos, and their own imaginations.

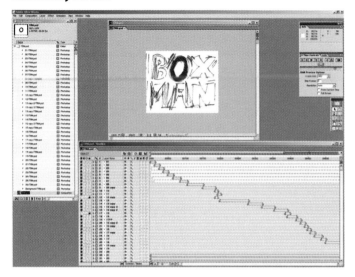

A hand-drawn storyboard was scanned in, chopped up in Photoshop, and sequenced in After Effects to get a feel for timing and scenes.

Open the comp [**02_Fido_Boxman_ storyboard**] to preview the storyboard Wahlstrom created for this spot. This was one of the later commercials Fido executed; they admit they were getting "a little experimental and surreal" at this stage, with throbbing hearts and huge flying lips. (One idea you'll see in the animated storyboard – Tina's head flying out of her own mouth – didn't make the final cut.)

After animation had started, Fido reports it was a normal process of showing the client the progress step by step. They found After Effects vital for this, because they could build half-finished versions quickly, render a QuickTime movie, and either email it or post it on a private Web page for the client to view. Since the look of the spots was so clean and graphical, the client was able to see what was going on even with a relatively small frame size.

Execution

Overall, perhaps the most interesting aspects of the Boxman spots were deciding when to execute a scene in 2D or 3D, and how Fido transitioned between the two worlds. Here are details of some of Fido's choices.

Veins

Each of the spots start with the O element from the Boxman logo. Since the song chosen for Tina Turner was "When the Heartache Is Over," it was natural that the first scene was a heart. Fido created the O by using a pair of masks in After Effects, then animated the mask shapes to match the shape of the heart that appeared in the first scene.

This outline of a heart was then "pumped up" by first tracing out a series of veins, then filling the heart into a solid shape. Although the look of the final effect was 2D, Fido decided to execute it in 3D using

To morph from the logo's O to a heart (above) only required animating a pair of mask shapes in After Effects (below).

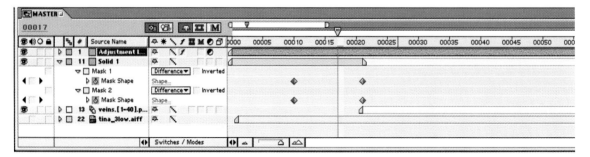

Softimage 3.8. Fido felt it was easier to perform the spline deformations needed to create the veins and fills inside Softimage than animating multiple mask shapes inside After Effects. Plus, the next scene would definitely be 3D; the transition was made easier by already using the same 3D model shape. Comp [**03_Fido_Boxman_veins**] shows a wireframe test of this animation and the final result side by side.

Harpooned Heart

The next scene – of arrows eventually causing the heart to shatter – was executed in Softimage, with a bit of sleight of hand courtesy of After Effects. Although both this scene and the prior one were rendered out of Softimage, they had very different looks: graphical 2D versus shaded 3D. When you play the spot all the way through, you probably didn't notice this transition as you were carried along by the song. Look again at comp [**01_Fido_Boxman_TinaT**], go to comp marker 2, and step forward a frame from there; now you'll see how abrupt the change really is. This serves as a great reminder of how much you can get away with when dealing with motion (especially coupled with sound), compared with a still image the viewer can study for a while.

In this same comp, preview the areas between comp markers 2 and 5 (refresher course: type 2 to locate to comp marker 2, press B to set the beginning of the work area, type 5 to locate to marker 5, press N to set the end of the work area, then press 0 on the extended keypad to preview). Notice how the heart flexes each time it is hit by an arrow: a nice touch to sell the effect.

You'll also notice some drops of blood flying when one of the arrows hits; this touch adds variety to keep the scene from becoming too predictable. The blood drops were simple models following arcs plotted in Softimage.

The animation of the veins growing and the heart filling to become solid were executed by deforming splines inside Softimage 3.8. Although the final look was 2D, building the model in 3D made it easier to transition to the same shapes in the next scene, which was definitely 3D.

When the arrows pierce the heart, it is deformed briefly to give the impression of natural resistance as the arrows pass through it.

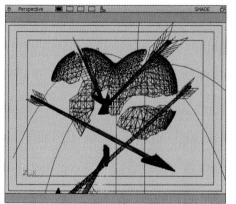

The harpooned heart set up in Softimage. The arcs leading away from the heart are the paths the drops of blood follow. Here, you see the fragmented version of the heart in Perspective view (far left) and from the Right view (left).

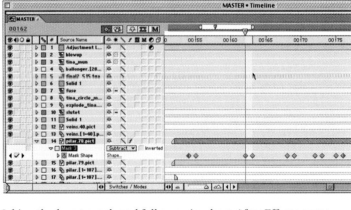

The transition from whole to cracked heart took place in After Effects. A mask was animated to reveal an already fully cracked version of the heart.

Making the heart crack and fall away is where After Effects came back in. Whole and fully cracked versions of the heart were rendered out of Softimage, with the whole version placed in front of the cracked version in After Effects. A mask was then animated for the whole version to reveal the cracked version behind. After the reveal was finished, the 3D cracked heart then fell away.

Floating Faces

After the heart falls off the bottom, a caricature of Tina pops down from the top and starts singing. "The design of the head was eventually decided upon after much consternation," noted Fido, and was created in Illustrator. Notice how it incorporates the signature O of the logo.

A caricature of Tina's face was created in Illustrator, keeping the signature O. These 2D splines were imported into Softimage, where a set of very 3D lips were added.

These splines were then imported into Softimage. Despite being rendered in 3D, most of the face keeps a graphical 2D look, but a shiny pair of 3D lips were added (which will appear later, larger than life). The lips were synchronized to the soundtrack; other simple animations like hair and eye movement were also added.

After Tina's singing has been established, she later floats among 3D balloons. One advantage of rendering this all in 3D is you can see her ray-traced reflection in the balloons before she even enters the scene (marker 6 in comp [**01_Fido_Boxman_TinaT**]).

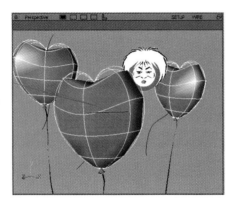

Tina's head floating among balloons was animated inside Softimage. Rendering these together allowed ray-traced reflections of her head to appear in the balloons, further selling the scene.

Bursting Balloons

The relative serenity of Tina floating among the balloons is shattered – literally – by the entrance of a giant set of lips. The last frame of the balloon scene was rendered in layers so each balloon and Tina could be treated separately in After Effects. They continue to drift through the use of Position keyframes, but the real action comes in blowing them up.

Each balloon is popped by first making it grow using the Production Bundle's Bulge effect, then bursting it using the Shatter effect from Atomic Power Evolution package (now included in After Effects 5 Production Bundle). Radial Blur is added to create a false sense of motion blur (since Shatter does not calculate motion blur). Tina's head is made to exit quickly by animating its position in After Effects; nice touches are animating its scale to make it seem to squash as it is blown off the screen, and enabling motion blur so it doesn't strobe as it moves.

If you have After Effects 5 Production Bundle, Fido has generously supplied a project that demonstrates this trick. Open the project **Fido_Boxman_shatter.aep** (or File>Import>Project to merge it with the current project) and step through the comp [**blowup**]. Notice that there are two copies of each balloon layer: one before the shatter, and one with the Shatter and Radial Blur effects. It is edited this way because the Shatter effect starts at the first frame of a layer.

Each balloon is popped using a combination of the Bulge and Shatter effects.

Lips!

When people think of Tina Turner, they think of big voice, big hair…and big lips. For the next scene, Fido took this to the extreme by having just a large pair of lips belt out the song. Again, this was animated in Softimage.

An unexpected problem was what to do with the rest of the mouth: As you look into it from the front, you expect to see teeth and the back of the throat, but these appendages didn't look right floating around behind the lips, especially when the mouth is closed.

To cure this, Fido rendered out a separate animation with just the front of the lips turned on. The main mouth animation then borrowed this second pass as its new alpha channel using the compound effect

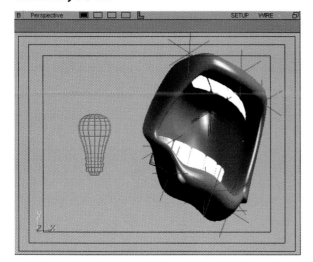

A giant set of lips was modeled and animated in Softimage. Notice the tooth sticking out behind the lip on the left; this and the back of the throat became a problem. A separate pass of just the front of the mouth was rendered and used as a matte to clean these up.

Channel>Set Matte, resulting in the excess appendages getting automatically cropped. Even with this, there were still some problems with gaps in alpha channel rendered from Softimage as the lips and teeth tore at each other. The third-party effect Miracle Alpha Cleaner from Pinnacle Systems Composite Wizard set helped cure this without resorting to hand repair of the mattes.

Da Bomb

The giant lips transitioned back to the familiar O element with more sleight of hand: They were animated into a roughly circular shape, then the video cut on another musical downbeat to a graphical O in After Effects. You can see this by going to comp marker 8 in the composition [01_Fido_Boxman_TinaT] and stepping forward frame by frame (remember you can use the Page Down key for this). Again: When things are moving fast, and timed to music, it's amazing what the eye and brain will accept as continuous. The subsequent throbbing was done with simple Scale keyframes in After Effects.

A fuse constructed of a simple solid suddenly appears, progressively hidden with a mask as it burns down. The sparks on the fuse were created with the ICE'd version of Final Effects Particle World. This proved faster than creating it in Softimage, and it certainly looks fine. As the

The final heart is blown up in Softimage using the Explode plug-in, in order to get more depth and perspective. A soft feathered mask then reveals the Boxman logo underneath.

fuse burns down, the masks that form the O were animated to form the recurring heart shape. The heart then suddenly contracts, which covers the switch back to a 3D heart.

This 3D heart was then blown up in Softimage using a plug-in called – appropriately enough – Explode. Fido opted for a 3D explosion this time because they felt the need for the extra depth and perspective that a real 3D package gave them. This explosion covers an animated heart-shaped mask with a large feather opening up to reveal the Boxman logo. Since they had already established the throbbing O and the heart shape as common motifs, they decided to continue to use them here for visual interest, and to help lead into the final transition.

The fuse is a simple solid; the sparks were created in After Effects using ICE'd FE Particle World from Media 100.

CD Cover

Each Boxman commercial ends with the CD of the music it's promoting. The question then becomes how you transition to it. As Fido explained, "The transition to the pack shot of Tina's CD cover turned out to be more complicated than it probably should have been, but it wasn't really clear what anyone wanted until we found something which looked good, and seemed to match the music."

The heart/circle steadily grew bigger with each throb, and over the last couple of frames turned into a rectangular-ish shape. At the same time, the CD case scene – modeled and rendered in Softimage – was faded in underneath as it was morphed in shape to match using the Production Bundle's Distort> Mesh Warp, which allowed the two to wipe together "as seamlessly as any two completely different things could."

The CD case was repurposed from another job Fido had done previously, which required far more detail than you get to see here. The fortunate bit was they had already figured out the lighting: Even though it looks like just one big specular hot spot, in reality a myriad of lights were employed to make it look like hard, cheap plastic.

The drop shadow from the CD case was a copy of the CD case, using Channel>Shift Channels to convert its alpha channel into RGB. It was then inverted, blurred, and tweaked using Channel>Levels to get the look Fido wanted.

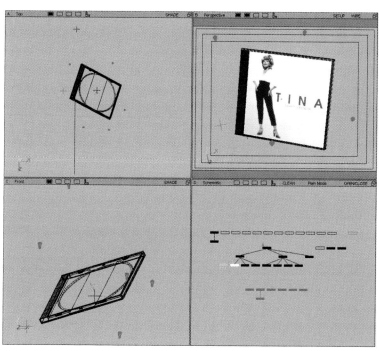

The CD case was also modeled in Softimage. Notice the large number of lights around it employed to fake the look of one big light hitting cheap plastic.

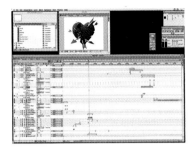

A high resolution screen dump (**Fido_TinaT_finalscreen.tif**) of the final Timeline window is included in the Sources folder in the project **[Fido_Boxman_ref.aep]** for you to study. Note the adjustment layer applied on top; Edge Blur from the Pinnacle Systems Composite Wizard set was used to even out the antialiasing and smooth some of the sharpness resulting from using all synthetic sources.

Parting Shots

The issue of color correction was considered from the very beginning, especially since the scenes bounced between 3D rendered out of Softimage and 2D created in After Effects, and Boxman's signature red color was so distinctive. In the end Fido decided to just be careful when modeling and texturing, and leave the 3D renders largely untouched when they were later brought into After Effects. If the color shift was too great, Fido preferred to re-render the offending sequence, rather than risk posterizing the image by trying to shift it too much with color correction in After Effects. (This is not as big a concern in After Effects 5 with its introduction of 16 bits per channel of color information.)

As a last step, Fido added an adjustment layer on top of the final composition, applying a small amount of CW Edge Blur from the Pinnacle Systems' Composite Wizard set. Because all of the images and sequences were very graphic and created digitally, Fido feels it is often necessary to apply a blur over the top to take away the unnaturally sharp look of all the layers, and to even up the different levels of antialiasing which were created by different programs and techniques.

Fido notes that it may seem a lot of cheats were used and corners cut, but that several factors allowed them to get away with it. One was that it was a relatively fast-paced commercial. There were lots of things going on, and new images would jump up and disappear before anyone would really have a good look at them. Another reason was that the whole job was synchronized to an obvious music track which had a strong beat to it. The mere presence of a strong beat helps propel the user from scene to scene, and the transitions are perceived as bridges, rather than new scenes unto themselves.

Postscript

Fido produced four spots for Boxman in a period of eight weeks, noting that this resulted in "not much time to dwell on each." As we all do, they admit they look at it now and wish they had more time. But the results were still effective: By the spring of 2000, Boxman was one of the most visited Web sites in Sweden, with 200,000 unique visitors a month (in a country of 8.5 million). The brand was known by 30% of Internet users in Sweden, and 15% of the general population.

Although everyone agreed that these spots succeeded in establishing the Boxman brand and selling CDs on a relatively modest media budget, Boxman went out of business during the Internet collapse of late 2000. Most analysts thought someone would pick up the name and start over, since the name was so well known, but it was not to be.

To see the other three spots Fido created for Boxman – Elvis, Cher, and Tom Jones – in the project **Fido_Boxman_ref.aep** open the folder **Other Spots**, double-click on each movie, and play. See if you can you spot similar tricks employed by the TinaT spot as they progress from scene to scene.

Fido

Fido Film is perhaps the most complete animation and special effects company in Scandinavia today. It is the result of a merger of four companies including Softmotion and Trick Film & Form. These companies specialized respectively in 3D animation and graphic design 2D effects; compositing and editing animatronics; models, pyro and other physical effects; and effects make-up and creature design. For projects that demand large-scale shoots, Fido cooperate with other production companies.

Fido's goal is to run a creative house where the idea always comes first. Fido tries to avoid technical discussions during a project's initial phase. The decision concerning technical approach is taken only when it is clear what the objective with the commercial or movie is.

Fido's clients include roughly 50% advertising agencies, 35% production companies, and 15% others (such as corporations and event organizers). Fido supplies full services as a production company for animated commercials. Movies are a growing part of Fido's commitments; it is currently in discussions with companies in Scandinavia as well as central Europe.

Fido today consists of twelve full-time employees and about the same number of freelancers, varying as required by the current workload. Their main tools are Maya and Softimage XSI for 3D and animation; After Effects, Commotion and Combustion for 2D and compositing; Media 100 and Softimage DS for off-line and on-line. Fido also recently built a workshop for its physical department where new materials are constantly being tested. Fido is pioneering the use of new ultrarealistic silicons in Europe, but it continues to use traditional materials.

Contact:

Fido Film AB
Stadsgården 17, 116 45
Stockholm, Sweden
Tel: +46 (0) 8 556 990 00
Fax: +46 (0) 8 556 990 01
www.fido.se

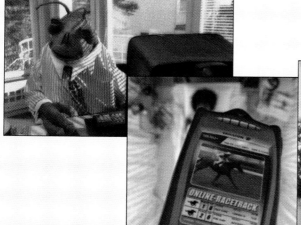

CyberMotion : PAX TV Promo

Filling the frame with light through a mixture of 3D rays and 2D compositing tricks.

The cable network PAX recently had its on-air image redesigned by The LePrevost Corporation. They developed a different look for daytime, primetime, and weekends. We worked with Creative Director/Designer John LePrevost of the LePrevost Corporation and Art Director/Designer Wendy Vanguard of Manna-Design to execute the prime-time promotional graphics. The central concept was to create a feeling of wonder using radiating, prismatic lights.

Although most of the elements – such as the PAX logo – originated as print-like 2D, the overall look had to be very dimensional. This seemed to call for working in 3D. But the way individual elements were to evolve and interact went well beyond what is easy to control inside most 3D programs. Therefore, a diorama of the logos and various light effects was created in 3D, rendered a piece at a time, and reconstructed inside After Effects. In the end, these layers faded in and out over time, were transfer-moded together, and even acted as mattes for each other.

The final design is the result of compositing numerous individual 3D elements – the letters, each individual light ray and beam, and even the separate surface colors and specular highlights – inside After Effects to maintain maximum control of how they blended together.

Exploring the Spot

Open the project **CyberMotion_PAX_ref.aep**. Now open the composition **[01_CyberMotion_PAX_Final]**, and RAM Preview (0 on the keypad). This is the opening bookend for the string of shows being promoted during a given evening. Since this sequence goes by very quickly, in many cases it will be easier to step through it frame by frame to see what's happening. Using the comp markers in After Effects (hit the numbers 1–8 on your keyboard), look for these details in particular:

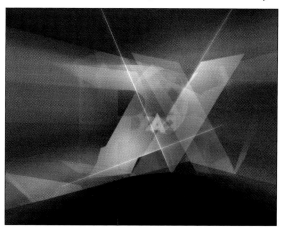

1 Pieces of characters that ultimately form the PAX logo unfold as laser beams shoot through the frame. Note that these beams alter their path to always trace along the edge of these logo pieces.

2 The light rays emanating from the logo – which started as sharp search beams, streaking off to the left and right – evolve over time: They become softer rays emanating from the ends of the character pieces. This is the result of crossfading between hard-masked versions of the beams to the beams in their original form. A smaller version of the logo also starts to unfold from inside the larger logo.

Both large and small versions of the logo unfold, while laser beams trace their edges and light rays emanate from their surfaces.

3 Both logos snap into their final shape as a set of four laser beams trace the X in the small logo. The spark in the middle of the X is created by a "scratch" plug-in from an old version of special effect wizard John Knoll's Lens Flare plug-in set, so named because the effect was originally created by scratching the film frames. (Through the generosity of Knoll's distributor Pinnacle Systems, a more capable version – LightFactory LE – is included on the CD that came with this book in the **Free Plug-ins** folder.)

4 Copies of the slogan – "share the wonder" – start appearing at different angles and trajectories, while the larger logo slowly spreads apart.

5 & **6** Sprays of prismatic light shoot through the logos as the overall shape continues to evolve. Also note the colored shards tumbling inside the broader light rays. We'll discuss both of these effects in more detail below.

7 Reprising the earlier action, four lasers intersect the small X again while a spark in its center flares up. This is the motivating moment as the entire construct flies apart.

8 As the logos and slogans fly apart, a final spark is cranked up in intensity until the entire frame flares out in white. This is the transition to the promo segments of the shows that are edited in afterward, and changed as needed from week to week.

The end of the sequence reprises the beginning, where four laser beams cross the X in the small logo. After these frames, the entire construct flies apart and toward the viewer in a blaze of light.

Style frames were created for client feedback by Creative Director/Designer John LePrevost (left) and Art Director/Designer Wendy Vanguard (right) before we started the animation. Our job was to blend these ideas with the client's own, and animate them.

One of Manna-Design's early guide storyboards for the project. At this stage, we were performing tests of how to execute the overall motion. Vanguard would then take one of our test frames, and add graphic elements on top for the client to get an idea of what the final would be like – thus her notations as to who was doing what.

Artistic Overview

Before we were hired, John LePrevost and Wendy Vanguard had already worked up design ideas to present to the client. LePrevost does a lot of his work in the 3D program Electric Image, which we also use; Vanguard does most of her design work in Photoshop.

The client liked aspects of both designs. The interesting challenge to us as the project progressed was finding ways to integrate all the bits different people liked so that they flowed together cohesively. We came to the conclusion that we would not be able to do this by just building one model or set in 3D and animating it: Instead, we would be fading elements in and out, practically morphing the elements as the overall spot progressed.

We have worked with Wendy Vanguard of Manna-Design on several jobs before. She always provides us with an informal storyboard of how the elements should generally move. Sometimes this "storyboard" even takes the form of a cardboard or plastic model that Vanguard constructs so she can illustrate physically how the camera moves around

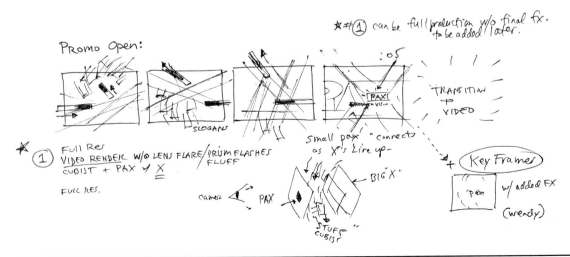

a scene, or a particular element animates. In this case, she divided the characters such as the main X of the logo into pieces and rejoined them to give us an idea of how they were supposed to swivel together.

Execution

Far from being just a production job from this point forward, many of the details were left for us to fill in. A common exchange when we and Manna-Design work together is for us to ask "and how do we get from this point to the next?" and for the reply to be "Well, that's for you to figure out, isn't it?" – usually resulting in much laughter all around.

As a result, we always plan for a week or two for R&D (research and development) at the start of these projects. Manna-Design is also very open to seeing alternate ideas or interpretations, and working them into the overall design. The result is quite collaborative. Below we'll give some behinds-the-scene looks at some of the R&D and problem solving this project required.

Faux Cubist

Part of working with Manna-Design is developing a shorthand language for visual concepts, which usually ends up being a melding of our individual and shared experiences. For example, a central part of Vanguard's design included shards of glass that loosely formed a pyramid in the center of her frame. We happened to be into the artist Picasso at that time, so this was christened the "cubist" effect.

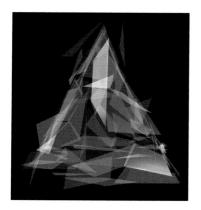 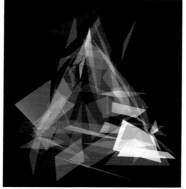 

We were initially petrified at the idea of having to animate each of these shards by hand. Whenever we're trying to create a scene containing numerous semi-random objects, it's a good idea to see if there is some physics simulation engine that can help out. We turned to one inside our main 3D application at the time – Electric Image – called, appropriately enough, Mr. Nitro.

As you can guess by its name, Mr. Nitro is normally used for blowing up models into little pieces. After some experimentation, we found that if we started with simple geometry like a pyramid, kept the polygons as large as we could, and balanced off the Force, Gravity, and

The animated shards were the result of exploding a simple pyramid model in Electric Image, reducing the Force parameter so the pieces would not fly out of the frame too quickly. These example frames are from just after the explosion; the resulting pieces were allowed to fly around for a few seconds to randomize their position before they appear in the PAX spot.

Rotation parameters so the resulting pieces would tumble but otherwise not fly too far away, we ended up with a look remarkably close to what Vanguard had hand-built in her style frames.

The next challenge came in coloring those shards. Chris had read that the music group Ultravox once toured with a completely gray stage and instruments, and did all of their dramatic coloring solely through the use of lights. As a result, a lot of our 3D work starts with white or gray models, and uses lights – as opposed to surface textures – to color them.

In this case, a half dozen lights were arrayed around the Nitro'd pyramid, using colors chosen from a palette Manna-Design provided. As the pieces tumbled and faced different lights, they would reflect different colors back to the camera. The overall object was semi-transparent, so you could see through individual shards to others behind. An additional three lights of different colors were positioned behind, and aimed at the virtual camera to cast multicolored light rays through the shards. The resulting surface color of the shards (known in Electric Image as the diffuse color pass), the specular highlights on them, and the light rays were all rendered separately and reblended to taste in After Effects.

The resulting cubist composite was used throughout the spot as a background element, often matted by other layers or objects. We also blurred a copy of the result to use as a fill for the text elements: We felt this was far more interesting than white text, and the resulting color washes tied in nicely with the animation already happening in the background, as they were derived from it.

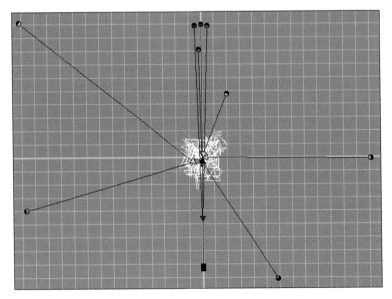

Manna-Design provided us with a color palette for the overall look (above). We used these colors as the starting points for the array of lights aimed at, and projecting rays through, the exploding pyramid (below).

In the project **CyberMotion_PAX_ref.aep**, open the comp **[02_cubist element]**. This includes a version of the final cubist/shards animation. You can RAM preview, play, or step through this to get an idea of the overall movement. Select the layer **CM_PAX_cubist.mov** and apply a blur-type effect to it, such as Blur>Fast Blur, Channel>Minimax, or the Foundry plug-in Tinderbox-Blurs>T-LensBlur that came free on this book's CD, and experiment with turning the image into a colorful wash. Then turn on the Video switch (the "eyeball") for the layer **Text Mask** and preview to see how your wash works as a fill for another element.

Mysterious Text

The logos originated as simple Illustrator artwork. For the beginning of the spot, it was decided to have pieces of each character swivel into place to create an origami-like unfolding. To do this, we broke the characters down into simpler shapes in Illustrator, and converted them into 3D models using Zaxwerks' EPS Invigorator plug-in for Electric Image. A simple animation was then set up to have the pieces swivel in different dimensions as they unfolded.

To impart more of the sense of wonder the client was after, we paid attention to the surface properties and lighting applied to the logos. We used narrow spotlight cones and reduced the size of the specular hot spots to just hint at portions of the overall characters, rather than illuminate them evenly. As the pieces animated, the lights played across them. The P was also slightly bowed with a deformation to increase the amount of light play. The letters were more opaque over time to make them more substantial as the spot progressed. As with the cubist shards, surface color and specular highlights were rendered separately, so we could later decide in After Effects how they blended, and animate their intensity.

Narrow spotlights and reduced specular sizes contributed to just portions of the background logo's characters being lit, increasing the sense of mystery and wonder. Note that the P is also slightly bowed to make the light play across it in a more interesting manner.

The laser beams that slash through the frame at the beginning and end of the spot were thin 3D tubes, attached to the logo pieces and textured with bright, fully self-luminescent colors. We then revealed them by animating a "clip" map quickly along their lengths.

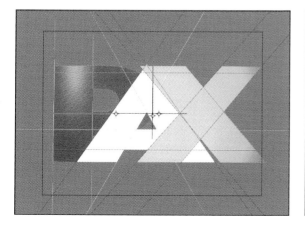

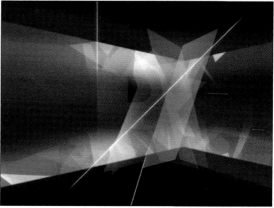

As the pieces swiveled into place, laser beams shot across the frame, outlining the edges of the pieces. To make sure the lasers tracked the movement of these pieces, we constructed them out of very thin tubes in 3D, and attached them to the logo pieces. The surfaces of these tubes were made to be self-luminant; a clipping map was then animated along their lengths to simulate the effect of a beam shooting across the frame – when in fact it was a solid model, merely having its transparency animated.

There was a desire to make the laser beams as thin as possible. However, as we made the model pieces smaller in Electric Image, the beams started to break up into aliased lines. Our solution was to use thin tubes, but render the frames from Electric Image at double the size needed, then scale them back down in After Effects – the thin lines held up better. A combination of the Add transfer mode and the Production Bundle plug-in Stylize>Glow finished the transformation from boring tubes into slashes of light.

Blending Rays

Next came the light rays that emanate from the surfaces of the logo. These were created with additional lights in Electric Image. The lights were attached to the character pieces, so they animated along with them, causing the light rays to sweep across the camera as the logo unfolded. Since the design called for a prismatic effect, we used a number of small rays of different colors, allowing them to overlap and give us prism-like gradients between the colors.

3D light rays take a very long time to render. Although we had a color palette from Manna-Design to use as a guide, we knew there was a chance the client might want the colors changed. Therefore, we "animated defensively" by rendering each ray out separately, so we could later reblend and even change colors inside After Effects.

To see this technique in action, in the project **CyberMotion_PAX_ref.aep** open the comp [**03_light rays**]. This includes a still of each ray as a separate layer – temporarily click on the Alpha swatch at the bottom of the Comp window to see their combined transparencies. Go ahead and turn individual layers on and off to get a feel for which is which. To alter the color of one of the rays, select it, and choose Effect>Adjust>**Hue/Saturation**. Change the Hue value in the Effect Controls window to get different colors.

A number of small, differently colored light rays were employed to give a prismatic effect. Each was rendered separately so we could later change their color, transparency, and blend modes to taste in After Effects.

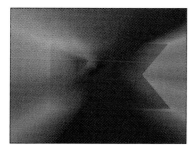 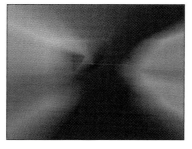 

Transfer modes result in different ways these individual beams mix. Make sure the Switches/Modes panel in the Timeline window is set to Modes (click at the bottom of the panel or use the keyboard shortcut F4 to switch between the two), select all the ray layers, and experiment by selecting different transfer modes from the Mode popup menu – they should all change together. (In After Effects 4.1, you need to hold down the Option key on the Mac (Alt key under Windows)to change transfer modes for all selected layers.) Screen mode is considered the normal way light rays would blend, and it's the look we settled on in the end.

These rays illuminate a considerable portion of the frame. As the design evolved, it was decided we needed more black space early on, opening into more light later. We accomplished this by creating two versions of the ray composite: one with the rays in all their glory, and one masked down by a large X which animates in the background during the length of the spot. We then blended between the two over the duration of the open.

Even this X was not left unmolested. At the beginning of the spot, its center is masked out. This mask was then faded over time to reveal a more solid X shape. The light rays were also re-used as an alpha matte for the cubist layer, to prevent it from dominating the frame. These cubist layers were then given the same crossfade treatment of first being matted by the X, and then later being allowed to open up into its ray-matted version.

By using elements already contained in the animation to matte out each other, we ensured the entire animation tied together, even though disparate elements were being layered.

Different transfer modes result in different blendings between the rays. Illustrated here are (left to right) the modes Normal, Screen, and Add.

To create more black space in the frame, the light ray and cubist elements were often masked by other elements in the animation. At the beginning, they are masked by a hollowed-out version of a large X that scissors open throughout the spot.

  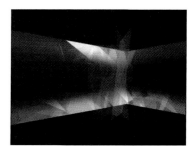

Shooting Light

A central theme for this spot was finding different ways to shoot light around the frame. In the composition [01_CyberMotion_PAX_Final], go to markers 5 and 6 and observe the prismatic light rays that travel quickly from the middle of the frame out through the logo. These were added to create a bit more excitement in the middle of the spot. Animating these rays to "shoot" rather than just fade on and off again required a combination of 3D and After Effects.

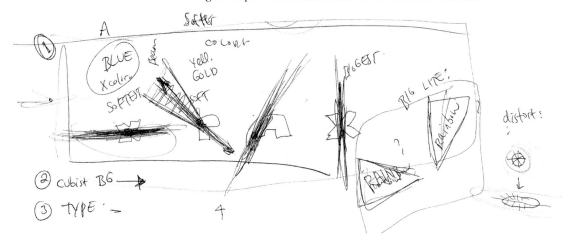

Vanguards's sketch of how she wanted the prismatic light rays to appear in the middle of the spot. Part of the instructions were for a spark or flare to mark their origins, distorted in a way that pointed in the direction of the beams.

Electric Image has options to create volumetric (visible) lights. These can either form a solid cone emanating from the light source, or become visible once they hit a 3D model. We used both types, rendered as separate passes. To further the sense of dimension, we composited the "from the light source" version behind the logo, and the "from the surface of the model" version on top. In both cases, these rays were used as mattes for a prismatic wash element John LePrevost had also created for the PAX daytime promo package – otherwise, we would have had to use several lights per layer or a different technique to create the desired rainbow effect.

The light rays acted as mattes to reveal the prismatic wash element Creative Director/Designer John LePrevost had created for the daytime promos he was working on.

It is possible to set and animate the overall length of rays and the size of their cone, but it is far more difficult to make them start from a particular point other than the light or the model. Therefore, half of the effect – the lengthening of the rays from their start point – was rendered from Electric Image, while the other half – shortening the back end, so the ray would appear almost

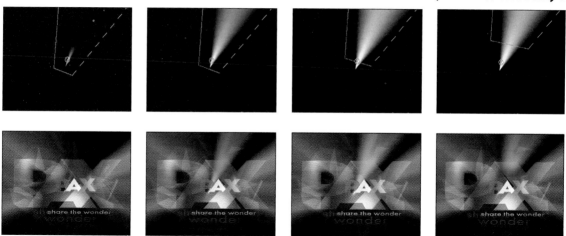

as a physical object that was shot through space – was faked by animating a mask in After Effects.

The sparks the rays originated from were another application of our old friend, the old Knoll Scratch Filter. We scaled and rotated them in After Effects to elongate them into more of a beam that pointed in the direction the rays were shot. A slight problem is these plug-ins did not give us much control over the direction the various spikes extended. Therefore, we pre-rotated them using the Transform effect (found under Effect>Distort in 5, Effect>Perspective in 4.1) to alter the orientation of the spikes. We then squished and rotated them into their final shape using After Effect's normal geometric transformations.

Light rays were animated in Electric Image to shoot out from a point in space. They were then masked in After Effects (the thin gray lines in the top set of images) to chase the light blasts off the screen, giving the illusion that they were a physical object that was shot through the logo.

Whiteout

This animation acted as a header that ran before previews of other shows. To make the transition, it was decided to end the open with a flare-out that ended in an all-white frame. We also provided a solo version of the ending flare as a matte, as an alternative way to dissolve on the first show to be promoted.

To realize this, we fell back on the Knoll Scratch Filter yet again. After the second crossing of the laser beams on the X of the small logo, the scratch dips in intensity, but then increases in brightness and size

The spot ends with a flare-out to an all-white frame. By using the Add transfer mode for the flare, the underlying elements appear to be overexposed, instead of just obscured.

until it engulfs the entire frame. To make sure we ended in pure white, a white solid was placed on top and also faded up over the last few frames.

The scratch was composited using the Add transfer mode. Rather than just obscuring the layers underneath, this instead caused it to "expose" those layers to a brighter and brighter virtual light, which creates a nice bloom that looks like film being progressively overexposed. Even relatively transparent elements such as the large X lurking in the background are illuminated. To add to the sense of drama, some of the 3D elements were also animated to fly apart or toward the camera.

We also created a bookend animation designed to end the promo segment. It came out of an all-white frame by reversing the flare-out described above, and resolved to an exploded "cubist" version of the logo. This endcap was much simpler, leaving room for the network and its affiliates to superimpose their program line-up over the animation, and hold it for as long as necessary.

Postscript

One of the reasons we used a 3D program to render essentially flat elements is that we applied a subtle overall camera move to the entire scene, adding to the weightless feeling of the piece. With the addition of 3D space to After Effects 5, many jobs like this one can now be executed almost entirely inside After Effects.

Why not just do the entire job in a 3D program? Flexibility, and time. The 3D elements alone took about 24 hours to render across two machines. If the spot was to be finished inside 3D, every change or tweak would require a time-consuming re-render. Instead, we could accommodate most changes by altering just the transparency or color of already rendered elements inside After Effects, or by altering the way the individual elements blended together through the use of mattes and transfer modes.

Since the motion in this spot was so quick, and we wanted to create a surreal smoothness to the movements, we field-rendered the final. We rendered all the 3D elements at 60 frames per second (fps) and conformed down to 59.94 fps (the field rate) in After Effects, so we could scale and position them as needed without worrying about messing up fields rendered out of 3D. Delivery was as frame sequences, loaded into a discreet flame* for final color correction. Since no video captures were used

Manna-Design

Wendy Vanguard is Creative Director of Manna-Design, a Los Angeles-based firm providing image design and production for the entertainment and broadcast industry. Vanguard's career in television began designing television titles for shows like *Rockford Files*, *Six Million Dollar Man*, and *Planet of the Apes*. She was part of the award winning design team of Charles and Ray Eames in the creation of the film *Powers of Ten*. Wendy was also an Art Director for Universal Television and a Design Director for the renowned broadcast designer Harry Marks.

During her tenure as Creative Director of California Film, Vanguard's team created award-winning image campaigns and corporate design packages for CBS Entertainment, CBS News, HBO, The Walt Disney Company, ABC *Prime Time Live*, National Geographic, TBN , The Movie Channel, and computer imagery for LucasFilm's *Return of the Jedi*. After a break, she formed Manna-Design, whose clientele for image campaigns and collateral marketing include Time Warner, The Roadrunner Group, The LePrevost Corporation, The Fremont Street Experience, and Microsoft.

Contact:

manna-design

Manna-Design
17525 Ventura Blvd.
Suite 108
Encino, CA 91316
Tel: (818) 789-7688
Fax: (818) 789-7091
Email: wvanguard@manna-design.com
www.manna-design.com

		#	Source Name	Mode		T	TrkMat	
▷	■	1	whiteout solid	Add	▼			
▷	■	2	spark out	Add	▼		None	▼
▷	■	3	spark mid2	Screen	▼		None	▼
▷	■	4	spark mid1	Screen	▼		None	▼
▷	■	5	spark in	Screen	▼		None	▼
▷	■	6	X rayflash 2.15-> D1/60.ei	Normal	▼		None	▼
▷	■	7	Daytime 500x338.ei	Hard Light	▼		Luma	▼
▷	■	8	P rayflash 2.05-> D1/60.ei	Normal	▼		None	▼
▷	■	9	Daytime 500x338.ei	Hard Light	▼		Luma	▼
▷	■	10	slogan main 1.f D1/60.ei	Normal	▼		None	▼
▷	■	11	01.4 blurred cubist	Add	▼		Luma	▼
▷	■	12	01.1 rays composite	Add	▼		None	▼
▷	■	13	PAX sml beams v1.06 2D1/60.ei	Add	▼		None	▼
▷	■	14	PAX sml beams v1.06 2D1/60.ei	Add	▼		None	▼
▷	■	15	PAX sml spec v1.06 D1/60.ei	Screen	▼		None	▼
▷	■	16	PAX sml diff v1.06 D1/60.ei	Hard Light	▼		None	▼
▷	■	17	PAX sml diff v1.06 D1/60.ei	Hard Light	▼		None	▼
▷	■	18	Hue/Saturation adjustment layer	Normal	▼		None	▼
▷	■	19	slogan ribbon 1.f D1/60.ei	Normal	▼		None	▼
▷	■	20	01.4 blurred cubist	Overlay	▼		Luma	▼
▷	■	21	slogan ribbon 2.f D1/60.ei	Normal	▼		None	▼
▷	■	22	01.4 blurred cubist	Overlay	▼		Luma	▼
▷	■	23	PAX lrg beams v1.10 2D1/30.ei	Add	▼		None	▼
▷	■	24	PAX lrg beams v1.10 2D1/30.ei	Add	▼		None	▼
▷	■	25	slogan main 2.f D1/60.ei	Normal	▼		None	▼
▷	■	26	01.4 blurred cubist	Screen	▼		Luma	▼
▷	■	27	PAX lrg spec D1/60.ei	Screen	▼		None	▼
▷	■	28	PAX lrg diff D1/60.ei	Screen	▼		None	▼
▷	■	29	X raycone 2.15-> D1/60.ei	Normal	▼		None	▼
▷	■	30	Daytime 500x338.ei	Hard Light	▼		Luma	▼
▷	■	31	P raycone 2.05-> D1/60.ei	Normal	▼		None	▼
▷	■	32	Daytime 500x338.ei	Normal	▼		Luma	▼
▷	■	33	02.1 cubist through rays	Normal	▼		None	▼
▷	■	34	02.2 cubist through X	Normal	▼		None	▼

The final composite consisted of 34 layers, many of which acted as mattes for other layers. Also notice the constant use of transfer modes to blend the layers together.

in the final, we were also able to re-create select frames at print resolution (3240×2430 pixels) for marketing materials.

The final composite required 34 layers, including seven sub-comps which blended additional layers such as the individual rays. Virtually all of the layers either had a transfer mode applied, or were acting as mattes for other layers. The use of transfer modes are what lent the highly luminescent quality to the final piece. Mattes helped ensure that no one element blotted out the others and left some black space. Using elements already in the animation to matte each other added another layer of interaction between elements which makes the final composite feel like a cohesive whole, rather than a hodgepodge of individual ideas.

Vanguard emphasizes that every successful and innovative project has been a collaboration of people with various skills and talents. She has especially enjoyed teaming up with CyberMotion since "they never seem to be intimidated by impressionistic ideas but find creative solutions to actually birth them into reality."

The LePrevost Corporation

The LePrevost Corporation was founded in 1975 by John C. LePrevost in Los Angeles. Considered pioneers in the industry, they were one of the first to combine graphic design with computer technology.

LePrevost has created and designed sixteen national campaign graphic packages for CBS, NBC, PBS, PAX, TCI and USA Network. Clients have included Americast, Democratic National Convention, CBS News, EMI Capitol, Greenpeace, MCA, Metromedia, Microsoft, NBC News, Paxson Communications, TBS, Travel Channel/Discovery Networks, Warner Bros. and World Cup Soccer. Their work has been honored with four Emmys, numerous gold medals from some of the world's most prestigious designs shows, the Monitor Award and an "Andy" from the Advertising Club of New York.

"We approach each client and project on an individual basis, by first understanding and evaluating their needs…then by working with them to solve problems" states LePrevost. "Our commitment to excellence in conceptual design and service enables us to create both classic and cutting edge solutions for all projects."

Contact:

The LePrevost Corporation
6781 Wildlife Road
Malibu, California 90265
Tel: (310) 457-3742
Fax: (310) 457-6142
www.leprevost.com

L e P R E V O S T

MEDIA CREDITS

We would like to acknowledge and thank the companies and artists who provided the media we used in the illustrations and projects throughout this book. To find out more about these companies and what they have to offer, check out the Credits and Info folder on the CD-ROM.

AB	**Artbeats**	www.artbeats.com
BS	**Bestshot**	www.bestshot.com
CL	**Creative License**	www.creative-license.com
DV	**Digital Vision**	www.digitalvisiononline.com
EW	**EyeWire**	www.eyewire.com
PC	**Perception Communications**	www.pcomm1.com
VS	**Pixélan Software**	www.pixelan.com

Please read and understand the End User License Agreements (EULAs) included on the CD; you are agreeing to abide by these whenever you use the content on the CD.

Note: *Sources prefixed by* **CM** *originated at CyberMotion, www.cybmotion.com*

Thanks to Our Team

Only two names end up on the cover, but in reality, scores of people are involved in the creation of a book like this. We greatly appreciate everyone who worked with us to create *After Effects in Production,* including:

• Everyone on our team at CMP Books, including Matt Kelsey, Dorothy Cox, Paul Temme, Frank Brogan, Shannon Crossman, Michelle O'Neal, and Brandy Ernzen, who gave us the tools we needed to realize the book we wanted to make.

• Guest artists Alex Lindsay and Kristin Harris, who designed two of our tutorials: *3D Mechanic* and *Flamingo 4.* We appreciate the variety these tutorials added to this book. Thanks as well to Carolyn West, who composed the music for Kristin's tutorial.

• All of the guest studios – ATTIK, Belief, Curious Pictures, The Diecks Group, and Fido – who willingly shared their tricks and techniques for the benefit of their fellow artists, and who dug deep into their archives to provide us with screen shots and production imagery so we could better detail their process.

• Testers extraordinaire Beth Roy and John Asbacher, who worked through every tutorial and gave us detailed feedback. Additional thanks to Michael Natkin and Leila Toplic of Adobe, who also checked the expressions tutorials.

• Fellow user JJ Gifford, who created a great tutorial web site on expressions, which he allowed us to include on our CD.

• *DV Magazine,* for whom we write the monthly *Motion Graphics* column plus the occasional feature, for giving us permission to reproduce some of those articles on our CD.

• Every one of you who bought *Creating Motion Graphics* – your positive response and support are what convinced us to write this companion volume.

• All of our motion graphics clients who have waited patiently while we immersed ourselves in yet *another* book.

• And of course, the entire After Effects team, for crafting this wonderful piece of software from which we derive our livelihood. You changed the motion graphics industry, and the lives of so many people who work in it.

Production Credits

• The book layout, cover, and CD art were designed by Trish Meyer.

• Typesetting and page layouts were performed in QuarkXpress by Trish Meyer and Stacey Kam.

• The text was copyedited by Mandy Erickson and proofread by Liza Niav.

• The Tip, Factoid, Gotcha, PB, and Connect icons were designed by Trevor Gilchrist.

• Whenever we created elements for these tutorials outside of After Effects, we have endeavored to explain how they were made through sidebars in their respective chapters. This includes the sources Chris Meyer used when arranging the music used in virtually all of the tutorials. Information on Chris' musical ensemble, *Alias Zone,* is included in the **Credits and Info** folder on the CD.

INDEX

Note: BT = Bonus Tutorial.

Numerics

2D/3D interactions, 161, 167, 181, BT8B

2D, faking 3D, 246–247

3:2 pulldown
  magnification issue, 88
  removing, 84–86
  rendering with, 101

3D Camera. *See* Camera

3D Layer
  3D Layer switch, 79, 133–134, 158, 167, 179, 194, 243
  Anchor Point, 180, BT8B
  auto-orienting to camera, 192
  axis arrows, 150, 158–161, 192
  Collapse Transformations, 179–180, 188, BT8B, BT11B
  combining with 2D Layers, 161, 167, 181, BT8B
  effects issues, 180
  intersections, 176
  Orientation/Rotation properties, 79–80, 174–175, 244–245, BT8B
  precomposing, 178–180, BT8B
  Rotation versus Orientation, 174–175, 198
  shadows, issues with, 161, 182
  Z depth sorting, 136–138, 159–161, 167–168, 180, 195

3D Material Options
  Casts Shadows, 134, 141, 181
  described, 134, 141
  Diffuse, 143
  Shininess, 143
  Specular, 143

3D multipass render, 108, 327–333

3D Studio MAX, 290

3D Views
  multiple views workaround, 169, 190–191, 195, BT8B
  switching, shortcuts, 136, 149, 159–161, 171, 186
  using Track Camera tools, 165–166, 168, 186–187
  using Zoom tool, 166, 169

A

Action Safe. *See* safe areas

Active Camera. *See* Camera

Add mode, 30, 34, 98, 103, 218, 329

Adjustment Layer
  in use, 81, 100, 104, 119, 180, 217, 226, BT7B, BT8B
  renaming, BT7B
  versus Expressions, 146

Advanced 3D Rendering Plug-in, 176, 179

aFraktal shader for Electric Image, 193

alpha channels
  Comp window display, 113, 206, BT8B
  edge issues, 109, 113–114
  interpretation, 97, 109
  straight versus premultiplied, 200–201

alpha matte, 116, 214–215, 329–331

Alvarez, Lloyd, BT8B

Anchor Point
  Anchor Point Path, viewing in Layer window, 25
  for 3D layers, 180, BT8B
  for character animation, 308
  scaling from, 25, 77, BT8B
  setting, 43–44, 77, 79, 237, 240, 252–253, BT7B

Anchor Point tool. *See* Pan Behind

animation
  character, 259–263, 305–309
  puppetry, 302–310
  slam style, 77–78
  stop motion, 305

antialias layers. *See* Quality

arrays. *See* Expressions

Attention To Detail, 107

ATTIK biography/gallery, 301

audio
  Audio Preview, Duration preference, 71, 259
  driving expressions, 235–240, 248–249, BT11B
  exporting to SWF, 269–270
  previewing, 8–9, 72
  shortcuts, 72, 259

spotting, 72, 260–261, BT8B

switch, 54–55

timing effects to, 36

timing keyframes to, 259–263, 275, BT7B, BT8B

timing The Wiggler to, 27–29, 102–103

timing video to, 312–313. *(See also CD>Goodies folder.)*

waveform, 9, 72, 261, 275, BT7B, BT8B

Audio Spectrum effect, 270

Audio Waveform effect, 270

Auto-Orientation
  camera, 171, 185–188
  collapsing with, 188
  dialog box, 171, 187, 192
  expression, BT8B, BT11B
  layers, 191–192
  lights, 189–190

Automatic Duck, 47

Avid, 47, 87, 200, 305

axis arrows. *See* 3D Layer

B

background color, 4, 126

Bacon Advertising Agency, 313

Basic Text effect, 103, 280

Belief, biography/gallery, 293

Bevel Alpha effect, 246, 249, 307, BT11B

Block Dissolve effect, 213–215

bluescreen, 306–307

Boris Mosaic effect, 68–69

Boris Tint-Tritone effect, BT2B, BT8B

Bulge effect, 317

C

Camera
  Active Camera explained, 170–171, BT8B
  Angle of View, 162–164
  animating, moving, 164–173, 187, BT8B
  Aperture parameter, 199
  Auto-Orientation, 171, 173, 185–186
  banking, 198
  Bezier path, editing, 168–169, 172, 187–188

Blur Level, 199

Camera Settings dialog, 162–164

creating new, 162

default comp camera, 136

depth of field, 199

expressions to follow, 247, BT8B, BT11B

Focus Distance, 199

multiple cameras, 170–171, BT8B

multiple views, 169, 190–191, BT8B

one-point model, 170–172

orbiting, 173

Orientation/Rotation, 171–173, 198

orienting layers to, 192

Position and Point of Interest, 164–173, 187–188

Presets, 162–164

switching between, 170–171, BT8B

two-point model, 164

Zoom property, 163–164, 170

CE Grid effect, 103

character animation, 259–263, 305–309

Collapse Transformations, 98, 179–180, 188, BT8B, BT11B

Color Burn mode, 81

color coding layers, 261

color correction, 288, 297–298, 305, 307, 320, 332

Color Dodge mode, 34

Color mode, 18

color palettes, 274, 326

colors
  animating, 147, 67–68
  color wheel issues, 147
  driven by expression, 147, BT11B
  master color. *See* master color

Color Theory effect, 148

comp markers. *See* markers

Composite Wizard effects package, 115, 289

comp proxies. *See* proxies

Note: BT refers to Bonus Tutorial.

Example: BT8B = Bonus Tutorial from Tutorial 8.

Note: BT refers to Bonus Tutorial.
Example: BT8B = Bonus Tutorial from Tutorial 8.

Note: BT refers to Bonus Tutorial.

Example: BT8B = Bonus Tutorial from Tutorial 8.